Joseph A. Schumpeter

SCHUMPETER

A Biography

Richard Swedberg

Princeton University Press
Princeton, New Jersey

Published by Princeton University Press,
41 William Street, Princeton, New Jersey 08540

Library of Congress Cataloging-in-Publication Data

Swedberg, Richard, 1948–
    Schumpeter : a biography / Richard Swedberg.
      p. cm.
    Includes bibliographical references and index.
    ISBN 0–691–04296–9 (acid-free paper)
    1. Schumpeter, Joseph Alois, 1883–1950.   2. Economists—United
States—Biography.   I. Title.
HB119.S35S94 1991
330'.092—dc20   91–16190
[B]   CIP

Printed in Great Britain

Contents

Acknowledgements   vi

Introduction   1

1 Childhood and Youth   5

2 Early Economic Works   21

3 In Politics   46

4 The Difficult Decade   65

5 Excursions in Economic Sociology   90

6 In the United States   108

7 Capitalism, Socialism and Democracy   136

8 Last Years, Last Work   167

Appendices

  I   Aphorisms from Schumpeter's Private Diary   199

  II Schumpeter's Novel *Ships in the Fog* (a Fragment)   207

  III Letters by Schumpeter   209

Bibliography of Schumpeter's Works   239

Notes   251

Index   286

Acknowledgements

First of all I would like to thank two people who have played a key role in this project: Anthony Giddens and my wife, Marta Cecilia Gil-Swedberg. Anthony Giddens suggested that I should write this book; and Cecilia gave me love, support and inspiration while I wrote it.

Most of the material for this book was gathered during the academic year of 1987–8 which I spent as a visiting scholar at Harvard University, where the Schumpeter Collection is to be found. I am very grateful to Mr Clark A. Elliott, Associate Curator of the Harvard University Archives, and to his most helpful staff, especially Mike Raines. Some of the other scholars working in the Archives were also very helpful to me, especially William Buxton and Larry Nichols. I must in addition thank the Schlesinger Library, Radcliffe College, where Elizabeth Boody Schumpeter's papers are housed, and the staff at the Kress Library and the Baker Library at the Harvard Business School. While in Cambridge I interviewed many people who had known Schumpeter in one capacity or another, including Abram Bergson, James Duesenberry, John Kenneth Galbraith, Carl Kaysen, Wassily Leontief, Richard Musgrave, Paul A. Samuelson, Robert Solow, Paul Sweezy and James Tobin. All of them gave freely of their time and knowledge. I also met and/or corresponded with a number of other scholars and have benefited very much from their insights and information relating to Schumpeter, including Hugh G. J. Aitken, Robert Loring Allen, Bernard Barber, Daniel Bell, Thomas C. Cochran, Lewis A. Coser, Regis A. Factor, Richard M. Goodwin, Gottfried Haberler, George C. Homans, David Landes, Edward S. Mason, Robert K. Merton and Chris Prendergast. A special mention must be made of Wolfgang Stolper, who for several years has answered my questions about Schumpeter with authority and kindness, and of Mark Granovetter who always teaches me new things in economic sociology.

Back in Sweden in the autumn of 1988 I continued to gather material, this time from Europe. Many people helped me at this stage, including Karl Acham, Massimo M. Augello, Gunnar Boalt, Erik Dahmén, Karl Eschbach, Herbert Giersch, Dirk Käsler, Hans Lutz Köllner, Dieter Krüger, Wolfgang Mommsen, Kurt Mühlberger of the Archives at the University of Vienna, Olle Persson (Inforsk), Galina Petkova, Günther Roth, Wolfgang Schluchter, Paul Schmidt at Archiv der Rheinischen Friedrich-Wilhelms-Universität, Yuichi Shionoya, Georg Siebeck, Michael J. Stevenson, Chuhei Sugiyama, Shigeto Tsuru and Lars Udéhn. I also received much fine information from various institutions, including Allgemeines Verwaltungsarchiv in Vienna, Karl-Franzens-Universität Graz, the Library of the University of Reading, the Royal Library in Stockholm, and the Library of Stockholm University. For intellectual inspiration I would like to single out Jürgen Osterhammel, who has written a couple of excellent articles on Schumpeter. Eckhart Kühlhorn and Harry Dahms helped me by checking my German translations. György Lengyel organized a fine seminar on comparative economic sociology in the spring of 1990 at Dubrovnik which inspired some of the ideas in chapter 7.

Finally, I most gratefully acknowledge financial support at various stages of this project from the American Council of Learned Societies, the Foundation of Ruben Rausing, and the Foundation of Magnus Bergvall (Skandinaviska-Enskilda Banken). The finishing touches to the manuscript were made in the autumn of 1990 while I was at the Russell Sage Foundation in New York. Many people at the Foundation helped me with various tasks, such as Sara Beckman, Vivian Kaufman and Pauline Rothstein. At this stage of the process I also benefited from very careful readings of the manuscript by Murray Milgate, Mark Perlman and Jack Repcheck. All three made many valuable suggestions for how it could be improved. A careful reading and copy-editing was also made by Sue Ashton. Finally, I hope that I have ended up by writing the kind of book that the reader will enjoy.

Introduction

Why a book on the life and work of Joseph A. Schumpeter? There are several reasons, some of which are more legitimate than others. For one thing, Schumpeter's ideas are very close to the temper of our time. Keynesianism has fallen into disrepute and economic liberalism has taken its place as the dominant economic ideology. The market and the entrepreneur are seen as essential not only to a well-functioning economy but also to a well-functioning society; and this means that what Schumpeter said on these topics is avidly studied today. There are many examples of this, from the business press to the academic journals. *The Economist*, for example, often takes a Schumpeterian stance in its editorials and articles. Those who are quick to sense an ideological ally in Schumpeter should, however, beware. Schumpeter may have celebrated the entrepreneur – but he also thought that socialism was around the corner and that monopolies could be superior to the free market.

Another reason for the current interest in Schumpeter is that mainstream economics is experiencing something of a crisis, and a number of economists feel that Schumpeter may have some relevant answers. Schumpeter spent much time on some of today's most important puzzles: the role of technology in the economy; how to incorporate social factors into economic theory; and how to develop a truly dynamic theory. Finally, there is also an increased realization that Schumpeter's life as well as his work are much richer than has commonly been understood. During the past few years, for example, a number of important unpublished texts by Schumpeter have been located and made available. These include not only a number of interesting economic writings but also some personal letters and political writings, which show that Schumpeter was a much more complex person and thinker than we thought. The same message comes through again and again in the conferences arranged by the recently created International Joseph A. Schumpeter Society. In brief: Schumpeter's legacy is very much alive and worthy of our attention.

A central theme in this book is that Schumpeter, in his various writings, tried to work out solutions to economic problems within a division of labour in the social sciences which is very different from the one we have today. When Schumpeter was young he was heavily influenced by Max Weber's attempt to create a new and broad type of transdisciplinary economics, called *Sozialökonomik* or 'social economics'. This type of economics was Weber's answer to the *Methoden-streit*, an academic feud between German-speaking economists which started in the 1880s and dominated the economic scene till some time in the 1910s. In Weber's opinion, this 'battle of methods' had had a disastrous impact on economics by polarizing it into a theoretical part and a historical part. Economics, Weber said, had been split into '*two* sciences': one that was overly abstract and non-historical and one that was overly historical and non-theoretical.[1] This was unacceptable to Weber; and to get out of this deadlock, he suggested a new type of economics – *Sozialökonomik* – which tried to synthesize economic theory and history. Sociology was also included in Weber's alternative; it constituted more or less the mediating link between history and theory. All of this had a great impact on the young Schumpeter who was a colleague of Weber and often took his side in public disputes. In short, Schumpeter made the Weberian notion of *Sozialökonomik* his own.

One key to Schumpeter's work is consequently his effort to work out his own analysis within this Weberian paradigm for economics, which is now since long forgotten. Sometimes he leaned more towards pure economic theory (this was especially true during the early part of his life when he endorsed mathematical economics) and sometimes (as in later life) he tried to counterbalance the exaggerated use of mathematics in economics with economic history. Always, however, Schumpeter was intensely aware that even if there exist several social sciences, there is only one social reality. To cite the famous opening lines of Schumpeter's classic, *The Theory of Economic Development*: 'The social process is really one indivisible whole. Out of its great stream the classifying hand of the investigator artificially extracts economic facts.'[2]

This book, however, is not only about Schumpeter's work, it is also about his life. The decision to include material about Schumpeter's life was taken despite the fact that the biographical information about Schumpeter is rather meagre, especially for his early years and his first academic appointments in Europe (for various reasons we know more about Schumpeter's American period). The fact that this study includes biographical material should, however, not be interpreted to mean that in order to appreciate Schumpeter's work, a knowledge of his life is absolutely necessary. It is clear that Schumpeter's finest intellectual achievements can be fully appreciated without any knowledge whatsoever of his life. Still, there is the fact that Schumpeter's personality is very much present in everything he wrote. In an article about Pareto, Schumpeter wrote as follows (and he might as well have been describing himself): 'But into everything that was not a theorem in the pure logic of economics the whole man and all the forces that conditioned him entered so unmistakably that it is more necessary than it usually is in an appraisal of scientific performance to convey an idea of the man and of those forces.'[3]

It is also true that just as our fascination with, say, someone like Max Weber is heightened by a knowledge of the various facts of his life, this is also the case with Schumpeter. The reader, one may say, would be cheated out of half the story if he did not get to know something about Schumpeter's life. For this is a very fascinating story indeed. Here we have the brilliant young economist who pulls off the feat of producing a major work in economics (in addition to writing its history) at an age when the average economist has barely finished his thesis. And then there is the conservative Schumpeter, who accepts a position as finance minister in a government led by the socialists in the young Austrian republic, only to be fired a few months later. And then, of course, there is Schumpeter the showman and the snob, entertaining his followers with his wit, such as the following infamous statement: 'Early in life I had three ambitions: to be the greatest economist in the world, the greatest horseman in Austria, and the best lover in Vienna. Well, in one of those goals I have failed.'

But there is also a less well-known side to Schumpeter. Here is the man who had to struggle in desperation to pay off a mountain of debts that he had incurred during an unsuccessful foray into the Viennese business world. And when things started to go well a few years later, his mother and his beloved young wife suddenly died. In order to counteract his profound sorrow, Schumpeter started to worship the memory of his mother and of his wife, turning them into his personal saints in a peculiar kind of private cult. Resigned and weary, Schumpeter eventually decided to move to the United States where he was offered a position at Harvard. The despair that he felt, however, did not go away; indeed, it increased even more in the 1940s, because of the impact of the Second World War. A sombre and sinister side to Schumpeter's personality now came to the fore. What to some friends was just crude anti-semitism and naive pro-fascism appeared in a different light to other friends, who swore that Schumpeter was just being outrageous and shocking. Who is correct? Well, with the help of Schumpeter's diary and other documents we can today get a little bit closer to the truth. After the war Schumpeter gave way to greater despair, and he now started to prepare for his death. In various ways he tried to summarize his life during these last years; he was feverishly working on a giant history of economic thought and he often set down his view of life in the form of terse, hostile aphorisms in his private diary (reproduced in Appendix I). He often asked himself why he was so unhappy. Perhaps it was because he never became the great economist that he had always wanted to be. Or maybe it was just that some old conflicts, which had always been there, were now activated with a vengeance. It is hard to know. In any case, all of this is part of the story which we are now about to tell.

1

Childhood and Youth

'Early in life I formed an idea of a rich life to include economics, politics, science, art, and love.' To this he drily adds today, 'All my failures are due to observance of this program and my successes to neglect of it; concentration is necessary for success in any field.'
(Interview with Schumpeter in *The Harvard Crimson*, 1944)

Schumpeter never wrote about himself and only touched upon his own life in anecdotes and witticisms as the one cited above. As will become clear later on, this penchant for using anecdotes and witticisms is an interesting fact in itself. Indeed, it constitutes a clue of sorts to Schumpeter's enigmatic personality. For the moment, however, let us leave this issue aside and instead introduce some of the basic facts about Schumpeter's early life. For this purpose consider a letter that Schumpeter wrote in 1934 to Stewart S. Morgan, a professor of English who had just told Schumpeter that one of his essays had been singled out for inclusion in a collection to be used in courses of composition. Schumpeter was clearly pleased with this acknowledgement of his handling of English, which after all was a foreign language to him ('I muddle along all right both in writing and in talking'), and he wrote happily back to Morgan:

You want to have some facts about myself. Well, I am an Austrian by birth, born in 1883 in a village called Triesch in what was then a province of the Austro-Hungarian Empire, viz. Moravia, which now forms part of the Czechoslovakian Republic. I was educated in Vienna, and following up an impulse which very early asserted itself, I then travelled about for a few years studying economics from various standpoints and began to give lectures on Economic Theory at the University of Vienna in 1909, in which year I also was appointed to a chair of Economics in Czernowitz, then the most eastern town of Austria, now belonging to Roumania. I was called to the University of Graz in 1911, and in 1913–14 I acted as what was called an exchange professor to Columbia University, when I first made acquaintance with and fell in love with this country. Later on I entered politics and took office as Minister of Finance in Austria after the war. I did not return to scientific life until 1925, when I accepted a professorship at the University of Bonn, Germany. In 1927–8 and again in 1930 I visited Harvard University, which I joined as a member of her permanent staff in 1932. I think this is as much as you will want to know about my past history and type of life.[1]

I

Schumpeter never wrote much more than this about his own life. There exists no autobiography or autobiographical articles in his giant production, which has been estimated to be around 250 items. What this means for our purposes is that Schumpeter's life has to be reconstructed bit by bit from official documents, recollections of friends, and the like. It may also be noted that Schumpeter never made any particular effort to save material about his life, such as letters or interviews. Indeed, when he in 1932 decided to emigrate to the United States, he left behind most of his correspondence, private library and public documents in Germany. He even left some of his own writings in economics. His wife Elizabeth says that he 'always regretted' that he did this and that various logistical problems prevented him from having his things shipped to the United States.[2] But Schumpeter could have sent for them whenever he wanted – they were all neatly stored in a number of trunks in a house outside Bonn. One gets the distinct impression that Schumpeter preferred to leave his European past behind and in this way be free from it.

Because of the lack of written records, what we know about Schumpeter's childhood is rather limited. According to his birth certificate 'Joseph Aloisius Julius Schumpeter' was born on 8 February 1883 in Triesch.[3] A few days later he was baptized into the Roman Catholic faith. His father, Josef Schumpeter, is described in the birth certificate as a *Tuchfabrikant* (cloth manufacturer) and so is his grandfather, Alois Schumpeter. The mother, Johanna Schumpeter (born Grüner), came from a well-known doctor's family in Iglau, a town close to Triesch. According to other official information, Joseph was the only child in the Schumpeter family; a second son was born dead on 10 April 1884.[4] At the time of Joseph's birth, his parents had been married for a little more than a year – their wedding had taken place in Iglau on 3 September 1881.

Triesch, where Schumpeter was born, is today called Trest and is a small town of about 6,000 people, situated in Moravia, Czechoslovakia. In those days Triesch was part of the Austro-Hungarian Empire and the population was around 4,000. The predominant language was Czech but there was also a small German minority, which controlled most of the economic and political life of the town. Most of the German-speaking inhabitants were Jewish, but some were Catholic. The Schumpeter family was a prominent and successful bourgeois family of the Catholic faith, which belonged to the German minority. Exactly when the family arrived in the region is unclear, but there exist records of the Schumpeters in Moravia since at least 1523. This means that Joseph Schumpeter was the eleventh generation of Schumpeters residing in Moravia. Schumpeter himself seems to have speculated that the Schumpeter family, before arriving in Moravia, had lived in Italy and that 'Schumpeter' was a German corruption of 'Giampietro'. No reliable confirmation of this has been found. Neither is it known whether there is any truth in the colourful legend about an early Schumpeter being a nobleman who was decapitated in the thirteenth century. In the Schumpeter family, however, this legend was apparently believed. To cite a letter (written in charming but faulty English) that Elizabeth Schumpeter received from one of her husband's relatives some time after his death:

The family is said to descend from barons of the Roman Empire of the German Nation; one of them was decapitated at Nüremberg as a robber knight under the Emperor Rudolph (1273–1291). The whole posterity was sentenced to lose its nobility and to be 'banished for ever from the country'. At Nüremberg, so it is told, there is a little church in which there is a sepulchre of a 'Reichsfreiherr' Schumpeter ... Then the Schumpeters appear in the Böhmerwald as glassblowers and later in the Sudetengebirge as clothweavers. Then they settled at Triesch about 200 years ago and acquired a big fortune, houses, factories, fields and forests. I am born there and I remember clearly the house, the furniture, the garden, the horses and the old servants. It is certain that the Schumpeters were an old patrician family with high freemanspirit and democratic feelings, and they refused several times titles of nobility, offered them by the Austrian Emperor.[5]

The factories referred to in the letter had been founded by Schumpeter's great-grandfather, Josef Schumpeter (1777–1848). In the early 1830s, according to a local chronicle, he established the first textile mill in Triesch.[6] This event, we are told, helped to trigger industrialization in the town. Josef's entrepreneurial feat was continued in the late 1840s by his son Alois Schumpeter (1813–98), who expanded and rationalized the factory. Alois Schumpeter, like his father, also served as Mayor of Triesch for several years. He and his wife were apparently very popular. To cite another passage from the letter to Elizabeth Schumpeter, already referred to: 'Alois was nicknamed 'Djedouschek', which signifies 'Little old grandfather' in Czech. He was a very good and wise man and his wife Maria was considered the angel of the workers. She installed a gratuite lunch for them in her home and was a great benefactor of the poor.'[7]

It is obvious that Schumpeter's great-grandfather and grandfather were the kind of entrepreneur about whom Schumpeter would later write so glowingly. So also, in all likelihood, was Schumpeter's own father, Josef Schumpeter (1855–87), even though we cannot be certain. The reason why we know so little about Schumpeter's father is that he died at an early age – when he was only 31 years old. At the time of his father's death, which happened on 14 January 1887 and which seems to have involved a hunting accident, Schumpeter was only four years old. It is clear that this event was not only a terrible shock to him, but that it would also have very important consequences for his whole future life. If his father had lived to a mature age, Schumpeter may very well have spent the rest of his life in Triesch and become a factory-owner like the other men in his family. But, as we know, that was not to be; and the life of Schumpeter was to take many unexpected turns.

Schumpeter's mother Johanna (1861–1926) was 25 years old when her husband died suddenly. She first seems to have moved back to her parents' home in Iglau. In October 1888, however, she and her little son moved to the much larger town of Graz. The reason for the move is not known. Johanna may possibly have wanted to be near the man she was later to marry, the recently retired Lieutenant-fieldmarshal Sigismund von Kéler. She may also have just wanted to move away from a small place like Iglau, which cannot have presented many opportunities for a young widow. In any case, von Kéler represented something new for Johanna: he was more than 30 years older than she; he was an aristocrat; and he was the son of a court dignitary. In 1885 von Kéler had retired to Graz, where his mother lived. He was not particularly wealthy (though he is supposed to have had a generous pension), but he had excellent connections in Vienna and elsewhere due to his family background.

Graz was where the young Schumpeter went to primary school. In September 1893, a few months after he had completed his four years of *Volksschule*, the whole family moved to Vienna where his mother and von Kéler immediately got married. The family moved into a spacious apartment on Doblhofgasse 3, which was an excellent address. Through his stepfather's connections, Schumpeter was promptly admitted to Theresianum, the famous preparatory school for the aristocracy. A new and important period of his life had begun.

But before recounting what we know about Schumpeter in Theresianum, a few words should be said about the people who influenced

Schumpeter the most during his early years. The three most important people in Schumpeter's childhood were clearly his father, his mother and his stepfather. His grandfather Alois, who lived till 1898, may also have played an important role – grandparents often do when one parent is missing – but about this we know very little. There exists next to no information about Schumpeter's father. According to one of Schumpeter's life-long friends, it was from his father that Schumpeter had inherited his 'dark features'.[8] Some people, however, have challenged even this and pointed to the 'persistent rumour' that Schumpeter was the illegitimate son of 'a very highly placed Austrian noble'.[9] If this rumour were true, von Kéler would be the obvious candidate as Schumpeter's real father. There is, however, nothing whatsoever to confirm this rumour. In any case, it is clear that Josef Senior mainly had an impact on his son by virtue of his absence.

That Schumpeter had an uncommonly close relationship with his mother is also obvious. And von Kéler does not seem to have intruded on this. When Schumpeter later spoke of his stepfather, he did so in a very relaxed manner; and he clearly did not look upon him 'as a father', according to a friend.[10] The adult Schumpeter, however, liked to hint that von Kéler was a bit more powerful than he actually was. To several of his friends Schumpeter apparently suggested that von Kéler was the commander of all the troops in Vienna, which at this time was the capital of the giant Austro-Hungarian Empire. Von Kéler, however, never commanded the troops in Vienna. The last position he held, before retiring to Graz (presumably because of bad health), was as the commander of the infantry troop division at Terezin (now Theresienstadt).[11]

But if von Kéler did not influence Schumpeter very much by virtue of his personality, he certainly did so by virtue of his class position. By marrying von Kéler, Johanna Schumpeter had in one stroke moved from the provincial bourgeoisie into an aristocratic family that was both well-known and respected in the capital. This, no doubt, made a great difference to her. She could now escape the not too enviable role of being a young bourgeois widow with a small child to care for and enter her new husband's aristocratic circles. On her son, of course, all of this made a different and ultimately more profound impression. He had originally been brought up to become an ordinary man with a specific social and psychological niche in bourgeois society. Suddenly, however, this path was altered when he gained an aristocratic stepfather and was placed with other aristocratic children in Theresianum.

Undeniably, the key person in Schumpeter's childhood was his mother. She was forever to be the emotional centre of his life. Several friends and acquaintances have testified to how extremely attached Schumpeter was to her, even long after her death. One friend describes the influence of Johanna Schumpeter on her son like this: 'Without doubt, his mother was the most important personal influence in Schumpeter's life. She was handsome, talented, and ambitious for her son. His devotion to her continued without diminution or disillusion not only to the end of her life but to the end of his.'[12] Schumpeter never mentioned his mother in any of his writings but in a thinly veiled autobiographical novel (which was never completed) he describes her as 'an excellent woman, strong and kind'. 'To make him an English gentleman was the one aim in life [and] she had connections she resolutely exploited for her darling.' She was *the one great human factor in [his] life*.[13]

Where does all of this leave us in so far as Schumpeter's personality is concerned? On an emotional level, how did he react to being at the centre of this triangle, consisting of an absent father, an aristocratic elderly stepfather, and a mother who was first widowed and then remarried? Well, there is first the exceedingly close relationship with his mother. Johanna Schumpeter seems to have doted on her son, brought him up as her little prince, and inculcated in him great designs for the future: he *should* succeed. Throughout his life, Schumpeter always feared that he would disappoint her. There was also the double opportunity for male identification – with the absent father (who one could fantasize about) and with the present stepfather (who was a real aristocrat and a military man). On some level it is clear that Schumpeter succeeded in fusing these two male influences in his vision of the bold and aristocratic entrepreneur, but it seems to have been more difficult to handle them on an emotional level. Beneath the brilliant and well-constructed surface that he loved to display in public, Schumpeter would always feel lost and unhappy. Why this was so is hard to say. There had perhaps been too many new and competing influences on his individual psyche before it had had the time to grow strong on its own. And when he was older, these conspired to make him feel that he did not really have an authentic self. The hero of his semi-autobiographical novel keeps saying that there was no place where he really 'felt at home': 'Certainly not in Germany or what had been the Austro-Hungarian Empire'. And even worse: 'he did not with subconscious allegiance belong either to society or the business class or the professions or the trade union world, all of which provided such comfortable homes for everyone he knew.' There was only one thing he could do that would help him. And that was to *work*: 'for modern man his work is everything.'[14]

When Schumpeter wrote the outline to this novel, which was to be called *Ships in Fog*, he was probably in his fifties and the contours of his life were by now fairly clear to him. In our story we shall, however, now return to 1893 when Schumpeter was ten years old and about to enter Theresianum. This famous school had originally been founded by Empress Maria Theresa in 1746 as a 'knight's academy' but had evolved into a school for the children of the high aristocracy and the top officials of the empire. When Schumpeter became a student this was still very much its task, even if the First World War would soon put an end to such pretensions. Theresianum was, one might say, a kind of Austro-Hungarian Eton and its main function more to teach the students how to govern the empire than to impart knowledge to them in a utilitarian fashion. The unofficial motto of the school was, according to the school boys, '*A bisserl blöd is vornehm*' or, freely translated, 'Being a bit stupid just shows you have the right background'.[15]

Schumpeter seems to have liked Theresianum quite a bit, and according to a friend he always remembered it 'fondly'.[16] He was a day student (*externer Schüler*), like many of the boys whose parents lived in Vienna. This was clearly less prestigious than being a regular boarder. On the other hand, it meant that Schumpeter could keep his distance from this new aristocratic world more easily than if he had lived within its walls day and night. Apart from teaching the students how to fence and ride, the emphasis in the curriculum was on classical education, especially Greek and Latin. In addition, the students were taught French, English and Italian; and Schumpeter soon spoke all of these languages fluently. According to an autobiographical note, it was also at Theresianum that he started to read on his own: 'My interest for sociology and philosophy was awakened already in high school.'[17] Exactly which books he read we do not know. At one point in a later essay he says that he studied Gumplowicz's 'racial theory of classes', but that is all.[18]

Schools like Theresianum are usually more important for what they teach the students informally than for what they impart to them formally, and this seems also to have been true for Schumpeter. It was during the eight years at Theresianum, Haberler says, 'that he acquired his agreeable, sometimes quaintly overpolite old-world manner'.[19] As we recall, the main function of Theresianum was to prepare the children of the top circles for the day when they were to take over the administration of the Austro-Hungarian Empire with all its multiple nationalities and ethnic groups. This necessitated a capacity in the administrator to rise above the separate interests and not to get bogged down in any particular perspective. For someone as unsure of himself as the young Schumpeter, this type of aristocratic education could possibly have had a damaging effect; it could have tipped his emotional balance towards insincerity and opportunism. And this is perhaps what happened – or at least that is what Felix Somary, a lifelong friend, thinks happened to Schumpeter at Theresianum:

Schumpeter ... never seemed to take anything in life seriously. He had been educated in Theresianum, where the pupils were taught to stick to the issue and not let personal feelings interfere. One should know the rules of all parties and ideologies, but not belong to any party or believe in any one opinion. And Schumpeter knew how to play all political games superbly, from the extreme left to the extreme right.[20]

II

In 1901 Schumpeter graduated from Theresianum with high honours. Later the same year he enrolled at the University of Vienna as a law student. He apparently already knew that he wanted to study economics. 'From the very beginning', he was later to write, 'I had decided to devote myself to economics.'[21] Economics, however, did not have its own separate department at the University of Vienna, so he had to enrol in the Faculty of Law and Political Science. This meant that he had to take obligatory courses not only in economics but also in law and political science. In addition, he attended lectures and seminars in statistics and mathematics. And, finally, he read voraciously on his own, especially in economics but also in the other social sciences, such as history and sociology.

At first Schumpeter seems to have enjoyed his studies in law. He took courses in Roman law, canon law and the history of law, and he was especially impressed by the Historical School of Jurisprudence. 'The first area I chose to work with at the university', he was later to recall, 'was legal and social history.'[22] Later on, however, as he became increasingly fascinated by economics, he found studying law to be a heavy burden. The way of thinking in law and in economics were just too different, he felt, and it was impossibly hard for a student to be properly trained in both of them simultaneously. As he put it in retrospect:

> That the student cannot master jurisprudence and the social sciences at the same time seems to have been experimentally demonstrated: There is no use denying that the holder of a law degree (*Referendar*) knows nothing about economics, and that the economist (*Diplomvolkswirt*) knows nothing about jurisprudence. No one who has himself experienced the fundamental difference of the two modes of thinking and the unmanageability of the combined material, can dispute the contention that this is not due primarily to accident or to avoidable mistakes.[23]

Virtually nothing is known about Schumpeter's studies in political science, apart from the fact that this subject played an important role in the course programme he was enrolled in. One of his law professors seems, however, to have had an important influence on Schumpeter's thinking in political questions. This was Heinrich Lammach, a conservative man with excellent connections at the imperial court. Schumpeter attended Lammach's lectures in foreign policy and international law and it was to him that Schumpeter would later turn for political advice during the First World War.

That Schumpeter also studied statistics and mathematics at the University of Vienna was directly connected to his interest in economics. Mathematics was not taught as part of economics in those days, so it was on his own initiative that Schumpeter attended lectures in this topic. Two statisticians who made an important impression on him were Karl Theodor Inama-Sternegg and Franz von Juraschek. The former was a prominent economic historian as well as the head of the Austrian Central Statistical Office. Juraschek was mainly a statistician and he eventually became Inama's successor at the Austrian Central Statistical Office. During the years 1903–5, Schumpeter participated in these two professors' seminar for three terms. During each term he presented a major paper and all three were published in *Statistische Monatschrift*. The titles were: 'The Method of Standard Population', 'The Method of Index Numbers', and 'International Pricing'. When these publications appeared in 1905 – they were Schumpeter's first – he was only 22 years old.

Schumpeter's main intellectual passion, however, was not statistics but economic theory. At the turn of the century, the University of Vienna was one of the most exciting places to be for a young economist. The faculty was under the strong influence of Carl Menger, who together with Jevons and Walras had set off the marginal utility revolution in the 1870s. The new type of economics, which Menger helped to develop and which in many ways constitutes the foundation on which modern economics still rests, was very different from the type of economics which was taught in the German-speaking universities around the turn of the century. Influenced by history and jurisprudence, German economists had since the mid-nineteenth century developed a kind of economics which was very critical of the abstract methods of British political economy and which mainly saw as its task to analyse unique economic events and economic institutions. Menger, who preferred the British kind of economics, wanted to break with historical economics, and had been since the mid-1880s embroiled in a stormy academic quarrel – the so-called *Methodenstreit* – with Gustav von Schmoller, the leader of the Historical School. For Schumpeter, all of this meant that he was primarily trained in the new kind of analytical and non-historical type of economics that Menger championed.

When Schumpeter arrived at the University of Vienna in 1901 Menger had just retired, though he would not formally give up his chair till 1903 when it was given to von Wieser. Schumpeter is reported to have met Menger only once or twice (he lived in seclusion) though it is clear that Schumpeter had a very high opinion of Menger's work. The three people most responsible for Schumpeter's education in economics were, however, Eugen von Philippovich, Friedrich von Wieser and Eugen von Böhm-Bawerk.

The first of these three had written an important textbook on economics, which Schumpeter appreciated very much, but, apart from this, Philippovich does not seem to have made any deeper impression on Schumpeter. It was different with both von Wieser and Böhm-Bawerk. Together with Menger, these two were the pioneers in what soon was to become known as the Austrian School in economics. This version of marginalist economics focused more on the subjective dimension of 'utility' and was less concerned with mathematics than Jevons and Walras. Schumpeter respected von Wieser very much, both as a scholar and as a person. On von Wieser's seventieth birthday in 1921 Schumpeter was one of the three key speakers, and he also wrote a moving obituary of his teacher a few years later. At von Wieser's seminar, as well as at the one led by Philippovich, Schumpeter presented papers which were early versions of chapters in the book on the history of economic theory which he would publish in 1914, *Epochen der Dogmen- und Methodengeschichte (Economic Doctrine and Method: An Historical Sketch)*.

Though Schumpeter always emphasized his debts to Philippovich and von Wieser, it was clearly Böhm-Bawerk to whom he felt closest. Schumpeter regarded Böhm-Bawerk as one of the 'great masters' in economics and he felt 'sincerely and personally devoted to him'.[24] Schumpeter especially admired Böhm-Bawerk's attempt to grapple with the concept of the economic process. The two sometimes also disagreed, and a few years after Schumpeter's graduation they got involved in a famous controversy over the nature of interest. According to some sources, Schumpeter and Böhm-Bawerk had a serious falling-out over this debate, and from 1913 onwards Böhm-Bawerk tried to keep Schumpeter out of the Austrian university system. Whether there is any truth to this is not clear.

Böhm-Bawerk served several times as finance minister in the Austro-Hungarian Empire, and it was not until he resigned from one of his appointments in 1904 that Schumpeter was able to participate in his famous seminars. The only seminar that we know he attended took place in 1905–6, and Schumpeter was only one of a number of outstanding students. There were, for example, Ludwig von Mises and Emil Lederer, both destined to become famous economists. There were also Felix Somary and the two outstanding Marxists, Otto Bauer and Rudolf Hilferding. Otto Bauer would soon become the leading theoretician of the Austrian Social Democratic Party and also serve as foreign minister. It was supposedly Bauer who recommended Schumpeter as finance minister in 1919. Rudolf Hilferding later wrote *Finance Capital* and was twice finance minister in Germany. The debates at the seminar were apparently quite stormy, which is not surprising since Böhm-Bawerk a few years earlier had written a withering critique of Marxian economics which Hilferding had tried to rebut. The key question, which was probably raised during the seminar, was whether Marx's theory of value was really useful as an analytical tool for understanding price movements. Böhm-Bawerk said emphatically 'no' and Hilferding 'yes'. Whose side did Schumpeter take? According to one of the participants in the seminar, 'Schumpeter attracted general attention through his cool, scientific detachment. The seemingly playful manner in which he took part in the discussion ... was evidently mistaken for a lack of seriousness or an artificial mannerism.'[25]

Schumpeter also studied on his own during these years as a student at the University of Vienna. Through his excellent language skills he could read all the great economists in the original and this opened up new worlds of exciting ideas to him. After what he called a 'sharp turn' away from his initial interest in legal and social history, Schumpeter began to study the 'economic theory of the Austrian (Menger) kind, whose representative (and *enfant terrible*)' he now became, at least for a while. But he soon went in his own direction and was especially inspired to do so by reading 'Walras, Pareto, and Edgeworth ("the mathematical school")'.[26] In Schumpeter's eyes, Walras was always 'the greatest of all theorists' and he considered Walras's general equilibrium theorem to be one of the finest achievements ever made in economic theory.[27] He was also very attracted to the efforts by people like Pareto and Edgeworth to develop economics with the help of mathematics. In 1906 Schumpeter published his first major paper on this topic, 'On the Mathematical Method in Theoretical Economics'.

On 16 February 1906, after five years of study, Schumpeter graduated from the University of Vienna with a doctorate in law. No thesis was necessary to gain the degree, but he had to pass a number of rigorous tests. He had also fulfilled the requirement to participate in a number of seminars, where he had made approximately 30 presentations. Schumpeter knew perfectly well at this stage of his life that he wanted to be an economist. Still, he was only 23 years old and in no particular hurry. And one thing that he had always wanted to do was to travel. During the summer of 1906 he went to Germany, where he took part in an economics seminar at the University of Berlin. He then continued to England via France and other countries. He remained in England for about a year. According to a friend, the young Schumpeter enjoyed himself tremendously while he was there: 'Many of the doors of English society were open to him. He lived as a fashionable young man in London, visited country houses and intermingled his social life with occasional visits to Oxford and

Cambridge. I have always felt that that year in England was the happiest in his life.'[28]

Schumpeter did not spend all of his time hunting foxes and riding his private horse in Hyde Park, he also worked very hard. He was associated with the London School of Economics as a 'research student' and he spent long hours at the British Museum, mainly working his way through the classics and works which had not been available to him in Vienna. The copious notes that he now took would be of use to him many times later in life, not the least in the 1940s when he sat down to write his enormous *History of Economic Analysis*. He also attended a number of lectures in London, including some by Karl Pearson in statistics and by Edward Westermarck in sociology. He made excursions to other British universities, and he paid respectful visits to the grand old men in the economics profession, such as Edgeworth and Marshall. One of the better anecdotes from this period tells how Schumpeter was advised by Marshall *not* to become an economic theorist. Or, in Schumpeter's own, mocking formulation:

> It is as I saw him [Marshall] when I looked at him across his breakfast table in 1907 to tell him: 'Professor, after our conversation (about my scientific plans) I feel exactly as I would if I were an indiscreet lover bent on an adventurous marriage and you a benevolent old uncle trying to persuade me to desist.' He answered: 'And this is as it should be. For if there is anything to it, the uncle will preach in vain.'[29]

To judge from the metaphor he used in the conversation with Marshall, marriage was on Schumpeter's mind. This was perhaps not so surprising since he was to top off his year in England by quickly falling in love and marrying a British woman. Her name was Gladys Ricarde Seaver and all that is known about her is that she was 'stunning' and the daughter of a high dignitary in the Church of England. The passion between the two seems however only to have lasted for a couple of months, and soon both of them began to have extramarital affairs.[30] Schumpeter was later to hint that the marriage had been a mistake from the beginning. To the perplexity of posterity Schumpeter also used to give different information about Gladys's age; to one close friend he said that she was 24 years older than he was and to another that she was 12 years older. Perhaps this was a way of portraying himself to friends as the innocent, young victim of an older and much more experienced woman – perhaps that was also how Schumpeter experienced the whole episode. In any case, Gladys was in all likelihood 12 years older than her husband and not 24.[31]

When Schumpeter arrived in England he seems to have toyed with the idea of studying law. He was not attracted to law *per se*, as he was already heavily committed to writing a book on economic theory. But he needed an income which would allow him to live like a gentleman. 'Schumpeter wanted an academic job but not an academic salary', as a friend put it.[32] But neither in Austria nor in England was it easy for an inexperienced law graduate quickly to find a well-paying job. For a while Schumpeter actually started to study English law, but he soon gave it up. ('As Schumpeter told it, he could not stand eating the required meals in the Temple.')[33] In the end, however, one of his many social contacts must have paid off, for late in 1907 we find him practising law in an Italian law firm in Cairo. The reason why he chose Cairo was that no earlier legal experience was needed to practise law at the so-called International Mixed Court of Egypt. As gleaned from various anecdotes Schumpeter liked to tell, he enjoyed himself enormously in Egypt and had a number of exotic experiences. One of his most important clients was, for example, an Egyptian princess whose business he dramatically improved simply by not stealing from her, as her previous legal adviser had done. For this he was amply rewarded, which was also the case when he helped to reorganize a huge local sugar refinery. Of course, there was a down-side to living in Cairo as well – Schumpeter was nearly whipped by a Moslem for wanting him to accept interest.

In the evenings, after work, Schumpeter was feverishly trying to finish off the manuscript to his first book. This he did in March 1908, and the manuscript was immediately sent to Germany. The book was called *Das Wesen und der Hauptinhalt der theoretischen Nationalökonomie* (*The Nature and Essence of Theoretical Economics*) and it was quickly to establish Schumpeter's reputation as a brilliant young economist. The work, incidentally, was dedicated to his mother and not to his wife. Around this time Schumpeter also fell ill of Malta fever, a serious infectious disease. This was the first time that Schumpeter had been seriously ill and it must have greatly frightened him. He decided that it was time to return to Vienna.

Once Schumpeter was back in Austria, after a few weeks of rest in England, he immediately took a series of steps to secure a teaching position. In October 1908 he submitted his book to the Faculty of Law and Political Science at the University of Vienna as his *Habilitationsschrift* so that he might acquire the right to lecture at the university as *Privatdozent*. No salary was attached to this position, which was the first step in the academic hierarchy. In the list of lectures that Schumpeter included with his application, he stated that he was planning to give courses in economics, sociology and statistics. He enumerated six possible courses, including 'Introduction to Political Economy', 'The Theory of Gold Markets', 'The Foundations and Contemporary State of Sociology', and 'Problems in Modern Statistics'.[34] Von Wieser and Böhm-Bawerk were his two

referees and they recommended that the faculty should approve
Schumpeter's request, which it did in December 1908. Schumpeter
gave his Habilitations-lecture in February 1909 on 'The Verification
of Abstract Theorems by Means of Statistics'. He was awarded the
title *Privatdozent* in political economy with effect from 16 March
1909. He was the youngest economist in Austria ever to have been
awarded this title.

During the spring of 1909 Schumpeter lectured at the University of
Vienna, and in the autumn of the same year he advanced further in
his academic career when he began to work as an associate (*ausseror-
dentlicher*) professor at the University of Czernowitz. This made him
the youngest professor of economics in the country. Still, it is clear
that the 26-year-old Schumpeter must have wanted an appointment
at a more prestigious university, and that he cannot have been too
happy with this move to a small-town university. Czernowitz was
in those days the capital of the Duchy of Bukowina in the eastern-
most province of the Austro-Hungarian Empire (today it is called
Chervotsy and is part of the Ukrainian Socialist Republic). The
University of Czernowitz was quite young – it had been founded in
1875 – and it had the reputation of being a place for exiled young
Turks.

But, despite the fact that he had come to a second-rate university,
Schumpeter soon took a liking to Czernowitz, and the two years that
he spent there were apparently happy ones. He would later entertain
his colleagues at Harvard with a string of stories about his 'extracur-
ricular activities' in Czernowitz which, according to Haberler, 'might
well have come out of the Arabian Nights'.[35] Haberler's statement
probably means that Schumpeter did his share of high-spirited
partying in Czernowitz; he also had a series of sexual adventures
with local prostitutes and the like.[36] Another memorable event from
these days was his duel with a librarian over the right of the students
to get better access to the books. Schumpeter, we are told, scratched
his opponent and won.

A clear drawback with Czernowitz was that Schumpeter did not
find his colleagues particularly interesting. Eugen Ehrlich, the
founder of the so-called sociological school of jurisprudence, was an
obvious exception, and there also seem to have been some other
interesting legal theorists in Czernowitz. But, on the whole,
mediocrity ruled, and Schumpeter was bored by his colleagues: 'He
used to shock them by appearing at faculty meetings in riding boots
and aroused unfavorable comment by dressing for dinner when he
and his wife were dining alone.'[37]

Despite being bored, however, Schumpeter's own work went exceedingly well in Czernowitz. He continued to write articles, and it
was here that he wrote the main part of his greatest work in economics, *Theorie der wirtschaftlichen Entwicklung* (1911; *The Theory of*

Economic Development). Besides teaching straight economics courses at the University of Czernowitz, Schumpeter also lectured on various social science topics. The sheer intellectual delight that pervades some of these lectures from Czernowitz can still be sensed by reading his excellent little pamphlet on the history of the social sciences, *Vergangenheit und Zukunft der Sozialwissenschaften* (*The Past and the Future of the Social Sciences*). The students also seem to have enjoyed Schumpeter hugely, and on some he made a lasting impression. A few days after Schumpeter's death in January 1950, his wife received a letter from a former Czernowitz student which reads: 'I still remember the good looking and elegantly dressed young man who ... entered our class room to deliver his first lecture at the University of Czernowitz and who immediately impressed us with the deepest respect for the brilliance of his delivery and the profoundness of his thought.'[38]

In 1911 Schumpeter moved to the University of Graz as a full (*ordentlicher*) professor in political economy. He now could add a third record to his collection: he was the youngest full professor in the empire. The University of Graz was also a cut above Czernowitz in terms of prestige. His appointment, however, was by no means uncontested. Before Schumpeter arrived in Graz, economics was taught by a member of the Historical School, Richard Hildebrand (son of the famous Bruno Hildebrand), who was firmly against having a theoretical economist like Schumpeter as his successor. In his referee report Hildebrand said the following:

> Unfortunately, there do not exist Austrians who could be considered to be in any sense at par with *Schachner* and *Pohle*. Take, e.g., *Schumpeter* (Czernowitz) from the younger generation. He adheres to a barren, abstract, and formalistic approach, only toying with mathematical or mechanistic concepts and analogies without any relationship to real life. His book *Das Wesen und der Hauptinhalt der theoretischen Nationalökonomie* contains nothing but empty commonplaces and trivialities – presented, however, with great self-indulgence and emphasis as if they were important findings. So far, he has nothing to offer that could be considered scientific research.[39]

Hildebrand's and his colleagues' decision to appoint a local nonentity was, however, overruled through an imperial decree from Vienna. Presumably Böhm-Bawerk, who had excellent connections in the highest administrative circles, was behind this move. In any case, in the autumn of 1912 Schumpeter began teaching at the University of Graz. The students were initially hostile to their new professor and for a couple of weeks they boycotted his classes. They felt that he demanded too much from them and they did not like the fact that he so often made disparaging remarks about his predecessor, Richard Hildebrand. Things, however, were eventually smoothed out and the students soon came to appreciate Schumpeter.

Schumpeter had a very heavy teaching load in Graz. During part of his appointment he also taught at the Graz University of Technology and it was not uncommon for him to lecture 14–16 hours per week. As often as he could, he would escape to Vienna which was only a three-hour train ride away. The year 1913–14 he succeeded in spending in the United States, at Columbia University as an Austrian exchange professor. Schumpeter went alone, since Gladys preferred to spend the year in England. At Columbia Schumpeter taught economic theory, held a seminar, and gave a course on social classes. He also gave special lectures at a number of American universities and met several prominent economists, such as F. W. Taussig, Irving Fisher and Wesley Clair Mitchell. The trip, Schumpeter felt, was a great success.

Back in Graz in 1914 Schumpeter had the pleasure of seeing his third book appear, an excellent little history of economic theory called *Epochen der Dogmen- und Methodengeschichte* (*Economic Doctrine and Method: An Historical Sketch*). Schumpeter now also joined the editorial board of *Archiv für Sozialwissenschaft und Sozialpolitik*, which was the most prominent social science journal in Germany. According to a letter he wrote in 1916 to the publisher of *Archiv*, Paul Siebeck, he had several other projects in mind as well. Some of these would later materialize, such as a small book on social classes. But others did not, including a thin volume called *Finanzpolitische Vorlesungen* (*Lectures in Public Finance*), another book about the credit system, and an interesting sounding two-volume set of essays on such topics as the woman's question.[40]

One explanation of why Schumpeter did not finish some of the projects he mentioned to Siebeck was the advent of the First World War. It is true that Schumpeter never took part in the fighting; he had undergone military examination in December 1914 but been exempted on the ground that he was the only professor of economics in Graz. Still, the First World War was to change all of Europe as well as Schumpeter's own world in many unforeseen ways. A few years later he decided to leave the academic world and pursue a career as a politician. Before we discuss Schumpeter the politician, however, we shall first take a closer look at Schumpeter's economic writings from these early years.

2

Early Economic Works

The social process is really one indivisible whole. Out of its great stream the classifying hand of the investigator artificially extracts economic facts.

(Joseph A. Schumpeter, *Theorie der wirtschaftlichen Entwicklung*, 1911)

From 1906, when Schumpeter graduated from the University of Vienna, to 1916, his research production was enormous. Not only did he produce a series of important articles in economic theory, some of which have become minor classics, but he also published three major books. There was first *Das Wesen und der Hauptinhalt der theoretischen Nationalökonomie* (1908; *The Nature and Essence of Theoretical Economics*), which is a study in economic methodology that Schumpeter finished in Cairo. Three years later, while teaching in Graz, he published *Theorie der wirtschaftlichen Entwicklung* (1911; *The Theory of Economic Development*), which is generally regarded as Schumpeter's most important work. And a couple of years after that, *Epochen der Dogmen- und Methodengeschichte* (1914; *Economic Doctrine and Method: An Historical Sketch*) appeared. This last work is a dense, superb little history of economic theory. As Arthur Spiethoff has said, 'One scarcely knows which is the more amazing: that a man of twenty-five and twenty-seven should shake the foundations of his chosen science, or that a man of thirty should write the history of that discipline!'[1]

What was the source of Schumpeter's creativity during these years? This is a difficult question to answer; intellectual creativity comes in many different forms, and Schumpeter's was just one of them. Schumpeter himself was convinced that the third decade in a scientist's life was something special; he often referred to it as 'the decade of sacred fertility', and he thought that during the rest of his life a scientist basically worked out the ideas he had had in his youth.[2] Schumpeter's own experience confirms this: his later works in economics, such as *Business Cycles* and *History of Economic Analysis*, are essentially elaborations of ideas already explored in his youth.

At times, of course, it could be difficult to be so young and so brilliant, something which his meeting in 1909 with Léon Walras illustrates. Before going to visit the aged Walras, the 26-year-old Schumpeter had sent him a copy of *Das Wesen und der Hauptinhalt der theoretischen Nationalökonomie*. When Schumpeter arrived at Walras's home in Clarens, near Montreux in Switzerland, the following happened: 'upon greeting the youthful Joseph Schumpeter, [Léon Walras] asked him to thank his father for the book. In vain Schumpeter tried to correct the misunderstanding. As Schumpeter took his leave, L. W. again complimented Schumpeter's father on the excellent book.'[3]

When Schumpeter's early works are discussed by economists, they tend to focus on *Theorie der wirtschaftlichen Entwicklung* and especially on the theory of economic change as developed within it. Much less has been written about Schumpeter's two other books and about his early production as a whole. What has been written has also been rather simplistic. As a rule, it is suggested that Schumpeter's great ambition as an economist, from his very first work onwards, was to revolutionize economics with the help of mathematics. Sometimes it is added that Schumpeter also did some work in non-economic subjects, such as political science and sociology. Exactly how all of these disparate interests fit together we are never told. A case in point is Erich Schneider's important article 'Schumpeter's Early German Works, 1906–1917'.[4] Schneider opens his article in the following way: 'It is significant that Joseph Schumpeter entered our field in the year 1906 with a study on mathematical methods in theoretical economics. This, his very first work, contains the points from which his own original research took its departure.'[5]

This picture of Schumpeter's early work is, however, a bit of a myth. It is no doubt correct that Schumpeter – especially at one point of his life – had extremely high hopes for the use of mathematics in economics. But to portray this as *the* major theme in his life-work as an economist is misleading. Schumpeter received his education as an economist at a time when it was considered self-evident that economics should be broader than just theoretical economics and this was always reflected in Schumpeter's writings, including his earliest ones. It is true that the emphasis at the University of Vienna was primarily on the need to use abstract methods as opposed to the historical type of analysis. After all, Carl Menger had been at the University of Vienna and he was Gustav von Schmoller's main adversary in the *Methodenstreit* debate. Still, people like Menger, Böhm-Bawerk and von Wieser all acknowledged that history and sociology had important roles to play in economics.[6] Schumpeter was brought up in this atmosphere of methodological pluralism, and it was also to become his belief that economics should be a broad-based social science, encompassing not only theoretical economics but also sociological and historical approaches. 'The social process is really one indivisible whole', to cite the famous opening line in *Theorie der wirtschaftlichen Entwicklung*.

The great problem for Schumpeter, as for some of his colleagues in Vienna such as von Wieser, was how to put all of these different approaches together. What role, for example, should history play in relation to economic theory? And what exactly was the role of sociology and statistics? During his career as an economist Schumpeter would answer these questions in different ways; sometimes he emphasized the role of abstract theory and at other times the role of economic history. But he always addressed these questions, and it is the way that he worked out these problems in his various writings which constitutes *the* major theme in his life-work as an economist. That it also constitutes the major theme in his early economic writings, is something we shall try to show in this chapter.

I

During his first years at the University of Vienna, Schumpeter was mainly interested in social and historical approaches to economic phenomena. He participated in a series of seminars in economic history which were led by Siegmund Adler, the brother of Max Adler. Siegmund Adler was primarily a historian of administrative law, but he was also interested in taxation, and under his guidance Schumpeter started to work on a history of taxation in Lower Austria.[7] Schumpeter does not seem to have completed this task, but he did get some experience in archival work. He was also awarded a prize for his work during these seminars in economic history.

We know that Schumpeter participated in several seminars led by von Inama-Sternegg as well. Besides being a prominent statistician, Inama was a recognized authority in economic history and the emphasis in his seminars was on a combination of statistics and historical economics. That Schumpeter quickly assimilated Inama's viewpoint is clear from a paper he presented in the 1904–5 seminar on the world economy and which was later published in *Statistische Monatschrift*.[8] A variety of approaches to the world economy came under discussion during the seminar, including Gustav von Schmoller's idea that the world economy constitutes the highest stage in the evolution of the economy. Von Inama-Sternegg himself argued that one could also view the world economy as a kind of sociological entity, similar to the way that a *Volk* constitutes an organism. Schumpeter, to judge from his paper, did not side either with Schmoller or his teacher. Instead, he just noted that world prices presuppose a world market. His concept of the world market was taken from economic history rather than from economic theory: 'In our empirical research we do not use a general concept of "the world market"; we rather look at the concrete geographical centra where these prices are formed, at concrete power factors and at interest groups.'[9] In the paper itself Schumpeter carefully analysed how four different raw materials – wheat, coffee, cotton and wool – were priced on the international market. He noted the central role of cities like New York, London and Chicago in this process; he made quick references to the historical formation of the various markets; and he noted the role of speculation and similar phenomena in the ongoing 'price struggle'.[10]

After a few years at the University of Vienna Schumpeter began to lose interest in the historical approach to economics. He had begun to read mathematical economics and he soon experienced, as he put it, 'a sharp turn' in his interests, away from Schmoller's type of historical economics.[11] All that mattered to him now was the idea that one could make economics into a real science with the help of mathematics. Economics, he thought, would finally be able to take its place at the side of chemistry, physics and the other real sciences. 'Dropping early sociological and historical interests', Schumpeter later wrote in a letter, 'I became an economic theorist and the work of my youth is summed up in a book I published in 1907.'[12]

The work that Schumpeter was referring to in his letter was *Das Wesen und der Hauptinhalt der theoretischen Nationalökonomie* or, as he himself translated the title, *The Nature and Essence of Theoretical Economics*. This book can best be characterized as a treatise in economic methodology with the emphasis on 'theoretical economics' or 'pure economics'. Schumpeter stressed that his work was by no means a textbook in theoretical economics, nor that it had been his intention for it to be complete. The aim of the book was rather to provide an adequate picture of the field of theoretical economics. To cite the introduction: 'The following account belongs to the family of purely theoretical works, and it tries to carefully examine the foundation, the methods and the major results of pure economics as well as its nature, value and potential.'[13] Schumpeter realized that much of what he had to say was already available in other works, but he felt that these were not very much known in Germany: 'One of my goals is to make the German audience familiar with a host of things – concepts, theorems and perspectives – which have remained alien to it, because it has not sufficiently followed the development of economic theory. German economics does not really know what "pure" economics is all about.'[14]

The reason why German economists at the turn of the century did not know very much about theoretical economics had much to do with the *Methodenstreit*. In the 1880s Schmoller had been so angered by Menger that he had decided to try to keep all economic theory out of the German universities. Schmoller was such a powerful person in German academic life that he largely succeeded in his quest. It was actually not until the 1920s, when Schumpeter was appointed to a chair at the University of Bonn, that theoretical economics was properly taught at a German university. That the *Methodenstreit* was still alive when Schumpeter wrote *Das Wesen* is also clear in many other ways from his book. At each point of his argument Schumpeter first introduces the position of the Historical School, which he then confronts with the viewpoint of theoretical economics. The parameters of the discourse of his book, in other words, were set by the *Methodenstreit*.

The general position that Schumpeter took on the *Methodenstreit* was that this dispute had been a disaster, that it belonged to the past, and that both sides had been correct, each in their own way. Whether a historical approach or a theoretical approach was needed, could never be decided *a priori* – it depended on the subject and the purpose of the analysis. Indeed, what in Schumpeter's opinion had caused 'the whole history of the *Methodenstreit*' was the erroneous assumption that because a certain type of analysis was applicable to *some* topics, it was *a priori* applicable to *all* topics.[15] Schumpeter also emphasized that the Historical School had been right in criticizing the kind of economic theory that was being produced during the mid-nineteenth century. At this time classical economics had suffered a serious decline and displayed many weaknesses. Later, however, when marginal utility theory made its appearance, there was much less justification for this type of criticism.

Despite Schumpeter's attempt to be fair to both sides in the *Methodenstreit*, it is clear that at this stage of his life he basically sided with the theoretical economists (later he would move towards a Weberian-type synthesis). Each time, before describing how he viewed some specific aspect of economics, Schumpeter always spelled out which errors must be avoided. And on every issue, he ended up taking a position that was diametrically opposite to that of Schmoller and the Historical School. It was, for example, imperative to Schumpeter that theoretical economics should not take a political stance or in any other way be connected to a political ideology. Schumpeter did not explicitly mention Schmoller's name in this context (or anywhere else in the book for that matter), but it was of course well-known that Schmoller had tried to use economics for various reform purposes, especially in the *Verein für Sozialpolitik*. For Schumpeter, however, this was absolutely inadmissible and already in the preface to *Das Wesen* he made his position clear: 'I am not interested in practical politics and my only ambition is knowledge.'[16]

This theme recurs time and again throughout the book. At one point Schumpeter talks sombrely about 'the crown of thorns of practical interests' and at another he says that the economist who wants to use economics for practical purposes is in reality its worst enemy.[17]

It is also important, Schumpeter argued, to resist the temptation to draw political consequences from economic theorems. The classical economists had clearly overstepped their boundaries when they portrayed perfect competition as an ideal; it was a theoretical assumption and nothing else. Schumpeter's famous concept 'methodological individualism' (which is coined in *Das Wesen*) also has its origin in a similar argument. According to Schumpeter, it was clear that in an economic analysis you often have to start the analysis with the individual as opposed to, say, the group or society in general ('methodological individualism'). This, however, must in no way be read as an endorsement of individualism as a *political* value ('political individualism'). As Schumpeter put it: 'It is impossible to deduct any argument either for or against political individualism from economic theory.'[18]

Also, when Schumpeter discussed the relationship between economic theory and history, he ended up on Menger's side. At first this may not seem to be the case since Schumpeter argues that the debate on induction versus deduction, which had been so hotly contested in the *Methodenstreit*, was basically a moot question – both of them were needed equally. But, after having said this, Schumpeter immediately advanced a series of arguments to the effect that the historian is only interested in describing individual cases while the economist wants to establish general laws. Schumpeter did not try to synthesize the two positions, as Weber had done a few years earlier with his concept of 'ideal types'.[19] Instead, Schumpeter presented an argument, which was basically partial to Menger. In both historical research and in economics, Schumpeter said, one has to start with concrete reality as opposed to *a priori* assumptions about what reality looks like. 'We start from the facts.'[20] To describe reality in all its multiplicity is, however, just as impossible for the historian as for the economist; both have to decide which facts are interesting and then concentrate on these. Once this has been done, however, the economist and the historian must part company since the latter is basically interested in 'cataloguing' some limited aspect of reality while the former wants to say something general about reality. Instead of just listing various facts, the economist now proceeds to make certain assumptions in order to get at the essence of a phenomenon. The economist, Schumpeter says, takes a short-cut by making assumptions, by abstracting and by isolating certain traits in a phenomenon. To the untrained eye it might look as if the result of all this activity has little to do with reality. But this is not the case; and with a few bold strokes the economist has actually created his own picture of reality. This picture is not identical to reality, but it captures its essence; and this is what matters. To use one of Schumpeter's favourite metaphors: an economic theorem fits reality just like a well-tailored coat fits the customer's body.

The conclusion one must draw from Schumpeter's argument is that theoretical economics and history have very little in common; they are essentially two different activities. Schumpeter, it should also be noted, took a similar stand on the relationship between economics and a host of other sciences. Theoretical economics, he argued, should be totally independent of these other sciences as well; and Schumpeter saw it as his duty to proclaim what he called 'a kind of Monroe Doctrine' for theoretical economics.[21] That economics should have nothing to do with metaphysics was perfectly obvious to Schumpeter. He also doubted that economics could learn anything from ethics. Economics does not take a stand on such issues as whether one should try to save a drowning man or not; all it can say is whether there exists an economic way of spending one's energy while swimming towards the drowning person. Economists should also stay away from philosophy. Theoretical economics is a science and it has no place for philosophical speculation.

In a similar manner Schumpeter declared the independence of theoretical economics from psychology, sociology, biology and ethnology. Economics – Alfred Marshall to the contrary – has nothing to learn from biology, nor from ethnology. The same is essentially true for sociology. On the one hand, Schumpeter says, it is clear that sociology is a young and interesting science whose further development economists should welcome. But, on the other hand, there is also the fact that many contemporary German economists are sociologists rather than economists; and for this reason it has to be clearly stated that from a principled point of view, economics and sociology have absolutely nothing in common. 'When it comes to our work, [sociology] has as little to offer us [economists] as we have to offer it.'[22] It was basically the same with psychology, in Schumpeter's opinion. Many economists, he says, feel that economics needs a psychological foundation. But this is wrong; the concept of utility is not a description of reality, and it does not describe what people actually feel. Utility, Schumpeter said, is a theoretical assumption. Schumpeter ended the chapter on the relationship between theoretical economics and the other sciences on an uncompromising note: 'This much we can say: All these assertions, which can be found in prefaces and occasional statements, that theoretical economics should be closely related to other sciences have little – or nothing – to offer us. In the interest of clarity we are obliged to proclaim their nothingness and throw this ballast overboard.'[23]

But if theoretical economics was to be so radically cut off from the other social sciences, what exactly was left for it to study? Schumpeter's answer was that even though theoretical economics covers a very small area, it is an important one. There exists a hole in our scientific knowledge when it comes to human behaviour, he said, and it is this hole that theoretical economics can fill. It holds out the promise, in brief, of being the first real science of human behaviour.

Schumpeter repeatedly said that when you look at the questions that theoretical economics deals with, these may seem rather dull in comparison to what is discussed in such fields as philosophy or sociology. In theoretical economics you do not address questions about the purpose of life, the course of history, and so on. Rather, its strength resides in its ambition to be absolutely scientific. In this sense, Schumpeter says, economics has much more in common with the natural sciences (*Naturwissenschaften*) than with the social sciences (*Geisteswissenschaften*). As Schumpeter put it: 'From a methodological and epistemological viewpoint, pure economics is a "natural science" and its theorems are "laws of nature".'[24]

The core of theoretical economics, Schumpeter says, consists of a few important but trivial-sounding statements. The basic assumption is the following one: 'At the foundation of our discipline is the understanding that all quantities, which we in all brevity shall call "economic quantities", are in such a state of mutual dependence that a change in one of them, leads to a change in all of them.'[25] When economic quantities are related to one another in this way, they constitute a system. This system is unambiguously determined if a change in one or several of the quantities leads to a specific change in the rest of them. When a change has worked itself out through the system, the system enters a state of equilibrium, which can also be defined as the tendency of the system to stabilize itself (on condition that there are no disturbing factors outside the system). The task of the economist is essentially to map out how one change in the system leads to another change. 'Explanation', Schumpeter says, is thus the same as a 'description' of the movements within the system.[26] The economic theorist essentially tries to establish economic laws, which are defined in the following way: 'The kind of explanation that is possible through our theory consists of functional relationships between elements in our system, established through the briefest and most general formula. These formulas we shall call "laws".'[27] Economic laws, Schumpeter emphasizes, do not constitute ideals; they are 'generalized observations' and non-political in nature.[28]

With the help of the equilibrium model, according to Schumpeter, one can only analyse a limited number of phenomena. Most importantly, one can study the process of price formation, but also exchange, savings and the process of distribution. There, however, also exist a number of economic topics that cannot be studied with the help of the static model. These fall into two categories, which must not be confused with one another. First, there are those that fall outside of the economic analysis by virtue of being non-economic in nature. And, secondly, there are those topics that cannot be analysed with the help of the static model and yet belong to theoretical economics. That socioeconomic facts fall outside the field of theoretical economics was self-evident to Schumpeter:

> Could it really be that the nature of a nation's economy would be indifferent to the economist? We do not hesitate to answer this question in the affirmative. Yes, we are ready to go even further and say that the nature of economic action is indifferent to us. We should only look at that which is our goal – and in this case this is how prices are formed – and we should only take into account what is absolutely essential to reach this goal.[29]

Some economic facts which cannot be analysed with the static model can, however, be analysed with the help of a dynamic model. The distinction between 'statics' and 'dynamics', which Schumpeter had probably picked up from John Stuart Mill and John Bates Clark, is absolutely crucial to his whole economic theory. Some changes in the economy would reach a state of equilibrium and not alter anything in the system itself. These changes, Schumpeter said (using an analogy from Walras), are like the waves in the sea: 'the surface of the sea is continuously disturbed but it always reestablishes itself.'[30] But then there are those changes which move the whole system in a novel direction, and these belong to the area of dynamics. And it is at this point that we arrive at one of Schumpeter's most important ideas, namely that after a process of disequilibrium, the system does not return to an equilibrium (the traditional position) but simply keeps on changing.[31] To try to analyse dynamic phenomena with the help of an equilibrium model would only be to impose a 'straight-jacket' on the analysis. They must be approached in an entirely different manner – one that sets an active individual in the centre as opposed to the passive 'equilibrium man' (Gleichgewichtmensch) of static theory. Schumpeter says apropos the latter type of person: 'What a miserable figure he is, this economic subject who is always looking so anxiously for an equilibrium. He has no ambitions and no entrepreneurial spirit; in brief, he is without force and life!'[32] One will not find a detailed account of what the dynamic type of analysis looks like in Das Wesen; this is something that Schumpeter saved for his next book, Theorie der wirtschaftlichen Entwicklung. It was, however, clear already from Schumpeter's first work that he attached a tremendous importance to the distinction between dynamics and statics and that he felt that all economic topics could be solved either through a dynamic analysis or a static analysis. While the equilibrium model was mainly applicable to the problem of price formation, the dynamic type of analysis covered economic development. Schumpeter summarized his ideas on this issue in the following way:

> This distinction [between statics and dynamics] is crucial. Statics and dynamics are two totally different areas. Not only do they deal with different problems, but they use different methods and they work with different materials. They are not two chapters in the same theoretical construction – they are two totally different buildings. Only statics has been worked on sufficiently, and this book mainly addresses this kind of problem. The analysis of dynamics is still in its beginnings; it is a 'land of the future'.[33]

Schumpeter's comments on dynamics in *Das Wesen* are brief, and they have been highlighted only in order to show how Schumpeter viewed dynamics at this early stage of his life. The main bulk of the book, however, is devoted to static analysis and how this type of analysis can be used to solve a series of economic problems. Schumpeter ends his book with some thoughts about the future of economic theory, especially in its static version. He emphasizes that very little has yet been accomplished and that progress will probably be slow also in the future. Still, using the static model is the correct way to proceed and that is ultimately what matters. The last few sentences of the book sum up Schumpeter's purpose in writing it:

> If the reader by now has come to believe that there exist strong and healthy forces in our discipline ... and that these will have something to say also in the future, then I have accomplished what I set out to accomplish, even if I have to admit that there only exists a limited number of interesting theorems today. Nevertheless, this small group of confirmed truths constitute a beacon in a sea of darkness.[34]

Das Wesen was reviewed in several of the major economic journals and 'locally [it] made something of a hit', according to Schumpeter himself.[35] As one might have guessed, the reviewers who were close to Menger's type of analysis approved of Schumpeter's book, while the ones who identified more with Schmoller's school found it wanting on many points. Von Wieser devoted a long article to Schumpeter's book; and in a letter to a colleague, Walras described *Das Wesen* as a 'very handsome and important work'.[36] On the other hand, Othmar Spann, who represented the opposition to Menger, felt that Schumpeter's work had a number of weak points: *Das Wesen* was too theoretical; the analysis was ahistorical; and so on.[37]

Schumpeter himself seems to have grown disenchanted with his book rather quickly. He never allowed a second edition to be printed and he did not even take a copy with him when he emigrated to the

United States in 1932. In an interview from the 1940s, Schumpeter said that 'I have no copy and have been trying to atone for this effort of my youth since it was issued.'[38] Schumpeter never elaborated on what he felt was wrong with the book.

Das Wesen, of course, does have a number of weaknesses. Von Wieser, for example, felt that Schumpeter had tried to take on too much. 'One gets the impression', von Wieser said jokingly, 'that the author has not yet reached his own equilibrium.'[39] Othmar Spann was critical of Schumpeter's whole enterprise and argued that Schumpeter had reified economics in an unacceptable manner by eliminating all references to economic action and by replacing it with sterile statements about relationships between quantities.

There is no doubt some truth to the criticisms of both von Wieser and Spann. Schumpeter's greatest error, however, was that he had drawn a much too narrow picture of theoretical economics by purging from it so radically all social and dynamic elements. This mistake was also accentuated by his unfortunate tendency, throughout the book, to talk in the name of 'economics', when he actually meant 'theoretical economics'.[40] As a result, the reader is left with the impression that economics could only develop if all of its connections with the other social sciences were cut off. This was definitely not a position that Schumpeter wanted to defend later in life. In fact, only a few years after *Das Wesen* was published, he would change his mind on this point. He did this when he was struggling with his next Herculean task: to complement Walras's type of static analysis with a dynamic one of his own.

II

In the letter accompanying a copy of *Das Wesen* that Schumpeter sent to Léon Walras in October 1908, he described his book as 'a work of a disciple' and he said that 'I shall always try to work on the foundations that you have laid and to continue your efforts.'[41] But it seems that parallel to this admiration for Walras's type of economics, Schumpeter also had some serious doubts about it. These evidently grew stronger the more he tried to grapple with the problem of economic development. The turning point came when he discovered that Walras's type of analysis was not only static in nature but that it could only be applied to stationary processes.[42] 'Static' in this context simply means that an economic phenomenon can be analysed as if it is always seeking an equilibrium. 'Stationary', on the other hand, means that the economic process can never change by itself; if it changes, it is only as a result of forces outside the economic system. Schumpeter's suspicion that Walras's type of analysis indeed had this limitation was confirmed when he met Walras in his home in Clarens. On this occasion Walras told Schumpeter that 'of course economic life is essentially passive and merely adapts itself to the natural and social influences which may be acting on it.' Walras also said that the theory of the stationary process constitutes the whole of theoretical economics and that economists cannot say anything about historical changes.[43] To Schumpeter this was unacceptable:

> I felt very strongly that this was wrong, and that there was a source of energy within the economic system which would of itself disrupt any equilibrium that might be attained. If this is so, then there must be a purely economic theory of economic change which does not merely rely on external factors propelling the economic system from one equilibrium to another. It is such a theory that I have tried to build.[44]

Schumpeter's theory of economic change is to be found in *Theorie der wirtschaftlichen Entwicklung* or *The Theory of Economic Development*, which appeared in 1911 (and not in 1912 as it says on the title page). According to the preface, the book had its origin in work that Schumpeter had done in 1905 on economic crises. After having looked at a series of problems in economic theory, which could not be solved through Walras's type of analysis, Schumpeter became increasingly convinced that there existed a common theoretical key to all of them. He presented his solution in his 1911 book, which in many ways can be seen as a sequel to *Das Wesen* or as a second volume of a larger work. That Schumpeter nevertheless decided against calling *Theorie* a sequel or a second volume he explained in the following way: 'my way of handling the material as well as the material itself [are] essentially different.'[45] Actually, he was so worried that *Theorie* might be seen as a 'refutation' of his earlier book, that he felt impelled to state explicitly that this was *not* the case.[46]

Despite Schumpeter's affirmations to the contrary, the differences between Schumpeter's first book and his second book are striking. While in *Das Wesen* Schumpeter had tried radically to isolate economics from the rest of social science through his 'Monroe Doctrine', in *Theorie* the focus is on an attempt to grasp the whole economic process with the help of economic theory *in combination with the other social sciences*. Throughout his new book Schumpeter also kept pushing back the area where static theory could be used; and he kept adding new topics which could only be analysed through the dynamic approach. At one point in the book the reader is even told that 'the capitalist economy' cannot be analysed through static theory; the latter is only applicable to 'non-capitalist production'. This meant, of course, that the more advanced a society is, the less you need the static type of analysis! There were good reasons, in other words, for Schumpeter to fear that some readers might see his new book as a 'refutation' of *Das Wesen*.

The first chapter of *Theorie* contains the famous ideal-typical portrait of the static economy as a 'circular flow of economic life'. Schumpeter here says that the static type of analysis is suitable only for one type of problem: to determine prices and quantities of goods under given conditions. These conditions are essentially the following. Let us imagine a perfectly isolated society with private property, division of labour and free competition. Nothing new ever happens in this society: the same goods are produced and consumed year in and year out. For every supply, there is always a demand. The amount of money in the system is exactly what is needed to carry out the customary transactions. Since people always do the same thing, they usually behave in a rational way. But they do not think about what they do – everything is done out of habit. There exists a tremendous resistance to anything new, and the 'static economic subjects' ('*statische Wirtschaftssubjekte*') are only capable of repetitive work.[47] They are also thoroughly traditionalistic: they put in a certain amount of work and they expect to be paid the exact equivalence in money. No leaders are necessary in Static Society because nothing new ever needs to be done. This also explains why the consumer is so powerful in this type of society:

> Under our assumptions ... the means of production and the productive process have in general no real leader, or rather the real leader is the consumer. The people who direct business firms only execute what is prescribed for them by wants or demand and by the given means and methods of production. Individuals have influence only in so far as they express a demand. In this sense indeed every individual takes part in the direction of production.[48]

Immediately after this highly stylized picture of the static economy comes Schumpeter's famous chapter on economic development. This chapter constitutes the heart of *Theorie der wirtschaftlichen Entwicklung* and it also represents Schumpeter's most successful effort to create an economic theory of his own. Schumpeter begins the chapter by making a distinction between dynamic theory and economic history. In the latter type of analysis one typically tries to explain a concrete incidence of economic development. In the pure economic theory of development, on the other hand, one tries to construct a model through which changes in the economy can be explained exclusively through the *inner* workings of the economy. The changes are, in other words, not the result of forces outside the economic system, as in the static model.

When Schumpeter talks about changes in the economy he means substantial changes and not just the kind of minor adjustments that always occur in an equilibrium model when one quantity is changed. Schumpeter contrasts qualitative changes, which are typical for a dynamic economy, with changes which are mere adaptations and typical of a static economy. The difference between the two can be illustrated by the following famous line: 'Add successively as many mail coaches as you please, you will never get a railway thereby.'[49]

To change the economy one basically has to put together already existing elements into new combinations. Indeed, Schumpeter defines the enterpreneur and enterprise with this very process in mind: 'The carrying out of new combinations we call "enterprise"; the individuals whose function it is to carry them out we call "entrepreneurs".'[50] The emphasis in Schumpeter's theory is consequently not on creating something new from scratch, but on combining what already exists in new and unexpected ways. Schumpeter therefore draws a sharp conceptual distinction between 'innovation' and 'invention'. The entrepreneur innovates, but he never invents: 'Economic leadership in particular must hence be distinguished from "invention". As long as they are not carried into practice, inventions are economically irrelevant.'[51]

According to Schumpeter, economic change can come in many different forms. It is not only a question of new goods or new technologies – Schumpeter's notion of economic change is much broader and more interesting than that. One can, he says, distinguish between five major categories of 'new combinations':

> (1) The introduction of a new good ... or of a new quality of a good. (2) The introduction of a new method of production ... (3) The opening of a new market ... (4) The conquest of a new source of supply of raw materials or half-manufactured goods ... (5) The carrying out of the new organization of any industry, like the creation of a monopoly position ... or the breaking up of a monopoly position.[52]

According to Schumpeter, someone is an entrepreneur only when he is putting together a new combination. This means, among other things, that no one is an entrepreneur forever and that there can be no social class of entrepreneurs. One may inherit an entrepreneur's money, but never 'the claws of the lion'.[53] It is equally impossible for the state to 'nationalize the brain of an entrepreneur'.[54] Still, in Dynamic Society it is the entrepreneur who dominates what is going on and not the consumer as in Static Society:

> Innovations in the economic system do not as a rule take place in such a way that new wants first arise spontaneously in consumers and then the productive apparatus swings around through their pressure. We do not deny the presence of this nexus. It is, however,

the producer who as a rule initiates economic change, and consumers are educated by him if necessary; they are, as it were,
taught to want new things.[55]

The entrepreneur must be someone special because he has to be
able to break through the resistance to change that exists in any
society. Most people are unable to do this; they can only handle what
is familiar to them. The entrepreneur, on the other hand, has the
strength and the courage to challenge the accepted ways of doing
things and to sweep aside the forces of tradition. There are naturally
very few people who can do this, according to Schumpeter, since
they have to have 'super-normal qualities of intellect and will'. But
these 'Carusos' of economic life do exist, and all changes in economic
life are ultimately due to their actions.[56] That there exist some simi-
larities between Schumpeter's heroic entrepreneur and Weber's char-
ismatic leader is obvious.[57]

What is it then that makes creative individuals take on the forces
of tradition and behave in such a way as to attract the disapproval of
most people? It is definitely not hedonism, Schumpeter says — if one
just wants to enjoy oneself, there is no reason to challenge the traditional way of doing things. According to Schumpeter, there exist
three major non-hedonistic motives for the entrepreneur:

> First of all, there is the dream and the will to found a private
> kingdom, usually, though not necessarily, also a dynasty ... Then
> there is the will to conquer: the impulse to fight, to prove oneself
> superior to others, to succeed for the sake, not of the fruits of
> success, but of success itself ... Finally, there is the joy of creating,
> of getting things done, or simply of exercising one's energy and
> ingenuity.[58]

After the chapter on economic development Schumpeter proceeds
to analyse a series of topics which all, he argues, fall within the area
of the dynamic type of analysis. These are credit, capital, interest,
profit and the business cycle. Credit is absolutely essential to the
entrepreneur who, in Schumpeter's scheme, by definition lacks capital. It is always the capitalist who must assume the risk by backing
the entrepreneur who, of course, needs the credit (or capital) to be
able to put together his combinations.[59] In the static system, on the
other hand, credit is not needed since nothing new ever happens. In
order that the entrepreneur can attain capital, some existing means
of production has to be diverted from its habitual use. This is done,
Schumpeter says, with the help of the banker who creates new
money via deposit banking, exchange bills or some similar technique. The banker thus plays a key role in Schumpeter's scheme.

Indeed, without banks there can be no economic change; and Schumpeter dates the emergence of capitalism to the time when massive credit creation via the banking system became possible for the first time.

Also profit, according to Schumpeter, only exists in a dynamic economy. In a static economy there are managers who receive wages, but there is no surplus to be distributed. An entrepreneur, on the other hand, typically does something novel and 'entrepreneurial profit' is his reward. Take, for example, a textile mill, Schumpeter says, where everything is done by hand. If an entrepreneur now begins to mechanize the production (like one of the Schumpeters had done in Triesch, for example), he will probably be able to produce the same merchandise at a much lower cost. And as long as he can sell the goods at the old price, he will be making a handsome profit. It is this latter sum (minus what the entrepreneur has to pay his workers, his banker, and so on) that constitutes profit in Schumpeter's scheme.

The last major topic that Schumpeter proposed to solve through his theory of economic development was the business cycle. He realized, while writing the book, that he had not developed his ideas as much as he would have liked to and that his theory was little more than 'a torso'.[60] Still, he seems to have been convinced that he had grasped the basic structure of the business cycle well enough. According to Schumpeter, the very essence of capitalism is expressed through the wavelike movements that the modern economy goes through; and these must somehow be accounted for in economic theory. The scientist who had come the closest to doing this was, in Schumpeter's mind, Clément Juglar. His idea was that cycles of 7–11 years' duration occurred naturally and unavoidably in capitalist society. Schumpeter liked to cite Juglar's statement that 'prosperity is the cause of depression', and there was also in Schumpeter's own theory a close link between the ups and downs in the business cycle; one implied the other.[61] More precisely, a cycle would start up when an entrepreneur put together a new combination. The profits that the entrepreneur now made would immediately attract other entrepreneurs, who would find it much easier to put together new combinations of their own, once the initial resistance had been broken down. With this 'swarmlike appearance' of entrepreneurs, as Schumpeter liked to phrase it, the economy would soon enter a boom: wages would rise, interest rates would shoot up, new jobs would be created, and so on. After some time, however, there would 'necessarily' also be a depression. There were several reasons for this. For one thing, there would be much less interest in new credits after a while. And when the entrepreneurs paid off their initial bank loans, there would be more downward pressure on the interest rate. The stronger the boom was, the harder it would also be for businessmen to make accurate calculations. And, finally, while old enterprises could always fall back on accumulated resources, new enterprises were very sensitive to changes in the economic climate and would easily go bankrupt. Under certain conditions, Schumpeter said, the depression might turn into a crisis, but this was not a necessary stage in the business cycle. It was, however, written into the very logic of the capitalist system that after some time of depression, new entrepreneurs would emerge in some industry. And then there would be a new 'swarm' of entrepreneurs. A wave of prosperity would start up and the whole cycle would roll on towards a new boom, a new depression, and so on.

Schumpeter's *Theorie der wirtschaftlichen Entwicklung* ends with a chapter entitled 'The Overall Picture of the Economy'. This chapter is very important since it is devoted to the theme of the opening line of the book, viz. that 'the social process is really one indivisible whole.' Schumpeter was later to feel that this chapter detracted from his attempt to present a new economic theory and that it should be eliminated. He was also annoyed that he received so many inquiries about his 'book in economic history'.[62] When he revised the second edition (which was the one that was later translated into English), the last chapter was not included. But since it gives a fine picture of how the young Schumpeter envisioned the relationship of economic theory to the whole socio-economic phenomenon, there is good reason to pay attention to it here.

Schumpeter does not present a general theory for what the socio-economic phenomenon looks like in the last chapter of *Theorie*. Instead, he discusses several different ways of approaching it, which allow the economist to get successively closer to 'the whole economic process'.[63] First of all, the economist can use statics and dynamics; By combining these two approaches, Schumpeter says, one gets a much better picture of the economic process than by exclusively relying on static theory: 'Our picture [then becomes] much closer to reality and also more simple than the usual [static] one; it makes it unnecessary to rely on many fictions ... and it helps to explain several neglected phenomena.'[64] The improved picture that Schumpeter talks about here is actually the combined result of six distinct elements: (1) the static process; (2) the dynamic process; (3) the interaction between statics and dynamics; (4) the secondary reaction of the static process to the economic development; (5) the influence on the economic system caused by internal developments within the population, within technology, and the like; and (6) disturbances in the economic system caused from the outside by war, political interference, and so on.[65]

But it was also clear to Schumpeter that one could not capture the whole economic process just with static and dynamic theory. There was too much left to explain, he felt, especially the social dimension. How was one then to analyse these missing bits? Schumpeter's answer to this question began with the reflection that it is clear that the economic structure always leaves an 'imprint' on the social structure.[66] The entrepreneur, for example, is not only a key figure in the economy but also in society at large. For one thing, economic power often leads to social and political power. There is also the fact that many people look up to an entrepreneur: 'His success impresses and fascinates.'[67] Still, one cannot just 'translate' from economic theory to social reality; and it is definitely wrong to assume that just because a certain assumption is useful in economic theory, it also depicts things as they are in society. According to economic theory, for example, all wage earners belong to the same economic class. In reality, however, we find wage earners in several different social classes. It would also be wrong to assume that social reality is just some kind of superstructure, erected on top of the economic basis. Schumpeter does not mention Marx's name in this context, but it is clear that he had Marx in mind and that his argument was intended as a refutation of the Marxian analysis of class. If anything, priority should, according to Schumpeter, be given to the social structure. To illustrate this idea, Schumpeter used the example of an economy devastated by war. If only buildings and material objects have been destroyed, the damage is not irreparable. As long as the authority structure and the general organization of the economy are intact, the economy will soon be running at full speed again.

In his next move to get closer to the social process Schumpeter focuses on certain independent areas of society, such as politics, art, science and morality. All of these phenomena, he says, display 're-markable analogies' to the economy in the sense that they have both static and dynamic elements.[68] Take, for example, art. On the one hand, art is the result of a certain milieu with its mixture of social and economic elements. But it also has a life of its own, which is much more important to grasp if one is to understand its essence. And it is the same with politics, morality, and so on: also they are the result of, on the one hand, a passive adaptation to a certain milieu and, on the other, a dynamic inner development. Schumpeter was very enthusiastic about his idea that everything in society could be analysed in terms of statics and dynamics. 'This insight', he said, 'constitutes the dawn in the scientific study of man.'[69]

According to Schumpeter, to each sphere in society there usually exists a corresponding group of people. Just as there is art and there is politics, for example, there are artists and politicians. Although each of these groups is relatively independent of all the others, together they make up what Schumpeter calls 'the social culture' of a country. And just as there exists a static and a dynamic dimension to each part of society, there exists a static and a dynamic dimension to a country's general culture. There exists a certain 'static unity of culture', but there also exists something else – 'that unexplained something which is the reason why all knowledge does not exhaust the totality of the social process'.[70] In the last instance, society is a single unity, just as Schumpeter had said in the opening line of *Theorie*. Schumpeter, however, cautions the reader in the very last sentence of his book to handle this truth with appropriate care: 'Our viewpoint is not a slogan nor the result of any *ad hoc* type of analysis. It is the result of a well-tried method.'[71]

Theorie der wirtschaftlichen Entwicklung did not get the reception it deserved when it was published. For one thing, the First World War was impending and soon people had other things on their mind than economic theory. A translation into English would no doubt have added many readers, but it was not until 1934 that a translation of *Theorie* appeared. There was also the fact that Schumpeter's book was just not very much appreciated by German economists. Schumpeter was later to write: 'When this book first appeared in 1911, both the general view of the economic process embodied in it and about half a dozen of the results it tried to establish, seemed to many people so strikingly uncongenial and so far removed from traditional teaching that it met almost universal hostility.'[72] When Schumpeter referred to the hostility that his book encountered, he must first of all have thought of an article from 1913 by Böhm-Bawerk which contained a devastating attack on the interest theory in *Theorie*. Böhm-Bawerk admitted that Schumpeter had 'a fine theoretical mind', but he still devoted a massive 60-page article to tear apart Schumpeter's argument piece by piece.[73] Böhm-Bawerk had himself devoted considerable energy to developing a theory of interest, so he no doubt had an axe to grind. And while Böhm-Bawerk's theory was centred around the problem of why there had to be a positive rate of interest in a stationary state, Schumpeter claimed that the rate of interest in a stationary state is zero. Schumpeter tried to defend himself against Böhm-Bawerk's onslaught in a 40-page article, where he argued that his theory of interest was in reality part of a much broader theoretical attempt to look at 'the totality of the economic process'.[74] But Böhm-Bawerk was not impressed and reiterated his original charge in a 20-page article, which ended the exchange. Böhm-Bawerk's verdict: Schumpeter's theory of interest was useless and a disservice to economic science.

Eventually, Schumpeter's book came to be recognized as a classic, and when it was about to be translated into English in the 1930s, Schumpeter wrote to the publisher that 'both the general view [in *Theorie*] and some of the individual theorems have been gaining ground and have exerted considerable influence on contemporaneous work in Germany.'[75] This was also to be the case in many other countries, when Schumpeter's work was translated into Italian (1932), English (1934), French (1935), Japanese (1937) and Spanish (1944).[76] Still, it is clear that by this time Western economics was very different from what it had been like in 1911, when *Theorie* was originally published. In the 1930s and 1940s it was increasingly felt that only economic theory which could be formalized and expressed in mathematical models was of interest. *Theorie* with its attempt to grasp the whole economic process now seemed a bit old-fashioned and quaint. This means that Schumpeter's major work never really got the reception it deserved.

III

Schumpeter's third book was published in 1914. It was called *Epochen der Dogmen- und Methodengeschichte* and it was later to be translated as *Economic Doctrine and Method: An Historical Sketch*. It is clear that this work is not in the same class as his earlier two books, in the sense that these were part of Schumpeter's ambition to establish himself as a major economic theorist. The history of economics had a much more humble origin: it had been commissioned by Max Weber for a handbook in economics, *Grundriss der Sozial-ökonomik*. Still, even if it is true that Schumpeter always attached more importance to his first two books than to *Epochen*, it is also a fact that Schumpeter would later spend many years working on a giant history of economics, which in many ways was an enlarged version of the 1914 book. We are probably correct in assuming that the young Schumpeter wanted to write a history of economics; and that Weber's request just provided him with an opportunity.

It should also be noted that even though it would be wrong to assign the same status to *Epochen* as to Schumpeter's first two books, his history of economics is quite important for an understanding of Schumpeter's major project as an economist. And this project was how to devise a way to encompass the whole economic phenomenon through economic theory *and* the adjoining social sciences. In *Theorie der wirtschaftlichen Entwicklung* we saw how Schumpeter had become interested in this problem and how he had been forced to change his earlier stance that economic theory should be radically cut off from the other social sciences. This development towards a broader conception of economics now continued in Schumpeter's book on the history of economics. Schumpeter would always insist on the importance of theoretical economics and this is also the case with *Epochen*; economic theory is absolutely essential to grasp the economic phenomenon. But he also continued to redefine the relationship of economic theory to the other social sciences so that all of them together, in some kind of combination, would be able to account for the whole economic phenomenon. An interesting novelty in *Epochen* in this respect is the importance that Schumpeter attaches to the 'sociology' of economists. Each time an economist is discussed, Schumpeter pays special attention not only to his contribution to economic theory but also to his attempt to complement economic theory with a general analysis of society ('sociology' in Schumpeter's terminology) and its economic institutions ('economic sociology'). It is true that in doing so, Schumpeter may have just been following the directions he received from Weber; the book, after all, was to be part of a general work in 'social economics' and not in pure economic theory. If this was the case or not, we do not know. What we do know, however (and we shall return to this in more detail in chapter 5), is that Schumpeter had by this time become very interested in sociology on his own.

Schumpeter's history of economics appeared as one of three contributions to the first volume of *Grundriss der Sozialökonomik*. The other two contributors were Karl Bücher, the economic historian, and Friedrich von Wieser, Schumpeter's old teacher from Vienna. Schumpeter's little book on the history of economics, it should be stressed, is a pearl of erudition; and it is clear that Schumpeter had read all the works he refers to in the original. Not all, to be precise: at one point Schumpeter mentions with obvious displeasure that 'as a result of an irreparable error I could not make myself familiar with this author in the original.'[77] It should immediately be mentioned that Schumpeter was referring to the work of Thomas Milles, a seventeenth-century British economist who must have been as little known in Schumpeter's days as he is today.[78]

Schumpeter divided his history into four major sections: one on the roots of economics; one on its birth; one on classical economics; and one on contemporary economics. In the first section Schumpeter suggests that economics actually has *two* origins: one in philosophy and one in the literature on practical economic questions. The philosophers who wrote on economics – the Greeks, the Scholastics, and so on – applied their habitual analytical skills also to economic problems, but they were not particularly interested in economics. There were other problems that fascinated them much more and they knew very little about concrete, economic matters. Many practical men of affairs, on the other hand, knew a lot about specific economic questions, such as exports, customs, gold, and so on. But they had no training in intellectual matters and therefore brought no analytical sharpness to their writings. Schumpeter writes very nicely on why this type of literature, which bloomed in England during 1500–1700, failed to become a contribution to economics. One major reason was that the topics were usually chosen with a practical end in mind:

Thus it is explained why in this branch of economic literature so
many excellent beginnings led to nothing because they were not
followed up beyond the concrete controversy which had occasioned
them. We also understand why we find side by side with many
diagnoses that were clearly and vigorously formulated some primitive prejudices, why it often happened that details were recognized
while the underlying principle was missed, and why analysis never
penetrated beyond what the occasion demanded and in most cases
did not attempt any clarification of the fundamental issues.[79]

In the second section of *Epochen* Schumpeter discusses how economics emerged as a science in the eighteenth century. His thesis is
that economics was born out of the meeting of the analytical–
philosophical tradition and the practical–concrete tradition. Schumpeter actually sees the two as coming together at one specific
point in history, more precisely in the controversy surrounding the
French corn laws in the eighteenth century: 'For the Physiocrats in
particular the controversy about the French corn laws ... was the
most important problem. It was in fact at this point that the two
sources of economics united. Never again has the investigation of
basic theoretical truths by the practical man and (shall we say) by
the philosopher been separated.'[80] It should also be stressed that
Schumpeter saw the Physiocrats, especially Quesnay, as the true
founders of economics. Their most important contribution was the
idea that one can conceptualize the economy as a giant circular flow,
where demand and supply always follow upon each other. It should
be noted that Schumpeter downplayed the importance of Adam
Smith and *The Wealth of Nations* in the founding of economics. He
agreed that Smith (as well as Turgot) had helped to bring together
the two sources of economics. But Schumpeter felt that Smith had no
original ideas of his own and that he had just 'that degree of super-
ficiality', which is needed when you have to make your way through
a huge material and cannot afford to be sidetracked by interesting
theoretical questions.[81] Schumpeter concluded: 'Today we can be
under no illusion about Smith's intellectual dimensions since we can
clearly enough distinguish between pedestal and monument.'[82]

The third section of *Epochen* is devoted to the classical period.
Schumpeter here discusses the development of economics from the
end of the eighteenth century to the mid-nineteenth century, first
and foremost in England, but also in France, Germany, Italy and
the United States. According to Schumpeter, there was a surge
of creativity during the first decades of the nineteenth century, primarily in connection with Ricardo's work. Towards the end of the
classical period, however, progress slackened and little new was
produced. As in the other sections of his book, Schumpeter pays
considerable attention to how the different economists saw society

and its economic institutions. One problem with the classical economists, he says, was that they had totally failed to produce a good
sociology. What caused this failure was their tendency to see society
as a mere collection of profit-seeking and isolated individuals: 'The
nations, as defined by the "classics", were merely additions of independent individuals of unchangeable natural characteristics who
were held together by economic interests. These natural characteristics the economists simply defined by the statement that each individual was guided merely by the desire for the greatest possible gain
with the least possible expenditure.'[83]

The attention that Schumpeter paid to sociology can also be exem-
plified by his analysis of Marx, which can be found in a giant footnote, nearly four pages long.[84] Schumpeter had not discussed Marx
in his earlier books, so this passage is of considerable interest.
Schumpeter first of all makes clear that even though Marx had a
tendency to fuse politics and science, he was a great economist. 'It is
true that the agitator shouts and gesticulates on every page of his
work, but underneath this form there is sound scientific work.'[85] He
then goes on to say that 'in the work of the *scholar* Marx we have to
distinguish between a sociological and an economic part – however
disagreeable such a distinction may be to his disciples.'[86] This is the
first version of an idea which is central to the well-known analysis of
Marxism in *Capitalism, Socialism and Democracy* (1942). Schumpeter
also singles out Marx's 'economic conception of history' (by which
he meant the theory that there was a close fit between economic production and social organization) as Marx's foremost sociological
achievement.[87]

The last section of Schumpeter's book contains a discussion of
historical economics and marginal utility theory. Schumpeter's presentation of the Historical School is respectful and very carefully
worded. While in his first book from 1908 he had allowed himself
some liberties when he referred to Schmoller and followers, there
was nothing of this in his history of economics.[88] Instead, Schumpeter
carefully enumerates the various contributions of the historical economists: they had helped to introduce the concept of evolution into
economics; they had drawn attention to the overall picture of the
economy; they had developed a much more realistic picture of economic motivation; and so on.

Still, Schumpeter felt that it was marginal utility theory and not
the historical type of analysis that represented the future in economics. The best of the contemporary economists had opted for the
analytical type of economics, which Ricardo especially had helped to
develop, and they had made a series of important contributions to
economic theory. Just as the classical economists had focused on the
theory of distribution, so had the new economists. But while the
concern of Ricardo and the other classical economists had primarily

been with determining the distribution of income between the various social classes, the new economists were basically interested in working out theorems about the factors of production. Schumpeter concluded that marginal utility theory constituted a solid foundation for further work in economic theory.

That Schumpeter personally identified very strongly with theoretical economics is clear enough from the last section in *Epochen*. It is, however, also obvious that he wanted to make a place for the other social sciences in the analysis of the economy. This comes out with particular force in the section on the *Methodenstreit*, which allows us to reconstruct how Schumpeter saw the relationship between economic theory and the other social sciences at this point of his scholarship. Schumpeter here says that the battle of the methods had been caused by a clash between two different ways of thinking, the historical approach and the analytical approach: 'it was a struggle between two methods of work, between people of different mental habits, who fought for elbow room or for domination.'[89] But this sharp opposition between the analytical method and the historical method was both superficial and wrong in Schumpeter's mind. He pointed out that Menger himself had said that history was necessary to solve many economic problems, and he added drily that if all economists who felt that historical material was needed to solve certain problems were to be called historical economists, then practically all economists belonged to this category. He also said that there will always be some economists who are more interested in history than in theory and vice versa: 'According to inclination and training some people turn to theoretical problems, while others apply themselves to historical and altogether descriptive ones ... without this in itself constituting a contradiction in principle.'[90] Explicitly referring to Weber's attempt to bridge the gap between history writing and theory construction through various epistemological devices, Schumpeter stressed that the differences between historical economics and analytical economics were not as radical as was commonly thought. 'Objects of cognition', as he phrased it, were clearly not the same as 'real objects'. This meant that both historical economists and theoretical economists were in reality trying to solve theoretical problems with the help of abstract concepts, albeit in different ways.[91]

It was also perfectly obvious to Schumpeter, and he repeatedly said so, that history was needed to complement economic theory. If there existed any real danger to economics, Schumpeter added in a little-noticed paragraph, it was rather that economic theory might one day get the upper hand in the economics profession and totally squeeze out history. The reason for this he ascribed to '*the general tendency of our time in favour of theory*'.[92] Schumpeter prophesized that '*we have every prospect of seeing the unpleasant spectacle that the historical school suffers the same injustice which in its time it had inflicted on the theorists.'*[93] Was Schumpeter correct in this prognosis? Later on in this book we shall try to answer this question. First, however, we shall take a look at Schumpeter's role in Austrian politics. After Schumpeter had finished his three books in economics he seems to have felt that there were other things he wanted out of life than just being a brilliant economist. Politics was a way of getting them. Or at least he thought so.

3

In Politics

Sir, I can add to your report on Schumpeter's ambitions. The version around Harvard Yard was that when Schumpeter was a dashing and thinner young man in Vienna, his ambitions were to be the greatest economist in the world, the greatest horseman in Austria, and the greatest lover in Vienna; but he failed to become the greatest horseman in Austria. Several of us young instructors invited him, in the late winter of 1943, to be our guest at a lunch to celebrate his 60th birthday. I asked whether the story of his three ambitions was correct. Actually, he said, he had had five: he wanted to be an accomplished connoisseur of art, and to be successful in politics.

(Letter to *The Economist*, 24 December 1983)

When Schumpeter was in his early thirties, he felt that the world was at his feet. And why not? He had just produced three exceptional works in economics, and his academic career was proceeding accordingly. In just a few years he had moved from being associate professor in Czernowitz to being full professor in Graz, and he was clearly one of the young stars of German economics. Schumpeter's confidence also seems to have extended to another of his ambitions during these years: to become a successful politician. It is not likely that he ever contemplated a career as a politician in general; rather, what he wanted to try was finance. This was not such an outlandish ambition for a young economist in the Austro-Hungarian Empire. Menger, von Wieser and Philippovich had all been connected to the Imperial Court as economic advisers, and Böhm-Bawerk had been finance minister three times. Early in his tenure at Graz, Schumpeter had probably set his eyes on becoming a successful finance minister as well as a brilliant economist. '*Faites moi de la bonne politique et je vous ferai de bonnes finances!'*, as he wrote in youthful exuberance in 1916.[1]

During 1916–19 Schumpeter would several times try to live out his political ambitions by actively taking part in various political enterprises. It, however, quickly turned out that he had little talent for practical politics; and his last effort in this genre became such a humiliating failure that he promised himself never to enter politics again. This must have been a hard decision for Schumpeter to make, because at heart he was a political animal. He loved to follow what was going on in the political world; he was always full of suggestions for how to improve things; and he would engage anyone in a political discussion at the drop of a hat. But a vow is a vow, and Schumpeter always stuck to his decision not to become active in politics again. 'I have made it a rule for myself', he later wrote to a colleague, 'not to take part in any public activity that is not directly related to the professional duties and competence of an economist.'[2]

Later in the United States, when people asked Schumpeter about his time as a finance minister and his other political experiences, he was reluctant to answer. Since he enjoyed telling anecdotes about his various adventures in Europe, we may assume that this reluctance was due to the displeasure of recalling earlier failures. As a result of this silence on Schumpeter's part, little was known of Schumpeter's ambition to become 'a successful politician', as he put it in 1943 when he was asked about his three ambitions in life. Today, however, this has changed, and we know much more about Schumpeter and his political activities. This is mainly the result of the work of a group of German and Austrian scholars, such as Stephan Verosta, Christian Seidl, Wolfgang Stolper and Eduard März. In the early 1970s Verosta found a series of letters by Schumpeter that showed that he had been very active in 1916–17 trying to influence the politics of the emperor of the Austro-Hungarian Empire.[3] Inspired by Verosta's research, Christian Seidl started to look for some memoranda by Schumpeter that were referred to in the correspondence, and he eventually found them in the Austrian National Library. In 1985 Seidl had these memoranda published in an anthology, co-edited with Wolfgang Stolper. Besides the memoranda, the anthology also contains several little-known political speeches, newspaper articles and the like by Schumpeter, as well as a detailed introduction by Stolper and Seidl on Schumpeter's political activities. At about this time Eduard März also presented some new and important findings on Schumpeter's time as finance minister.

The material that is available to us today allows us for the first time to assess Schumpeter as a politician. It also allows us to raise some interesting questions about Schumpeter. For example, to what extent was his failure as a politician due to personal incapacity or to difficult circumstances? And what do Schumpeter's political activities tell us about his personality? Was he really an opportunist, as many claim, or did he behave in an honourable manner? To answer these questions is the main purpose of this chapter. We shall begin by presenting some facts about Schumpeter's three forays into politics: as a self-appointed adviser to the emperor of the Austro-Hungarian Empire in 1916–17; as a member of the German Socialization Commission in early 1919; and as the finance minister in the newly founded Austrian Republic later in 1919.

I

What Seidl found in the Austrian National Library were three of Schumpeter's memoranda. There appears to be a fourth one – on the situation in Bohemia – but it still remains lost. The three memoranda that Seidl did find had all been written by Schumpeter in 1916–17 while he was teaching in Graz. Their purpose was essentially to galvanize the Austro-Hungarian aristocracy and its followers into action on several matters: to reject Germany's demand for a tariff agreement; to found a popular conservative party; and to guide the country through the difficulties that were expected at the end of the First World War.

Schumpeter's three memoranda are indispensable for anyone who wants to understand the evolution of his political ideas. But to perform this function they must be set in their proper context, and it is therefore important to take a look at the concrete political situation in which Schumpeter tried to intervene with his memoranda in 1916–17.

Well before the First World War, the Austro-Hungarian Empire had shown clear signs of being a tottering giant. It was easily Europe's largest country in terms of geographical size, but it lacked cohesion and stability. To some extent this was due to the fact that the empire had mainly been put together through the successful marriage strategy of the Habsburg family. But there was also the failure of the dynasty to impose a strong central government on the member states. The Austrian Empire consisted of many different ethnic groups and strong-headed local aristocracies, all of whom, for different reasons, resisted the weak attempts from the centre to introduce a unitary structure on the empire. After the Napoleonic wars, nationalistic sentiments were added to the centrifugal forces, and in 1867 Hungary's demand for constitutional independence was granted. But there were many other minorities and peoples in the Austro-Hungarian Empire who were just as discontent. These included the Czechs, Slovaks, Slovenes, Poles, Germans, Ukrainians, Romanians, Croats, Serbs – and a few others as well.

The Habsburg rulers also failed miserably during the nineteenth century to modernize the empire, politically as well as economically. By the First World War there was male suffrage, but since there was no parliamentary control of the Imperial government this was of little consequence. Unlike Germany, the Austro-Hungarian Empire failed to industrialize. While Germany had used all the advantages of an industrial latecomer, Austria, at the turn of the century, was a predominantly agricultural country with traditional landlord–peasant relations still in place.

Austria's helplessness at the outbreak of the First World War also extended to its foreign policy. Since Bismarck's days Germany had tried to dominate Austria's foreign policy. Bismarck had, for example, wanted the friendship between the two countries to be inscribed in their very constitutions. This did not occur, but when Bismarck was forced out by Emperor Wilhelm II in 1890 the pressure on Austria increased considerably. In the 'new course' that Wilhelm had devised to make Germany a world power, the Austro-Hungarian Empire was to be an ally of Germany's. The way in which the First World War started demonstrates Austria's lack of independence *vis-à-vis* Germany. When the Austrian archduke Francis Ferdinand and his wife were assassinated in Sarajevo in June 1914, the Austrians felt that they finally had a chance to settle the score with Serbia and put an end to Serbia's attempts to incite the Slavs within the Austro-Hungarian borders. Germany, however, quickly declared war on Russia and France, something which meant – according to a military agreement between Germany and Austria-Hungary – that Austria had to abandon its plan to conquer Serbia and instead use its army to protect the German invasion of France against possible Russian intervention.

For a variety of reasons, the Germans virtually took over the leadership of the Austro-Hungarian Army during the First World War. Inside Germany itself there was also much agitation calling for closer cooperation between Germany and Austria. This position was presented in a popular book from 1915, which had been written by an influential member of the German parliament, Friedrich Naumann. The book was entitled *Mitteleuropa* (*Middle Europe*) and the general idea was that all German-speaking minorities should rally around the German Reich. This way Germany would become strong enough to hold its own against the East as well as the West. Naumann's ideas soon became popular within the German leadership, and in November 1915 a brusque diplomatic note was sent to Austria in which Germany demanded much closer cooperation between the two countries. It was further said that the Slavs were threatening to overrun Austria and that this had to be stopped; the German-speaking minority must be supported. There also existed a secret appendix to the note in which it was argued that there ought to be a tariff agreement (*Zollbündnis*) between the two empires and that some time in the future there should also be 'a fusion [of Germany and Austria] into a single economic unit'.[4] The Austrian government reacted negatively to the German demands, but answered in a conciliatory and evasive manner. Schumpeter, however, became very agitated when he heard about the secret appendix; and he immediately decided that he must do something to the plans for a tariff agreement. His three memoranda of 1916–17 all have this as their primary purpose.

Schumpeter learned about the content of the secret appendix in early 1916 from a colleague at the University of Prague, Arthur Spiethoff, who had been asked by the German government to comment on the economic aspects of the plan. Schumpeter at once decided to do what he could to stop Austria-Hungary from entering into a tariff agreement with Germany, and with this in mind he turned to Heinrich Lammasch who had been his professor at the University of Vienna. Lammasch was the right person for Schumpeter to contact, since he had excellent connections with the people around the emperor and also with the emperor himself. Lammasch had represented Austria in various official contexts and been political advisor to Francis Ferdinand, among others. In July 1917 he was almost appointed president by Emperor Charles. In brief, if any one of Schumpeter's friends and acquaintances could get the ear of the emperor, Schumpeter must have felt, it had to be Lammasch. Since Schumpeter had stayed in contact with Lammasch after he had graduated from the University of Vienna and since the two used to meet now and then in Vienna, it would also be fairly easy to broach the issue of the tariff agreement with Lammasch.

On 21 February 1916 Schumpeter wrote a letter to Lammasch in which he warned that the proposed tariff agreement would be a disaster for Austria. It is clear, he said, that Germany's major war goal is to conquer Austria. 'Just imagine, honorable Herr Hofrat,' Schumpeter wrote, 'what all of this means: a Prussian–Lutheran–Militaristic "Middle Europe" with an attitude towards the rest of the world like that of a beast of prey, baring its teeth. The Austria we know and love would cease to exist.'[5] In order to prevent this from happening, Schumpeter said, Lammasch had to try to make the emperor realize how dangerous the proposed tariff agreement was. Lammasch must have agreed with Schumpeter's analysis because he encouraged Schumpeter immediately to write a memorandum about the tariff agreement, which he said he would try to show the emperor. Schumpeter complied, and in a few days he had finished the memorandum. All in all, he would write four secret memoranda on this matter, each of which was circulated in the utmost secrecy among the highest aristocratic circles in the empire.

In the first memorandum, dated 'Graz, early 1916', Schumpeter warned that the idea of a tariff agreement between Germany and

Austria was becoming dangerously popular in Austria. Journalists and various leading public figures were behaving in a very disloyal manner, he said, by openly supporting the tariff agreement. But all these people were wrong in believing that this was just an 'economic' agreement. On the contrary: 'such an agreement would mean a revolution in the economic life of the monarchy.'[6] Many industries in the empire would soon disappear and others would be seriously weakened. German finance capital would quickly knock out the weak Austrian banks and thereby make Austrian industry dependent on Berlin. Hungary would probably turn away from Vienna and come under Berlin's domination as well. Since 40 per cent of Austria's foreign trade was with Germany, while the equivalent figure for Germany was only 6 per cent, any increase in trade between the two countries, as envisioned in the tariff agreement, would result in Austria becoming more dependent on Germany. 'A common customs policy will force together our two economic areas with iron clasps and totally amalgamate them.'[7] In so far as the economic consequences of the tariff agreement were concerned, Schumpeter concluded, 'Austria-Hungary would become a German colony.'[8]

The political consequences would also be severe in Schumpeter's opinion. The Austro-Hungarian Empire would increasingly lose its capacity to conduct its own independent foreign policy. Its diplomats would soon be seen as 'German agents' and the empire would eventually not even be able to pay for its own administration and army. Step by step the Austro-Hungarian Empire would be forced to become part of Germany. A common organ for tariff matters would probably be created first; then there would be a demand for the coordination of consular activities; and finally there would be a clamour for a common stand in foreign policy. 'This "common stand towards other countries" ... will be the beginning of a new state, a new international legal person – and the end of Austria', Schumpeter wrote.[9]

Schumpeter argued that the internal political structure of the Austro-Hungarian Empire would be affected by the tariff agreement as well. The German-speaking minority would be pushing for Germany's interests and thereby force the other minorities, especially the Czechs, into a hopeless situation. And once Austrian patriotism had disintegrated, the whole empire would collapse into a number of different minorities with nothing in common.

What could then be done to stop the proposed tariff agreement? Schumpeter's answer was that a man had to be found who could rally the Austrians around the emperor. This could only be an aristocrat, 'a grand seigneur'. Schumpeter does not seem to have had a specific person in mind, but it had to be someone from the highest circles in the empire: 'Only a man with a historical name and who has the active support of the whole top aristocracy will be able to end the present disorganisation of all political will.'[10] Once a coherent programme had been worked out by this aristocrat and his followers, the parliament must be called in. When this was done, there would no doubt be much criticism of the state and quite a few tactless things would be said. But this was something one had to put up with ('there are tactless statements in all parliaments'), and the main point was that it was easy to control and dominate the general public via a parliament. In 'modern politics' it is always necessary to 'fascinate', to 'impress' and to 'engage' the general public, Schumpeter said, and a parliament was the perfect vehicle for this. What Schumpeter wanted, in other words, was not democracy in the sense of popular participation, but rather the kind of aristocratic democracy he had come to know in England:

> It is clear how important it is to systematically be able to control the press, to have a loyal and intimate cooperation with the administrative apparatus, and to have cabinet members who reach out to the general public – in one word, it is important to use that technique of public life which England has developed to its absolute perfection ...: *the technique of tory democracy*.[11]

Schumpeter's second memorandum is dated 'Graz, December 1, 1916', and it was according to Schumpeter 'as little as the earlier one ... intended for the general public'.[12] The main purpose of the new memorandum was essentially to outline the foreign policy consequences of the proposed tariff agreement and to present an alternative to this. In Schumpeter's mind, close economic cooperation with Germany would first of all mean that the Austro-Hungarian Empire would lose its capacity to have an independent foreign policy in the Balkans and towards Russia. Hungary would also try to break out of the empire and in most questions Austria would simply be following Germany's lead. This foreign policy was also bound to cause difficulties internally: it would make the German-speaking minority run Prussia's errands and make all the other minorities resentful and bitter. Austria would also end up being the enemy of the Western states, something which Schumpeter felt would be a great mistake.

The alternative foreign policy that Schumpeter proposed in his memorandum was that the Austro-Hungarian Empire should be on good terms with both Germany *and* with Russia. Russia was not Austria's natural enemy any more than Germany, Schumpeter said, and the empire could not afford to have either of these two neighbours as an enemy. Austria should also try to have a close relationship with the Western powers. England and France were especially important to Austria, not the least by virtue of their financial resources. In case Austria was forced to choose between Germany and Russia, it should pick the same side as the Western powers. 'The goal of our foreign policy can thus be expressed by means of a formula: we should be allied to the German Empire and to Russia; and when it is necessary to choose one particular side, we should join the one that the Western powers support.'[13]

Schumpeter's last existing memorandum is dated 'Graz, April 1917'. It deals with the possibility of restoring Austria to its former glory by playing a key role in the peace negotiations at the end of the First World War and with the need to create a viable conservative party in Austria. Schumpeter repeated that Austria must under no circumstances sign the tariff agreement, especially not now. To enter an agreement at this time would only make the Austro-Hungarian Empire look worse in the eyes of the West. Austria should instead try to seize the present momentum to peace – all the warring nations were close to exhaustion – and try to reconcile the two sides. By virtue of its history and its interests, Austria was ideal for the role as a mediator between Germany and the Allies. A bold act of this type would recall the memories of the Vienna Congress and also help the country to break with its servile attitude to Germany.

To do all of this, however, the Austro-Hungarian Empire first needed a good conservative party, led by an aristocrat. But nothing even close to such a party existed. The conservative forces were badly divided in Austria; landowners, industrialists and peasants were all antagonistic towards one another and did not realize how much they actually had in common. Once it was constituted, such a party would no doubt have to face many difficult problems, especially economic ones. A sound financial policy was particularly important but also bound to be unpopular with the general public; sound financial policy always was. A socialist might ignore and ridicule issues such as the public deficit and the weak Austrian crown. But it was different for a conservative party: 'A conservative party cannot do that. It would give itself up, if it did.'[14] Schumpeter's programme for a conservative party was basically the following one: taxes should be low; industry should be encouraged; and no additional funds should be spent on social welfare. A crowning of Emperor Charles in Prague might help to restore the popularity of the emperor. Through this symbolic gesture, reminiscent of the historical crowning of a Habsburg as King of Bohemia in 1723, the relationship to the Czech population might also be improved. Schumpeter emphasized, *'one has to have the political courage to be conservative in basic questions and to act from this perspective in a determined manner.'*[15]

In hindsight we know that little came of Schumpeter's political activities during the First World War. Not so much that he failed to get his message across – the emperor is supposed to have read one of Schumpeter's memoranda and probably also met him – but the whole empire was disintegrating so quickly that it did not very much matter what the emperor did. There were plenty of problems to deal with, and that of a tariff agreement with Germany was relatively minor. In 1916 Emperor Francis Joseph died and was replaced by his inexperienced grandnephew, the 29-year-old Charles. The new emperor tried to accommodate the various ethnic and national groups in the empire, which were all demanding independence, but it was too late. On 16 October 1918 Charles announced that Austria-Hungary was now a federal union, consisting of four basic components (German, Czech, South Slav and Ukrainian). Special provisions were also made for Poland and Hungary. The new national councils, however, immediately began to operate as national governments, and in a series of quick events the whole Austro-Hungarian Empire started to fall apart. On 22 October 1918 Heinrich Lammasch formed a new cabinet, and also tried to save the situation by steering Austria in a federal direction. But it was just not possible to reverse the turn of events, and the various nationalistic movements were growing stronger by the day. In early November Emperor Charles, on Lammasch's initiative, waived his political authority. And a few days later – on 11 November 1918 – Charles issued a declaration, which marked the formal dissolution of the Austro-Hungarian Empire and the end of the Habsburg era.

II

If one reads Schumpeter's memoranda from Graz without knowing anything of their author, one would probably think that they had been written by an earnest patriot, who had decided to try to address the emperor in order to save the country. But there was, of course, much more to the story than that. In reality, Schumpeter was a very ambitious man and his political behaviour was often contradictory and ambiguous. His participation in the German Socialization Commission in 1919 shows this very clearly.

By way of introducing this event, it should be noted that Schumpeter was in contact not only with Lammasch during the First World War; he also had his feelers out in several other directions. First there was the small circle of people who all received personal copies of his secret memoranda. And then there were those who Schumpeter had decided to cultivate just because they could help with his political career. This last category included such persons as Josef Redlich, a liberal professor who was to become finance minister in Lammasch's liquidation cabinet. In Redlich's diaries from 1908 to 1919, which constitute an often-used source for political life during the last years of the Austro-Hungarian Empire, there are a few references to Schumpeter. In October 1917, for example, when there was a rumour that Redlich might be appointed finance minister, Schumpeter immediately appeared on his doorstep, 'torturing him because of his alleged chances to become a minister'.[16] And a couple of months later, in June 1918, when there was a rumour that Redlich might become the minister of finance in a cabinet led by Ernst Graf Silva-Tarouca, Schumpeter again made his appearance:

> Yesterday morning Professor Schumpeter paid me a visit for two hours. I gathered from his talks that I am supposed to become a minister in a cabinet Silva-Tarouca, but that 'conservative' circles (whose advisor Schumpeter likes to regard himself) distrust me. He, however, had used his influence successfully so that they would not oppose me. Mere fantasies! Nothing to it! I took the pleasure of offering Mr. Schumpeter the position as secretary of state in the Ministry of Finance which he promised to take into serious consideration. His mixture of praise, flattery and bold disclosure that he distrusts me represents a curious mixture.[17]

Schumpeter, as we know, failed to gain a political appointment during the last years of the empire. Lammasch, for example, preferred Friedrich von Wieser to Schumpeter as minister of commerce in the cabinet he formed in October 1918. And, two weeks later, the whole Austro-Hungarian Empire was formally dissolved, which meant that Schumpeter's chances of *ever* taking part in an imperial cabinet had been brought to an end. But Schumpeter also had some contacts with the new men of power. As a prelude to what was to come, he received a request in January 1919 from two of his Marxist acquaintances. Would he be willing to join a Socialization Commission, which had just been formed in Germany? The answer was 'yes'.

The Socialization Commission had been created by the new socialist government in Germany in order to prepare for the takeover of certain industries. The Ministry of Finance had originally wanted the Commission to produce concrete plans for what the state should do, but this was rejected by its members who rather wanted the Commission to be a kind of fact-finding group. This was reluctantly granted, and the meetings of the Commission were conducted more or less as academic seminars with long discussions of various topics. The first commission, in which Schumpeter participated, met in the winter of 1918–19. The members consisted mainly of trade union leaders and economists (such as Rudolf Hilferding, Emil Lederer and Schumpeter); Karl Kautsky was its chairman and Eduard Heimann the secretary. Most of the members were socialists, but there were also a few liberal members. Kautsky and many of the trade union leaders were absent during most of the meetings, which as a consequence were dominated by the economists.

The task of the first Socialization Commission was to investigate the German coal industry and see if it could be socialized. According to one of the participants, the discussion was centred around three general questions. First: on the assumption that one wanted to keep the capitalist system, what would be the minimum amount that the state had to intervene in order to prevent obvious abuses, such as excessive profits and monopolies? Secondly: if one wanted to social- ize the whole German industry, how could this be done without the state stifling all economic life? And, thirdly: how could one get competent industrial leaders to work in socialized industries – what kind of incentives were needed? On 15 February 1919 the Commission issued a preliminary report, signed among others by Schumpeter.

There exist contradictory opinions about Schumpeter's behaviour in the Commission. According to one version, Schumpeter was very hostile to the socialist aims of the commission. When Schumpeter was asked how he, one who had always extolled the virtues of private entrepreneurship, could be part of something like the Socializa- tion Commission, he said, 'If somebody wants to commit suicide, it is a good thing if a doctor is present.'[18] This version of Schumpeter's attitude has, however, been challenged by one of the members of the Commission, Theodor Vogelstein. According to Vogelstein, Schum- peter was not at all negative to socialization:

> Certainly Schumpeter's presence added much brilliance and in- terest to our internal discussions and our very informal conver- sations outside the Committee Room. In fact Schumpeter sided mostly with the more extreme propagators of immediate and integral socialization, i.e., more with Lederer who, at that time, was rather radical and doctrinaire in his intention of bringing forth 'Socialism in our time', as against Hilferding who – as always in practical matters – was more compromising and willing to yield to the arguments of his opponents. In a private conversation with Schumpeter and some members, after the official close of a session, I expressed a certain surprise about his position, whereupon he answered: 'I don't know whether or not Socialism is a practical possibility, but I am convinced that it is impossible if not applied integrally. At any rate, it will be an interesting experiment to try it out.'[19]

Vogelstein's version of Schumpeter's behaviour is also supported by Felix Somary, who reports that 'Hilferding spoke repeatedly to me about how surprised he was by Schumpeter's radicalism [in the Socialization Commission].'[20]

What is one to make of this? Was Schumpeter against socialization or was he for it? According to Haberler, Schumpeter's contradictory behaviour was due to the fact that he often told people what they wanted to hear: 'His attitude ... can perhaps be explained by the

fact that he had one very Austrian vice, that is to say, he always
wanted to be nice to his friends; and since he was on good terms
with Lederer, he may have sided with him [in the Socialization
Commission].'[21] Somary explains Schumpeter's behaviour in a different way. He says that Schumpeter was 'anything but radical; [and in
this particular case] he only drew the conclusion, given the premiss:
if one wanted to socialize some industry after the war, one had to do
it in a certain manner.'[22] To decide what ultimately motivated
Schumpeter in a case like this is, of course, impossible. What
Schumpeter's position was on the socialization issue itself, however,
is easy enough to establish. Here we have the Commission's report
that Schumpeter signed.

There are three parts to the preliminary report of the Commission.
There are some sections which all of the members signed; there is the
majority report; and there is the minority report. What all of the
members of the Commission agreed on was that it was necessary for
the state to intervene in the coal industry and to socialize it. It was
absolutely crucial that this did not lead to a bureaucratization of the
industry; the goal was 'socialization' as opposed to 'nationalization',
in the Commission's terminology. The new managers must therefore
be given full freedom to make whatever decisions they thought were
necessary. The democratic rights of the workers, it was emphasized,
must also be respected.

The members of the Commission, however, disagreed over the
extent of the socialization. According to the majority report – which
Schumpeter signed – there existed in principle three general options
for the coal industry. It could be left to the free play of the market;
the state could take it over; and it could be socialized. The capitalist
option was rejected on political grounds and with the argument that
the war had made it hard for the market to operate properly. If the
state took over the coal industry, this would only lead to 'state
capitalism' or to a giant 'state cartel', neither of which was desirable.
The way to go was clearly 'socialization' or nationalization without
the state itself taking over the management: 'The workers want a
reconstruction along the following lines: democracy in all the enterprises of the industry in combination with firm leadership; the eli-
mination of capital as a ruling power; and that the enterprises are
managed with the help of creative personalities.'[23] That the workers
should take over the factories and run them on their own in syndical-
ist fashion was firmly rejected; this would only lead to chaos and
group egoism. 'Economic democracy' was one of the two basic principles of 'socialization' – the other was 'free initiative and individual
responsibility'.[24] The present organization of the coal industry in
Germany dictated that socialization had to be total and immediate.
When this operation was carried out, the majority report said,

powerful productive forces would be released, just as in the early
stages of capitalism. In this way, socialization would also help to
'realize the principle of socialism'.[25]

Why Schumpeter signed the majority report instead of the minority report is an interesting question. The minority report had been
authored by the two liberal members of the Commission, Vogelstein
and Francke, who argued that even though socialization might be a
good thing in the long run, its implementation must be a gradual
process. If one reads a bit between the lines, however, it is clear that
the authors of the minority report preferred capitalism to socialism.
This was also Schumpeter's position; in principle he was against any
kind of nationalization of private property. So why did Schumpeter
not sign the minority report but rather the pro-socialist majority
report? Was he insincere or was it rather that he wanted to please his
friends, as Haberler has suggested? There is really no way to know.
Most likely, however, Schumpeter felt that socialism, at this stage of
history, was premature and doomed to fail – but that if it was to be
tried out, it had to be done in a full-scale manner.

III

When the Socialization Commission was convened again in 1920,
Schumpeter was not among its members. Political events in 1919
had changed Schumpeter's political position considerably and he
had by now little interest in being part of the Commission. What had
happened was yet another interesting chapter in the life of Joseph
Schumpeter. In February 1919 an election had been held in Austria
and the Social Democrats, closely followed by the Christian Social
Party (a conservative Catholic party), were the two big winners.
Together these parties controlled a comfortable majority in the constituent national assembly and in March 1919 they formed a coali-
tion government, led by Karl Renner. Otto Bauer, who was the new
foreign minister, suggested (on the recommendation of Rudolf Hilferding) that Schumpeter should be appointed finance minister. This
was acceptable to the Christian Social Party, where Schumpeter had
some support especially in the circles around Ignaz Seipel. On 15
March Schumpeter moved into his new office, a magnificent baroque
building which had been built by Eugene of Savoy in the eighteenth
century.

Otto Bauer, as we know, knew Schumpeter from their days
together at the University of Vienna. He had probably been told
about Schumpeter's radical attitude in the German Socialization
Commission, something which must have pleased him since Bauer
thought that socialization (as opposed to a revolutionary uprising)
was the best road to socialism. It is sometimes also suggested that
Bauer picked Schumpeter as finance minister because he was very

impressed by Schumpeter's analysis of Austria's financial situation in a pamphlet called *The Crisis of the Tax State*. Perhaps Bauer had even been present when Schumpeter presented his original lecture on the tax state in Vienna in 1918. However this may be, it is clear that *The Crisis of the Tax State* gives an early view of how Schumpeter saw Austria's economic situation towards the end of the First World War, something which makes it of special interest to us.

The main message in *The Crisis of the Tax State* was that the capitalist state (or, to use Schumpeter's terminology, 'the tax state') was *not* going to collapse once the war was over. Schumpeter was convinced that socialism would eventually become a reality in Austria as elsewhere – but not quite yet. And if capitalism was going to stay for a while, so was its complement, the capitalist state. 'The hour [of socialism] has not yet struck ... Nevertheless, the hour will come.'[26] This message was no doubt palatable to the Austrian Social Democrats who also were convinced that socialism would become a reality in the long run, but that capitalism was necessary for the moment. They probably also approved of Schumpeter's recipe for how to get the economy going again, namely a huge capital levy. But while Schumpeter basically wanted to use the levy to release the entrepreneurial energies of the country and to induce countries like England and France to invest in Austria, Bauer and the Social Democrats saw the capital levy more as a weapon in the economic class struggle. Still, there were some points of agreement between what the Social Democrats felt should be done about Austria's economy and the programme that Schumpeter presented in *The Crisis of the Tax State*.

The centrepiece of Schumpeter's suggestions for how to restore Austria's post-war economy was clearly the capital levy. If one reads *The Crisis of the Tax State* carefully, however, it becomes evident that Schumpeter also had his doubts that a capital levy would do the trick. The reason for this, he said, was that he had increasingly become convinced that Austria's financial problems were just as much political as economic in nature. Only a government with a broad political basis would be able to convince the general public that a levy was the right thing. 'The man who is to solve this task', he concluded, 'needs real political and fiscal ability – and that glamour of word and action which commands the trust of the people.'[27]

Was Schumpeter such a person? Let us assume that he had the requisite technical skills for a finance minister. But was he really someone who would inspire trust in people? The answer that the Austrian newspapers gave when they found out that Schumpeter had been appointed finance minister, was a categorical 'no'. The day after Schumpeter's appointment, *Reichspost*, a Christian Social newspaper, wrote, for example, that all the political parties in Austria think that Schumpeter supports their particular policy 'and thereby we have said enough about his political character'.[28] A few days later the new finance minister could read a little verse entitled 'Schumpeter' in *Der Morgen*, in which he was portrayed as having 'three souls': one that was liberal, one that was conservative, and one that was to the left. 'How delightful it must be to have three souls in one!', the verse began.[29] And some time later Karl Kraus, the great Austrian satirist, wrote in his much-read *Die Fackel* that Schumpeter was a well-known opportunist. Making a pun on Schumpeter's earlier appointment as an Austrian exchange professor in the United States, Kraus called Schumpeter an 'exchange professor in convictions' (*'ein Austauschprofessor seiner Überzeugungen'*) and said that he 'had more opinions than were necessary for his advancement'.[30] In brief, all of Vienna – except for a few people in the Social Democratic Party, it seems – felt that Schumpeter was untrustworthy and opportunistic. Soon, however, Bauer and colleagues would change their opinion; and in October 1919 – only seven months after his appointment as finance minister – Schumpeter was dismissed for, among other reasons, disloyal behaviour.

When one tries to assess Schumpeter's accomplishments as a finance minister one must certainly take into account how impossibly difficult his task was. In early 1919 Austria was in a terrible state. The population was starving, especially in Vienna, and unemployment was sky-rocketing. The political situation was very unstable as well. The Austrian Social Democrats were committed to parliamentarianism, but the impact of the Russian Revolution was felt everywhere in Europe. During the spring of 1919 Soviet Republics were proclaimed in Hungary and Bavaria, and the Austrian communists made two attempts to take power by force. 'I held the ministership in time of revolution', Schumpeter was later to tell a journalist, 'and it was no pleasure, I may assure you.'[31]

The economic situation was also close to hopeless. There was first of all the giant war debt and rampant inflation. Austria's industrial equipment was old-fashioned and many industries were at a standstill due to lack of raw materials. The state had to pay out enormous sums for food subsidies and in unemployment compensation. The new Republic had also inherited most of the administrative apparatus of the Austro-Hungarian Empire, which had to be paid for. All of this made Schumpeter's task very difficult indeed. When he took office in March 1919 he quickly outlined the broad aims of his economic policy, but the fact that he had no real support in the cabinet for his proposals meant that the parliament could not act on Schumpeter's ideas. Schumpeter repeatedly tried to put pressure on the cabinet by arguing his case in parliament and in public, but without success. Instead he spent much of his time trying to encourage entrepreneurial activities and to remove bothersome state regulations from the economy.[32] On September 29 Schumpeter decided to force the issue and formally submitted his financial plan (*Finanzplan*) to the cabinet. The result, however, was disappointing: the cabinet rejected the whole plan after a long discussion. For all practical purposes this meant that Schumpeter was finished as finance minister, and about two weeks later he was dismissed.

In order to gain a fair picture of Schumpeter as a finance minister it is important to take a look at his financial plan, which was entitled 'The Basic Lines of Financial Policy for Now and the Next Three Years'. As opposed to in *The Crisis of the Tax State*, the emphasis had now shifted from the capital levy to encouraging foreign capital to invest in Austria. In order to get the country going, there had to be fresh capital from abroad: 'The problem of financial policy today is the problem of credit. All financial policy must be put at the service of credit.'[33] A capital levy was still needed – the deficit in the budget had to be covered somehow – but Schumpeter now subordinated this measure to the problem of providing foreign capital. Wealthy individuals who could arrange for foreign credits would, for example, be able to pay off their capital levy on very favourable conditions. Indirect taxes were also needed to cover the budget deficit but, again, the first task was to restore the confidence of local investors – and thereby foreign investors. Schumpeter finished his financial plan in the following way: 'Foreign countries must be shown that we are ready to help ourselves. Only then will they be prepared to help us.'[34]

But Schumpeter was not only fired because the cabinet disapproved of his *Finanzplan*, there were also two other important reasons: he opposed the Social Democrats' policy of bringing Austria closer to Germany, and he was accused of having tried to stop their socialization programme in an underhand way. That Schumpeter would be hostile to any attempt to bring Austria and Germany closer together is self-evident, given his stance during the First World War on the question of the tariff agreement. Otto Bauer, however, does not seem to have known about Schumpeter's wartime activities. Perhaps he thought that Schumpeter would be loyal enough to support the plans for an *Anschluss* between Austria and Germany which, after all, had been written into the new Republic's constitution in November 1918. And perhaps he thought that Schumpeter would be loyal enough to support the foreign policy of the government in which he was to serve, even if he disagreed with it personally.

On both accounts, however, Bauer was soon to be disappointed. Schumpeter very quickly set out to undermine Bauer's attempt to bring Austria and Germany together, especially his plans for a currency union between the two. In Schumpeter's opinion – which he apparently told to anybody who cared to listen – it was preferable for Vienna to be restored to its former position as a financial centre in Central Europe and for Austria to enter into agreements with the countries that had been part of the Austro-Hungarian Empire, such as Hungary and Czechoslovakia. Early in May 1919 Schumpeter made a particularly blatant attack on Bauer's *Anschluss* policy in an interview. Bauer immediately responded by writing a warning letter to Schumpeter. This, however, did not stop Schumpeter, either in public or in private. A few days after he had received Bauer's letter, he presented a secret economic plan to a British financial expert, Francis Oppenheimer, who was visiting Austria on behalf of the British government.[35] According to Oppenheimer, Schumpeter told him that Austria would be willing to give the Western states extraordinary powers over the country's economy in exchange for foreign capital. The Western states would also get control over the new central bank, which was to be created. How much Bauer got to know about this is not clear. A few days later, Bauer in any case wrote to Renner, the head of the government, that Schumpeter was disloyal: 'Schumpeter . . . carries on with his intrigues. I shall do nothing for the time being, but after the conclusion of the peace treaty it will be inevitable to force his resignation.'[36]

Bauer's resolve to get rid of Schumpeter can only have been strengthened by Schumpeter's behaviour in the so-called Kola Affair a few weeks later.[37] This incident did not so much involve the government's foreign policy as its stand on socialization. For a variety of reasons, not least to counteract the revolutionary strategy of the communists, the Austrian Social Democrats had taken a principled stand on the socialization of various key industries in Austria. Otto Bauer, especially, felt that socialization, as opposed to ordinary nationalization, was an integral part of the socialist strategy. Towards the end of May the government announced that it had decided to take over a number of key industries, including the country's largest ironworks, its power stations, and so on. One industry, which was bound to be taken over, was the Alpine Montan Gesellschaft. This company was the most important iron and mining industry in Austria; its management was notoriously anti-labour; and the workers had explicitly asked the state to take over the company. Luckily for the government, the shares of Alpine Montan were very cheap on the stock exchange at this time, so the whole thing would not be expensive for the tax payer. In June, however, their value suddenly trebled and it soon became clear that Fiat had bought a large number of shares in the company. This meant that Alpine Montan could not be socialized: one did not take over a company where one of the major shareholders was a firm located abroad.

Fiat had bought its shares in Alpine Montan via a Viennese banking firm called Kola & Co, which had continuously informed Schumpeter about its various transactions. Indeed, when Richard Kola approached Schumpeter to tell him (as he had to by law) that a huge amount of Italian currency would now be made available to the

Austrian government, he also explicitly told Schumpeter about his plans to buy shares in Alpine Montan for 'an Italian source'.[38] Bauer was always to feel that Schumpeter had acted in a disloyal manner by not telling the rest of the cabinet about these plans. Schumpeter, however, defended himself by saying that it was true that he had known about the plans, but that he had no authority whatsoever to stop them; and that even if he had had such authority, it would have been contrary to Austria's interest. Whatever one makes of Schumpeter's argument, it is not surprising that Bauer and others had had enough; and on 17 October 1919 they brusquely dismissed Schumpeter. The cabinet members of the Christian Social Party did not defend him, probably because he had offended their conservativism by proposing a capital levy and by advocating socialization.

To add insult to injury, Schumpeter also became very unpopular with the general public around this time.[39] As soon as he had been appointed finance minister, Schumpeter had begun to live in an extravagant fashion – he rented a castle, he acquired a stable of riding horses, and so on – and this was not very popular in a city where large parts of the population were suffering economically. Rumours soon began to circulate that Schumpeter was a callous person and that he did not care for the fate of ordinary people. One thing in particular that Schumpeter had said in an interview, stuck in people's minds: 'Krone ist Krone' or, freely translated, 'a crown is a crown, whatever it buys for you.' In saying this, Schumpeter was no doubt right from an economic point of view, but it was clearly not a very wise thing to say in a country which had been as hard hit by inflation as Austria.

IV

What conclusions about Schumpeter's personality and his skill as a politician can we draw from these experiences of 1916–19? In terms of Schumpeter's personality, perhaps it was just very difficult for him not to give a particular audience what it wanted. A few days before he was dismissed from the government, the Social Democratic Arbeiter-Zeitung, for example, accused him of 'adjusting his speeches to the audience: when he speaks before a workers' council, he does it as a Social Democrat; and when he addresses a peasants' assembly, he does it as a peasant.'[40] Did Schumpeter do this consciously? If one wants to be generous, one can say 'no' – Schumpeter may have felt that he sometimes should speak exclusively as a politician, at other times exclusively as an economist, and so on. But even if it may have been easy for Schumpeter himself to keep these roles apart, it is also understandable that he must have confused his audiences.

Apart from his personality, which was clearly a handicap for anyone engaged in serious politics, was Schumpeter a skilful politician?
The answer must be 'no'. Schumpeter usually backed losing causes;
he tended to misjudge situations; and he had too much of a taste
for intrigue. During his time as a finance minister he would often
completely misjudge a situation. For example, he probably counted
on support from the Christian Social Party in October 1919 – a
misjudgement which cost him his position. His behaviour towards
the British financial expert Francis Oppenheimer – trying to make
deals behind the back of his government colleagues – exemplifies
Schumpeter's willingness to get involved in intrigues. And his behaviour in the Kola affair and in the German Socialization Commission confused even the staunchest of his supporters. Schumpeter's
memoranda of 1916–17 are another example of how he could misjudge a situation politically. During these years the entire empire
was crumbling, but Schumpeter just continued to repeat in memorandum after memorandum how important it was to stop the tariff
agreement between Austria-Hungary and Germany. There is indeed a
curious dimension to these memoranda of 1916–17, which at times
gives the reader the impression that Schumpeter was something of a
Don Quixote in politics – with his notion that only a high nobleman
could save the Habsburg Empire, and with his plan for a symbolic
crowning of the Emperor in Prague, and so on.

Where does this leave us? That Schumpeter was just a bad politician? Perhaps. But it should immediately be added that Schumpeter
was also a political theorist of the highest calibre. That he had a
great talent for analysing politics is obvious from many of Schumpeter's articles from these days as well as his future masterpiece in this
genre, *Capitalism, Socialism and Democracy* (1942). Schumpeter, in
brief, was one of those people who have a superb theoretical grasp of
politics, but who fail miserably when they try to translate their ideas
into practical politics. Perhaps he was too subtle in his political
thinking for the real world; or maybe he just thought that he was
more subtle than everybody else – an error often made by academics
who get involved in politics. In any case, other people who fall into
this category of success in political theory and failure in practical
politics are Machiavelli and Max Weber. In other words, even in
his failures – and this is an irony which would have appealed to
Schumpeter -- he was in the best of company!

4

The Difficult Decade

If I have a function, it is to open doors, not to close them.
(Joseph A. Schumpeter in his farewell
speech at the University of Bonn in 1932)

The 1910s were good to Joseph Schumpeter. He had published a
series of important books and he had advanced very quickly in his
professional career from associate professor to full professor. His
appointment at the age of 36 as finance minister no doubt crowned
this series of youthful achievements. Unfortunately, it also marked
the peak of his career. A few months later, to recap, Schumpeter was
abruptly dismissed from the government. He, who had known so
many successes, now had to face defeat for the first time. And much
more was to come. Indeed, the 1920s were to be filled with serious
setbacks and difficulties for him. And this was true for virtually all
areas of life: in his work as an economist; in his professional career,
inside as well as outside academic life; and in his relationship with
his family. His life, which earlier had been so easy and carefree in
many ways, now seemed haunted. He went bankrupt when he tried
to venture into business; he failed to produce another book on economics despite giant efforts; and – most devastating of all – his
mother, his new wife and a newborn child all died. Towards the
end of the 1920s Schumpeter was in bad shape; he was tired, disappointed and disillusioned. The proverbial straw that broke the
camel's back came in the early 1930s when Schumpeter failed to get
a chair in economics at the University of Berlin. In 1932 he decided –
'in a mood of resignation', we are told – to accept an invitation to
teach permanently at Harvard.[1] Schumpeter, who was such a fervent
nationalist, would never return to his home country. And he, who

loved Europe so much, would never live there again. He had had enough.

That Schumpeter's intellectual activities would suffer from all these setbacks is understandable enough, and there is indeed a fragmentary character to his work from this period. During the early years of the 1920s he wrote very little because he was outside academia at this time, and later he failed to realize his number one project during this period, a book on the theory of money, which consumed large chunks of his time. But despite all of these failures, Schumpeter kept working away at the same set of problems as before, and he made some important progress. In 1926, for example, a new and much-improved edition of *Theorie der wirtschaftlichen Entwicklung* appeared. But first and foremost, Schumpeter succeeded in putting some order into his ideas about a broad-based economics and how economic theory should be related to the other social sciences. When working on *Theorie der wirtschaftlichen Entwicklung* Schumpeter had become convinced that there was something wrong with the traditional division of labour between economic theory and the other social sciences; and in his history of economics from 1914 he had explored this issue further. But he had not attempted to express a vision of what such a new and broad-based economics should look like; he knew what was wrong with static economics and the historical type of economics, but not much more than that. We find in Schumpeter's work from the 1920s a first attempt to find a solution to this problem, especially in his important essay 'Gustav von Schmoller and the Problems of Today' (1926). Using the term '*Sozialökonomik*' (which he had borrowed from Weber), Schumpeter here proposed a new and original way of looking at the science of economics. Theoretical economics, he argued, must be much more closely related to facts. This meant, among other things, that statistics should also be an integral part of economics. History and sociology had somehow to be incorporated into the scheme as well. A broad-based economics or *Sozialökonomik* should in other words consist of four parts: economic theory, statistics, sociology and history. These areas were all to be distinct from one another, but somehow also related to each other.

Schumpeter was fascinated by the task of how one could conceptualize the nature of these links; and this is also the central theme in the analysis of Schumpeter's writings in economics in this chapter. An analysis of Schumpeter's writings in sociology from these years appears in the next chapter – they raise so many interesting questions that they deserve a chapter of their own. Before looking in more detail at Schumpeter's writings in economics, we shall, however, take a look at what happened to Schumpeter himself during this difficult decade.

I

Exactly what Schumpeter did after he was dismissed from the government in October 1919 is not known. He probably stayed in Vienna for a while to see if any new and interesting possibilities would open up. But no interesting job must have been offered for, by the summer of 1920, we find Schumpeter back in Graz, teaching at the university. He, however, only taught at the University of Graz until the end of the year. In March 1921 he applied for leave for one year and some months later he handed in his resignation. In the meantime he had found a new means of support: he had become the president of a small but respected Viennese banking house, the Biedermann Bank.

Schumpeter probably went into business because he had lived far beyond his means as a finance minister. It is also likely that by 1921 he had spent whatever small fortune he had amassed during his stay in Cairo. Schumpeter, in brief, needed to make money quickly; and finance rather than entrepreneurship was the easiest way to do this in Austria. It must also have been hard for Schumpeter to go back to a place like Graz and just resume his normal activities as a professor, after having held an important position in the government. In any case, Schumpeter seems to have thrown himself body and soul into his new affairs because he wrote virtually nothing during the early 1920s. In 1921 Arthur Spiethoff asked him if he would be willing to write a book on economic theory for an encyclopaedia he was helping to edit, *Enzyklopädie der Rechts- und Staatswissenschaft*.[2] Schumpeter agreed, but it soon became obvious that his other duties were so demanding that he had no energy left to write a book. Early in 1924 Spiethoff had to tell Schumpeter that he had decided to look for another writer, since Schumpeter showed no signs of progress. Schumpeter answered Spiethoff in a letter, dated 17 April 1924, which was resigned in tone and in which he said that these days he 'saw science and scientific work a little bit like a distant and unreachable native country'.[3]

Schumpeter's involvement with the Biedermann Bank arose as follows.[4] After he had been dismissed as finance minister in 1919, he was rewarded by the parliament – more precisely, by the conservative members of the parliament – with the right to dispose of a concession to establish a bank. These banking concessions were difficult to obtain and consequently quite valuable. The Biedermann Bank was an old private banking firm, which was in the process of becoming a public corporation and therefore in need of a concession of the type that Schumpeter owned. In 1920–1 an agreement was reached between the Biedermann Bank and Schumpeter through which the bank obtained the concession while Schumpeter became

the chairman of the board, acquired some shares in the new corporation and received a huge salary (about $15,000 in 1921 dollars). He
also – most important – was allowed to make sizeable overdrafts.
Schumpeter was not involved in the everyday running of the bank;
he had primarily been brought in because he had the sought-after
banking concession and because it looked good to have a former
finance minister on the board. For his part, Schumpeter was not
particularly interested in banking: he wanted to make money.

Schumpeter used his credit line at the Biedermann Bank to invest
heavily in a series of different business enterprises. The basic idea
was apparently to borrow money from the bank and then repay it
with whatever his investments brought in, while keeping the difference. This scheme worked very well during the first three years that
Schumpeter was involved with the Biedermann Bank. Most of his
investments paid off, and Schumpeter soon resumed his former
extravagant life which, it may be noted, also extended to his love life.
A friend recalls, for example, how Schumpeter, when told that he
should be more discreet and not display himself publicly in Vienna
with prostitutes, just laughed: 'In response ... he rented a pair-
drawn open *Fiaker* [carriage] and rode up and down Kärtnerstrasse –
a main boulevard in the inner city – at midday with an attractive
blonde prostitute on one knee and a brunette on the other.'[5]

In 1924, however, things quickly turned sour. Austria was hit by a
severe economic crisis and many banks and industries went bankrupt. In a few months Schumpeter lost all of his investments. It also
turned out that one of his business partners – a trusted, former
Theresianum student – had been involved in shady, if not illegal,
dealings. The Biedermann Bank itself was in serious trouble, and late
in 1924 the bank had to be restructured to survive. To strengthen the
bank, a new partner was brought in, who demanded that Schumpeter immediately be fired. On 11 September 1924 Schumpeter was
abruptly dismissed as the chairman of the board of the Biedermann
Bank. Suddenly, he was without a job, without a salary and with a
mountain of debts.

Schumpeter's situation was close to desperate in 1924. Not only
did he owe money due to his failing investments, but he apparently
also had other debts from his time as finance minister and he owed
the Austrian state a considerable amount in back taxes. Friends tried
to help him in various ways, but he had to carry the main burden
himself. For the next ten years he would desperately try to pay off his
debts the only way he knew: by giving speeches and writing articles.
He even tried to put together a general textbook on economics, but
never succeeded in completing it. In 1924 it was also unclear what
Schumpeter would do next: he had no capital; he had a poor
reputation as a businessman; and he was very unpopular in political

circles. Things, indeed, looked black. In 1925, however, his luck changed and he was offered the chair in public finance at the University of Bonn. He immediately accepted.

The person who was responsible for Schumpeter's appointment in Bonn was his old friend Arthur Spiethoff, who had informed Schumpeter during the First World War of the German plan for a tariff agreement with Austria. In those days Spiethoff was at the University of Prague, but he had since moved to the University of Bonn. In 1924 preparations were started at the University of Bonn to replace Heinrich Dietzel, a well-known liberal economist who among other things had helped to introduce the notion of *Sozialökonomik* into Germany.[6] The faculty submitted two names – Fritz Karl Mann and Franz Gutman – but neither was acceptable to the Prussian Ministry of Education.[7] Instead the faculty was asked by the Ministry to suggest three new candidates and in particular to express its opinion about Ludwig von Mises. In its answer, dated 2 July 1925, the faculty suggested the names of Schumpeter and Walter Lotz of the University of Munich; von Mises was accused of being so caught up in his own ideas that he was unable to relate to other viewpoints in economics. Effective as of 15 October 1925, Schumpeter was appointed Professor of Public Finance at the University of Bonn.

It had not been easy for Spiethoff to push through Schumpeter's appointment. Schumpeter was apparently not very much liked at the Prussian Ministry of Education, something which was probably related to Schumpeter's open hostility to a close relationship between Germany and Austria. Spiethoff's colleagues in Bonn were also worried by all the rumours about Schumpeter, and they kept asking Spiethoff if there was anything to all these stories about the flamboyant ex-minister and ex-banker who might become their colleague. To calm them down, Spiethoff wrote a letter to Gustav Stolper, a well-known publisher and public figure, and asked him for his opinion about Schumpeter. Stolper answered Spiethoff on 22 August 1925 that he too had heard many stories about Schumpeter and that Schumpeter had 'many enemies'.[8] Stolper, however, felt that this was only natural since Schumpeter had advanced so quickly in his career and since his lifestyle was so provocative and 'un-Austrian' in many ways. 'Ordinary people', Stolper wrote, 'can simply not understand why a university professor from Graz refuses to frequent the local pub and why he mechanically repeats whatever political slogans are in the air, be they to the left or to the right; and why a bourgeois minister in a petty bourgeois government must have handkerchiefs and shirts of silk or own a riding-horse.'[9] According to Stolper, Schumpeter was simply not suited to be in politics and he was even worse of a disaster in business. Schumpeter belonged in the academic world, Stolper said, and added that he found it shameful that Othmar Spann had succeeded in blocking an appointment for Schumpeter at the University of Vienna. 'It would be a crime', Stolper emphasized, if Schumpeter was denied a position at a German university just because of malicious gossip. Schumpeter had a superb scientific talent, Stolper concluded, and he still had much to give.

Stolper's letter apparently did the trick for by the autumn of 1925 Schumpeter could start his new appointment. Since he was professor of public finance, he was responsible for giving lectures in this topic as well as in the theory of money. Schumpeter also taught history of economic theory and social theory. His main specialty, of course, was economic theory, but Spiethoff kept this topic for himself. Spiethoff had been an assistant to Gustav von Schmoller; and even though he was not hostile to theoretical economics of the type that Schumpeter represented, he probably thought it would be wiser if Schumpeter was not responsible for the main lectures in economic theory. Schumpeter, however, quickly began to lecture on economic theory as part of his courses and seminars on other topics. Schmoller had succeeded in keeping modern economic theory out of the German universities for nearly three decades, but this now came to an end with Schumpeter's lectures at Bonn. A well-known German economist, who gained his education from Schumpeter at the University of Bonn, has described the importance of Schumpeter's lectures in the following way:

> The assumption of teaching by Schumpeter in Bonn was a sensation for the academic world of economics. For the first time since decades, theory was taught again at a German university. Names like Cournot, Walras, Pareto, Wicksell, Böhm-Bawerk, Wieser, Edgeworth, and others now became daily fare. The use of the language of mathematics was no longer confined to a small sect, but became a matter of course in lectures and seminars. In a next to incredibly short time Bonn became a Mecca for economists from all over the world. What Göttingen was for mathematics and physics, Bonn now became for economics – and this in spite of the fact that Schumpeter did not officially represent economic theory as a field.[10]

At first Schumpeter seems to have felt somewhat alien being back in academia. After a few weeks as a professor he wrote to a friend that, 'it has felt a little odd to be among all these young people and these professors with the same mentality as young people. I feel older and more experienced and – how should I say – it is not so easy for me to take *seriously* what is seen as important in this "world".'[11] But the University of Bonn was a charming, old university and Schumpeter was probably relieved to be back in an academic setting. 'Academic activities ... are perhaps the least distasteful ones to indulge in, in the world as it is', as he once put it.[12] Schumpeter also resumed his research, and within a short time he sent off several important articles. He began to work very hard on a new major theoretical project, which was to be of the same order as his first two books. This was his book on the theory of money.

Schumpeter established good relationships with the students and his lectures were highly appreciated. A couple of students have given the following description of how Schumpeter appeared to them during these years in Bonn:

> The first impression you had of Schumpeter when he came into the lecture hall ... was of a fairly small and even slender man, at least in comparison to the way that his colleagues, Spiethoff and Herbert von Beckerath, looked. He was dark-skinned, had black hair, a broad forehead and a receding hairline. There was something wrong with his hip – according to what people said, he had once had a fall when riding – and he held his body in a rigid way. But despite this he had a slightly springy walk, which gave a controlled and elegant impression. Schumpeter's facial expression was clear and open. At first he would give the impression of being amiable, but you immediately became aware of something searching and very firm about him. His eyes were calm, steady and often some-what mischievous, as you would quickly notice. In a discussion he would be calm and contemplating while he was listening; he would quickly come alive when he answered; and he was full of fire when his counterattack led to victory.[13]

The lectures themselves were apparently quite an event since Schumpeter was an accomplished actor. The description continues in the following way:

> Schumpeter would start his lectures in a very composed manner, always without a manuscript. Occasionally he would search through his jacket pockets for some small notes, which never seemed to be in any particular order and which were about twice the size of a matchbox. While he kept on lecturing he would laughingly put them all back but one, which would have the formula he was looking for and which he then would proceed to explain with all the nonchalance of an artist who is perfectly in control.
>
> Schumpeter spoke in a clear and amiable manner as the Vien-nese tend to do; he was a little playful, but also measured and emphatic. He gestured quite a bit when he was lecturing, which he did either while leaning against the pulpit or, less frequently, while walking around it with one hand in his jacket pocket. His hands were calm and firm; his handwriting was grandiose – the letters looked interesting but were often unreadable and his drawings were clumsy.[14]

II

Schumpeter remarried in 1925.[15] As we recall, Schumpeter had been married before to an Englishwoman called Gladys Ricarde Seaver. When Schumpeter returned in 1914 from his year as exchange professor in the United States the first Mrs Schumpeter was in England and she refused to accompany him to Austria. At this point there was probably little affection left between Schumpeter and his wife, so her decision to remain in England was no great tragedy for either of them. After the First World War broke out, Schumpeter apparently made a half-hearted attempt at reconciliation – he wanted them to meet and sort things out in Switzerland – but Gladys was not interested and she definitely did not want to live in an enemy country. After this second refusal, Schumpeter appears to have regarded himself as unmarried and he let this be known in his various social circles. No formal divorce ever took place between Schumpeter and Gladys. But when the City of Vienna, shortly after the First World War, announced that a simplified form of divorce was possible if one spouse wanted it, Schumpeter immediately applied. He did not tell Gladys about his application, and it is quite likely that she would have been able to challenge the legality of the divorce in an Austrian court.

While married, Schumpeter had had a series of extramarital affairs, and after the break with Gladys he continued to seek out women. Most of his new relationships seem to have been rather short-lived, but there were also exceptions, such as his relationship with a Viennese prostitute who insisted on presenting herself publicly as Schumpeter's wife ('Nelly Schumpeter').[16] These, however, all pale in comparison with the romance that started up in 1924 and was to become the great love affair of Schumpeter's life.

The object of Schumpeter's affection was a young woman from Vienna called Anna ('Annie') Josefina Reisinger. As Schumpeter himself used to tell the story, he met Annie when she was still very young, arranged with her parents to marry her at a later date, and in the meantime sent her to school in France and Switzerland. In the words of Richard Goodwin, a friend and colleague whom Schumpeter sometimes confided in: 'When in Bonn he [that is, Schumpeter] fell in love with a porter's daughter, who was only 12 or so years of age, and he asked that he be allowed to arrange for her education and to marry her when she came of age.'[17]

Thanks to the fact that Annie kept a detailed diary we know, however, that the truth is somewhat different.[18] In reality, Annie was the daughter of the concierge in the house on Doblhofgasse in Vienna where Schumpeter's mother lived and where Schumpeter had grown up. Annie was 20 years younger than Schumpeter and came from a modest working-class family. As a teenager, she had apparently had a crush on Schumpeter ('Schumy'). And when she was seventeen she and Schumpeter started to see each other, first in secret and later with her parents' permission. Soon, however, they broke up. In a letter that Annie wrote to Schumpeter in September 1920, she accused him of being a womanizer; she knew that he was married; and she also thought that he was 'a big egoist'.[19] Schumpeter does not seem to have been particularly upset by Annie's decision to stop seeing him, and he apparently made no attempt to contact her during the next two and a half years which she spent as a maid in France. When she and Schumpeter met again in December 1923 in Vienna, however, they decided to stay in touch. At first, nothing much seems to have happened between the two; and both were actually seeing other people as well. Soon, however, they realized that they were deeply in love with one another.

Schumpeter's friends, who were used to seeing him with a variety of women, could at first not believe that he was serious about a young working-class woman like Annie. But he was serious indeed, and in May 1925 he proposed marriage. Early in October 1925 he triumphantly telegraphed Annie that he had secured the professorship in Bonn ('*Bonn erobert*'), which meant that they could now afford to marry. The marriage itself took place in a Lutheran church in Vienna on 5 November 1925; and Annie as well as Schumpeter had to convert to Lutheranism in order to marry. Neither Schumpeter's mother nor Annie's parents were present at the wedding, since they disapproved of the marriage between the 22-year-old bride and the 42-year-old groom.

Schumpeter himself was clearly very, very happy to be married to Annie and he was later to describe her as '*the great wonder of my life*'.[20] All of Schumpeter's friends also testify to his profound love for Annie. Their residence in Bonn on Coblenzerstrasse 39, which was a magnificent house overlooking the Rhine, soon became known for its lavish parties, and the elegant Mr and Mrs Schumpeter were very popular guests as well. Within a short time Annie became pregnant, and it is clear from Schumpeter's correspondence that he liked the idea of becoming a father. It is in the midst of all this happiness, incidentally, that Schumpeter wrote his most important work of the period 1919–32, the essay 'Gustav von Schmoller and the Problems of Today' (1926).

But the good times were not to last. The first blow came on 22 June 1926 when Schumpeter's mother died. She had been the most important person in Schumpeter's life and her death was clearly a hard blow for him. Earlier we noted that after Schumpeter left for the United States in 1932, he would never return to Austria again. In fact, he is supposed to have visited his native country only once after

his appointment to Bonn in 1925 – and that was to hurry to his
mother's deathbed in June 1926. More sorrows were, however, soon
to come. About a month after the death of Schumpeter's mother,
Annie suddenly died in childbirth. This tragic event took place on 3
August 1926. Her pregnancy had been difficult from the beginning,
and she had haemorrhaged irregularly for some time before giving
birth. Annie's condition was further aggravated by a series of quarrels between her and Schumpeter, set off by Gladys's threats to sue
Schumpeter for bigamy. The child to which Annie gave birth was
baptized 'Joseph Schumpeter', but only became '3 and ¾ hours' old,
according to the death certificate.[21]

At Annie's death, she and Schumpeter had been married for less
than a year, and Schumpeter was totally devastated by what had
happened. The same day, the fateful 3 August 1926, he wrote in
despair to a friend, 'I had been prepared that anything might happen
but not that I, old man, would survive a 23-year old wife ... I may
deserve a lot, but not this.'[22] The funeral of Annie and the child was a
profoundly moving event. A friend recalls how 'Schumpeter stood
speechless, yet manly at the side of the coffin, which he had decor-
ated with red roses, and in which his young and beautiful wife was
lying, like a madonna with her little boy in her arms.'[23] The scene at
the funeral etched itself into Schumpeter's memory, and some time
later he wrote in a letter that 'the main thing is that I can work and
that when I do that, I regain my equilibrium, in spite of the image in
my mind of the agonizing expression in her eyes during the last
hours ... Even in the last seconds she was so esthetic looking, so
beautiful – and then with such calm majesty in the coffin. And with
... the little child in her arms.'[24]

The time after the deaths in his family was terrible for Schumpeter. A series of personal letters have survived from these difficult
years in the mid-1920s, and they show the agony he felt.[25] He wrote:
'My sorrow knows no limits ...'; 'I sometimes suffer as if I were
condemned to hell ...'[26] How deeply affected Schumpeter was by his
wife's death is also evidenced by the fact that for years he would not
change anything in her room, not even remove her clothes.[27] A death
mask of Annie and the little son were from now permanently on
display in Schumpeter's home. Every morning he walked to the
nearby churchyard, where Annie was buried, and placed a rose on
her grave. Another, more curious habit now also developed. Each day
Schumpeter would meticulously copy passages from Annie's diary,
even imitating her handwriting and faulty punctuation. When he had
copied the whole diary, he would start all over again, at times adding something he felt that Annie had failed to mention. Slowly,
Schumpeter began to transform Annie and his mother into his private saints or guardian angels. The term he often used for the two of
them was *Hasen*, which literally means 'hare' or 'rabbit' but which

also denotes a person who is inordinately and passionately loved. According to those who have studied these parts of Schumpeter's writings in detail, he eventually created a whole, rather strange cult around 'die Hasen'.[28] Whenever he was about to do something difficult, he asked for their support; and when something had gone well, he thanked them profusely. Schumpeter would typically ask 'Mami' and 'Annerl' for protection against physical dangers, such as train and boat accidents, or ask them for help with a lecture or a manuscript. The cult around Annie and Schumpeter's mother seems to have had certain religious overtones. Schumpeter, for example, sometimes wrote 'Hasen sei Dank' ('The Hasen be thanked'), reminiscent of 'Gott sei Dank' ('God be thanked'). And each day Schumpeter started his diary entry with the same invocation: 'O Mutter und Herrin, o seid über mir!' ('O Mother and Mistress, please protect me!')

Schumpeter also tried to counter his sorrow with work. But he did not accomplish very much. He wrote to a friend some time after Annie's death:

> I work hard but I fail all the time. All my thoughts are blurred and I can't even get the most simple thing done for the text book. You must not think that I *want to* perish ... I myself do not understand how it came about – how it could come about – that science, which was so generous to me during my best years, now refuses me. I say to myself that this must be madness, that it just can't be – especially not for a man who does mental work – that another human being is his everything and that when he has lost her, he is finished.[29]

Schumpeter was unable to overcome Annie's death for many, many years and he increasingly withdrew into his work. But he had lost his old capacity to concentrate and to create:

> It is dissatisfying how paralyzed and unhappy I always am when I do not work. The vacation was too short. And when I resumed work [on the book on money], there was only a sense of impotence, failure and anxiety ... that I definitely was finished. I am depressed and continuously feel restless and tormented. Even if I accomplish something, the old ease with which I used to create is gone. When I dictate, I often have to stop or to continue in pain.[30]

His friends also noted that Schumpeter had changed as a result of the deaths in his family. 'After that time', Gottfried Haberler later wrote, 'a streak of resignation and pessimism was unmistakable in his character.'[31]

It is no doubt true that Schumpeter's failure to concentrate on his scientific work was also connected to the fact that he now had to write and lecture for money in order to pay off his debts. The amount he owed actually increased in 1926–7, when the Biedermann Bank finally went under.[32] Schumpeter soon began to hate lecturing whenever he was offered some money, and he developed a strong antipathy for his audiences, which usually consisted of local politicians, members of trade associations, and the like. As an intellectual he had always been used to explore any problem just because it was interesting, and he resented having to write for money tremendously. In a letter from 1927 we read, for example: 'this activity [of writing] which used to be pleasurable to me now only fills me with oppression and repulsion. I can't any longer follow my interests, and I have to tell myself: you should stop at this point, because it won't bring any money to continue. I can't tell you how much I hate it . . . .'[33] And in a letter from 1928 Schumpeter says that it is a form of 'prostitution' to have to write and give speeches for money all the time. He adds in despair that 'this slave chain has no end – this forced labor can last for another 20 years.'[34]

Given the circumstances of Schumpeter's life in the late 1920s, it is not surprising that he failed to realize his plans to produce a third major work in economic theory. By the mid-1920s, as we know, Schumpeter had decided to write a book on the theory of money, and after Annie's death he continued to work hard to finish it. His efforts culminated in the autumn of 1929; and on 19 September 1929 Schumpeter wrote to Spiethoff that 'I have made a desperate attempt to finish my book on money . . . but only to fall back into a state of exhaustion.'[35] In a letter from April 1930 Schumpeter wrote to Spiethoff that 'I work every day as a mad bull on my book on money and I am doing everything I can to have it ready by September 9, the day of my departure [for the United States].'[36] But the book was not finished by September.

Schumpeter was not the only one who was trying to recast the theory of money in the 1920s. In 1930 J. M. Keynes published *A Treatise on Money* and it was immediately recognized as a major work. Schumpeter, who seems to have regarded Keynes as his main rival all through life, reacted violently to this news. For example, he told one of his students in Bonn that Keynes had upstaged him and that 'all that was left [for him] to do was to destroy the manuscript'.[37] According to Edgar Salin, Schumpeter actually burnt his manuscript.[38] And on and off, for the rest of his life, Schumpeter would continue to work on his book on money – but without being able to finish it. Two months before his death in January 1950 he wrote, 'within a year or two I hope to write a book on money that will give my latest views.'[39]

Schumpeter would slowly learn to recover from the shock of having lost his whole family at one blow. But his longing for what had been taken away from him was still there. 'I recall a very illustrious local gathering', one of Schumpeter's students in Bonn once said, 'where he conversed only with the 6–10 year old children of the host.'[40] Schumpeter was also extremely friendly and affectionate to his students in Bonn, and several of them – such as Wolfgang Stolper and Erich Schneider – would always feel very devoted to him. According to Stolper, 'he lived for us [students] and treated us somewhat like his children.'[41] The following story that Stolper tells from his days as a student in Bonn shows how well Schumpeter treated his favourite students and how he tried to turn his relationship with them into something like a replacement for the family he had lost:

> I had the good fortune of being probably Schumpeter's only tutee [in Bonn]. This procedure, too, he deliberately introduced from England. Every Monday evening I appeared to read and discuss a paper he had assigned to me the week before. But that was really only a small part of my education. Every Monday noon I had to appear to order dinner and select a wine, for this too was part of the education of a gentleman. In the evening Schumpeter would approve of my choice (since his wine cellar was excellent that was not really too difficult) and we would discuss anything that came to his mind: Goethe's poems or his letters to Frau von Stein, Gothic cathedrals about which he knew an enormous amount, Picasso and Braque. I do not remember ever discussing music, however, which was my special love. At about ten o'clock we would retire to the glassed-in veranda with a magnificent view of the Rhine and the Seven Mountains (Schumpeter had rented the house used by the Emperor as a student) and until one in the morning we would discuss economics, Schumpeter exercising a heavenly patience with his somewhat obtuse and totally inexperienced pupil.[42]

Another way that Schumpeter tried to compensate for his losses was by travelling a lot and by staying away from Bonn as much as possible. In 1927–8 Schumpeter was a visiting lecturer and tutor at Harvard University and he returned in the autumn of 1930. During the latter occasion he helped to found the Econometric Society, which is today a thriving and influential organization. The initiative for the society came from Europe – more precisely from Ragnar Frisch in Norway – and some of the preparatory meetings were actually held at Schumpeter's home in Bonn. Schumpeter was very enthusiastic about the possibility of 'a unification of the theoretical–quantitative and the empirical–quantitative' (to cite the constitution of the society). He also had the honour of being the chairman at the historic founding meeting of the Econometric Society on 29 December 1930 in Cleveland, Ohio.

On his way back from the United States in early 1931 Schumpeter stayed for some time in Japan, where he gave a series of lectures.

Schumpeter had had several Japanese students in Bonn and a relative of his, Hugo Schumpeter, had been consul-general to Japan. So when he arrived in Japan, he already had some links with the country. But he cannot have been prepared for the enormously enthusiastic reception that he received from the Japanese scholars. Everywhere he lectured, it was a triumph. Schumpeter quickly fell in love with Japanese culture in return and especially with its temples, these 'temples that grow out of their natural surroundings – a moving beauty', as he would later describe them.[43] While still in Japan, Schumpeter wrote the following happy letter to a Harvard colleague:

> My trip has been a failure as far as the purpose of having a rest is concerned. For the time in Japan was one continuous rush of addresses and excursions of all sorts arranged by friends and pupils very much against my will. Yet I have enjoyed it greatly and I carry away with me a very good impression not only of Japanese colleagues and students, but also business leaders and politicians. As to the latter, it is perhaps the aristocratic element in Japanese culture that makes them show up so very well as compared with what one meets in Europe.[44]

But even if we can sense a certain *joie de vivre* in Schumpeter's letters from Japan, he was still suffering very deeply from Annie's death. In a letter from Singapore, dated 31 March 1931, he wrote to a close friend ('G...'):

> There are no travels, dear G... – one is always imprisoned in oneself. And there is no true liberation ... Difficult memories and premonitions haunt me. It is interesting in this context to note that from a psychological viewpoint all my faults, failures, calamities, and so on, are never as present to me as when I am on board a beautiful ship and travel across the calm sea in what would seem to be a pleasant manner. But a feeling of decline, both mental and physical, always accompanies me, and it is sometimes condensed into a premonition of imminent death.[45]

Connected to Schumpeter's despair was, as we know, a strong desire to get away from Bonn.[46] The universities in Kiel, Prague and Freiburg had all made offers to Schumpeter in the late 1920s, but he turned them down. When in the early 1930s several positions were opened up at the University of Berlin – Germany's most prestigious university – Schumpeter, however, immediately let it be known that he was interested. He particularly wanted to get the chair in economic theory, which was to become vacant when Werner Sombart retired. But Schumpeter was not the one selected, and Sombart's chair went instead to Emil Lederer, Schumpeter's colleague in the German Socialization Commission and in the *Archiv für Sozialwissenschaft und Sozialpolitik.* Nor did Schumpeter get a second chair at the University of Berlin, which became vacant at around the same time. It is not clear why Schumpeter, who was probably the most competent of the candidates, was passed over in both cases. In all likelihood it was due to a combination of two factors. First, Schumpeter was intensely disliked by the economists in Berlin; and, secondly, it was feared that his huge personal debt would interfere with his scholarship. According to one source, most of the economists at the University of Berlin were mediocre scholars and well aware that Schumpeter had great contempt for them.[47] And because of this, so the story goes, they did everything they could to stop Schumpeter, including spreading malicious rumours about him. However this may be, Schumpeter was deeply disappointed at his failure to get a chair at the University of Berlin. As a result he made it known at Harvard, where the economics department had tried to woo Schumpeter for a long time, that he was willing to consider an offer. Such an offer was soon forthcoming, and by 1932 Schumpeter could leave Bonn for good.

III

The 1919–32 period was not a very creative one for Schumpeter. But the pressure to produce – in order to pay off his debts – was there, and during these years Schumpeter wrote more than 70 articles. Of these, only ten were written before the trouble at the Biedermann Bank in 1924; and the remaining 60 or so afterwards.[48] Most of Schumpeter's articles from these years appeared in trade journals and general economics magazines, such as *Der Arbeitsgeber*, *Die Chemische Industrie* and *Berliner Börsencourier*. For just one magazine – *Der Deutsche Volkswirt* which was published by Gustav Stolper (Wolfgang Stolper's father) – Schumpeter wrote nearly 20 articles. But he also tried to keep his own research alive, and some of his articles from these years appeared in good scientific journals, such as *Schmollers Jahrbuch*, *Economic Journal* and *Archiv für Sozialwissenschaft und Sozialpolitik*. As opposed to the articles he wrote for money, Schumpeter's scientific articles dealt less with day-to-day topics. There were three scientific topics that especially fascinated Schumpeter while he was at the University of Bonn: the theory of money, the theory of economic change, and the general structure of a broad-based economic science or *Sozialökonomik*.

To some extent it can be said that Schumpeter failed to accomplish what he had set out to do for himself during these years. This was particularly true for his book on money, which he never succeeded in completing. Still, his writings from 1919 to 1932 also contain some very valuable insights and this is especially true for Schumpeter's analysis of *Sozialökonomik*. This concept is mainly developed in his article 'Gustav von Schmoller and the Problems of Today' (1926), which is a seminal essay in many ways. Here Schumpeter indeed succeeded in 'opening up new doors', to cite his farewell lecture from 1932.

Throughout his life it was always Schumpeter's ambition to produce a major work on the theory of money. He never succeeded in doing this and when he summed up his work in this field, just a year before he died, he had to admit that 'I have never treated the problems of money per se: my views of money have been presented only incidentally in works of mine which were primarily devoted to other subjects.'[49] There was, however, one exception and that was an article from 1917–18 entitled 'Money and the Social Product'.[50] Schumpeter, however, soon became dissatisfied with this article: 'I do not think much myself [of it]', as he wrote to a colleague in the 1940s.[51]

As we know, Schumpeter worked furiously to finish his book on money in the late 1920s, only to discover that he had been upstaged by Keynes. And when Schumpeter realized how similar Keynes's *Treatise* was to his own book, so the story goes, he destroyed his manuscript. But Schumpeter must have kept a copy, because after his death a manuscript was found among his papers which has been identified, beyond any shadow of a doubt, as the manuscript that Schumpeter worked on in 1929 (and, as it turns out, tried to amend in the early 1930s when he had just arrived in the United States). Schumpeter's manuscript was published many years later as *Das Wesen des Geldes* (1970) or *The Nature of Money*. The editor, Fritz Karl Mann, felt that the title of the key chapter – chapter 9, 'Das Wesen des Geldes' – was preferable to the original title, *Geld und Währung* (*Money and Currency*). Mann also decided that Schumpeter's manuscript could be published, despite its occasionally fragmentary nature and despite Schumpeter's own insistence that it must not be published until it had been thoroughly revised.

We should definitely be grateful to Mann for his decision to go through with the publication of Schumpeter's manuscript. *Das Wesen des Geldes* may not be a finished product or in a class with Schumpeter's major works, but it does contain some very interesting ideas. The book opens, for example, with some powerful statements about the way that money reflects the major social struggles:

> The great and often passionate interest that is evoked by practical questions relating to money and its value, can only be explained by the fact that the monetary system of a people reflects all that a people wants, all that it suffers, all that it *is*; as well as by the fact that a people's monetary system is an important influence on its economy and on the fate of society in general.[52]

According to Schumpeter, everything that influences society will also affect its monetary system: 'Every kind of politics can become monetary politics; every kind of event can become a monetary event.'[53] Indeed, in order to grasp the role that money plays in society we have to conceptualize it as part of the totality of society and to do this, a 'sociology of money' is needed. The similarity between Schumpeter's ideas on this point and those of Georg Simmel in The Philosophy of Money (1900) is striking. But even if Schumpeter's book contains a forceful argument for looking at money from a broad, sociological perspective, its main emphasis is elsewhere. What Schumpeter primarily wanted to provide with his book was a contribution to the economic theory of money. This was a task, he emphasized, which must not be confused with that of tracing the history of money. The latter may very well be a worthwhile task – but it would tell us little about money as an economic (as opposed to a social) phenomenon. In many cases, Schumpeter says, the earliest version of an institution is actually much more difficult to grasp from an analytical viewpoint than is its later, more developed form. An economic theoretician, as opposed to an economic historian, would therefore do best to focus on money such as it exists today in a modern economy.

Schumpeter's own attempt to develop a theory of money in Das Wesen des Geldes is centred around three major themes.[54] The first of these, which can also be found in 'Money and the Social Product' (1917–18), is that the theory of money should be part of general economic theory. This means, first of all, that there is no point in developing a separate monetary theory – it has to be linked to the theory of value and price. The second theme in Schumpeter's theory of money is that monetary theory has to include the theory of banking and bank credit. This idea is present already in Theorie der wirtschaftlichen Entwicklung (1911), where Schumpeter argues that money plays an essentially passive role in the circular flow while credit creation is absolutely necessary for there to be economic development.

The third theme in Das Wesen des Geldes is more difficult to summarize in a few words, but central to an understanding of Schumpeter's theory of money. It has to do with Schumpeter's idea, following Walras, that money can best be analysed from the viewpoint of social accounting. The argument is technical, but boils down to the following. In Eléments d'Economie politique pure Walras had proposed that in a closed economy the only things that matter (given free competition and a state of equilibrium) are price ratios and not absolute prices. To get at the latter, an arbitrarily selected multiplier has to be introduced into the analysis; and it is this multiplier (or 'kritische Ziffer' in Schumpeter's terminology) that is the key to

Schumpeter's theory of money. According to *Das Wesen des Geldes*, the 'critical figure' is always set in an indirect way:

> It is this indirect and basically arbitrary method which determines the nature of the social institution which we call money ... The money method is that social accounting method in which the critical figure of the economic system varies according to its own specific laws. Every such method creates accounting units which exist as such – physically or in the books. We call these accounting units money.[55]

To conclude, what characterizes Schumpeter's theory of money is that money is firmly connected to the theory of value and price and that money is seen as following its own specific laws.

During Schumpeter's time in Bonn he also worked on his theory of economic change. There were two aspects of economic development, which especially fascinated him during these years: the business cycle and structural changes in whole economic systems. During the 1920s, business cycles was a popular topic among economists, as the work of people like Spiethoff, Pigou and Wesley Clair Mitchell show. Part of the reason for this was that good economic statistics were now becoming available for the first time. Schumpeter himself, for example, wanted to develop his theory of business cycles in very close conjunction with statistical data. Indeed, one of the reasons why he was so keen to get a chair in economics at the University of Berlin, was that there existed excellent facilities for empirical research in the capital. His failure to get a professorship in Berlin may also explain why it took him so long to present his final version of the business cycle. Indeed, it was not until 1939 that his massive, two-volume work *Business Cycles* could be published. Still, it would be incorrect to leave the reader with the impression that Schumpeter's research on the business cycle did not advance during his time at the University of Bonn. It was, for example, during this period that he developed the idea that several different business cycles are in progress simultaneously. While in his work from the early 1920s he had only spoken of the Juglar cycle, he now also spoke of 'the long wave' and 'the forty-month cycle' as well.[56] For all practical purposes, this is the basic conceptual scheme that we shall later find in *Business Cycles* (1939).

During his years in Bonn, Schumpeter also worked on the topic of changes in the economic system *per se* and here as well he succeeded in 'opening up doors'. His most important work in this genre is an article from 1928 called 'The Instability of Capitalism'. The kind of changes that Schumpeter focused on here differs from those which make up the business cycle in the sense that they affect the economic system itself, something which a Schumpeterian business cycle never does. The economic system that Schumpeter had in mind in his 1928 article was capitalism which, as he put it, had a 'tendency towards self-destruction from inherent economic causes, or towards out-growing its own frame'.[57] Schumpeter emphasized that what he was talking about was *not* changes in capitalism due to political causes ('political instability') or changes due to social causes ('social insta-bility'). Instead, as he saw it, there existed an inherent 'economic instability' in the capitalist system itself, which had become accen-tuated when 'competitive capitalism' was replaced by ' "trustified" capitalism'. The main reason for the increase in economic instability was, in Schumpeter's opinion, that the entrepreneur was disappear-ing and being replaced by teams of researchers working for huge corporations. The last sentence of Schumpeter's article indicates, however, that he had a much broader explanation in mind:

> Capitalism, whilst economically stable, and even gaining in stabil-ity, creates, by rationalizing the human mind, a mentality and a style of life incompatible with its own fundamental conditions, motives and social institutions, and will be changed, although not by economic necessity and probably even at some sacrifice of economic welfare, into an order of things which it will be merely a matter of taste and terminology to call Socialism or not.[58]

'The Instability of Capitalism' is in many ways a remarkable article, as Paul Samuelson has made clear.[59] But even if Schumpe-ter's article deserves all the praise that Samuelson has lavished on it, there is also the fact that Schumpeter later upstaged himself by writing a whole book on the same theme, *Capitalism, Socialism and Democracy* (1942). For this (and for some other reasons as well) 'The Instability of Capitalism' is really no serious competitor to Schumpe-ter's most remarkable essay from this period, 'Gustav von Schmoller and the Problems of Today' (1926). What makes this latter essay so outstanding is that Schumpeter here tried to go beyond the *Methodenstreit* and develop his own positive synthesis of historical economics and analytical economics. In this sense, Schumpeter's essay is very similar to Weber's essay from 1904, ' "Objectivity" in Social Science and Social Policy'. But even if Schumpeter's solution to the battle of the methods is similar to that of Weber in some aspects, it is also different enough to be seen as a serious alternative to Weber's proposal as well as an original contribution in its own right.

In his 1904 essay Weber had introduced the concept of ideal type with its 'analytical accentuation of certain elements of reality', on the one hand, and its roots in serious historical research, on the other, as a solution to the 'apparently unbridgable gap' between historical research and analytical model-building in economics.[60]

Weber had also bemoaned the fact that after the Menger–Schmoller
fight economics had split into 'two sciences', and he had suggested
a solution in the form of a broad-based *Sozialökonomik* with a place
for conventional economic theory as well as economic history and
economic sociology.[61]

But this is also where Weber's vision ended. In his essay on
Schmoller, Schumpeter argued in a similar vein that a broad-based
Sozialökonomik was the answer to the destructive split between historical economics and economic theory. But he also picked up where
Weber had stopped and added some original thoughts of his own.
Schumpeter's most complete version of *Sozialökonomik* is to be found
in his posthumously published *History of Economic Analysis* and will
therefore be discussed later in this book. It was, however, in his 1926
article on Schmoller that Schumpeter formulated his basic ideas on
this topic for the first time. In brief, it was here that Schumpeter
made the breakthrough.

In the beginning of his essay on Schmoller, Schumpeter warns that
a new *Methodenstreit* seems to be brewing in the United States. As
an example he cites a speech that Wesley Clair Mitchell had given
in 1924 at the American Economic Association. But such a battle of
methods must be avoided at all costs, Schumpeter said, because it
would only have negative results. The very idea that there could exist
different 'schools' in economics was utterly alien to Schumpeter,
in whose opinion there only existed good work and bad work. The
original *Methodenstreit* had in particular distorted the work of Gustav von Schmoller, Schumpeter said, and his essay of 1926 was first
of all an attempt to vindicate Schmoller. But there is much more to
'Gustav von Schmoller and the Problems of Today' than this. In the
first part of the essay Schumpeter tried to show on what particular
points Schmoller had been misunderstood. But in the second and
more important part, Schumpeter outlined what he saw as Schmoller's real contribution to economics, namely his attempt to formulate
a new and much richer concept of economics. The essay is thus
centred on Schmoller's potential contribution to a '*Sozialökonomie* of
today and tomorrow'.[62]

As an example of how often Schmoller had been misunderstood in
the past, Schumpeter cited his own history of economics from 1914.
His characterization in this work of Schmoller and the so-called
Younger Historical School now seemed 'partly dissatisfying' to
him.[63] In particular, Schumpeter said, he had been wrong in assert-
ing that Schmoller had only been interested in detailed, historical
research and that Schmoller had questioned the value of abstract
theory. Failures to understand what Schmoller had really said were
plentiful in Schumpeter's opinion, and the time had now come to set
the record straight.

As part of his attempt to rehabilitate Schmoller, Schumpeter
singled out the three most common misinterpretations of his work:

that Schmoller was hostile to all forms of economic theory; that he was only interested in historical details; and that he had failed to distinguish between science and politics in most of his writings. To assert that Schmoller was hostile to all kinds of theory was quite naive, in Schumpeter's opinion. There existed at least three forms of economic theory – hardcore theory of Ricardo's type, general economic theory, and standard explanations of economic events – and Schmoller had often used the latter two. Even though Schmoller had felt alien towards the most abstract type of economic theory, it still deserved 'a room in the big house of economics' in Schmoller's opinion.[64] What Schmoller really had disliked about economic theory was not so much its abstract quality, Schumpeter said, as the tendency among certain economists to use it as a vehicle for all types of speculation and also to glorify the liberal type of economy ('*Manchestertum*').

Schumpeter also refuted the idea that Schmoller had only been interested in historical details. For one thing, as he pointed out, Schmoller had never shown any particular preference for just *historical* facts; rather, Schmoller was interested in looking at economic reality from a special angle. This meant that contemporary data were just as important to Schmoller as historical data. As an example of this, Schumpeter referred to the work by Arthur Spiethoff, who had been Schmoller's assistant and now was the editor of *Schmollers Jahrbuch*. Spiethoff mainly did research on business cycles and for this he used contemporary data. Schumpeter also rejected the idea that Schmoller had only been interested in facts as opposed to theory. For Schmoller as for Schumpeter, the very idea of, on the one hand, 'anti-descriptive theory' and, on the other, 'anti-theoretical description' was absurd.[65] Facts and theory, Schumpeter said, always interpenetrate.

It was also clear that no facts can be totally individualistic or they would lose all interest for the scientist: 'What is truly unique is impossible to understand and also uninteresting since it has no relationship to the observer.'[66] It should also be remembered, Schumpeter added, that over the years history has become increasingly scientific and analytical in character. While earlier historians often looked only at specific events, contemporary historians were much more interested in trying to explain historical processes. The activities of historians and of economists were in reality not so dissimilar:

> The economic historian who wants to explain things and to make them understandable, cannot go about his business in any other way than the economist; and the economist, for his part, cannot behave towards historical facts in any other way than the historian. To find relationships, to reflect on these, to formulate them and to explain them – that is something that both of them do.[67]

It had also been a mistake, in Schumpeter's opinion, to reject Schmoller's work on the ground that he had confused value judgements and facts. The major part of Schmoller's work was not at all political in nature but rather an attempt to make people understand their own social problems. In his writings Schmoller did not side with any particular class or party, but rather tried to see things from the viewpoint of society (which he equated with the state). The only reforms that Schmoller had been interested in promoting, were those that were already latent in people's minds and which only needed a bit of a push to become reality. These were not divisive measures, but reforms that tomorrow's generation would regard as totally self-evident. Many social scientists, Schumpeter noted, tended to exaggerate the conflicts in society between groups and classes. Schmoller, on the other hand, had correctly understood that there existed several issues that everybody could agree on. In his own intuitive way, Schumpeter concluded, Schmoller had sensed the possibility of 'scientific politics' as well as of 'scientific value judgments'.[68]

The main gist of Schumpeter's argument was, however, not so much to defend Schmoller against all these misunderstandings, but to stress the relevance of Schmoller's vision of economics for today. And to Schumpeter, Schmoller's programme was truly a *'program for the future'*.[69] What Schumpeter especially admired in Schmoller's work was its exemplary broad vision of the economic process and Schmoller's attempt to explain the totality of this process in an innovative and scientific manner. Schmoller, Schumpeter said, looked at everything that economic theorists tended to ignore, namely 'the concrete economic circumstances of a people, its natural possibilities, its capacities, its international economic relations; its social structure, its figures of production, the size and distribution of its social product, and its social and political constitution'.[70] Schmoller's programme consisted, first of all, in an attempt to document all of this and to explain how a country's economy had come about; how its institutions functioned; and what the past and future evolution of the whole economy might look like. As part of this formidable task, Schumpeter said, Schmoller had collected data (e.g. in *Acta Borussica*); he had put together statistics (e.g. financial statistics); he had made numerous concrete investigations (e.g. in *Schmollers Jahrbuch*); and he had even attempted a synthesis of all this empirical knowledge (in his *Grundriss der allgemeinen Volkswirtschaftslehre*). Schumpeter concluded:

> And just as he is the only one in our science who was not only interested in such an ambitious program, but who also tried to realize it in a conscious and concrete manner, he is the only one ... who through his own actions has been able to give us a real sense of what this type of economic science might look like.[71]

This far we have mainly tried to give a description of what Schmoller tried to accomplish, and we shall now look at Schumpeter's interpretation of Schmoller's work in order to understand Schumpeter's own contribution to *Sozialökonomik*. Here it should first of all be noted that Schumpeter interpreted Schmoller's work as a kind of general economics which includes several different, disciplinary approaches to economic reality – approaches, it should be noted, which often overlap with one another. There were no sharp boundaries, in other words, between the different fields:

> In scientific thinking logically disparate elements, which are often impossible to separate from one another, tend to mix; and the main viewpoint changes constantly. Instead of trying to establish sharp borders between disciplines and approaches, we must realize that everything flows together and that the knowledge of an epoch is no planned and unitary building, but essentially a non-systematic conglomeration of what partly implies double work, and which as to content and method is woven together on different levels....[72]

According to Schumpeter, Schmoller had not only *added* something new to economics – say the historical approach – but he had actually *transformed all of economics in a fundamental manner*. Schmoller, in brief, had created 'a new system [of economics]'.[73] To anticipate Schumpeter's argument a little, it can be said that Schmoller, as Schumpeter saw it, had transformed the very concept of economic theory by making it much more concrete; he had developed a new branch of economics which could be called 'economic sociology'; and he had convincingly argued that one must also include history and statistics into the science of economics. As to economic theory, Schumpeter argued that Schmoller had introduced a new kind of theoretical economics ('*theoretische Sozialökonomie*'), which was much more closely connected to facts than ordinary economic theory (or what Schumpeter had called '*theoretische Nationalökonomie*' in his first book).[74] This new type of economic theory Schumpeter sometimes referred to as 'concretized theory' and in the next chapter of this book we shall see what Schumpeter meant by this expression in more detail, since it was precisely this type of theory that Schumpeter himself tried to develop in *Business Cycles* (1939).[75]

As Schumpeter saw it, Schmoller had also taught economists to realize the importance of statistics and economic history. Both of these disciplines had their own, distinct tasks to fulfil within *Sozialökonomik*. But they also had to interact with one another and use concepts from economic theory. In Schumpeter's opinion – and this is an important point – it was necessary for *all* of the different sciences within economics to cooperate, if there was to be a good result. A certain autonomy for each discipline in combination with exchange over the borders (which were diffuse anyway) – that was Schumpeter's recipe for a successful *Sozialökonomik*.

A few words also need to be said about Schumpeter's discussion of economic sociology in the Schmoller essay. As already mentioned, Schmoller saw economic institutions and their functioning as an integral part of the economic process. By economic institutions, it may be added, Schmoller meant institutions such as property, inheritance and (in certain respects) the state. Schumpeter now singled out this part of Schmoller's thought and suggested that what Schmoller had really been trying to develop all along was something that could be called 'economic sociology' or '*Wirtschaftssoziologie*': '*Schmoller's lifework can then to a large extent be seen as the founding and development of such an economic sociology [of institutions].*'[76]

In a way that is strongly reminiscent of Weber, Schumpeter thus ended up by suggesting that 'economic sociology' might be seen as a kind of solution to the *Methodenstreit*. Economic sociology – which was partly empirical and partly generalizing in Schumpeter's opinion – was to bridge the tendency to over-emphasize theory, on the one hand, and the tendency to over-emphasize detailed descriptions, on the other. To what extent Schumpeter was directly influenced by Weber on this point (who after all had presented the same solution 20 years earlier) is not easy to determine. The impression one gets is that Schumpeter pretty much had to reinvent the wheel. The idea of 'economic sociology' was, of course, also in the air during these years, as, for example, the work of Werner Sombart shows.[77]

The situation, however, was somewhat different with the concept of *Sozialökonomik*. True, again it was Weber who had drawn up the broad lines for what the solution should look like: it was Weber who had suggested the idea of an overarching kind of economics, which should include not only economic theory but also economic history and economic sociology; and it was Weber who had tried to show what this new type of economics would look like more concretely in *Grundriss der Sozialökonomik*. But it was also true that Schumpeter had presented new and quite original additions to Weber's vision of *Sozialökonomik* in his essay on Schmoller. For one thing, Schumpeter here suggested that the different sciences, which were to contribute to the general field of economics, often *overlapped*. He also emphasized the need for *collaboration* between all these sciences. Economic history, for example, must use concepts from economic theory; economic sociology could provide data for economic theory; and so on. This process of interaction and exchange was similar (but not identical) to another important process, namely that of *coordinating* economic theory, economic history, economic sociology and statistics. And, finally, Schumpeter had sensed *the limits to integration* that were present in Weber's concept of a general economic science. The different fields could not simply be collapsed into one another, say sociology into economic theory or economic theory into sociology. Schumpeter's main contribution to *Sozialökonomik* in the Schmoller essay, in short, was to have brought Weber's vision out into the open and to have suggested some ways in which it could be further developed.

5

Excursions in Economic Sociology

Schumpeter is Weber's greatest successor in the role of an economic sociologist.
(H. Stuart Hughes, *Consciousness and Society*, 1958)

During the period from the First World War I to 1932, when he emigrated to the United States, Schumpeter also made an important contribution to a social science other than economics: *sociology*. It is true that Schumpeter saw his writing in this field primarily as a contribution to a broad-based science of economics, *Sozialökonomik*, but it is still important to note that Schumpeter had the intellectual vigour during these difficult years to make a contribution to a social science different from economics. Later in life Schumpeter was often to express a distinct satisfaction with two of his sociological essays from this period, 'The Sociology of Imperialisms' (1918–19) and 'Social Classes in an Ethnically Homogenous Environment' (1927). After his death, a note was found among his papers to the effect that these two essays (plus his four major books) were to be considered as 'his most important works'.[1] And at other occasions as well, Schumpeter made clear that he saw these two essays as his major sociological writings.[2] Why Schumpeter was so pleased with just these two articles is easy enough to understand; they are both excellent studies and well worth reading today. Why he excluded 'The Crisis of the Tax State' (1918) from his list of preferred sociological writings is, however, more difficult to grasp. This third essay broke important new ground by introducing (following Rudolf Goldscheid) the area of 'fiscal sociology'; and it also contains a number of brilliant observations in economic sociology. 'The Crisis of the Tax State' will therefore be one of the sociological writings discussed in this chapter; the other two being the essays on class and imperialism.

Even though Schumpeter wrote his most important sociological works when he was in his mid-thirties and early forties, it is clear that his interest in sociology went far back. Indeed, as a young boy at Theresianum, Schumpeter had started to read books on sociology and philosophy.[3] Exactly which sociological works he read during these years is not known, except that he came across Gumplowicz's books with their 'racial theory of classes'.[4] We know just as little about Schumpeter's study of sociology while he was at the University of Vienna. Perhaps it was here that he encountered the works of Weber, Marx and the Austro-Marxists for the first time. After having been awarded his doctorate in 1906, Schumpeter as we know spent some time in England. And here he followed the lectures of, among others, the prominent Finnish sociologist Edward Westermarck.[5] From Schumpeter's writings in the 1910s, we also know that he was familiar with the sociological writings of authors such as Emile Durkheim, François Simiand and Georg Simmel.[6] In 1909, when Schumpeter applied for his *Habilitation*, he suggested that besides economics and statistics, he was also competent to teach sociology. The course that he proposed to teach was entitled 'The Foundation and the Contemporary State of Sociology'. The way in which Schumpeter described the course conveys the impression that he was well versed in sociology:

1. How sociology emerged and why it is necessary. – 2. Its area and which facts belong to it. – 3. Its problems. – 4. Its methods and contemporary results. – 5. Main currents in sociology. – 6. Sociology of everyday life; the sociological knowledge of artists.[7]

It is clear that the boundaries between the different social sciences were not as sharp in Schumpeter's days as they are today. When Schumpeter, for example, taught at the University of Czernowitz in the early 1910s, he gave a course in 'State and Society' which was mainly sociological in nature. And when he was exchange professor at Columbia University in 1913–14, he taught a course on 'The Theory of Social Classes'. That Schumpeter himself had a broad interest in social science is also obvious from a fine little pamphlet that he wrote while in Czernowitz, called *The Past and the Future of the Social Sciences* (1915).

At this point, it should perhaps be stressed that by sociology Schumpeter did not mean social science in general, but a distinct approach with its own set of problems. This is, for example, one of the points that he made in his first book, *Das Wesen und der Hauptinhalt der theoretischen Nationalökonomie* (1908). Schumpeter here says that sociology 'is not – and must not be – just a term for social science in general; it is its own science with its own goals and methods.'[8] Even though economics, by virtue of Schumpeter's

'Monroe doctrine', should be clearly distinct from sociology, it was also stressed that 'no one could be more convinced than the economist of the necessity of this young science.'[9]

Schumpeter never felt that it was particularly important to give exact definitions of the different social sciences, and during his early years he often emphasized different aspects of sociology. In his history of economic theory from 1914, for example, he defined sociology as 'the theory of social institutions and principles of social organization'.[10] And in an article from about the same time, sociology is described as 'the doctrine about the interaction between individuals and groups of individuals within the social whole'.[11] Usually, however, when Schumpeter spoke of economic sociology, it was *institutions* that he had in mind. By this term he meant what is normally understood by the notion of institution, namely ways of doing things, as enforced by norms and sanctions. Schumpeter also insisted that while it was necessary always to start with the individual in economic theory, this was unsuitable in sociology since its basic unit is the group.[12]

A special chapter would be needed to describe the relationship between Schumpeter and Max Weber adequately.[13] When Schumpeter first heard of Weber and started to read his work is not known, but it was probably while he was a student at the University of Vienna. Perhaps the two met for the first time at one of the meetings of the *Verein für Sozialpolitik*, to which all the prominent German-speaking economists belonged, including Weber and Schumpeter. In any case, we know that Schumpeter backed Weber in the famous debate about value judgements in economics that took place during the years around 1910 in the *Verein*.[14] That Weber, for his part, early became aware of Schumpeter's work is clear from Weber's annotated copy of Schumpeter's *Theorie der wirtschaftlichen Entwicklung* (1911), which can still be inspected at the Max-Weber-Arbeitsstelle in Munich.[15] Weber, as we know, also commissioned Schumpeter to write a history of economic theory for *Grundriss der Sozialökonomik* in the early 1910s. When Weber was asked in 1918 to make a statement about which candidate he considered to be the most suitable for a chair in economics at the University of Vienna, he wholeheartedly supported Schumpeter over a host of other names.[16] Both Weber and Schumpeter were also editors together of the famous *Archiv für Sozialwissenschaft und Sozialpolitik* for a few years towards the end of the 1910s, more precisely from 1916 to Weber's death in 1920.[17]

While Schumpeter had personal difficulties with Sombart, he got on well with Weber.[18] There exists, for example, an account of a pleasant meeting in 1919 with Max Weber, Marianne Weber and Walther Tritsch.[19] But there were also differences, in temperament and political ideology, between Weber and Schumpeter, as the following anecdote from about the same time makes clear:

Both had met in a Vienna coffee-house, in the presence of Ludo Moritz Hartmann and Somary. Schumpeter remarked how pleased he was with the Russian Revolution. Socialism was no longer a discussion on paper, but had to prove its viability. Max Weber responded in great agitation: communism, at this stage in Russian development, was virtually a crime, the road would lead over unparalleled human misery and end in a terrible catastrophe. 'Quite likely', Schumpeter answered, 'but what a fine laboratory.' 'A laboratory filled with mounds of corpses', Weber answered heatedly. 'The same can be said of every dissecting room', Schumpeter replied. Every attempt to divert them failed. Weber became increasingly violent and loud, Schumpeter increasingly sarcastic and muted. The other guests listened with curiosity, until Weber jumped up, shouting, 'I can't stand any more of this', and rushed out, followed by Hartmann, who brought him his hat. Schumpeter, left behind, said with a smile: 'How can a man shout like that in a coffeehouse?'[20]

But this flare-up between Schumpeter and Weber did not mean that they did not appreciate each other. When Weber died in 1920, Schumpeter wrote a moving obituary for *Der Österreichische Volkswirt*. From this brief article it is clear that Schumpeter 'had fallen under Weber's spell', as Fritz Karl Mann has put it.[21] In the article, entitled 'Max Weber's Work', Schumpeter describes Weber in a rather exalted manner: 'he led [and] you submitted, whether you wanted to or not'; 'above all he was loved'; 'this Lohengrin with his silver moral armor'; and so on.[22] In terms of Weber's intellectual production, we already know that Schumpeter had borrowed the notion of *Sozialökonomik* from Weber and that Weber had also been instrumental in creating the field of economic sociology, which Schumpeter later became interested in as well.[23] In the obituary Schumpeter spoke very highly of Weber's contribution to the philosophy of the social sciences; he was clearly awed by Weber's immense mastery of historical facts; and he singled out 'The Protestant Ethic' and 'The Social Psychology of the World Religions' as 'the best sociological achievements of German science'.[24] But even if Schumpeter praised Weber as a sociologist, it should be noted, he did not have a high opinion of him as an economist:

> Weber was a sociologist above all. Even though he was a sociologist with a penchant for things that are primarily concerned with economics, he was an economist only indirectly and secondarily. His interest in economics does not focus on the mechanism of economic life as described by economic theory, nor on the real historical phenomenon for its own sake, but rather on the sequence of historical types and their socialpsychological profusion.[25]

In other words: Weber might be a superb sociologist, but he had little to contribute to the economic theory part of *Sozialökonomik*.

I

Of Schumpeter's three major essays in economic sociology, 'The Crisis of the Tax State' is the one that he wrote first, probably in late 1917 and early 1918. This essay contains, among other things, an important analysis of the difficult financial situation that was to be expected in Austria after the war. What Schumpeter had to say on this point has already been presented in chapter 3 on Schumpeter in politics. Some of the issues discussed here concerned whether a capital levy was needed to get the Austrian economy moving; how inflation could be stopped; and what role foreign capital might play in the reconstruction of the Austrian economy. The main part of 'The Crisis of the Tax State' is, however, not about the financial situation in Austria after the war. It is about the possibility of opening up a new field in sociology, called 'fiscal sociology', and what this might look like.

At this point it is necessary to pause for a moment to make one thing perfectly clear: in writing the essay on the tax state Schumpeter was not interested in contributing to sociology *per se*, say as an expression of his general erudition in the social sciences. Instead, this essay was part of Schumpeter's conscious programme to develop a broad economic science or *Sozialökonomik*. The main task of this article was therefore to *expand the domain of the economist*. In this sense, 'The Crisis of the Tax State' is no different from Schumpeter's two other essays in sociology which were also attempts to introduce new topics into economics. But in order for this to be possible, Schumpeter stressed, the economist had to give up his ambition to use a purely analytical approach and to lay bare so-called economic mechanisms. This was something you could only do when you were working on a small set of problems, such as price formation. But in order to be able to analyse such things as taxes, classes and imperialism, the economist must switch over to another approach: that of *economic sociology*.

One of the many things that an economic theorist could not talk about was the state. The reason was simply that the state was not an economic phenomenon: the political structure of a society belonged to those things that an economist *presupposed* and not to what he analysed. In reality, of course, the state is also an economic actor. The state is not (to use Weber's terminology) an 'economic organization' or an organization whose main purpose is economical; but it is still an 'economically active organization' or an organization whose activities are not primarily economic, but which include economic ones.[26] And one of the economic activities of the state is the handling of taxes: the collection of taxes and the spending of its revenue. Still, the economist (especially in the late 1910s when Schumpeter's article was written) could not analyse fiscal activities like this since they were so closely related to the political function of the state and thereby, by definition, did not follow an economic logic. The sociologist, on the other hand, lacked these restrictions; and since he could look at any kind of 'economic institution', he could also analyse fiscal phenomena. Through sociology, in brief, a whole new field of problems and facts could be opened up to the social economist (*Sozialökonom*), and it was this field that Schumpeter (following the Austrian sociologist Rudolf Goldscheid) called *Finanzsoziologie* or 'fiscal sociology'.

With the help of fiscal sociology, the economist could follow a series of interesting economic phenomena far into society. By its financial measures the state often affected the whole economic development of a country, Schumpeter said. 'Fiscal measures have created and destroyed industries, industrial forms, and industrial regions even where this was not their intent, and have in this manner contributed directly to the construction (and distortion) of the edifice of the modern economy and through it, of the modern spirit.'[27] One could also get a very realistic view of the state by looking at its budget; and Schumpeter liked to cite Goldscheid's words that 'the budget is the skeleton of the state stripped free of all ideology.'[28] The type of taxes that the state tried to enforce, and the way that the state went about collecting them, also influenced the various groups in society and their respective standing. A strong group might be able to resist the state; a weak group would be destroyed; and so on. 'The spirit of a people, its cultural level, its social structure, the deeds its policy may prepare – all this and more is written into its fiscal history, stripped free of all phrases.'[29]

Besides these general benefits which could be had by using the approach of fiscal sociology, Schumpeter also presented two general theses in his essay. The first was that the modern state had been born out of its fiscal needs; and the second that there existed an inherent tendency towards a fiscal crisis in the capitalist state. Again, to trace the history of the modern state was not something an economic theorist could do; this was clearly outside his competence. 'The Crisis of the Tax State', however, contains an excellent, ten-page account of the emergence of the modern state. The reader should note that Schumpeter was only interested in tracing the typical development of the state, since his article was not intended as a study in history but in sociology. In broad strokes, Schumpeter therefore described how the modern state had emerged in Central Europe towards the end of the Middle Ages as a result of the financial needs of the prince. The prince desperately needed money during this period for the following three reasons: he had mismanaged his affairs; he had to maintain a costly court (to divert the aristocracy); and – most importantly – he had to raise huge amounts of money for the war

against the Turks. The prince realized that the only way for him to be
able to obtain huge enough sums, was if he could get the estates to
assume responsibility for the war against the Turks. He therefore
proposed that he alone should not be responsible for the war; it was
really a 'common exigency' and the estates must shoulder their responsibility as well. The estates finally agreed, and 'out of this "common exigency" the state was born.'[30]

Schumpeter's thesis about the birth of the modern state – that
'without financial need the immediate cause for the creation of the
modern state would have been absent', to cite his article – has been
criticized for underplaying the role that the political element played
in this process.[31] With an explicit reference to this passage, Rudolf
Braun has, for example, argued that contrary to what Schumpeter
says, 'the financial needs [of the state] are symptoms and effects as
well as causes of new political, social and economic needs and of a
new quality of life, which is developing.'[32] Fritz Karl Mann concurs:
'Without political need the cause for the creation of the modern
finance and tax system would have been absent.'[33] There is, no
doubt, something to this critique. Still, Schumpeter was not so far off
the mark in stressing the role that the fiscal needs of the prince
played in this process; and it should also be noted that the distinction between 'economic' and 'political' causes can easily become
scholastic when one, after all, is talking about the actions of political
players.

In a somewhat similar manner, one may say that the obvious
critique that can be directed against Schumpeter's second thesis –
the idea that a fiscal crisis is inevitable as well as an integral part of
the decline of the capitalist system – should not be allowed to detract
from the originality of Schumpeter's thought. What Schumpeter was
saying was simply that there exists a definite limit to the fiscal
capacity of the state and that, if this limit is transgressed, the state
will collapse. Schumpeter drew up several scenarios for how this
situation could come about, while repeatedly stressing that they
were all unlikely to take place in post-war Austria. Schumpeter's
theory about the collapse of the fiscal state implied, first of all, a
long-term perspective. And in such a long-term perspective, it was
clear to Schumpeter that the tax state would fall apart due to the
general development of capitalism. At this point Schumpeter's argument fuses with a general feeling, on his part, that the time is up for
the capitalist system; and 'The Crisis of the Tax State' contains
indeed the germ of some of the ideas that were later to be more fully
developed in *Capitalism, Socialism and Democracy* (1942). We read:
'The hour has not yet struck [for capitalism]. Nevertheless, the hour
will come.'[34]

As compared to *Capitalism, Socialism and Democracy*, however,
Schumpeter's article on the tax state pays much more attention to

the role that fiscal policy can play in triggering off the final demise of capitalism. A severe crisis can actually be brought about in several different ways, all involving some kind of fiscal measure by the state. For one thing, the state can tax entrepreneurial profit in such a radical manner that the economic development will simply come to a standstill. The individual's motive to work hard and to be entrepreneurial would be affected by this; and capitalism grind to a halt. There was also the possibility that the state would just keep on increasing the taxes until they were far too high:

> The closer the tax state approaches these limits, the greater is the resistance and the loss of energy with which it works. A bigger and bigger army of bureaucrats is needed to enforce the tax laws, tax inquisition becomes more and more intrusive, tax chicanery more and more unbearable. The absurd waste of energy that this picture entails shows that the meaning of the organization of the tax state lies in the autonomy of the private economy, and that this meaning is lost when the state can no longer respect this autonomy.[35]

And, finally, there is a third kind of possible fiscal crisis, which is reminiscent of the second type, but which contains a new and original twist. This is the crisis that is brought about because the tax revenues are not sufficient to cover the expenses of all the measures that people feel entitled to by the state:

> If the will of the people is to demand higher and higher public expenditures; if more and more means are used for purposes for which private individuals have not produced them; if more and more power stands behind this will; and if finally all parts of the people are gripped by entirely new ideas about private property – then the tax state will have run its course and society will have to depend on other motive forces for its economy than self-interest. This limit can certainly be reached and thereby also the crisis which the state could not survive.[36]

That Schumpeter's ideas on this topic are still pertinent is, for example, testified to by the huge success that James O'Connor had in the 1970s with *The Fiscal Crisis of the State*. The general argument of this neo-Marxist book is that there exists a general tendency for the expenditures of the capitalist state to increase faster than it can raise money to finance them, and that this may lead to a fiscal crisis. Or, to phrase it differently: that there exists a dangerous contradiction between the task of 'accumulation' and the task of 'legitimation' in the capitalist state which may lead to a fiscal crisis. Though O'Connor does not acknowledge Schumpeter's role in framing this thesis – he actually downplays 'The Crisis of the Tax State' and lamely asserts that 'fiscal sociology has always been central to the Marxist tradition'[37] – it is obvious enough that O'Connor's main idea comes straight out of Schumpeter's essay.

II

'The Sociology of Imperialisms' was written around the same time as the article on the tax state and published in 1918–19 in two instalments in *Archiv für Sozialwissenschaft und Sozialpolitik*. Here also Schumpeter's main concern was to extend the science of economics to topics which were clearly outside the competence of the theoretical economist. And again, the way to do this was with the help of economic sociology, that is, through the semi-analytical, semi-empirical kind of approach that Schumpeter discusses in his essay on Schmoller. That imperialism was not a phenomenon which could be handled with conventional economic theory is clear enough from Schumpeter's famous definition: '*imperialism is the objectless disposition on the part of a state to unlimited forcible expansion.*'[38] More precisely, there are three elements to this definition, which makes imperialism fall outside the scope of theoretical economics. First, it involves the behaviour of a political actor, the state. Secondly (and this is to a certain extent connected to the first point), imperialistic behaviour always involves force, which is a taboo topic in economic theory.[39] And, thirdly, imperialist behaviour is not rational behaviour and economic theory only deals with rational behaviour.

That imperialism is profoundly irrational in nature is somewhat hidden behind the two words 'objectless disposition' in Schumpeter's definition of imperialism. At other places in his essay, however, Schumpeter clarifies that there exist no 'definite utilitarian limits' to imperialist behaviour.[40] Instead, 'non-rational and irrational' elements play a key role; and imperialist wars are often set off without any specific goal in mind.[41] For imperialism to work effectively and to be able to mobilize support, it has to be able to arouse 'the dark powers of the subconscious'; and to do this, it has to appeal to 'the need to hate', 'inchoate idealism', and the like. In brief, it has to appeal to a totally different set of motives than those referred to in conventional economic theory.[42]

The difference between imperialism, as Schumpeter sees it, and the behaviour that theoretical economics focuses on ('price–value–money'), is further accentuated by Schumpeter's idea that capitalism is in its nature absolutely antithetical to imperialism. Schumpeter's general idea was that in capitalism people put all their energy into work and have little energy left over for martial activities, including imperialist adventures. 'In a purely capitalist world, what was once energy for war becomes simply energy for labor of every kind',

Schumpeter writes.[43] In a capitalist society people also think in a rational manner, since the economic logic of capitalism is hammered into their minds on a daily basis, something which makes them resistant to irrational phenomena like imperialism. 'Everything that is purely instinctual, everything insofar as it is purely instinctual, is driven into the background by this development.'[44] Schumpeter summarizes his thesis about the relationship between capitalism and imperialism in one sentence: *capitalism is by nature anti-imperialist.*'[45]

From this quick overview of Schumpeter's theory of imperialism one might get the impression that this phenomenon, in Schumpeter's mind, has nothing to do with economics and is therefore of little interest to the economist. This, however, is not the case; and there are mainly two reasons for this. First, there already exists an attempt to account for imperialism on purely economic grounds. This is the Marxist theory of imperialism; and the economist needs to take a position *vis-à-vis* this argument. And, secondly, imperialism can in Schumpeter's mind be explained from an economic viewpoint, but it has to be an explanation which draws on economic sociology as opposed to theoretical economics. As to the first point, Schumpeter was mainly concerned to show that what he called the 'neo-Marxist theory of imperialism' was wrong. By this he meant the works of Rudolf Hilferding and Otto Bauer (but not Lenin's theory of imperialism as the highest stage of capitalism which was probably not available to Schumpeter when he wrote 'The Sociology of Imperialisms').[46] There were several reasons for Schumpeter's sharp rejection of the Marxist theory of imperialism. For one thing, Hilferding and others had nothing to say about imperialism in pre-capitalist societies, since they saw imperialism as closely connected to capitalism. This was a position that Schumpeter could not accept. The Marxist idea that capitalism would have some inherent tendency towards imperialism was equally unacceptable to Schumpeter, who felt that capitalism was inherently peaceful. And, finally, Schumpeter thought that it was far too simplistic to say that imperialism was caused by the economic structure or the relations of production; this type of argument ruled out the kind of complexity that Schumpeter felt was involved.

What then did Schumpeter's own theory of imperialism look like and, more precisely, how did he propose to link imperialism to economic behaviour so that it would be of interest to the *Sozialöko-nom*? The answer is that just as Schumpeter felt that there exist several types of imperialism – the title to his essay refers to 'imperialisms' in the plural – there also exist several types of explanations for this type of behaviour. Early in his essay Schumpeter, for example, discusses imperialism in antiquity and especially in Persia, Egypt and Assyria. In all of these empires, he said, imperialism was built into society via the social structure; they were all warrior nations which would collapse if they did not expand. The particular way in which they would fall apart, in the absence of expansion, varied from case to case. But the main point was that such expansion was absolutely necessary. Imperialist behaviour was linked to the social structure of the economy in such a way that certain social groups could not survive by their own labour; and they therefore had continuously to conquer new areas. 'In order to exhibit a continual trend toward imperialism, a people must not live on – or at least not be absorbed by – its own labor.'[47]

Since imperialism is irrational in nature, Schumpeter argued, it is strengthened by age. Tradition, in other words, plays an important role in imperialism; and this is particularly clear in Schumpeter's analysis of the imperialism of the absolutist state. Also this type of state, which was common in Europe during the seventeenth and eighteenth centuries, was a kind of war machine and the king was primarily a war lord. Schumpeter does not say very much more than this about the absolutist state, except that its ruling class was disposed to war and that the crown saw war as a way of maintaining its prestige. The reason for the brevity of Schumpeter's analysis on this point was probably due to the fact that he was discussing matters that were well known to the reader: the audience of *Archiv für Sozialwissenschaft und Sozialpolitik* was no doubt familiar with the history of Prussia and its neighbours in the eighteenth century. But even though Schumpeter was not very interested in discussing absolutism *per se*, the absolutist state plays a crucial role in his analysis of imperialism in capitalist society, as we soon shall see.

As we know, capitalism was, according to Schumpeter, 'by nature anti-imperialist'. This, however, only meant that there would be no imperialism in a *purely* capitalist society. In many contemporary capitalist states, however, there existed a tendency towards 'modern imperialism'; and this had to do with the fact that warlike elements from the absolutist state had survived and become part of capitalism. Schumpeter explains:

> Imperialism thus is atavistic in character. It falls into that large group of surviving features from earlier ages that play such an important part in every concrete social situation. In other words, it is an element that stems from the living conditions, not of the present, but of the past – or, to put it in terms of the economic interpretation of history, from past rather than present relations of productions. Since the vital needs that have created it have passed away for good, it too must gradually disappear, even though every warlike involvement, no matter how non-imperialist in character, tends to revive it.[48]

Schumpeter's argument was therefore that modern imperialism was linked in an indirect way to economic factors; it was caused by 'past rather than present relations of production'. What this meant, in more detail, was that modern capitalism had inherited a tendency to rely on certain restrictive economic measures which had originally been instituted by the absolutist state. One example was trade regulations. These particular measures distorted the economic logic of the market and in some cases even made a country prone to imperialism. Schumpeter especially singled out the role that tariffs played in this whole process. Tariffs had originally been used by the monarchy to provide some revenue, and they were clearly an example of 'artificial' economic measures in the sense that they went counter to the logic of capitalism. Tariffs were instrumental in fostering imperialism in the following way. They prevented free trade and created protective walls around nations. This made it possible for cartels and trusts to reap monopoly profits in the domestic market, while they dumped the rest of their production to lower prices abroad. And this led to 'economic aggression' between countries, which often ended in various imperialistic ventures.

Schumpeter's article on imperialism has been severely criticized by a variety of authors. In the opinion of the Marxists, for example, Schumpeter's theory of imperialism is more or less useless since it denies that there is a link between capitalism and imperialism.[49] Given the fact that Schumpeter's theory is diametrically opposed to the Marxist thesis of imperialism as a creation of capitalism, this verdict is not surprising. The Marxist tendency to reject Schumpeter's analysis *in toto* is, however, too radical and fails to do justice to the wealth of ideas in Schumpeter's essay. The Marxists also miss the point that Schumpeter's theory of the inherent peacefulness of capitalism is little more than a modernized version of Montesquieu's idea of '*commerce doux*' and the thesis of Saint-Simon and Herbert Spencer that in 'industrial society', as opposed to 'military society', there will be peace and not war.

Today very few people believe that industrialism will lead to peace, especially after two world wars and multiple colonial wars. This notion, however, also exists in a revised and more sophisticated version, which is quite similar to Schumpeter's idea that 'modern imperialism' is the result of a survival of absolutism. This is the notion, popularized among others by Barrington Moore in *Social Origins of Dictatorship and Democracy* (1966), that societies which industrialize and have a strong feudal past, will have more difficulty in establishing a democratic regime. In his Auguste Comte Memorial Lecture from 1957, entitled 'War and Industrial Society', Raymond Aron has also pointed out that, 'the facts which ... Schumpeter can quote in support of [his] theory are not open to doubt. The survivals of the *ancien régime* were stronger in Germany and Japan than in Great Britain or France. In both countries there was this combination of a property-owning class and a militaristic caste which can be regarded as the chief cause of imperialism.'[50]

It is, finally, also clear that Schumpeter's essay contains the germs of several other theories of imperialism. One of these can be found in Schumpeter's analysis of imperialism during antiquity. Schumpeter's main thesis here, to recall, was that groups which live by war are likely to be advocates of aggression and imperialism. Karl W. Deutsch explains how one can develop Schumpeter's argument on this point into a more flexible theory of modern authoritarianism and imperialism:

> Schumpeter's theory [of imperialism] has a second and more dynamic implication. Whenever new social changes create a set of military habits, politically influential groups or classes, and important social institutions, all dependent for their continued functioning on sustained policies of warfare or at least war preparations, there the pattern of seemingly irrational imperialistic behavior – in the crude Assyrian or the more polished Roman manner – may come to be acted out all over again. Where such warlike habits and institutions have once again been developed, rational discussion of aims of foreign policy might once again come to be beside the point. Only domestic changes in the distribution of economic and political influence and in popular habits of political behavior might then be able to deflect or reverse the drift to unending armed conflicts.[51]

III

Schumpeter's third major article in sociology, 'Social Classes in an Ethnically Homogenous Environment', was published in 1927 in *Archiv für Sozialwissenschaft und Sozialpolitik*. In the introduction Schumpeter says that the basic idea for his essay went back to 1910–11, when he had taught a course on 'State and Society' at the University of Czernowitz.[52] This was also the time when Schumpeter was putting the finishing touch to *Theorie der wirtschaftlichen Entwicklung*; and the parallels between the theory of entrepreneurship developed in this book and the basic thesis in the essay on social class are striking. In the 1910s Schumpeter continued to work on the concept of social class, but it was not until the mid-1920s that he sat down to write the essay on class, spurred on by the fact that he had to give a lecture in November 1926 on 'Leadership and Class Formation' at the University of Heidelberg. But even at this late point Schumpeter emphasized that it would be 'years from now' until he would be able to present a final version of his ideas on this topic.[53]

This final version, however, never appeared; and in his later works, Schumpeter always referred to his 1927 article.[54]

According to Schumpeter, the concept of class was extremely important and promised to solve a number of difficult problems in the social sciences. Schumpeter's description of the potentials of class analysis is nearly lyrical:

> The subject [of class] – and this is what constitutes its fascination – poses a wealth of new questions, offers outlooks on untilled fields, foreshadows sciences of the future. Roaming it, one often has a strange feeling, as though the social sciences of today, almost on purpose were dealing with relative side-issues; as though some day – and perhaps soon – the things we now believe will be discounted.[55]

In order to carry out this type of exciting analysis, however, it was necessary to use the sociological concept of class and not the one used in theoretical economics. This last point was crucial to Schumpeter, who argued that the economic concept of class was only to be used as an analytical tool, while its sociological counterpart denoted a distinct part of social reality. The economist, Schumpeter specified, used the notion of class to 'classify different things according to certain chosen criteria'; and the economic concept of class was consequently 'a creation of the researcher'.[56] Schumpeter used the following example to bring out the difference between the economic and the sociological concepts of class. Take a lawyer and a manual worker. From the viewpoint of economic theory, it is clear that both receive a wage and therefore belong to the working class. From a sociological viewpoint, however, wage earners can belong to several different classes; and it would be absurd to put a lawyer and a manual worker in the same class.

Just as in his earlier sociological essays, Schumpeter emphasized that the only way that an economist could hope to deal effectively with socioeconomic problems was to switch from theoretical economics to economic sociology. The concepts of theoretical economics were very useful for certain tasks, but it was not possible to use them for sociological purposes. The temptation to do so was however there: 'there is the fact that the economic theorist finds it exceedingly difficult to confine himself strictly to his problems, to resist the temptation to enliven his presentation with something [social] that fascinates most of his readers.'[57] But the only way to proceed for the *Sozialökonom* was to use the sociological concept of class, according to which class was a concrete entity, 'a special social organism, living, acting, and suffering'.[58] A social class, Schumpeter continued, typically had 'its own life and characteristic spirit'.[59] People preferred to interact with people from the same social class:

Class members behave towards one another in a fashion charac-
teristically different from their conduct toward members of other
classes. They are in closer association with one another; they
understand one another better; they work more readily in concert;
they close ranks and erect barriers against the outside; they look
out into the same segment of the world, with the same eyes, from
the same viewpoint, in the same direction.[60]

The most important consequence of this tendency to interact with
members from the same social class was that most people also married within their own class. This last point was very important to
Schumpeter, who saw the family as absolutely central to class cohesion: 'The family, not the individual,' he wrote, 'is the true unit of
class and class theory.'[61] This focus on the family, as opposed to the
individual, was finally a further reason why conventional economic
theory could not be used to analyse social classes. Methodological
individualism had a place – but not in sociology.

The huge number of questions that could be addressed through a
class analysis, Schumpeter said, made it imperative for him to limit
himself to one topic. The one he chose was that of 'class formation',
which he defined in the following manner: 'the question of why the
social whole, as far as our eye can reach, has never been homogenous, always revealing a particular, obviously organic stratification.'[62] The problems that Schumpeter wanted to deal with, in other
words, were fundamental to the very concept of class. A close reading
of his article also makes it clear that he felt that the existing literature on class theory – by Schmoller, Durkheim, Spann, Simmel, and
so on – was deficient in some fundamental manner. Though
Schumpeter does not say so explicitly, he seems to have felt that
there did not exist an acceptable theory of social class; and the task
that he set for himself was to construct such a theory. The way he
proposed to do this, as we soon shall see, was by linking the phenomenon of class to his own theory of economic change.

The main part of Schumpeter's article is devoted to an analysis of
three phenomena: intra-class mobility, inter-class mobility and the
rise and decline of whole classes. The kind of intra-class mobility
that Schumpeter had in mind was that of families. It is typical for
classes, Schumpeter said, that even though their basic structure
remains the same, they often contain different people. Or in a famous
formulation: 'Each class resembles a hotel ... always full, but always of different people.'[63] These turnover processes, however, were
slow and usually took several decades. The basic reason why they
took place at all had to do with the fact that certain individual
families could successfully adapt to new situations while others
could not. Looking at the industrial bourgeoisie, for example, it was
clear that the leading families in the 1920s were not the same as
those in the middle of the nineteenth century. In capitalist society,

Schumpeter said, a bourgeois family had to be innovative or it would automatically decline. The reason for this was that new profit was continuously needed to maintain a prominent position, and that this profit could only be gained through innovative business behaviour. At this point Schumpeter explicitly referred to his own theory of entrepreneurial profit; and the link between his economic theory and his sociological analysis is obvious:

> This decline [of bourgeois families] *is* automatic, for it is not a matter of omission or commission, but flows instead from the self-actuating logic of the competitive system, by the simple fact of profits running dry. As to the question why this is so, it is answered by [my] theory of entrepreneurial profit.[64]

In his analysis of inter-class mobility, Schumpeter was first of all concerned to show that contrary to what was often asserted, there did indeed exist some movement from one class to another. Schumpeter stressed that this process, just like intra-class mobility, only became visible in a long-term perspective. And, again, Schumpeter sought the explanation among the factors that he had highlighted in his theory of the entrepreneur: 'Those factors that account for shifts in family position within a class are the same that account for the crossing of class barriers.'[65]

The most impressive and imaginative part of Schumpeter's entire essay is his analysis of why whole classes rise and fall. Here as elsewhere, he focused mainly on ruling classes and in particular on the fate of the feudal class. Every ruling class fulfils a specific function, Schumpeter said, and the function of the feudal class was military in nature. During the Middle Ages, the feudal lord had taken care of this function himself: 'the lord would mount his horse and defend himself, sword in hand, against dangers from above or below.'[66] From the fourteenth century and onwards, however, the feudal class had started to decline. One reason for this was the gradual emergence of commercial society and the slow demilitarization which this led to. But there was more to the decline of the feudal class than this objective development. The aristocracy had also begun to lose interest in its military function. It increasingly preferred to hire mercenaries and to work in the administration of the state rather than in the army. The situation was soon such, Schumpeter said, that the lord 'was likely to don armor only when his portrait was to be painted'.[67] Schumpeter was clearly fascinated by the self-destructive element in this process, which was 'turning the nobility against its basic function, causing it to undermine the very foundations of its own military importance'.[68] The similarity between this analysis and the main thesis about the decline of the capitalist system in *Capitalism, Socialism and Democracy* is obvious.

Towards the end of the essay, Schumpeter summarized his findings and also presented his own theory of why social classes exist. The main reason for this, he suggested, is that the aptitude for innovating behaviour is distributed evenly throughout a population or nation. Once a successful innovation has been made, however, the innovator is surrounded as it were by an aura of success. This aura exerts a lasting effect on the surroundings and has a life of its own: 'It does not necessarily disappear when its basis disappears – nor, for that matter, does its basis readily disappear. *This is the very heart and soul of the independent existence of "class"*.'[69] The prestige and success, however, does not only attach to the innovator, but also to the family of the innovator. Several families soon cluster together: 'Coordinate families then merge into a social class, welded together by a bond, the substance and effect of which we now understand. This relationship assumes a life of its own and is then able to grant protection and confer prestige.'[70]

How well does Schumpeter's essay on class stand up today? Some of Schumpeter's assertions about inter- and intra-class mobility need no doubt to be corrected. This, however, is only to be expected since 'Social Classes' was written more than 50 years ago. Schumpeter himself, it should be added, realized very well how few good data he had at his disposal when he wrote 'Social Classes'; and he called explicitly for more empirical research, especially on the history of leading bourgeois families. The problems which beset Schumpeter's main thesis – that social classes and stratification basically exist because of entrepreneurial activity – are more serious. It should first of all be noted that this idea has not been accepted in contemporary sociology (even though Schumpeter's essay is well known in the stratification literature).[71] It is difficult to find anybody who has explicitly spelled out what is wrong with Schumpeter's thesis, but it seems more or less taken for granted that one cannot go very far with it. A weaker version of Schumpeter's theory about the entrepreneur might, however, be useful. Social classes are often treated as if they were the result exclusively of objective factors; and Schumpeter's focus on individual, creative action may be a healthy antidote to this tendency.

It should finally also be emphasized that Schumpeter's handling of historical material in 'Social Classes' is just superb. Schumpeter could draw on the sophisticated German scholarship in history from around the turn of the century, and as a result he displays a versatility in historical sociology that simply does not exist today, despite efforts by people like Barrington Moore, Charles Tilly and Theda Skocpol to revive it. In the long run, it might very well be precisely because of this quality that 'Social Classes' will still be read and appreciated during many years to come.

We have now come to the end of Schumpeter's 'excursions' into economic sociology and are in a position to summarize their importance for his vision of a broadbased *Sozialökonomik*. Schumpeter should, first of all, be applauded for the audacity of his enterprise: he was after all trained primarily as an economic theorist, but he still dared to venture out into another field of the social sciences. And when he did this, he produced three major articles in sociology which are still widely read and generally acknowledged as excellent contributions. Schumpeter, it should be noted, is unique among twentieth-century economists in this. It is true that Pareto also made a valuable contribution to sociology and saw sociology as a complement to economics. In Pareto's work, however, there was no attempt to establish a link between economics and sociology; and his works in sociology and in economics could for all practical purposes have been written by two different people. With Schumpeter this is not the case, and his three essays on the tax state, social classes and imperialism are the result of a conscious effort to bring economics and sociology closer to one another. 'These essays [by Schumpeter] build a bridge carrying two-way intellectual traffic between economics and sociology', as Robert K. Merton has said.[72]

The way that Schumpeter tried to construct this bridge or bring theoretical economics and economic sociology into contact with one another, differed from case to case. In one of his three essays Schumpeter experimented with the idea of introducing the theory of the entrepreneur directly into the sociological analysis – this is the basic idea behind 'Social Classes'. In another essay, he tried to make sociology of the old notion that economic activity is by nature apolitical and peaceful – this is the core argument of 'The Sociology of Imperialisms'. And in his third essay, Schumpeter was wise enough to follow Schmoller and rely more on historical data than on theoretical economics – and this is how 'The Crisis of the Tax State' was constructed. This last strategy – to use historical material, but to do it in an analytical manner – was probably the most successful. In any case, it was this strategy that Schumpeter would follow during the 1930s in his work on business cycles, as we shall see in the next chapter.

6

In the United States

Professor Schumpeter began to teach economics here in 1932, although maintaining his research program. This program 'varied but always stayed on the same plane – that of evolving a comprehensive sociology with a single aim'.
(Interview with Schumpeter in *The Harvard Crimson*, 1944)

There are many indications that Schumpeter left Germany in 1932 primarily because he wanted a radical change in his life. It is true that he would have preferred a position at the University of Berlin to the one at Harvard, but once it was decided that it was going to be Harvard, he embraced the decision. Within a few months of arriving in the United States, he, for example, made up his mind that he wanted to become a US citizen. On 24 February 1933 he announced his intention of becoming a citizen to the authorities in Boston, and on 5 April he handed in the formal application. One also gets the distinct impression that Schumpeter was making a huge effort to like the United States from the beginning and turn it into his new home country. He knew this was a crucial move in his life and he desperately wanted it to work. While Schumpeter had earlier been known to complain about the United States ('an incredibly uncongenial country', as he once described it), his letters from the first months at Harvard speak a different language.[1] 'I feel quite happy at Harvard which in fact is an old love of mine', he wrote in November 1932 to Adolph Löwe.[2] And to another acquaintance, Dennis H. Robertson, he wrote a few weeks later, 'Academic life goes its pleasant course as usual at Harvard. I like the place immensely.'[3] Finally, there was also Schumpeter's decision to leave behind a substantial part of his belongings in Germany. This was something of a symbolic action, indicating his desire to break with the past. His belongings were stored in a house in a small town called Jülich, outside of Bonn. The house belonged to the father of Mia Stöckel, Schumpeter's secretary at the University of Bonn, who had been a combination of house-keeper and companion to him after Annie's death. According to a type-written list which has survived, Schumpeter left behind 28 trunks of belongings in Jülich.[4] These contained a variety of items Schumpeter would naturally not have wanted to take across the Atlantic, such as a number of novels, material he had used for his books, and econ-omic literature which was 'not important'. But he also left behind a number of other items, which one would not have expected. These were described in the list as 'old manuscripts', 'old notebooks – very important', 'manuscript to the textbook – very important', and 'letters'. Schumpeter did not even take a copy of his first book to the United States, and he also left behind most of his articles in German.[5]

Why was Schumpeter so eager to break with his past? One answer would be that he wanted to be happy and this was impossible for him in Bonn. But anyone who has studied Schumpeter's personality knows that whatever drove him, it was not really the pursuit of happiness. Various clues in Schumpeter's writings, private as well as public, point to a different answer. What motivated Schumpeter to leave for the United States was first of all his desire to pursue his *work*.[6] After Annie's death, it seems that work had become his anchor in reality and his main reason to exist. From now on, he seems to have decided, everything should be subordinated to his work. More precisely, he wanted to complete the task he had set for himself in his youth: 'that of evolving a comprehensive sociology with a single aim'. 'After Schumpeter came to Harvard', Arthur Smithies has con-firmed, '. . . his main purpose was to build on the foundation that he had laid before the war, to test his earlier conclusions, and to modify them where necessary in the light of his historical and statistical research.'[7] Schumpeter would allow nothing to deflect him from this task and repeat what had happened in Bonn. While in the United States he worked ruthlessly all the time – during days, evenings, weekends and vacations – and some even say that he died from overwork. Each day he graded himself in his private diary and he married a woman he perhaps did not love, but who could provide him with a home and the comfort that was necessary for his work. 'My work is my only interest in life', as Schumpeter wrote to a colleague in the mid-1930s.[8]

Schumpeter was well aware of the dangers in subordinating every-thing to work: it wore you down and it tended to make you inhuman. That he became physically ill, Schumpeter accepted; that was a price he was willing to pay. Anyway, he could always cope with problems of this sort, since one can 'deal as rationally with one's organism as one does with one's motor car'.[9] He also tried to cope with the latter danger – that of becoming inhuman towards others – in various

ways. He treated students and colleagues with great friendliness
and politeness, as if he had nothing more important to do than to
chat with them and discuss their papers at great length. Schumpeter
was fully aware of how inhuman people can be who are totally consumed by their work; this is clear from the following passage from
Schumpeter's essay on John Maynard Keynes:

> In general, there is something inhuman about human machines,
> that fully use every ounce of their fuel. Such men are mostly cold
> in their personal relations, inaccessible, preoccupied. Their work is
> their life, no other interests exist for them, or only interests of the
> most superficial kind. But Keynes was the exact opposite of all this
> – the pleasantest fellow you can think of; pleasant, kind, and cheer-
> ful in the sense in which precisely those people are pleasant, kind,
> and cheerful who have nothing on their minds and whose principle
> it is never to allow any pursuit of theirs to degenerate into work.
> He was affectionate. He was always ready to enter with friendly
> zest into the views, interests, and troubles of others. He was gener-
> ous, and not only with money. He was sociable, enjoyed conversa-
> tion, and shone in it. And, contrary to a widely spread opinion, he
> could be *polite*, polite with an old-world *punctilio* that costs time.[10]

Did Schumpeter succeed in making the break with the period in
Bonn that he clearly wanted so much? The answer, in so far as his
work is concerned, has to be 'yes'. When Schumpeter came to
Harvard, he immediately began to work on his old manuscript on
money. After a while, however, he gave up and concentrated instead
on his new book on business cycles. 'The depression exhaling from
this manuscript [on money] has nearly spoiled my first year at Harvard which otherwise would have been very pleasant and all that I
could have wished or expected', he wrote to Gottfried Haberler in the
spring of 1933.[11] To stop working on the money book was a wise
decision, and from now on Schumpeter would not let himself be
sidetracked from the great task he had set for himself: to complete
the 'vision' from his youth.

During the time he was in the United States, Schumpeter toyed
with the idea of writing a book on money and another one called *The
Theoretical Apparatus of Economics*. But he never invested very much
energy into either of these two enterprises, and among his papers
from the American period one can find no huge manuscripts, like the
one on money from 1929 and the textbook that he presumably left
behind in Germany. The closest that Schumpeter came to turning a
side-interest into a full book was with his Lowell Lectures from 1941.
And the reason for this may well have been that he had promised to
co-author this book with his wife, and that he felt an obligation
towards her for all the work she had already put into the Lectures. Of

the projected eight chapters, however, only two were completed before Schumpeter gave the whole project up.

What makes it possible to state so affirmatively that Schumpeter did indeed succeed in making the break he wished for when he left Bonn, is that he produced three major works while in the United States. During his years in Bonn, to recall, he had not published any book. Each of the three books he wrote in America took something like 5–10 years of concentrated work. Together they add up to nearly 3,000 printed pages, and the effort that must have gone into writing them was just incredible. Two of them, *Capitalism, Socialism and Democracy* and *History of Economic Analysis*, are today regarded as classics, while the third, *Business Cycles*, has been forgotten. All three, however, are well worth remembering and each will be discussed in a separate chapter, starting with *Business Cycles* in this one. These three chapters will also include a discussion of Schumpeter's minor works from his years in the United States. These writings are often very interesting in their own right, and include an article Schumpeter wrote on rationality for a seminar he had started in 1939 (discussed in this chapter); his Lowell Lectures from 1941 (discussed in the following chapter); and his magnificent essays in economic history from the last half of the 1940s (discussed in chapter 8). In these three chapters on Schumpeter's American period we shall also discuss his personal life as it evolved from 1932 onwards. Schumpeter's overriding ambition during these years might have been to complete his *oeuvre*, but he was no human machine. For each step he advanced in his work, he also had to pay; and even though he did not have a major breakdown, like the one that Weber had in 1898–1903, he had to suffer tormenting depressions and minor crises on a fairly regular basis.

I

When Schumpeter arrived in Cambridge in the autumn of 1932 he was invited to stay with F. W. Taussig, the great old man of the economics department at Harvard. Taussig was in his early seventies and the owner of a pleasant house at 2 Scott Street, just a few minutes' walk from the Harvard campus. As it turned out, Schumpeter was to stay with Taussig for five years or until August 1937, when he remarried. The friendship between Taussig and Schumpeter was long-standing. There still exists a letter from 1912 in which Taussig compliments Schumpeter on his English and tries to answer some theoretical questions in response to a letter from Schumpeter.[12] From an intellectual viewpoint, it seems that what attracted Taussig to Schumpeter was his theory of the entrepreneur. Taussig himself was very interested in the role of strong individuals in the economy and wrote two famous studies on this topic, *Inventors and Money-Makers* (1915) and (together with C. S. Joslyn) *Origin of American Business Leaders* (1932). Schumpeter regarded both of these works as important contributions to economic sociology and was later to write apropos the latter book, 'He [that is, Taussig] was among those few economists who realize that the method by which a society chooses its leaders in what, for its particular structure, is the fundamental social function ... is one of the most important things about a society, most important for its performance as well as for its fate.'[13] Taussig, in other words, addressed some of the questions that Schumpeter himself was interested in.

From an emotional viewpoint, it seems that Taussig and Schumpeter developed a kind of father–son relationship, which was gratifying to both of them. Schumpeter, as we know, had lost his father when he was only four years old, and Taussig was probably in need of some company. When Schumpeter had taught at Harvard for a few months in 1930, he had stayed with Taussig. In a letter to a friend, written just after he had left Cambridge in early 1931, he wrote:

> I quickly fell in love with my friend and householder [when I was at Harvard]. What do you think of that? He is no elegant little Jew but the famous 72 years old economist from the economics department at Harvard, who has helped to turn this place into what was perhaps the first hotbed for economics in the world; and who also has taught here for nearly fifty years.[14]

According to reliable sources, it was Taussig who was behind Harvard's invitation to Schumpeter to become a permanent member of the economics department, not only in 1932 but also in 1927. This should not be interpreted to mean that Taussig had succeeded in imposing his will on the rest of the department, as Spiethoff seems to have done at the University of Bonn. From the internal correspondence of the department, it is clear that Schumpeter was popular with many people at Harvard. When Schumpeter turned down the offer in 1927, 'all [the members were] very much disappointed', according to a letter from the chairman to the Dean.[15] The department was generally understaffed and several professors, such as William Z. Ripley, Charles J. Bullock and Thomas Nixon Carver, were about to retire.[16] The department members had all agreed that 'an *outstanding* man' was needed; and in the vote that accompanied the discussion, Schumpeter easily came in first, followed by Gustav Cassel and Edwin Cannan. Slightly worried by the fact that Schumpeter would demand his full market price even though he was a foreigner ('he knows what the general scale of salaries in this country are'), the chairman of the economics department summed up his impression of Schumpeter to the Harvard bureaucracy in the following way:

Schumpeter, beyond doubt, is the most distinguished of the younger generation of economists on the continent of Europe. He is a
former Finance Minister of Austria, and was also at one time the
head of a large bank. He is, I imagine, about forty-five years old.
His English is good ... He is well-known in America, and his
coming to this country would create a great deal of interest among
American economists, and would be very distinctly a feather in our
cap.[17]

When Schumpeter finally accepted Harvard's offer, he insisted on
receiving a very good salary. One reason for this was that he still
owed quite a bit of money in Europe. During the next few years
Schumpeter would regularly send money to his creditors in Austria
and Germany. By 1935 he had paid off all his debts, and he must
have felt a great sense of relief.

In 1935 Taussig also resigned (at the age of 75 years!), and Schumpeter was assigned to take over his graduate course in economic theory,
the famous 'Ec-11'. This was a course that Taussig had started to give
in the 1880s and it came to acquire great fame in the United States,
where it was copied at many universities and colleges.[18] The basic
idea behind Ec-11 was that the teacher would try to impart a special
way of looking at economic problems to the students through class
discussions. Taussig first introduced a problem; and he then skilfully
steered the students towards the solution, without ever himself
supplying the answer. He apparently did this with unequalled artistry
– at least until Schumpeter replaced him. Schumpeter, however, was
an artist of a different temperament than Taussig. Paul Samuelson,
who was present when Schumpeter taught Ec-11 for the first time (he
was later to give it up for more advanced theory courses), has described how the new teacher/actor made his entrée:

The class met at 2 o'clock in Emerson Hall. After, and not before,
the students had assembled for the class hour, in would walk
Schumpeter, remove hat, gloves, and topcoat with sweeping ges-
tures, and begin the day's business. Clothes were important to him:
he wore a variety of well-tailored tweeds with carefully matched
shirt, tie, hose, and handkerchief. My wife used to keep track in
that period of the cyclic reappearance of the seemingly infinite
number of combinations in his wardrobe: the cycle was not simple
and far from random.[19]

There were about 50 students in Schumpeter's class, Samuelson
says, and most were confused by what their new teacher had to say.
Taussig had mainly stuck to the British economists and was not well
read in contemporary economic theory. Schumpeter, on the other
hand, spoke about people like Pigou, J. B. Clark and Ragnar Frisch.

To the ears of the American students, there was a thick Viennese accent to Schumpeter's voice, which it took some time to get used to. Otherwise his language was accurate, witty and somewhat flowery. At first Schumpeter tried to continue Taussig's tradition in Ec-11 of using the Socratic method, but apparently without much success. 'He called on people in the class', Samuelson says, 'and he was constantly interrupted by his audience. If anything, he tolerated too many interruptions from grade-chasers, fools, and exhibitionists.'[20] The end result was rather uneven, as in most classes that Schumpeter taught. A few students thought they had learned a great deal, and a few later realized that they had indeed learned a great deal. Most, however, were bewildered and amused in different combinations. All agreed, however, that Schumpeter was 'a great showman', as Samuelson put it.[21]

'Schumpy', as the students called him, soon became popular on the Harvard campus. One reason for this was no doubt the friendliness he showed towards the students. Or at least towards the graduate students; undergraduates were basically a nuisance in Schumpeter's eyes, and he never really understood why there had to be undergraduates at Harvard or any other university: it was more than enough with scholars and graduate students. Schumpeter encouraged the graduate students to come and talk to him, and he had plenty of time for each of them. In the afternoon Schumpeter often went to a coffee shop across the street from the Widener Library, where the students knew that they could talk to him. The fact that Schumpeter was an easy grader also added to his popularity. The joke was that Schumpeter only gave 'A's' to three categories of students: to all the Jesuits; to all the women; and to all the rest.[22] Schumpeter, it seems, entertained his students with a never-ending stream of jokes and amusing anecdotes. What, for example, was the definition of the middle class? Those that can only afford two servants, of course! This did not mean that you should underestimate the value of a servant, Schumpeter added; anybody knows that a good servant is worth more than a thousand gadgets. Take the mail, for example. When he first arrived in the United States, Schumpeter said, he did not even know what a mail-box was; in Europe, you just place your letters on the silver tray in the hall, and then they are gone in the morning. But it was, of course, expensive to live properly, Schumpeter would add reflectively. If you wanted to live the life of a gentleman, it would cost you something like $50,000 (or $500,000 in today's value). When the students looked bewildered at their teacher for these and similar remarks about the stimulating effect of inequality, Schumpeter would happily point out to them that each year many egalitarian-minded young Americans travel to Europe to enjoy the sights of the monuments of despotism.[23]

Soon Schumpeter had an admiring circle of young students. Several of these would later be among the world's leading economists and receive the Nobel Prize and other honours. There was, for example, Paul Samuelson whom Schumpeter once described in the following way: 'Now here is a man whom nature has obviously made for scientific achievement and who not only takes to an abstract argument as a duck takes to water, but also brings to bear upon it a fertile and independent mind.'[24] Other students who admired Schumpeter included James Tobin, Richard Musgrave, Richard Goodwin and Wolfgang Stolper (who had transferred from Bonn to Harvard). Schumpeter was also popular with some of the young instructors, especially Paul Sweezy and John Kenneth Galbraith. Sweezy was one of the few sophisticated Marxists in the United States as well as the son of a wealthy banker, a combination that appealed to Schumpeter. Galbraith was very curious about Schumpeter – he, for example, sat in on Ec-11 – but he was also disturbed by Schumpeter's conservatism.

Apart from taking over Taussig's class, Schumpeter also contributed to the instruction of economics at Harvard by introducing mathematical economics into the curriculum. The background to this important development was as follows. At the time that Schumpeter arrived at Harvard, the economics department was in a stage of transition. Economic history was traditionally very strong at Harvard, and the publications in the Harvard Economic Studies Series were overwhelmingly in this field.[25] The economics department had also been in charge of instruction in sociology till 1931, when Sorokin (brought in by the economics department) became the first chairman of the newly established department of sociology. That economic history and sociology should play an important role in economics was, however, increasingly being perceived as anachronistic; and it was generally understood that much more emphasis had to be placed on modern economics if Harvard was ever to become a world-class department. Schumpeter, who ever since his youth had been convinced that theoretical economics must make use of mathematical methods, felt that the time had come to introduce mathematical economics at Harvard.

Schumpeter threw himself a hundred per cent into this new project. Several of the other ivy league schools had already started to teach mathematical economics, such as Yale (Irving Fisher), Columbia (H. L. Moore) and Chicago (Henry Schultz).[26] Schumpeter sensed that Harvard was ripe for the same thing and it was clear to him that Harvard, as opposed to the University of Bonn, had the required infrastructure to make a success out of it. As he wrote to Henry Schultz in early 1933:

As long as I was in Germany I took it as a matter of course that exact methods had really no room in the curriculum of the average

student and I was quite content to give occasionally a course on
mathematical methods to a small group which I apprehended was
drawn towards it much more by the novelty of the thing than
by any wish to make serious use of it. But as I believe and as is
undoubtedly the fact that at the best American universities economic teaching is at a much higher level, I really feel it a duty to
do whatever is in my power in order to help the teaching of our
science over the difficult and dangerous transition which it goes
through at present.[27]

Around the same time Schumpeter put together a Committee on
Instruction in Mathematical Economics, which consisted of himself,
Leonard Crum and E. B. Wilson. What was mainly discussed in the
committee was how to make doctoral students understand enough
mathematics to become capable theorists. The group worked out a
proposal for a course in mathematical economics to be given in the
autumn of 1933 and also got the department to accept mathematical
economics as a 'special field' in the doctoral degree. When the course
catalogue for the academic year 1933–4 appeared, it contained a
course called 'Introduction to Mathematical Treatment of Economics'. The course was described in the following way: 'The aim
of this course is to acquaint such students as may wish it with the
elements of the mathematical technique necessary to understand the
simpler contributions to the mathematical theory of Economics.'[28]
According to the catalogue, the course in mathematical economics
('Ec-8a') was to be taught by 'Prof. Schumpeter and other members
of the Department'. In 1933, however, Schumpeter was the only
teacher. After he had finished the course, he described the experience
in a letter to E. B. Wilson in the following manner:

> It occurs to me that it might be useful to tell you what I am doing
> in Ec. 8A. The humble aim of this course is, as you know, to provide
> beginners with so much of mathematical tools as to enable them
> not to do anything in that line themselves but at least to under-
> stand their Marshall. The course carries them so far that they are
> able to understand such major contributions as it is necessary to
> understand for the general economist. To put the thing in terms of
> authors, I try to make them understand and handle with facility
> Cournot, Walras, Marshall, Edgeworth, Pigou, some of the more
> acceptable propositions of Pareto and most of Irving Fisher ...
> The course is primarily intended for undergraduates as a sort of
> collateral to Taussig's Ec. 7A, but of course it was mainly all the
> members of the staff who came to it last year.[29]

Schumpeter also taught Ec-8a during the next academic year. From
1935–6 onwards, however, he was replaced by Wassily Leontief.
Schumpeter does not seem to have minded; he knew he was not

much of a teacher in mathematics and he had a very high opinion of Leontief ('a young genius').[30]

It is clear that Schumpeter had extremely high hopes for the introduction of mathematics into economics. Economic theory, as he often said during the 1930s, was in a difficult stage of transition from being an inexact philosophy to becoming a science using exact methods.[31] Mathematics was absolutely essential in this transition, Schumpeter felt. Most mathematics, however, was a result of attempts to solve problems in physics and as a consequence not particularly suited for economics. Real progress would come first when mathematical methods were explicitly created for economic purposes.[32] Schumpeter kept advocating these ideas not only at Harvard, but also at the Econometric Society where he was very active. In 1938 and 1939 he was its vice-president and in 1940 he became president. In 1946 Schumpeter published a textbook in mathematical economics, *Rudimentary Mathematics for Economists and Statisticians*. The book was co-authored with Leonard Crum, a colleague in the economics department with a PhD in mathematics. The book was essentially a revised and enlarged version of a supplement that Crum had published in 1938 in *The Quarterly Journal of Economics*. Since Schumpeter had made substantial additions to the supplement, Crum insisted that Schumpeter should stand as co-author. The book, as the title indicates, was rudimentary in character, and Schumpeter used to refer to it as 'from creeping to crawling'.[33]

The main reason why Schumpeter was replaced by Leontief in 1935 as the teacher for Ec-8a was that it was soon realized at Harvard that Schumpeter was not much of a mathematician. He loved mathematics and he was convinced of its usefulness in economics, but he had no particular talent for it himself. Abram Bergson, who had both Schumpeter and Leontief as teachers at Harvard, has described their difference in the following way:

> I had a sense that Schumpeter was not really at home in mathematical economics. He was not at home in the sense that he could manipulate with it and do fresh things. I had the impression that he was inspired by his conviction that this is the way economics would become a science – by the increased use of mathematics – and that he must be a champion for it. But nevertheless he was not an adept practitioner, and I think this tended to make the course not as exciting as it might be. I don't like to make invidious comparisons, but I later took a course with Leontief in price theory and analysis. And Leontief was completely at home with mathematical formulations. And it was for me a much more useful course and much more interesting.[34]

Schumpeter, of course, knew about his limitations in mathematics and that he had the greatest difficulty even in getting anything right in class, despite daily exercises. But he does not seem to have been particularly depressed about this. In a letter to a colleague from 1933, he referred to his incapacity in mathematics in such a magnificent manner that one somehow gets the impression that it was a virtue. 'I sometimes feel', he said, 'like Moses must have felt when he beheld the Promised Land and knew that he himself would not be allowed to enter it.'[35] Schumpeter's colleagues were also quick to spot that Schumpeter did not use mathematics in his own writings. According to Schumpeter, the reason for this was simply that it was difficult for him to express his ideas in mathematical language. There exists 'a living piece of reality' behind all of my ideas, Schumpeter used to say, and it is this that 'makes ... my theories so refractory to mathematical formulations'.[36] To Schumpeter, in brief, the lack of mathematics in his work was nothing negative; mathematics was supposed to be part of economic theory, not synonymous with it. 'Nothing is further from our minds', as he wrote in a programmatic article in the first issue of *Econometrica*, 'than any acrimonious belief in the exclusive excellence of mathematical methods, or any wish to belittle the work of historians, ethnologists, sociologists, and so on.'[37]

It should also be mentioned that Schumpeter does not seem to have been aware at this time that by backing mathematical economics, he might also have helped to unleash forces that were hostile to his own project of a general *Sozialökonomik*. What upset him already by the mid-1930s, however, was the way the graduate students and the young faculty members at Harvard were looking forward to the publication of Keynes's new work. In 1935 the department had been visited by a young Canadian economist, Robert Bryce, who had participated in Keynes's seminar in England and who was full of enthusiasm for the ideas that Keynes was soon to make public in *General Theory*.[38] 'Keynes is Allah', Schumpeter sourly noted, 'and Bryce is his Prophet.' When Keynes's book was published in 1936, the graduate students in the economics department at Harvard banded together and put in a collective order for their copies, so they would arrive faster in Cambridge. And when *General Theory* finally arrived, it was read with veneration and admiration. In 1937 Schumpeter noted with dismay in a letter to a colleague that 'the majority of our very best young people are almost fanatically for Mr. Keynes' book.'[39]

And it would get worse. Some of the faculty members soon became Keynesians as well, such as John Kenneth Galbraith and Alvin Hansen. The star-student of the department, Paul Samuelson, also converted. In the end, Harvard not only became the centre for Keynesian economics in the United States, but also the place from where Keynes's ideas were to spread all over the world, via the writings of Alvin Hansen and Paul Samuelson's famous textbook on economics.[40] The older economists at Harvard, including Schumpeter, remained, however, unflinchingly hostile to Keynes. 'In the Harvard Department', Schumpeter noted in 1944, 'perhaps the majority is opposed to the ideas of Keynes and Hansen.'[41] Schumpeter also did his best to counter Keynes's ideas. He, for example, wrote a very negative review of *General Theory* in which he attacked Keynes for giving policy advice in the name of science; for constructing a multitude of artificial definitions; and for giving the false impression that one particular case – that of England – could be elevated into a general norm for economic theory.[42] In his private correspondence Schumpeter was less restrained. Here he criticized Keynes for 'shirking all real problems' and for having missed everything in the economic literature since the 1830s.[43] Schumpeter was flabbergasted by Keynes's success and noted sourly that 'in the essay on the sociology of success which I shall never write, I shall use the case [of Keynes], if not as an illustration, yet as part of my laboratory material.'[44] When Keynes died in 1946, Schumpeter wrote a long article about him for *The American Economic Review*, which is filled with acid statements: Keynes only generalized from the English experience; the real attraction of *General Theory* had to do with its simplicity; the analysis in *General Theory* is static and only valid in the short-run; and so on.[45] The only work by Keynes that Schumpeter seems to have genuinely liked, was his *Essays in Biography*.

An additional reason why Schumpeter reacted so negatively to *General Theory* may have been that Keynes had again succeeded in upstaging him. All through the 1930s Schumpeter had worked incredibly hard with only one goal in mind: to finish his giant study of business cycles and complement the ideas he had put forth in *Theorie der wirtschaftlichen Entwicklung* (1911). Schumpeter had hoped to have his work ready by the mid-1930s, but failed; and it was not until 1939 that the massive, two-volume set of *Business Cycles* could be published. By this time, however, another world war was starting in Europe and Keynesianism had already swept the Harvard department of economics. *Business Cycles* will be discussed in detail later in this chapter, but it can be noted here that the reviews of Schumpeter's book were polite and friendly, but not very much more than that. No one that counted thought that *Business Cycles* was a major work or on a par with *General Theory*. *The American Economic Review* actually contained a devastating critique of Schumpeter's work by Simon Kuznets, in which many of the basic ideas of *Business Cycles* were challenged.[46] The graduate students at Harvard also decided to have a seminar on *Business Cycles* to which they invited Schumpeter. It soon became clear, however, that they did not have a very high opinion of Schumpeter's book. Schumpeter, who rarely could be coaxed into discussing his own work, nearly lost his temper. The whole thing was a disgrace; in Wolfgang Stolper's opinion: 'the book was simply not taken seriously.'[47]

II

The picture of Schumpeter during the 1930s that emerges from the memoirs of Harvard faculty members and graduate students is mainly one of Schumpeter the showman and Schumpeter the snob. These include anecdotes about how Schumpeter always wore spats, how *outré* he was at parties, and how bored he was at faculty meetings (he used to sit and solve mathematical problems). This, no doubt, was also the image that Schumpeter wanted to project. But all these anecdotes should not be allowed to detract from the fact that Schumpeter, first of all, worked tremendously hard during these years. He drove himself incessantly, both when it came to his duties as a teacher and in his own scholarship. He taught more than the average professor and he complained bitterly about it in his private correspondence. 'The teaching load is terrible and enough to kill a bull', he wrote to a friend in the late 1930s.[48] The main bulk of his energy, however, went into completing *Business Cycles*, and when this work finally appeared in 1939, it was more than a thousand pages long and contained a multitude of carefully crafted charts. A massive study of this type is usually the result of a large research machine, fed by huge grants and many junior researchers. Schumpeter, however, had had very little assistance, only small grants, and he more or less had to do everything himself.

One price that Schumpeter had to pay for working so hard, was that he had very little social life. The only people he met were his colleagues at Harvard and their wives. About once a week, often on a Friday, he had a meeting with one of the many study groups he belonged to. Schumpeter was, for example, a member of a group at the economics department called the Seven Wise Men and he often took the initiative himself to start informal seminars and study groups. These weekly meetings often included good dinners and good conversations, but little of emotional sustenance. They were typically men's gatherings with discussions, amusements and banter of a particular kind. Robert Loring Allen, who has interviewed many of Schumpeter's friends from these days, gives the following picture of a typical dinner:

> The usual Friday night meeting place might be Lochobers, the Oyster House, or some other good restaurant in Cambridge or Boston. After a few drinks and a good meal, followed by some brandy and talk, the group retired to the house, apartment, or rooms of a participant. When it was Schumpeter's turn to host the group, it met most often in the upstairs room of the Harvard Faculty Club. Although discussions of economics ruled these evenings, all was not serious. The members initiated Schumpeter into the joys of American burlesque by attending the Old Howard, with

its striptease, at Scollay Square in Boston. These gatherings were later followed by more drinks and even more talk into the night.[49]

Schumpeter soon established something of a reputation as a womanizer on the Harvard campus. He apparently had a number of affairs, but they did not mean very much to him.[50] His love life, it seems, was mainly a form of distraction; it also helped to counteract the pressure of his work. And this latter was something he desperately needed, not the least to prevent his depressions from turning into major breakdowns. By the end of each academic year, he felt deadly sick and as if he was about to collapse. When doctors were consulted, they typically found nothing wrong with him, something which irritated Schumpeter who knew that all was not as it should be. In 1936 he, for example, wrote to Irving Fisher:

> When I try in the summer to get into working form again and for the purpose consult some doctor, the result has been so far invariably that there is nothing organically the matter with me and that hence nothing ought to be done. This is precisely the reverse of the truth. It is before a definite breakdown has occurred that investigation ought to show the weak points in order to take them in hand while there is time.[51]

A few weeks after he had sent off the letter to Fisher, Schumpeter wrote in his private diary, 'funny, how quickly my organism reacts to decent treatment'.[52] The entry was signed 'Taconic' and referred to a visit he had just paid to Elizabeth Boody Firuski in Taconic, Connecticut. Elizabeth was a Radcliffe economist in her mid-thirties who met Schumpeter shortly after he had arrived in the United States and who soon fell in love with him. As opposed to his male colleagues, Elizabeth had no difficulty in discerning that Schumpeter was in poor emotional shape; and she soon made it her task to try to make life better for him. Schumpeter, whose ideas of femininity were along rather conventional lines, did not know how to react to a serious and non-glamorous person like Elizabeth. As the reader already knows, the two eventually married; and Elizabeth would take care of Schumpeter and nurse him for the rest of his life. It was very much because of Elizabeth, in other words, that Schumpeter could carry out his research programme in the United States and that we today have such works as *Business Cycles, Capitalism, Socialism and Democracy* and *History of Economic Analysis*. For this and other reasons, Elizabeth Boody Schumpeter is worthy of a tribute.

Romaine Elizabeth Boody was born on 16 August 1898 as the daughter of Maurice Boody, and his Swedish-born wife, Hulda Hokansen.[53] The Boody family was well off, but not wealthy. Elizabeth grew up in Lawrence, Massachusetts, where she also went to

high school. She was admitted to Radcliffe College in 1916 and
received her AB in 1920. She received the first *summa cum laude* in
economics that Radcliffe awarded. She also earned her MA and
PhD in economics at Radcliffe. After receiving her MA, she spent two
years in England, doing archival work for her thesis. What particularly interested her was British trade statistics from the eighteenth
century, and she was soon totally immersed in economic history.
During her years in England she also attended the London School of
Economics and was heavily influenced by Harold Laski. When she
returned to the United States, she was for several years prevented
from working full-time on her thesis. During this time Elizabeth
taught, and she got married to a radical bookseller and teacher by
the name of Maurice Firuski. She also found out that she had severe
diabetes. Elizabeth divorced Firuski after eight years of marriage in
1933 and the next year she presented her doctoral dissertation at
Radcliffe, *Trade Statistics and Cycles in England, 1697–1825*. In 1935
she was employed to lead a project on Japan, sponsored by the
Bureau of International Research at Harvard and Radcliffe.

When Schumpeter and Elizabeth first met in Cambridge, he was
around 50 and she was 35. Elizabeth was a slender woman of
medium height; she had hazel eyes and brown hair. Photographs
show a serious, dignified face with a compassionate look. Most of
the students who belonged to Schumpeter's fan club soon, however,
began to dislike her very strongly. She was a reactionary, they said,
and a prune. She also tried to use them to get closer to Schumpeter,
something which they resented very much.[54] Elizabeth's female
friends and colleagues had a very different impression of her. To
them she had succeeded in uniting the role of being a professional
and a woman. She was 'a scholar all her life [but] her professional
interests never diminished her essential femininity', as one of them
put it.[55] Elizabeth is described by her friends in such terms as
'forthright', 'honest', 'staunch' and 'loyal'. Her nicknames were 'Lizzie' and 'Lizzie Bee' (a pun on 'busy bee' or just short for Elizabeth
Boody?).

Elizabeth soon invited Schumpeter to her home in Taconic, Connecticut, where she had a lovely big house called 'Windy Hill'. 'A
great lover of the outdoors', a friend of Elizabeth has said, 'she was
an eager and successful gardener, as the beautifully kept terrraced
lawns and flowers [at Windy Hill] attested to.'[56] She was also an
excellent hostess, as Schumpeter soon found out for himself. And
many of her interests were similar to his. She once described herself
in a questionnaire as being interested in 'books, bridge, dogs, tennis,
walking, international relations, current economic and political
problems'.[57] Still, Schumpeter hesitated to get too much involved
with her. His reason for this is not clear, but a few letters from
Elizabeth to Schumpeter show that a real drama went on in 1937
before things settled down and the two became a couple for good.

Schumpeter apparently swayed backwards and forwards in his feelings for Elizabeth, who responded with anger and hurt to his ambivalence. In a letter from the summer of 1937 Elizabeth writes,

> Almost the most difficult thing about you is the way you swing back and forth like a pendulum ... You mellow in my society and then you go away and think dark thoughts. I have been willing to try to draw you back again and again because I love you and because it seemed to me that almost any life would be preferable to the one you are now leading with its concomitant state of mind. It is, of course, your mind much more than your body which makes you feel ill and weak.[58]

According to another letter from about the same time, Schumpeter had refused to visit Elizabeth – presumably in a half-hearted effort to break off the relationship – and Elizabeth responded in anger: 'You really will have a breakdown if you go on leading the ridiculous existence you lead at present.'[59] Whatever the problem between the two may have been, a few weeks later – on 16 August 1937 – Schumpeter and Elizabeth got married in Community Church in New York.

An important consequence of Schumpeter's decision to marry Elizabeth was that he could now leave Taussig's house and finally get a home of his own. Elizabeth and Schumpeter first lived at 15 Ash Street in Cambridge. In June 1938 they moved to 7 Acacia Street, which was to be their permanent home (besides Windy Hill) till Schumpeter's death in 1950. The house on Acacia Street was partly chosen because it was situated on a peaceful side street. Elizabeth did everything she could to accommodate Schumpeter's 'nerves and health', as she put it.[60] The only telephone in the house was, for example, placed in the kitchen so that the ringing would not disturb Schumpeter. And when a neighbour started to change his driveway, with the result that it came a bit closer to the Schumpeters' house, Elizabeth immediately contacted an attorney to put a stop to the whole thing. In her letter to the attorney Elizabeth cited Schumpeter's nerves as the main reason why it was impossible for them to have a driveway so close to their house:

> He [that is, Schumpeter] has had many heavy responsibilities and many difficult situations to face in the past. As a consequence his nervous system has become more or less disorganized. He is able to carry out his work at Harvard only if he has fairly long periods of complete quiet and rest. He is, of course, being subjected to careful medical treatment.[61]

Slowly Schumpeter and Elizabeth started to grow close to one another. Unable to have children, Elizabeth lavished her affection on

Schumpeter; and both of them lavished it on their Irish setter, Peter. Elizabeth took care of Schumpeter's practical needs: she was his chauffeur, his research assistant and his householder, all in one. 'Elizabeth is managing my worldly affairs', as he used to say.[62] Elizabeth also saw to it that he had his own rooms at Windy Hill (two studies and a separate bedroom); that he could play tennis whenever he wanted; and that his physical health did not deteriorate too much. A little note from Elizabeth to Schumpeter signed 'Auntie' has survived, where she lovingly inquires whether 'the world's most charming and distinguished economist' is 'eating and sleeping adequately'.[63]

And how did Schumpeter react to all the affection that Elizabeth showered on him? No doubt positively. But Schumpeter was a difficult and complex personality, as Elizabeth must have discovered quickly. Even though he was now married to Elizabeth, he continued meticulously to copy Annie's diary and in other ways cultivate the memories of his second wife and of his mother.[64] He kept a photograph of Annie on his bedside table, and he would regularly write, with Annie in mind, 'you are my first and last thought.' Every day Schumpeter also addressed his mother and Annie in his diary, asking them for help when he was in trouble, and thanking them when things went well. They were more and more becoming his private saints, and even though Schumpeter was not a religious man, it is clear that by now he had created some kind of private, semi-religious cult of his own.

Given Schumpeter's strange obsession with his memories of Annie and his mother, it must have been rather difficult for Elizabeth to live with him. And, in a sense, all of Elizabeth's love and care was just used by Schumpeter to carry out his punishingly hard research programme. Still, it was presumably satisfying for Elizabeth to realize that, without her, Schumpeter would have fallen apart. As Arthur Smithies has written about her role: 'Without her companionship and single-minded devotion he might well have sunk into a state of intolerable melancholy and loneliness.'[65] Tragically, Schumpeter's mental condition would deteriorate rather quickly during the 1940s; and during these years there were long periods when even Elizabeth's care was not enough to draw him out of his depressions. Before we discuss what happened during these years, however, we shall first present Schumpeter's scientific work during the 1930s and in particular his *opus magnum* from this time, *Business Cycles*.

III

When one looks at Schumpeter's scientific production from the time of his arrival in the United States in 1932 till the end of the decade, one is struck by how very few articles he wrote. The reason for this, as we know, was that Schumpeter was trying to focus all the energy he could possibly muster on his enormous book on business cycles. Apart from a few book reviews, interventions at conferences and the like, Schumpeter only produced a handful of articles in the 1930s. The most important of these is probably 'The Common Sense of Econometrics' (1933), although 'The Analysis of Economic Change' (1935) is cited quite often as well. In the former article, which is programmatic in nature, Schumpeter explains in broad lines why econometrics is necessary and what it can be used for. In the article on economic change, Schumpeter gives an early summary of the ideas he would present in much more detail a few years later in *Business Cycles*. A special mention should also be made of the fact that an English translation of *Theorie der wirtschaftlichen Entwicklung* (2nd edn, 1926) appeared in 1934. Schumpeter had not made the translation himself – it was made by Redvers Opie, a personal friend and Taussig's son-in-law – but he wrote a brief new preface for the American edition. Much more important, it should be noted, is the preface that Schumpeter wrote for the Japanese translation of the same work, which appeared in 1937.[66] This latter preface contains an uncommonly succinct account of the main ideas in Schumpeter's work, which authors had influenced him the most, and the parallels, as he saw them, between his own ideas and those of Marx.

One project, which Schumpeter began during these years, but which was never finished, was a work entitled *The Theoretical Apparatus of Economics*. This project had its roots in some work Schumpeter had done in 1927–30 in Bonn.[67] Schumpeter was apparently quite dissatisfied with the draft he had finished in Germany (and left behind when he emigrated?), because when the project was revived in the mid-1930s, he made little reference to it. According to Schumpeter's correspondence, *The Theoretical Apparatus* was supposed to replace his first book, *The Nature and Essence of Theoretical Economics* (1908).[68] While the emphasis in Schumpeter's earlier work had been on the philosophy and methodology of economics, the new work was to be much more practical and quantitative in nature. In a letter from 1936 to the Rockefeller Foundation, in which Schumpeter applied for funds, he gave a one-line description of the new book: 'in [this work] I want to overhaul and improve the quantitative methods of modern economics.'[69] In the main application, dated 3 February 1936 and addressed to the Committee on Research in the Social Sciences at Harvard, Schumpeter provided a fuller description: 'The grant is applied for in order to enable applicant to carry to completion a work on Economic Theory ... The object of this work is, among other things, to contribute towards the creation of a more useful type of Economic Theory, every concept and method of which should carry statistical meaning and prove an efficient tool of quantitative factual analysis.'[70] With his usual optimism Schumpeter said that the book would be finished within a year or two. This, however, was not to be the case and in 1938 he applied for more money, stating that the attempt to give economic theorems their 'statistical complement' meant that 'the project continues applicant's work on Business Cycles'.[71] Schumpeter would continue to work on *The Theoretical Apparatus of Economics* in the 1940s, but despite occasional assurances to the grant authorities that 'the main ideas are worked out', nothing ever came of the project.[72]

That Schumpeter had many good ideas brewing during the years when he was trying to finish *Business Cycles* is also evident from his work on rationality. The concept of rationality, Schumpeter said, was one of those concepts that he had never been able to resolve fully to his satisfaction.[73] Early in 1939 a paper by Chester Barnard triggered off a decision by Schumpeter to put together a discussion group on rationality, formally referred to as the Seminar on Rationality in the Social Sciences. The participants came from different departments at Harvard, and it was clear that Schumpeter wanted it to be an interdisciplinary group. The members included Talcott Parsons and Wilbert E. Moore from sociology; David McGrannahan from psychology; and Gottfried Haberler, Wassily Leontief and Paul Sweezy from economics. There were about ten meetings, starting in October 1939 and ending in April 1940. An attempt to put together a book from the papers that had been presented failed to materialize, partly because the appointed editor, Parsons, lost interest.[74] Schumpeter, however, made both a presentation and wrote a paper. Schumpeter was not completely satisfied with his paper, which was entitled 'The Meaning of Rationality in the Social Sciences', and told Parsons that once the projected volume on rationality was closer to being finished, he would rewrite it. This, however, never happened.

The version of Schumpeter's paper that exists ('still only a sketch') gives, however, a good idea of how Schumpeter looked on rationality.[75] We know already from Schumpeter's essay on imperialism, that Schumpeter did not think that all social phenomena were rational. Indeed, to some extent one can say that what fascinated Schumpeter so much about rationality was exactly the problem of where to draw the line between rational and irrational behaviour. In the version that Schumpeter presented to the discussion group, he tried essentially to get at this problem by introducing different types of rationality. The two key distinctions were, on the one hand, between 'rationality in the observer' and 'rationality in the observed', and, on the other, between 'conscious or subjective rationality' and 'subconscious or objective rationality'. Any kind of scientific inquiry, Schumpeter explained, must by necessity be rational ('rationality of the observer'). But this does not mean that the object of the study also has to be rational ('rationality in the observed'). A common problem with economics, he said, was that economists much too often assume that economic actors behave in a consciously rational manner ('subjective rationality'). In many cases, however, it was not only wrong to make this assumption, it was also unnecessary. People often act in such a way that the theorist is justified in making the assumption that the actor is behaving according to a rational scheme, regardless of the actor's intentions ('objective rationality'). This was about as far as Schumpeter got in his paper; and he was not particularly happy with the result. It is clear that Schumpeter's discussion does not represent any major breakthrough in the study of rationality. Still, the distinctions he introduced are useful to bear in mind, especially nowadays when rational choice is becoming popular again. Schumpeter, incidentally, would probably have disapproved very sharply of 'economic imperialism' or the current attempt to apply the economic concept of rationality to a host of non-economic problems. According to Schumpeter, it is not possible even to solve all *economic* problems with the help of economic theory, let alone historical and sociological problems.

Schumpeter's major work from these years, however, was *Business Cycles*. He had not published a book since the 1910s – more than 25 years – so *Business Cycles* can be seen as an attempt on Schumpeter's part to make a comeback as an economic theorist. The topic that Schumpeter picked for his new book was in line with his main theoretical interest, and *Business Cycles* was in many ways intended by Schumpeter as a sequel to *Theorie der wirtschaftlichen Entwicklung* from 1911. In *Theorie*, as Schumpeter phrased it in the preface, he had worked out the basic theoretical tools ('the scaffolding') and he now turned to the construction of the actual 'house'. However: 'It took longer than I thought to turn that scaffolding into a house, to embody the results of my later work, to present the historical and statistical complement, to expand old horizons.'[76] The reason why it took such a long time to finish was because of the extremely ambitious way in which Schumpeter had formulated his task, namely to explain the development of capitalism, from its origin till today, in full historical detail and with full logical stringency.

To complete a work of this type was obviously very taxing, especially if one insisted on absolute historical accuracy, as Schumpeter did. No short-cuts were acceptable to Schumpeter. For example, in a letter to Wesley Clair Mitchell from 1937, he wrote:

It is my conviction that this situation [of carefully tracing the historical development of capitalism] must be faced and that an immensely laborious analysis of every historical pattern within the reach of our material must be undertaken. My trouble was that I have neither the means nor, within the plan of work which I have cut out for my remaining years, the time to do more than to scratch the surface of that herculean task and it sometimes makes me quite melancholy to think that what I have really to say will have to remain unsaid forever.[77]

As the reader knows, *Business Cycles* has not survived as a major work in economics, despite the enormous labour that went into it. Some years ago, Galbraith said that *Business Cycles* 'is now only a scholastic oddity' and this is probably how most economists think of it today.[78] To some extent this judgement is justified; Schumpeter's two-volume work is often long-winded, repetitive and simply not on the same level as his best works. Still, there is much more to *Business Cycles* than is commonly thought. Schumpeter's work has its problems, but it also contains some extremely fine parts. Add to this that it is one of the few original histories of modern capitalism; that it cleared the ground for Schumpeter's next great work, *Capitalism, Socialism and Democracy*; and that it allowed Schumpeter to develop further his vision of a broad-based science of economics, and we have more than enough reasons to question the habitual rejection of this work.

If *Business Cycles* has its theoretical roots in the early 1910s, the idea of 'complementing' *Theorie der wirtschaftlichen Entwicklung* with historical and statistical material goes back to the 1920s. It was during this decade that Schumpeter had re-evaluated the work of Gustav von Schmoller and developed a more positive attitude to historical research. He had also argued that economic theory should be developed in close conjunction with empirical data and that, thereby, a new and superior type of economic theory would become possible ('concretized theory'). In this context, Schumpeter used to refer to the work of Arthur Spiethoff on business cycles. Spiethoff had, in Schumpeter's opinion, been highly successful in his attempts to 'fuse' empirical results and business cycle theory. Spiethoff's work, Schumpeter said, showed 'what the *Sozialökonomik* of the future will look like'.[79]

Just like Spiethoff's studies, *Business Cycles* was an attempt by Schumpeter to show what a realistic science of economics could accomplish. Schumpeter, however, emphasized that he did not want to span 'the entire range of the economics and sociology of capitalism'.[80] This would have meant that capitalism was analysed with the help of all the four components of *Sozialökonomik*: economic theory, economic history, economic sociology and statistics. But to trace the purely economic development of capitalism and also to look at the social structure and the institutions of capitalism was simply too much; and Schumpeter was only willing to pursue 'a purely economic argument'.[81] *Business Cycles*, to cite its subtitle, is consequently 'a theoretical, historical and statistical analysis of the capitalist process'.

The decision to exclude sociology, it can be noted, obviously made *Business Cycles* more manageable. But it also made Schumpeter's analysis less realistic in several ways. For Schumpeter, contemporary capitalism was in a stage of institutional transition from 'Competitive Capitalism' to 'Trustified Capitalism'; and this whole development now had to be abstracted from, since economic sociology (or the analysis of economic institutions) was to be eliminated from the analysis. *Business Cycles* covers the evolution of capitalism from the late eighteenth century to the 1930s, and for this long historical stretch Schumpeter made the assumption that the institutional structure had remained the same.[82] This made it possible for him to focus exclusively on the 'economic mechanisms' involved – that is, on the business cycles – but he also had to cut away many interesting ideas. This was especially the case the closer he came to his own time, because contemporary capitalism was in Schumpeter's mind going through some extremely important institutional changes. The reader, however, would have to wait till *Capitalism, Socialism and Democracy* for a discussion of these.

Having explained why sociology should be excluded from the analysis, Schumpeter went on to discuss the relationship that ought to exist among economic theory, economic history and statistics. This is mainly done in chapter 2 of *Business Cycles* and represents one of the high points in the book. The discussion draws heavily on German philosophy of social science, in particular on Weber and Schmoller, and is of very high quality. Schumpeter first defends the use of theory against empiricism. 'Raw facts', he says, 'are a meaningless jumble'; and it is impossible to get anywhere in economics without a theory.[83] To believe that one can proceed just by generalizing on the basis of data, Schumpeter calls 'Nonsense Induction'.[84] But this must not be understood to mean that theory should be cut off from data. On the contrary, theory must be developed in very close contact with data; it must be '*interpenetrated*' by data. To view theory as something one simply confronts data with to verify it, is superficial. Theory is not to be identified with explanatory hypotheses but is rather something which enters the analysis on a deeper level. At heart, theory is a way of ordering reality in a creative manner by way of scientific concepts. These 'tools of analysis', as Schumpeter liked to call them, include such concepts as 'price level', 'demand' and so on. He summarized his argument in the following manner:

> If we are to speak about price levels and to devise methods of measuring them, we must know what a price level is. If we are to observe demand, we must have a precise concept of its elasticity

... No hypotheses enter into such concepts, which simply embody methods of description and measurement, nor into the propositions defining their relations (so-called *theorems*), and yet their framing is the chief task of theory, in economics as elsewhere. This is what we mean by *tools of analysis*. Obviously, we must have them before we take hold of the material we wish to measure and to understand.[85]

Each historical event, Schumpeter continued (again following Weber), was a 'historical individual' and as such irreducible to a general group of phenomena. Theory, on the other hand, had to be analytical, generalizable and not constructed with individual facts in mind. One way to bridge the gap between theory and individual events, Schumpeter argued, was to let them interpenetrate via historical and statistical material. Economic theorists, he said, could for example not afford to ignore the increasingly rich statistical material that existed. On the other hand, much statistical material had been constructed on the flimsiest theoretical grounds and was only of limited value. There was also the unfortunate tendency among economists to use aggregates far too often and thereby gloss over important differences. 'Beware of averages!', as Schumpeter used to say. Historical research was also far more sensitive to individual actors such as entrepreneurs; and it was absolutely necessary for the economic theoretician to be well versed in economic history. It was only when he was familiar with economic history, that the economic theorist was in a position to handle conventional statistics in a satisfactory way. 'It is always of the utmost importance for us', Schumpeter said, 'to be thoroughly masters of the economic history of the time, the country or the industry, sometimes even of the individual firm in question, before we draw any inference at all from the behavior of time series.'[86] Economic theory and statistics, he continued, could simply not be used in isolation from economic history. Since it is often asserted that Schumpeter became an advocate of economic history only *after* the Second World War, it deserves to be emphasized that the following key passage can already be found in *Business Cycles*:

We cannot stress this point sufficiently. General history (social, political, and cultural), economic history, and more particularly industrial history are not only indispensable but really the most important contributors to the understanding of our problem. All other materials and methods, statistical and theoretical, are only subservient to them and worse than useless without them.[87]

Schumpeter's actual analysis of business cycles further illustrates what he meant when he said that theory and empirical data must

items as interest rates, price levels, production levels in different
industries, and the like. Schumpeter uses the statistical material
mainly to delineate his three kinds of business cycles. This is done
for three countries during the 1787–1938 period: Great Britain,
Germany and the United States. Schumpeter finds three giant
Kondratieff Cycles during this period and a multitude of minor cycles.
Schumpeter has conveniently summarized some of his major findings in a letter to Simon Kuznets:[91]

The phases of the Kondratieff of the Industrial Revolution I date as
follows:

Prosperity	1787–1800
Recession	1801–1813
Depression	1814–1827
Revival	1828–1842

The phases of the bourgeois Kondratieff are:

Prosperity	1843–1857
Recession	1858–1869
Depression	1870–1884/5
Revival	1886–1897

The phases of the Neo-Mercantilist Kondratieff:

Prosperity	1898–1911
Recession	1912–1924/5
Depression	1926–1938

To this should just be added that towards the end of the book
Schumpeter makes a great deal of the peculiar structure of the Juglar
Cycle, which was due in 1935. According to Schumpeter, this cycle
should have shown a much stronger 'prosperity' than it did. And
more importantly, phase two, or the recession, was practically eliminated and replaced by a strange rush directly into a depression.
This was all very odd, Schumpeter said. Should it perhaps be seen as
an indication that the capitalist system was on the verge of exhausting itself? Not at all; there were plenty of signs that capitalism was
doing very well from a purely economic point of view. If one, however, included sociological factors in the analysis, Schumpeter said,
the whole thing suddenly looked different. Many economic institutions were, for example, in an early stage of decay. This did not mean
that capitalism would disappear from the historical stage within the
next few years. 'But the sociological drift cannot be expected to
change', as the book ends.[92]
    Most of the reviewers acknowledged the tremendous amount of
work that had gone into *Business Cycles*; and adjectives like 'stupen-
dous', 'monumental' and 'formidable' were frequently used.[93] The

reviews were on the whole positive, but they were not written by the people who counted; and the book, as we know, did not become the trend-setter for which Schumpeter had hoped.[94] One very negative review appeared in the prestigious *American Economic Review*, written by Simon Kuznets. Since Kuznets's article was to set the parameters for the debate about *Business Cycles* for many years to come (it is still often referred to), we shall discuss its argument at some length.[95] Kuznets begins by describing Schumpeter's three 'approximations' in *Business Cycles*. Schumpeter's fine introduction about the relationship among theory, history and statistics is, however, passed over in silence, as well as Schumpeter's decision to eliminate sociology from his analysis and the consequences that this has for the argument. After having reduced *Business Cycles* to manageable size in this way, Kuznets says that his reading of the book has left him with some 'disturbing doubts' about Schumpeter's analysis. These doubts, he says, centre on three key propositions in *Business Cycles*: that innovations come in bundles; that there are four phases to the business cycles; and that three cycles go on simultaneously.

As to the first proposition, Kuznets argues that there is no reason why there should be discontinuity in the stream of innovations. 'Why should we not conceive these applications of high entrepreneurial ability', he asks, 'whether represented by one man or several, as flowing in a continuous stream, a stream magnified in a constant proportion by the efforts of the imitators?'[96] As to Schumpeter's proposition about the four-phase model, Kuznets says that in order for Schumpeter to prove his point, he would have to use something better than inflection points (a statistical measure introduced by Ragnar Frisch) in order properly to establish departures from the equilibrium line. In general, he adds, Schumpeter seems to scorn the help of formal statistics. Kuznets concludes: 'The difficulties encountered in the matter of inflection points and the paucity of formal statistical analysis in the treatise lead to a doubt whether Professor Schumpeter's concept of equilibrium and of the four-phase model of business cycles are such as to permit of application to statistical analysis.'[97] As to Schumpeter's three-cycle schema, Kuznets finds that Schumpeter has not succeeded in dispelling the doubts that surround the existence of Kondratieff Cycles. He also notes that since 'the cycle is essentially a quantitative concept', it is questionable whether historical records of the type that Schumpeter introduces ('qualitative records') can contribute anything of substance to the analysis.[98] Schumpeter, Kuznets says, actually ends up by using the most simple-minded methods to construct his time series; and Schumpeter then just vaguely states that the curves affirm his thesis about the various cycles. 'The failure to follow articulate methods of time series analysis reduces the statistical methods to a mere recording of impressions on charts.'[99] Kuznets sums up his review by saying that a critical evaluation of Schumpeter's work yields 'disturbingly destructive results'.[100]

It is clear that Kuznets has put his finger on several weak points in *Business Cycles*. There is something seriously wrong with Schumpeter's long chain of causation, which starts with the single, powerful innovation and ends with the three simultaneous cycles. Schumpeter may very well have intended merely to use his cycles as an illustrative device, but he definitely finishes by taking them much more seriously. As the book progresses, Schumpeter dissects cycle after cycle after cycle till the whole thing 'begins to smack of Pythagorean moonshine', to cite Paul Samuelson.[101] Erik Dahmén, a Swedish economist who has spent many years working on Schumpeter's ideas, has made the point that Schumpeter should perhaps have looked at the transformations brought about by economic change rather than on change exclusively in the form of business cycles.[102] Indeed, there exist many good ideas in *Theorie*, which Schumpeter could have focused on. He could, for example, have looked at the differences between entrepreneurs and managers; at the fights between old firms and new firms; and at the emergence of giant corporations. Some of these ideas Schumpeter would discuss a few years later in *Capitalism, Socialism and Democracy*. In *Business Cycles*, however, Schumpeter tried to squeeze all of economic change into his three cycles, and the result was a relentless account of every cycle there has been in Great Britain, Germany and the United States since 1787.

Still, *Business Cycles* has a worse reputation than it deserves, and it will not do to treat *Business Cycles* as if it contained just a couple of verifiable hypotheses and nothing else. We have already mentioned the interesting discussion in chapter 2, where Schumpeter tries to disentangle some difficult methodological problems in a very ingenious way. Scattered throughout *Business Cycles* one can also find evocative accounts of economic innovations. Schumpeter is sometimes treated as if he equated innovations with technological innovations, but this is not the case. In *Business Cycles* Schumpeter covers a huge array of innovations, including organizational, locational and political innovations.[103] It must finally also be acknowledged that compared to today's business cycle experts, who often work with extremely abstract models based on rational expectations ('new equilibrium business cycle research'), Schumpeter's goal was much more in line with that of classical political economy and social science in general. And this goal, to cite a memorable phrase from *Business Cycles*, was to present the reader with '*a reasoned (=conceptually clarified) history ... of the economic process in all its aspects and bearings*'.[104]

7

Capitalism, Socialism and Democracy

> I have first to say that I am not running a drugstore. I have no pills
> to hand out; no clear-cut solutions for any practical problems that
> may arise. For these problems are largely political and it is up to
> you to say what you want to do and to fight for it, to say what you
> will extol and what you will destroy. The economist has no particu-
> lar qualification to speak about that aspect of any subject. What he
> can do and what I want to do, to the best of my ability, is to present
> the problem ... as I see it.
>
> (Schumpeter in a speech in Detroit, April 1941)

After Schumpeter had completed *Business Cycles*, he immediately
began to work on *Capitalism, Socialism and Democracy*, which was to
become his second great work in the United States. On one level,
Capitalism, Socialism and Democracy is clearly a political work – a
treatise in political philosophy or political sociology. But it was also
intended to complement *Business Cycles* and to be a sequel of sorts
to this work. In *Business Cycles*, Schumpeter had stressed that he
was not going to cover 'the entire range of the economics and sociology of capitalism', because it was too large a task.[1] It was difficult
enough to take economic history, statistics and economic theory
into account; and sociology had to be excluded. This meant that
Schumpeter had to make the assumption that the economic institutions of capitalism had remained the same under the period of investigation, that is, from 1787 to 1938. As Schumpeter saw it, this
assumption facilitated the analysis for most of the period. But the
nearer he came to the 1930s, the more difficulties there were. The
Juglar in the mid-1930s, for example, did not behave at all the way it
was supposed to do. And the reason for this – as Schumpeter was to
explore in his Lowell Lectures from 1941 as well as in *Capitalism,
Socialism and Democracy* – was that the institutions of capitalism

were slowly being transformed. Capitalism was in a stage of transition – from what Schumpeter called 'Competitive Capitalism' to 'Trustified Capitalism'; and this made a conventional economic analysis in many ways incomplete.

Capitalism, Socialism and Democracy is written with so much vitality and elegance that the reader easily gets the impression that the years during which Schumpeter worked on it (the bulk was written during 1938–1941) were very happy and successful years for him. But that was not the case. The years from 1939 to 1945, which constitute the focus of this chapter, were actually among the worst that Schumpeter experienced during his entire life. There were many reasons for this. By the late 1930s Schumpeter was, for example, quite unhappy at Harvard; he felt snubbed by the administration and not much appreciated by his colleagues and students. And as the Second World War drew closer, he became increasingly tormented by political events. It is true that he became a US citizen in 1939, but in his heart he was still very much a European. And, finally, in the early 1940s he went through a difficult personal crisis, feeling that his life was coming to an end and that it was time for him to sum things up. The way that Schumpeter responded to all of these pressures was the usual one – with work. According to Galbraith, Schumpeter was 'very unhappy during World War II' and 'he secluded himself over in the library of the Business School, reading and working away [while] the Europe he knew and loved, was tearing itself to pieces.'[2] The events surrounding Schumpeter's personal and professional activities during 1939–45 will be the main topic of the following section. Then comes a section which is exclusively devoted to Schumpeter's political philosophy. It is generally recognized that Schumpeter was a sophisticated political thinker, but very little systematic attention has been paid to his ideas; and this section is an attempt to remedy this. There is, of course, also the fact that Schumpeter has been accused of being a fascist and pro-Nazi; and these charges need to be discussed. The chapter concludes with a presentation and analysis of Schumpeter's masterpiece, *Capitalism, Socialism and Democracy*.

I

If we take a look at the courses Schumpeter taught during the war and compare them with the ones he taught during the early to late 1930s, we find continuity as well as change. Schumpeter had been taken on by Harvard mainly as a theoretician, and he taught courses in economic theory and business cycles on a regular basis in the 1930s as well as in the 1940s. During the war, however, he also began to teach the history of economics, money and banking, and the economics of socialism. The last course ('Economics of Socialism') was connected to his work on *Capitalism, Socialism and Democracy*, which includes a detailed discussion of the workings of socialist economies. The course on the history of economics ('History and Literature of Economics since 1776') was connected to Schumpeter's decision, taken in the 1930s, to expand and rewrite his *Economic Doctrine and Method* from 1914. The course on money (usually entitled 'Principles of Money and Banking') was probably inspired by Schumpeter's desire during the late 1930s and early 1940s to revive his money book. Around this time, for example, an advertisement appeared in *The American Economic Review* which said that a book by Schumpeter on money was soon to be published.[3]

That Schumpeter tried to renew himself during the war is also evidenced by the fact that he gave a course of public lectures in the spring of 1941 at the famous Lowell Institute in Boston. The Institute had been founded in 1836 and its main activity consisted in hosting a series of prestigious public lectures each year at the Boston Public Library. Ten courses were given in 1940–1, including one by André Maurois ('Mes Souvenirs de Guerre'), one by Pitirim Sorokin ('The Twilight of Sensate Culture') and one by William Langer ('The Rise of the European Conflagration of Ideas'). The topic that Schumpeter had chosen was 'An Economic Interpretation of Our Time', and the course consisted, as was the rule at the Lowell Institute, of eight lectures. The titles of the individual lectures give an indication of how Schumpeter viewed his topic: 'The Economic and Political Structure of Modern Society' (Lecture 1), 'The Impact of the World Crisis' (Lecture 3) and 'International Trade' (Lecture 7). Schumpeter's lectures essentially dealt with the same set of topics as *Capitalism, Socialism and Democracy*, namely the institutional change that contemporary capitalism was going through. This meant that the emphasis was on '*the socio-economic analysis*' as opposed to the purely economic analysis.[4] Some important differences, however, also exist between *Capitalism, Socialism and Democracy* and *An Economic Interpretation of Our Time*, which in fact was supposed to be a book on its own. The Lowell Lectures contain, first of all, a much more concrete analysis of the political and economic events in Europe between 1871 and 1940 than can be found in *Capitalism, Socialism and Democracy*. They give a very good picture of how Schumpeter saw some of the key events between the wars, and we shall therefore draw quite a bit on the Lowell Lectures in the section on Schumpeter's political philosophy.

Despite Schumpeter's efforts to renew his scholarship, he was not happy at Harvard during these years. Schumpeter had, for example, become used to an admiring circle of students in the 1930s, but this changed when Keynesianism became popular.[5] The students now began to desert him and flock to other teachers. Schumpeter blamed himself for this development and wrote unhappily in his private diary: 'I am vexed at my inability to convey my message to youngsters.'[6] Schumpeter was also very discontented during these years with his colleagues. 'Though outwardly affable, congenial and charming', Galbraith says, 'he secretly and sometimes not so secretly regarded many of his Harvard economist colleagues as clods.'[7] This, of course, did not endear him to some of his colleagues. He also had several clashes with the people who controlled the department. In particular, Schumpeter disliked Harold Burbank, who was the chairman of the department for many years. 'Burbie' was apparently a rather bitter man, a mediocre scholar and strongly anti-semitic.[8] He had complete power over the junior faculty appointments which he used to keep down the number of Jews in the faculty.[9] One of the people Burbank prevented from obtaining a job at the Harvard faculty was its star student, Paul Samuelson. In 1940 there was a big dispute at the department around this issue and Schumpeter was totally infuriated by Burbank's decision to block Samuelson's appointment.[10] Coming out from a stormy faculty meeting, where the matter had been discussed, Schumpeter was heard to proclaim in a loud voice on the stairs of the Littauer Center, 'I could have understood if they didn't want to hire him because he is a Jew. But that wasn't it – he was just too brilliant for them!'[11]

Schumpeter was so discontented with the economics department in 1940 that he seriously contemplated leaving Harvard. It was apparently well known at other universities that Schumpeter was unhappy and that he was thinking of leaving Harvard for good. At Yale University the economics department was very eager to have Schumpeter. Yale had a smaller department than Harvard, and the main attraction that Yale held for Schumpeter was probably that he would be able to influence the department much more than he could ever hope to do at Harvard. On 1 May 1940 the provost at Yale made a formal offer to Schumpeter to become Sterling Professor of Economics with a salary of $10,000. On 18 May, he raised the offer to $12,000 (to match Harvard) and wrote, 'Our Department of Economics supports this invitation unanimously and enthusiastically, as do the University officers. If you come to Yale we shall look to you for leadership in the department of our graduate work and rely upon your counsel in selecting personnel to carry out the program.'[12] Schumpeter answered a few days later that he was considering the offer very seriously, but that he needed some time to think it through. In the meantime it became known at Harvard that Schumpeter might leave, and efforts were quickly set in motion to persuade him to stay. On 3 June Schumpeter was handed two petitions, one signed by all the senior members of the economics department and the other by the graduate students and some junior faculty members. The senior members wanted Schumpeter to know that they felt a 'deep concern at your projected departure from Harvard in favor of Yale University'.[13] They stressed: 'We value you as a colleague, we need you and we want you to stay.' The students and the young instructors emphasized that 'rightly Harvard has been regarded as a world center of research and teaching in the fields of economic theory and business cycles, and in large measure this has been your achievement.'[14] They also stressed how much Schumpeter had helped them and how generous he was with his time: 'Above all, you have been more than a teacher to us; we have always been proud to think of you as a true friend. We feel that your departure would be an irreplaceable loss to us and to future Harvard students.' This show of affection apparently did the trick because Schumpeter decided to stay. Leontief wrote happily to Schumpeter that 'it was a relief to hear that you have decided not to trade your Harvard birthright for a Yale porridge.'[15] And many years later Elizabeth Boody Schumpeter noted that 'it was the Yale offer which made his [that is, Schumpeter's] future at Harvard tolerable.'[16] But apart from the show of support from faculty members and students, nothing of substance was really accomplished and Schumpeter was soon unhappy again, complaining bitterly in his private diary about '[the] stifling atmosphere at Harvard'.[17]

A few years later Schumpeter was again infuriated by the economic department's appointment policy. This time it was a question of choosing between John Dunlop and Paul Sweezy, one of Schumpeter's favourites. Sweezy had been on military leave from Harvard since 1942, and in 1945 he was ready to return and resume his teaching, if he was given tenure. The department had to make an appointment very quickly, and Sweezy and Dunlop were the only candidates. Schumpeter backed Sweezy's case very strongly and wrote to the Dean that Sweezy's major work *The Theory of Capitalist Development* (1942) was 'a masterly exposition of the Marxian system of thought' and that 'this task ... has been attempted by dozens of economists of all countries [but] has never before been done so well.'[18] In comparison to Sweezy, Schumpeter argued, Dunlop had not accomplished very much. Schumpeter was not impressed by Dunlop's major work up till this time, *Wage Determination under Trade Unions* (1944). 'This book', he said, 'cannot rank high as a scholarly achievement.'[19] Schumpeter was well aware that it was to Sweezy's disadvantage to be a Marxist, and he wrote in his letter to the Dean, 'The book [by Sweezy] has been criticized for his wholesale acceptance of Marxian propositions, but this criticism misses the nature of the performance. Whether we accept Marxian economics or not, it is of sufficient importance in economic thought to justify the task of propounding it from the standpoint of which it was conceived.' Dunlop, however, was finally chosen, and it was fairly clear to everybody – or at least to Sweezy – that the main reason was that Sweezy was a radical while Dunlop was not.[20]

But even if these quarrels at Harvard depressed Schumpeter, it was the war itself that put the heaviest strain on him during the early 1940s. The Second World War seems to have released a stream of feelings in him, which he did not understand but which filled him with anguish. 'Why, why do I *grieve* so much about this war?', he asked himself in his private diary.[21] He realized that he experienced the war differently from other people, and as a result he felt isolated and apart: 'This is no longer my world. I am a stranger to the mortals and their doings....'[22] Also, it seems that the war made Schumpeter lose his emotional balance; and he now started to behave in an erratic manner, both in public and in private. Schumpeter's behaviour had always been on the eccentric side, but it was fairly harmless and inoffensive. He was a snob and a bit of a fool, even if his wit could also be cutting. But now his behaviour changed, and many of Schumpeter's public statements from these years have a sinister and hostile quality to them. According to one of the graduate students in economics, Schumpeter frequently made 'pro-Hitler' statements, 'saying to anyone who cared to listen, that Roosevelt and Churchill had destroyed more than Jenghis Kan'.[23] Gottfried Haberler, a close and loyal friend, has described a scene from a party that Schumpeter attended towards the end of the war:

> In 1944, when Roosevelt was running for his fourth term as president, a lady who was unaware of Schumpeter's intense aversion [for Roosevelt] asked him at a cocktail party whether he would vote for Roosevelt. He answered: 'My dear lady, if Hitler runs for President and Stalin for Vice President, I shall be happy to vote for that ticket against Roosevelt.'[24]

Reading Schumpeter's private diary of the 1940s, it is clear that he was mentally out of balance. He had always been a prejudiced man – he had, for example, grown up in a deeply anti-semitic milieu – but he also took a certain pride in not letting his prejudices interfere with his better judgement. During the war years, however, his prejudices rose to the surface with a vengeance. In his private diary we find outbursts against 'niggers, Jews and subnormals' and statements of the following type: 'Just as the nigger dance is the dance of today, so is Keynesian economics the economics of today.'[25] Schumpeter knew very well that he might get into trouble if he said some of these things in public and he told himself to be cautious: 'never attack the Jews and the Catholic Church ... Attack on these spell defeat.'[26]

Schumpeter's obsession with his memories of Annie and his mother also became more intense during these years.[27] The more depressed he became, the more he pleaded with *die Hasen*, as he affectionately called them, for help. While he earlier had had imaginary dialogues with Annie and his mother, there was now a shift in the direction of monologues. Schumpeter addressed *die Hasen* in an increasingly formal and ritualistic manner, which further underscored their elevation into some kind of distant, private deities. As one commentator has noted, 'Annie and his mother had become more remote, more holy.'[28]

It seems that Schumpeter and Elizabeth grew closer to each other during the war. One reason for this was that Elizabeth was also isolated due to her political opinions. Before the war she had been known for her violent hostility to Roosevelt and for being very right-wing in general.[29] When in the late 1930s, as a result of her work for the Bureau of International Research at Harvard and Radcliffe, she started to oppose the administration's policy towards Japan, it was apparently too much for some people. In 1939 she wrote to a publisher,

> As a result of this work [for the Bureau of International Research] I am convinced that Japan is much stronger economically than is commonly supposed and that the present war could not be stopped by economic action on the part of the United States within shall we say two years. I have expressed this view from time to time at the School of Public Affairs at Charlottesville, Virginia, and at the Detroit meeting of the American Economic Association. As a consequence I am extremely unpopular in certain Far Eastern circles which are anxious to have the United States take this action whatever the consequences may be. I am accused of being anything from merely 'pro-Japanese' to a 'Japanese spy'. I like the Japanese people but I have no sympathy whatsoever with the Japanese Army and its aspirations in China. I do believe, however, that even where your sympathies are concerned, you should be somewhat realistic.[30]

A little later Elizabeth wrote in a letter that she was 'practically ostracized' at the Institute of Pacific Relations, where she had been a member since 1934.[31] As a result she finally resigned from the Institute in 1940. At about the same time the result of her work for the Bureau of International Research appeared, an edited volume entitled *The Industrialization of Japan and Manchukuo, 1930–1940*. Elizabeth's own contributions amounted to more than 300 pages and quickly established her as an expert on contemporary Asian economic and political affairs.[32] In November 1941 Elizabeth received a telegram from the Office of Production Management in Washington about a possible job. This pleased her since she wanted to contribute to the war effort; she also wanted a government job in case anything happened to Schumpeter. A few weeks later, however, she received a message saying that she was not needed. Elizabeth was convinced that Washington in the meantime had been told that she had the 'wrong' opinions about Japan.[33] After a while it also became clear to

her that the FBI was keeping an eye on her, which meant that she
was considered a security risk. The same was true for Schumpeter,
who was primarily suspected of being pro-German. But even though
the FBI investigated the Schumpeters rather thoroughly, no evidence
was ever found that either of them had done anything illegal.[34]

For a long time Elizabeth tried to find out who her enemies were
in Washington and why she did not get the government job, but she
never succeeded.[35] She continued for a while to write articles and
give public speeches about the economic and political problems
of Japan. But few were interested in her viewpoint and after a
while she withdrew from these activities. Increasingly, she helped
Schumpeter in his research and writings. In particular, she assisted
him with material for *Capitalism, Socialism and Democracy* and the
Lowell Lectures.

Schumpeter appreciated Elizabeth's support, but it was not
enough to stop him from plunging into a deep depression during the
war. If one follows Schumpeter's diary from the 1930s and onwards,
there is a noticeable change in tone in the early 1940s. While in the
1930s Schumpeter had mainly been concerned with how to muster
forces for his work ('Oh, give me passion for my task!'), in the early
1940s he began seriously to question the meaning of life and to think
about death.[36] In the 1930s Schumpeter had shown a certain appetite
for life, even though he felt that he should repress it and concentrate
on his work. He had, for example, toyed with the idea of writing a
novel or a play. ('A few plays and novels bubble in my brain – well, I
suppose I better do my work.')[37] Nothing came of these plans, except
for a few pages on a projected novel called *Ships in Fog* (reproduced in Appendix II). Sometimes, however, Schumpeter wrote autobiographical poems, and the following one from the 1930s captures
his mood during this decade quite well:

> Waving weary through my day
> like a cab horse tired of trotting
> everything is gray and low
> and my plans are lying rotten
> steam of energy wont flow
> I am far from being gay
>
> But the day wears on and on
> and our task goes with another
> Why should after all I bother
> . . .
> And it is not so bad.[38]

In the 1940s, however, Schumpeter's mood changed and he now
became increasingly preoccupied with his own death. In 1941 he
wrote the following poem:

My death comes like the servant
who walks about the room to blow out the candles
after the feast.
Wouldn't do to blow them earlier
While life and joy goes on.
Wouldn't do to leave them burning
After the feast.
So it's all right.
It would have been a pity
to have blown them out before.
But neither should they go on burning
After the feast.[39]

The idea that his death was imminent had haunted Schumpeter before and it now returned with full force. There is entry after entry in his private diary about death; how death is coming soon and how he welcomes death. 'Death is much in evidence', he wrote in December 1941.[40] Sometimes he elevated his premonition of death into an aphorism – 'death is involuntary as pleasure', 'the essential fact about life is death' – and sometimes he fused it with his scholarship: 'The doctor who is dying and who puts down the symptoms – *that* is man at his best.'[41] Another note in his diary reads: 'The truth is that the will to live is dying within me.'[42]

The idea of death also made Schumpeter look at his own life and try to sum it up. One day, for example, he carefully went through his main interests in life and enumerated them to himself: 'Women – Art – Sport – Science – Politics – Travel – Money'.[43] Often he felt that his life had been a waste; he had been 'worthless', 'frivolous', 'vain' and a 'snob'.[44] Schumpeter knew he had made a mark on economics, but that was not enough – he still felt like a failure. What especially plagued him was his lack of leadership qualities; he might be famous all right, but other economists did not look to him for solutions. One entry begins like this:

funny, when I survey my life and my present situation I see that I was favored in many respects and I also see a mosaic of many successes. Yet, as a whole and in a worldly sense, and quite apart (tho' perhaps not so 'apart' after all) from the fact that subjectively I was unhappy most of the time, it was a failure. And the reason is quite clear – even in my scientific activity and in spite of an 'oeuvre', a fraction of what would have been enough for 'fame', I do not carry weight.

The rest of the entry is hard to decipher but it is clear that Schumpeter felt he did not carry weight because he lacked 'leaderly' qualities; he was 'a man without an aura' and 'without an antenna'.[45] 'I lack the quality of leadership', he gloomily noted, and 'with a fraction of my ideas a new economics could have been founded.'[46] In the end, however, Schumpeter does not seem to have minded. He felt that he was going to die soon and from the perspective of death these matters lost much of their importance. All he wanted was 'coexistence with the All', as he wrote in his diary in 1942.[47]

II

It would be wrong to take some of the more outrageous statements Schumpeter made during the Second World War, when he was embittered and off balance, and present these as his political philosophy. There exists a certain continuity to Schumpeter's political philosophy from the First World War onwards; and it is this philosophy that needs to be assessed if we are to understand the political analysis in *Capitalism, Socialism and Democracy*. No general study of Schumpeter's political philosophy exists as of yet. It is, however, possible to gain a fairly good picture of the development of Schumpeter's political ideas by just going through his articles from the 1910s onwards. The Lowell Lectures are especially interesting in this context since they contain a detailed analysis of the interwar period. Schumpeter's political ideas during the First World War are well known today through his secret memoranda from 1916 to 1917, which were discussed in chapter 3. We also know something about Schumpeter's political stance in 1919, when he was finance minister; and we are familiar with many of his provocative statements during the Second World War. But there exists a gap for most of the period between the wars, and it is primarily this gap that the following account will try to fill.

A certain continuity to Schumpeter's political philosophy exists from the First World War onwards; throughout his life he would basically stand by the beliefs that he had expressed during the Great War. What Schumpeter's political opinions were like before the First World War, we do not know. During the war, however, he defined himself as a conservative, as a nationalist, as pro-British and as a royalist. Throughout his life Schumpeter would continue to identify with conservatism (albeit his own rather odd brand of conservatism), but never with fascism nor with Nazism. He would also remain a nationalist; Austria should in his opinion be an independent country and not part of Germany or under German domination in any way. During the First World War Schumpeter had urged the Emperor to look to England and its tory democracy for inspiration. And many years later he would still proclaim that England had 'the very best political system'.[48] As to Schumpeter's royalism, it is true that after the First World War he felt that it was unrealistic to continue to be a royalist; Austria had become a republic and the Empire was gone for good. 'I liked those times [before the war]', as he said in one of the Lowell Lectures, 'but since there is no use in wishful thinking, I realize that that world is dead and buried and there is no way back to it.'[49] Still, an important component of Schumpeter's political philosophy was precisely his longing for the world that had existed before the First World War; and we can only understand his hatred for the new world that emerged after 1918 if we remember that he always compared it in his mind to the days of the Empire. Schumpeter's political ideas merged very strongly at this point with his cultural likes and dislikes. He was disgusted by the post-war world, which he would describe in terms like the following: 'All standards were lowered in everything, art – witness dadaism and the expressionist excesses – and sexual morals included, down to rules of civilized behavior in private life. A world had crashed. A Jazz civilization emerged. And this was so everywhere.'[50] At one point in the 1930s Schumpeter referred to his allegiance to something he called 'cultivated conservatism'; and this term no doubt captures something essential in Schumpeter's political philosophy with its mixture of traditional conservative beliefs and cultural preference for the bourgeois world as it had existed before the First World War.[51]

Even though Schumpeter participated in a government led by the Austrian Social Democrats in 1919, he always detested socialism. His behaviour as a finance minister, for example, only makes sense if we assume that he stuck to his conservative ideology and his belief that Austria should be independent of Germany and close to the Western powers, especially England. Even though Schumpeter was convinced that the long-term trend was towards socialism, he felt very strongly that the time was not yet ripe. This was true for Austria as well as for Germany, and even more so for Russia.[52] The Soviet Union, as Schumpeter saw it, had introduced socialism through a coup d'état and could only maintain it with the help of a repressive army. Lenin was 'a bloodstained mongol despot' and the Soviet Union an example of oriental despotism.[53] By the late 1920s the Soviet Union had become a powerful state and there was little chance that it would fall apart by itself. In the 1920s Schumpeter feared that Russia would expand and he was very disappointed by 'England's failure to bring the powers of Europe into line against Bolshevism'.[54] This disappointment, it should be noted, was not only inspired by Schumpeter's fear of socialism. He also detested the Slavs as an ethnic group and was worried about their high birthrate. In one of the Lowell Lectures, he gloomily predicted that 'white humanity, if it keeps to its behavior, will maintain itself – only they will all be Russian some day; all others are going to die out.'[55]

As to Austria, Schumpeter bemoaned the 'wanton destruction' by the Allied powers of the Austro-Hungarian Empire through the peace treaties after the First World War.[56] If the Empire had been kept intact by the victorious nations, he argued, it could have become an effective counterweight to Germany. Instead, they had created 'the little wreck of a state that the victors persisted in calling Austria'.[57] The political and economic structure of the new Austria was quite peculiar. On the one hand, there was Vienna which was a huge urban enclave and a sophisticated financial centre. On the other hand, there was just the countryside plus a handful of large industries. For many years, Schumpeter said, a kind of balance existed between these two parts: the countryside was conservative while Vienna was run in a very competent manner by the Social Democrats. In February 1934, however, when the Austrian Chancellor Dollfuss suddenly made an armed attack on the Social Democrats, this balance was destroyed. Schumpeter was very worried by this development and he was convinced that, 'if the Nazis should come into power, Austria would be governed from Berlin.'[58] Schumpeter despised the Austrian Nazis and was very upset by the Anschluss in 1938. It was understandable, he felt, that many Austrians would want to join Germany since the new Austria mainly consisted of ethnic Germans. Still, the Anschluss was a disaster for independent Austria.

As an Austrian, Schumpeter always had mixed feelings towards Germany. On the one hand, he admired German culture and its people. But, on the other hand, he feared that Germany, by virtue of its superior economic and military strength, would dominate Austria. It would have been a good idea, he thought, if the Allied powers had decided to clip Germany's wings a bit by giving Eastern Prussia to Poland.[59] However that may be, Schumpeter also felt that Germany had been severely mistreated in the peace negotiations after the First World War. The victorious nations, he said, had behaved abominably; they just 'drew up a plan for how to divide the loot'.[60] Germany clearly got a rough deal in many ways, including the decision that it must disarm. This decision meant 'national dishonor' for Germany. 'But again the arrow was turned round in the wound by the fact that, rightly or wrongly, the Germans understood that their disarmament was to be part of a scheme of general disarmament and that the world for the time being was obviously not prepared to give effect to this plan.'[61] The reparations imposed on Germany were a form of 'economic warfare'. They forced Germany into autarchy, Schumpeter felt, in the same way that Roosevelt would later encourage militarism in Japan through economic sanctions.

When Schumpeter left Germany in September 1932 he had no inkling of Hitler's seizure of power the next year.[62] Indeed, a few years before, he had written an article on Germany where he emphatically stated that no political catastrophe was on the horizon and that increased stability was to be expected.[63] Schumpeter would later acknowledge that 'it is not much to my credit as a political analyst that I had no idea whatsoever of Hitler's impending rise to power.'[64] Still, one should not exaggerate Schumpeter's misreading of the situation. It is, for example, clear that he had a sense that a new world war was brewing. In a speech he made at Yale University in 1928 on 'The Problem of Europe', he stressed that 'it is impossible to deny the existence of the danger of a new catastrophe, from which European culture may or may not emerge.'[65]

In the United States Schumpeter soon became very critical of Roosevelt and the New Deal. He particularly feared that the Depression would do to the United States what the First World War had done to Europe, namely accelerate the inevitable trend towards socialism. In private as well as in public Schumpeter advocated that the Depression must run its course; and that one should not interfere with the workings of the business cycle.[66] 'Recovery is sound only if it does come of itself', as Schumpeter phrased it in a book that he co-authored with some of his Harvard colleagues, who were generally regarded as equally hostile to the New Deal.[67] In his private correspondence from the 1930s Schumpeter often made violent attacks on Roosevelt, and he was especially afraid that Roosevelt would get the United States involved in the war. The United States should in his opinion stay out of the war; Europe was ready for a readjustment – the Versailles Treaty was unacceptable – but that was none of America's business. A war would also accelerate the drift towards socialism. As he wrote to a friend some months before Pearl Harbor:

> When I see how the government [in the United States] goes about defense and when I consider what kind of fiscal policy and what kind of government control over industry is likely to emerge once the President becomes absolute on our entry into the war, I cannot help feeling that this will be the end of the American way of life. A ten-year's war and a ten-year's Roosevelt dictatorship will completely upset the social structure. That the likes of us will disappear from the picture is, of course, in itself of small moment.[68]

When news reached the United States of Hitler's accession to power in March 1933 Schumpeter did not know how to react. In the summer of 1932, when he was about to leave Bonn, he had said in a farewell speech that Germany was facing 'catastrophe or glory' in the near future.[69] In March 1933 he repeated this opinion in a letter to Haberler: 'As to Germany, I find it very difficult to form an opinion. Recent events may mean a catastrophe but they also may mean salvation.'[70] But even if Schumpeter was not sure of how to react in his own mind, he was quickly angered by the attacks on Hitler in the American press. Personally he had contempt for Hitler and thought that Hitlerism was a kind of religion, but he did not like to see Hitler criticized in an indiscriminate manner.[71] 'I know something of the government which preceded Hitler's', he wrote in a letter in 1933, 'and I can only say that I am quite prepared to forgive him much by virtue of comparison.'[72] When German refugees began to arrive in the United States, Schumpeter helped them as much as he could. In his correspondence we find letter after letter written on behalf of former colleagues and other academics who needed help. Some people owed their careers to Schumpeter and perhaps their lives as well. But Schumpeter also felt uneasy about helping the refugees, most of whom were Jews. This comes out very clearly, for example, in the following letter, which was written as part of an attempt to form a committee to help German refugees:

In order to avoid what would be a very natural misunderstanding, allow me to state that I am a German citizen but not a Jew or of Jewish descent. Nor am I a thorough exponent of the present German government, the actions of which look somewhat differently to one who has had the experience of the regime which preceded it. My conservative convictions make it impossible for me to share in the well-nigh unanimous condemnation the Hitler Ministry meets with in the world at large. It is merely from a sense of duty towards men who have been my colleagues that I am trying to organise some help for them which would enable them to carry on quiet scientific work in this country should necessity arise.[73]

At the beginning of the war Schumpeter was convinced that Hitler would win.[74] For how long he thought this, is hard to tell. In one of his Lowell Lectures, delivered in March 1941, Schumpeter argued that there were two possibilities. One was that England would win the war. The other was that the world would split into four blocs: an Anglo-American bloc, a European bloc, a Russian bloc and a Japanese bloc. The European bloc – presumably Continental Europe led by Hitler's Germany – would have around 400 million people.[75] It would need some raw materials from abroad, but this problem could to a certain extent be solved by seizing Asia Minor. The four blocs, Schumpeter said, would be largely self-sufficient, but they would also trade with one another. From an economic viewpoint, the split of the world into four blocs was a perfectly feasible arrangement. It also implied, as Schumpeter saw it, 'a very tolerable future of international relations'. At some later point – probably in the spring of 1943 – Schumpeter realized that Hitler would lose; and he now became obsessed with the idea that the Bolsheviks would take over the world. Paul Samuelson has said that, 'when Schumpeter realized that he was wrong [about Hitler winning the war], he came increasingly of the opinion that the tragedy was that we fought the wrong enemy [and that] Stalin was the one who was going to pick up all the pieces at the end of the war.'[76] Judging by Schumpeter's notations in his private diary he was quite out of balance in 1945 when Hitler was finally defeated. He thought that the British and the Jews had won the war with the help of the United States. The whole thing was a 'Jewish victory' and the Americans had accomplished what Hitler had originally set out to do: to conquer the world.[77] He wrote in anger: 'The world civilization is at the mercy of a giant – in terrible armor – without a brain.'[78]

Because of the genocide of the Jews during the Second World War, it is important to establish whether Schumpeter was anti-semitic or not. There exists a multitude of stories about remarks Schumpeter made at one time or another about the Jews.[79] It was clearly not beneath him, either in anger or in jest, to make a crack about the Jews. When confronted with the accusation of being anti-semitic, Schumpeter however firmly denied it. 'Nor am I nor have I ever been an anti-Semite', as he once wrote to Ragnar Frisch.[80] According to Galbraith (who feels that Schumpeter was *not* anti-semitic), 'Schumpeter had a strongly ethnic vision of Jewish preeminence and monopoly of economic thought [and he] had a strong vision that Jewish intellectuals were imperialist.'[81] As Paul Samuelson has testified to, Schumpeter was also of the opinion that Jews were early 'bloomers'. While non-Jews would take some time to mature and show their talent, Jews were much faster and therefore had an unfair advantage in academic life.[82] In conclusion, one can say that Schumpeter had a series of prejudices about the Jews. He did not, however, incorporate these into his political philosophy. He would occasionally vent his personal rage against the Jews, especially when he was off balance and depressed, but this is also where he stopped.

If we sum up this overview of Schumpeter's political philosophy from the First World War till the end of the Second, it is clear that there exists a certain consistency to Schumpeter's views. From early on he was a nationalist, a conservative and an anglophile in political matters. If we wish to divide his political thought into periods, we can say that he was a conservative and a royalist during the First World War. After the war, till the early 1940s, he was a 'cultivated conservative', if by this term (used by Schumpeter to describe himself) we mean a conservative who longs for the world as it existed before the Great War. During much of the Second World War (roughly from 1941 and onwards) Schumpeter was angry and off balance; and his conservatism occasionally turned into reactionary fury. By this time, however, *Capitalism, Socialism and Democracy* had already been written, and this work is much more balanced in tone than most of Schumpeter's statements from 1941 to 1945. According to Galbraith, Schumpeter was 'the most sophisticated conservative of this century'.[83] Paul Samuelson has summed up Schumpeter's political philosophy in a less respectful way: 'For all his tone of objectivity, Schumpeter was a reactionary. But as Holmes said of Spengler, he is the kind of rascal who gives you a run for your money.'[84]

III

Capitalism, Socialism and Democracy is by far Schumpeter's most famous work; it keeps appearing in new editions, and as of 1990 it had been translated into sixteen languages, including Persian, Korean and Hindi. The famous part called 'Can Capitalism Survive?' was already written in 1935, when Schumpeter gave a speech with this title in Washington, DC. The main bulk of the book, however, was written in 1938–41. 'As soon as the proofs of his book on *Business Cycles* were out of his hands', Schumpeter wrote about himself in a grant application from 1940, 'he turned to the task of completing a little volume on certain problems of modern socialism.'[85] His wife, Elizabeth, describes the birth of *Capitalism, Socialism and Democracy* like this: 'After herculean labor, J.A.S. had finished his monumental *Business Cycles* in 1938 and sought relaxation in *Capitalism, Socialism and Democracy*, which he regarded as distinctly a "popular" offering that he expected to finish in a few months.'[86] But the book turned out to be more time-consuming than Schumpeter had thought, and, even though he was on leave from Harvard in 1940, the book could not be completed before some time in 1941. And at this stage it was not 'a little volume' any longer, but had grown into a volume of nearly 400 pages. When the book was published in 1942 it only received notice in a relatively small circle.[87] It was not until 1947, when the second edition appeared, that it was widely acclaimed. And in 1950, when the last edition appeared which Schumpeter had overseen, it was clear to everybody that *Capitalism, Socialism and Democracy* was a huge success. From the various prefaces that Schumpeter wrote, it is obvious that he was quite pleased that his book had received so much attention. Still, the fact that *Business Cycles*, which he had had such high hopes for, had been so ignored, while *Capitalism, Socialism and Democracy*, where Schumpeter's scientific ambitions were lower, was so popular, seems to have hurt him. Galbraith has said that, 'Schumpeter ... once told me that among his books this one [that is, *Capitalism, Socialism and Democracy*] inspired his special loathing. It lacked, he said, scientific depth and precision.'[88] Galbraith, however, sensed that this was not the only reason for Schumpeter's aversion: 'a more important reason was his vanity. This required that he disavow any work that had won a popular audience. He wrote for the elect.'

In his correspondence from 1939 to 1940 Schumpeter referred to *Capitalism, Socialism and Democracy* as 'a little volume ... on socialism'; and in the preface to the first edition he says that, 'this volume is the result of an effort to weld into a readable form the bulk of almost forty years' thought, observation and research on the subject of socialism.'[89] But, as the title of Schumpeter's book indicates, he ended up by taking on more topics than socialism. According to the original preface, there exist 'five central themes' in *Capitalism, Socialism and Democracy*: Marxism, the future of capitalism, the future of socialism, socialism and democracy, and the history of socialist parties.[90] That Schumpeter had difficulty in melding all of these topics into 'a well-balanced treatise', as he put it, is obvious to any reader of *Capitalism, Socialism and Democracy*. Schumpeter wrote: 'Links and bridges between them have been provided of course and something like systematic unity of presentation has, I hope, been achieved. But in essence they are – though not independent – almost self-contained pieces of analysis.'[91]

The first task that confronts the reader of *Capitalism, Socialism and Democracy* is to try to locate the central theme that underlies Schumpeter's analysis of these five topics. Here we shall suggest that this central theme is Schumpeter's concern with *the role of institutions in the economy*. As we know, Schumpeter felt that economic theory should deal with 'economic mechanisms' and economic sociology with 'economic institutions'. In most of Schumpeter's works the emphasis is on the 'economic mechanisms', but he also had the ambition to cover the whole economic phenomenon. The last chapter of *Theorie der wirtschaftlichen Entwicklung*, for example, was devoted to this topic; and Schumpeter also explicitly stated in *Business Cycles* that 'capitalism is ... essentially one process, with the whole earth as its stage.'[92] Schumpeter was somewhat ambivalent concerning how to go about an analysis of the whole economic phenomenon, and usually settled for a study of the institutions involved. These, it should be noted, were not only economic (such as property and contract) but could also be political or social; the only condition was that they were in some way related to the economy.

Capitalism, Socialism and Democracy exemplifies Schumpeter's profound interest in the different types of institutions that are part of economic life. In the part called 'Can Capitalism Survive?' (Part II), Schumpeter was mainly concerned with the fact that the economic institutions of capitalism were undergoing a radical change which threatened to undermine the whole system. The part entitled 'Can Socialism Work?' (Part III) addressed the question whether an economic system, based on socialist institutions, can function as efficiently as a market economy. In the part called 'Socialism and Democracy' (Part IV) Schumpeter tried to see if a socialist economy is compatible with the kind of political institutions that are necessary for there to be democracy. In 'The Marxian Doctrine' (Part I) Schumpeter suggested that the best way to approach Marx is to split up his work into different parts; one dealing with economic mechanisms ('Marx the Economist'), one dealing with institutions ('Marx the Sociologist'), and so on. Why Schumpeter included 'A Historical Sketch of Socialist Parties' (Part V) as the last part of *Capitalism, Socialism and Democracy*, is somewhat unclear. According to Schumpeter, one reason was that he wanted to provide a background to his earlier discussion of socialism in the book; he also said that he was fascinated by the way different types of socialist organizations are related to different strands of socialist thought. Finally, it may be noted that one of the most fascinating qualities of *Capitalism, Socialism and Democracy* is that Schumpeter does not always stick to his habitual separation of the economy into 'mechanisms' and 'institutions'. The reader is often not quite sure whether Schumpeter is talking about one or the other. On a deeper level, this raises the question whether this separation is not artificial – an interesting idea to keep in mind when one reads *Capitalism, Socialism and Democracy* or when one tries to evaluate Schumpeter's concept of a broad-based economic science.

The first part of *Capitalism, Socialism and Democracy* contains a famous analysis of Marxism. Schumpeter was the only economist of any stature in the United States who took Marxism seriously; and this is one reason why this section is of particular interest. Another reason is that it contains a provocative and novel interpretation of Marx. Schumpeter, as we know, had been fascinated by Marxism since his youth. As an economist, however, he had some difficulty in incorporating Marx into his analytical scheme, which was inspired by people like Walras and Böhm-Bawerk. This comes out very clearly in Schumpeter's history of economic thought from 1914, where the discussion of Marx is relegated to a giant, 4-page footnote which begins with the statement that 'it is not possible to produce a penetrating analysis of Marx's life-work within the framework of this study.'[93] The idea that one can split Marx's work into a sociological and an economic part is, however, already present here.[94] In the 1920s, Schumpeter touched upon Marx's work now and then, but mainly in his writings on socialism and not in his articles on economic theory.[95] Another attempt to deal with the question of how to incorporate Marx's ideas into economics, can be found in Schumpeter's famous preface from 1937 to the Japanese translation of *Theorie der wirtschaftlichen Entwicklung*. Schumpeter here says that he has slowly come to realize that his own project of producing 'a purely economic theory of economic change' is actually very similar to Marx's project: 'this idea and this aim are exactly the same as the idea and the aim which underlie the teachings of Karl Marx.'[96] Even though there clearly exist some differences between his own and Marx's theory, Schumpeter says, both shared 'a vision of economic evolution as a distinct process generated by the economic system itself'.[97]

The main novelty in *Capitalism, Socialism and Democracy*, in so far as Schumpeter's interpretation of Marx is concerned, is that Schumpeter had now discovered a way to handle Marx's ideas and relate them to his own view of economics. The way to do this, Schumpeter says (again following a suggestion by Weber), is to analyse Marx's work in terms of the general scheme of *Sozial-ökonomik*.[98] This means, first of all, that one has to conceptualize Marx's contribution in terms of economic theory, economic history, economic sociology and statistics. Marx's overall synthesis cannot be accepted since it fuses these four fields in an unacceptable manner and thereby fails to respect their individual independence. Indeed, it is exactly Marx's insistence on the unity of his ideas that makes it so hard to place him in the history of economics and to make use of his insights. But there exists a way to liberate the creativity inherent in Marx's ideas, Schumpeter says, and that is to split up his vision.

And this is exactly what Schumpeter proceeds to do in *Capitalism, Socialism and Democracy*. As to statistics, he notes that in Marx's days statistics was not much developed, so Marx did not have to struggle with this issue. On the other hand, Schumpeter was extremely impressed by Marx's knowledge of economic history and by the way he had integrated it with economic theory. Schumpeter wrote:

> Economists always have either themselves done work in economic history or else used the historical work of others. But the facts of economic history were assigned to a separate compartment. They entered theory, if at all, merely in the role of illustrations, or possibly of verifications of results. They mixed with it only mechanically. Now Marx's mixture is a chemical one; that is to say, he introduced them into the very argument that produces the results. He was the first economist of top rank to see and to teach systematically how economic theory may be turned into historical analysis and how the historical narrative may be turned into *histoire raisonnée*.[99]

Schumpeter devoted one special section to Marx's sociology and one to his economics. Schumpeter was clearly very impressed by Marx's sociology, especially his theory of classes and his 'economic interpretation of history'. Marx's sociological theory of classes, Schumpeter stressed, must however be separated from his economic theory of classes. Here Schumpeter repeated some of the ideas that he had first presented in his 1927 essay on social class, namely that while class is a classificatory concept in economic theory, it denotes a living reality in sociology. Schumpeter had also a very high opinion of Marx's 'economic interpretation of history', which he described as 'one of the greatest individual achievements of sociology'.[100] This particular theory boiled down to two major propositions: that the forms of production have a logic of their own, and that the forms of production determine the social structure, social attitudes and the like. Schumpeter was very much taken by Marx's ideas on this score and, as we know, the title he chose for his Lowell Lectures was 'An Economic Interpretation of Our Time'. He, however, did not accept Marx's idea that the economy determines the social structure and social attitudes. Just as the economy may influence the social structure, Schumpeter said, the social structure may influence the economy. There is in other words interaction and causation both ways. The reason for this is basically that once social structures and attitudes have come into existence, they tend to persist. To cite a memorable phrase from *Capitalism, Socialism and Democracy*: 'Social structures, types and attitudes are coins that do not readily melt.'[101]

Schumpeter appreciated Marx as an economist, but it is fair to say that he had a higher opinion of Marx's sociology than of his economics. Marx's labour theory of value was 'dead and buried'; his doctrine of surplus value 'untenable'; and he had no theory of business cycles – Marx's theory of accumulation was 'essentially prosperityless and depressionless'.[102] But what more than made up for all of these drawbacks, Schumpeter said, was that Marx had succeeded in developing a purely economic theory of change. As opposed to the static theory of Walras, Marx had created a kind of truly dynamic theory, which explained changes by the inner working of the economic system itself. According to Schumpeter, Marx was 'the first to visualize what even at the present time is still the economic theory of the future for which we are slowly and laboriously accumulating stone and mortar, statistical facts and functional equations'.[103]

In his discussion of Marx's economic and sociological ideas Schumpeter repeatedly pointed out that Marx had mixed economics and sociology in an unacceptable manner; they were 'wedded by force and neither of them could breathe'.[104] To make a synthesis in the social sciences was extremely difficult, Schumpeter said, and it could definitely not be accomplished simply by collapsing economic theory, sociology and history into one another. But this is exactly what Marx had done, and to a large extent this was also why Marxism was so popular. It basically responded to people's need for simplistic answers; and it provided a kind of *Ersatz* for religion. But what to so many activists and intellectuals was Marx's greatness was in reality his weakness; and in the last instance he had only succeeded in 'weaving together those extra-rational cravings which receding religion had left running about like masterless dogs, and the rationalistic and materialistic tendencies of the time ... which would not tolerate any creed that had no scientific or pseudo-scientific connotation'.[105] In brief, Marxism was a kind of religion, disguised as science.

The analysis of Marxism in *Capitalism, Socialism and Democracy* is followed by a long section entitled 'Can Capitalism Survive?' This is by far the most celebrated part of the book, and it is also the one that has generated the most research among economists. What has become known in the economics literature as 'the Schumpeterian hypothesis' – briefly defined as the proposition that monopoly furthers innovation – is developed here. It should also be noticed that Schumpeter's ambition in 'Can Capitalism Survive?' was essentially to complement *Business Cycles*. This latter work had ended with a statement that the institutional structure of capitalism was changing and that it was therefore necessary to extend the analysis beyond pure economics. And it is precisely this that Schumpeter attempts to do in this part of *Capitalism, Socialism and Democracy*: he looks at the institutional changes in capitalism and tries to determine how they will affect the economic processes or the economic mechanisms of capitalism.

There are two parts to Schumpeter's argument that capitalism is unlikely to survive. He first raises the question of whether capitalism, *from a purely economic point of view*, is likely to go under. His answer is 'no'. He then expands the analysis and looks at the institutions of capitalism. And when he does this, the answer changes. In the first part of the argument Schumpeter says that if we assume that the US economy will do as well during 1928–78 as it did during the 50 years preceding 1928, it will do very well indeed. Assuming a 2 per cent increase in output per year and a normal increase in population, Schumpeter says, we can safely predict that by 1978 Americans will be about twice as well off as they were in 1928. There is no evidence to support the idea that capitalism is running out of steam: whether we look at population, technology or vanishing investment opportunities in general, it is perfectly clear that capitalism still has a lot to give.

As part of his argument that capitalism is still very strong from a purely economic viewpoint, Schumpeter makes an attack on the idea that the competitive market is the key to the success of capitalism. Whatever welfare there exists today, he says, is mainly due to something else, namely the monopolistic practices of big business. The perfectly competitive market has never existed, Schumpeter says, and it never will. 'Perfect competition has at no time been more of a reality than it is at present.'[106] And if a perfectly competitive market did exist, it would not be very efficient anyway. The notion that a competitive firm would tend to maximize production in a perfectly equilibrated stationary condition, Schumpeter says, is 'almost, though not quite, irrelevant'.[107] The main reason for this is that in reality, as opposed to in economic theory, the economy always changes. New firms start up; old firms die out; new technologies are introduced; and so on. '*Capitalist reality is first and foremost a process of change*', as Schumpeter put it.[108] At this point Schumpeter also introduces his famous concept of 'creative destruction', by which he means that capitalism contains forces 'that incessantly revolutionize the economic structure *from within*, incessantly destroying the old one, incessantly creating a new one'.[109] A 'perennial gale of creative destruction' is going through capitalism.[110]

According to Schumpeter, monopolistic practices are often very positive for the economy. There are several reasons for this: only big corporations can afford the enormous investments that are needed for a new product, say a car; many risks can only be handled by big corporations; big business tends to attract 'the better brains'; and so on. What may look like a monopoly position is also in many cases something else. The mere thought that some other capitalist might discover a way to produce a merchandise cheaper or introduce a new technology has a disciplinary effect on big business. 'A monopoly position', as Schumpeter says, 'is ... no cushion to sleep on.'[111]

It is at this stage of his argument that Schumpeter develops the ideas that have become known in the literature as 'the Schumpeterian hypothesis'. By this term is actually meant two propositions, namely (1) that innovations tend to be more frequent in monopolistic industries than in competitive ones; and (2) that large firms are more innovative than small firms.[112] The first proposition can be broken down into a number of more precise hypotheses, for example that a firm with monopoly power is in a position to prevent imitation; and that a firm which can reap monopoly profits is better able to finance research and development. The idea that large firms are more innovative than small firms is also associated with Galbraith's book *American Capitalism* (1952). It entails, for example, the notion that a large firm is often in a position to finance more research and development than a small firm, and that it is easier for a large firm to exploit unforeseen innovations. Schumpeter's idea that there is a positive relationship between monopoly power and innovations has also inspired what is known in the economics literature as the 'demand-pull' hypothesis and the 'technology-push' hypothesis. The former emphasizes that innovations are often a response to an economic opportunity, while the latter focuses on the fact that innovations tend to grow out of a strong technical basis. To summarize all the research that has been done on the Schumpeterian hypothesis since the 1940s is obviously a difficult task. Yet, in a recent survey, an attempt was made by Morton Kamien and Nancy Schwartz, and they conclude that economic opportunity is more important than technological strength as a spur to innovation.[113] They also found convincing evidence that neither perfect competition nor monopoly are as conducive to innovations as a situation with moderate to large firms.

The main thrust of Schumpeter's argument in 'Can Capitalism Survive?' has, however, little to do with the Schumpeterian hypothesis and claims instead that capitalism is in the process of decline. There are many reasons why this is the case, according to Schumpeter, and most of them have to do with changes in the institutional structure of capitalist society. The feudal elements, for example, which have given bourgeois society a certain stability, are on their way to disappearing. And the huge corporations, which are so efficient in many ways, also help to undermine capitalism by eliminating the need for the individual innovator through their giant research and development departments. There is less and less room in modern society, in other words, for the type of entrepreneur that Schumpeter had celebrated in his early works. The huge corporations also tend to be run by managers, who have little in common with the old type of entrepreneur. In terms of mentality, Schumpeter said, the modern manager lives in a totally different world; he is basically 'just another office worker'.[114]

Not only the capitalist firm, but also such institutions as property and contract are in the process of decline, according to Schumpeter. The old-fashioned capitalist had a direct and physical relationship to his property; he would walk around in his factory and touch the walls, just like a peasant would smell the earth. Today, however, you own shares and not concrete objects; and the property owner is being replaced by distant shareholders. During the nineteenth century, the institution of the contract was also quite different from what it is today. In those days, you made a contract that was valid as long as the two parties agreed. Today, on the other hand, the original capitalist contract is being replaced by such oddities as the modern labour contract, where the two parties are bound to each other in a very different manner and for an indefinite period. In general, Schumpeter said, there exists an attitude of hostility in bourgeois society to capitalism. This hostility is fanned by the ever-increasing number of intellectuals, who are all basically resentful of capitalism. The intellectuals do not form a class of their own, according to Schumpeter, but they like to spearhead other classes and tell workers what to think. As a result, demoralization is spreading in capitalist society. The bourgeoisie is also being undermined by its own defeatist attitude and general lack of vitality. While having a family had been perfectly self-evident to the nineteenth-century bourgeoisie, today's members of the ruling class often look at children in terms of costs. They thereby introduce 'a sort of inarticulate system of cost accounting' into their private life, as Schumpeter noted with clear distaste.[115] The twentieth-century bourgeoisie is also convinced that all people are equal; and its members prefer to live in simple apartments rather than in the kind of house that is suitable for a true industrialist. Today's bourgeoisie, Schumpeter said, is not ready to fight for its rights; it does not even dare to 'say boo to a goose'.[116] 'The only explanation for the meekness we observe is that the bourgeois order no longer makes any sense to the bourgeoisie itself and that, when all is said and nothing is done, it does not really care.'[117] The bourgeoisie is in a stage of 'decomposition', Schumpeter gloomily concluded.

Schumpeter's analysis of capitalism in *Capitalism, Socialism and Democracy* is usually applauded for being both brilliant and insightful, even if it is also realized that it was probably wrong on a number of points.[118] Schumpeter's analysis of socialism in the same book, however, has not attracted much attention. Gary Becker, for example, rejects Schumpeter's analysis of socialism as 'naive'.[119] And, according to Gottfried Haberler, it constitutes 'the most controversial and ... questionable part of Schumpeter's book'.[120] Here we shall argue the opposite of Becker and Haberler: that Schumpeter's analysis of socialism is insightful, occasionally wise and always thought-provoking. This is true when it comes to the analysis of the economic institutions as well as the political institutions of socialism.

Schumpeter emphasized very strongly that socialism is possible only if the capitalist system has exhausted itself. If that is the case, we will have 'socialization in a state of maturity'.[121] If not, there will be 'socialization in a state of immaturity'. This is an important distinction to Schumpeter. By capitalism exhausting itself, he essentially meant that the economic potentials of capitalism have been realized. The economy now consists of a small number of giant corporations, which run everything in a very efficient but mechanical manner. Entrepreneurs have become ordinary managers and innovations are mainly carried out within the giant corporations. The rate of interest is converging towards zero and the whole economic system is becoming increasingly static. This does not mean that the capitalist machine will stop – but it no longer changes.

It is in this historical situation (which Schumpeter felt was not very far off in the 1930s and the 1940s) that socialism has a real chance. Both 'things and souls' are now ready for socialism.[122] The majority of the people in all social classes will peacefully cooperate in the transition to socialism, and it is very unlikely that there will be a violent revolution. The transition to socialism will go 'firmly, safely and gently', and there will only be 'a minimum of loss of energy and injury to cultural and economic values'.[123] Those who are trained to run the economy will support the new state of things in a positive spirit: 'there will be a group of experienced and responsible men ready to put their hands to the helm.'[124]

But if 'things and souls' are not ready, and if capitalism has not exhausted itself, then the situation is very different. In a state of immaturity, there might very well be a chance for a socialist party to take power by force. But if it does this, there will be plenty of difficulties. Things and souls will have to be forced, since many social groups will not be ready to cooperate. There will be 'ruthless treatment' and 'criminal ferocity towards opponents' from the new government's side.[125] The Soviet Union was in Schumpeter's mind a perfect example of a society which had attempted a transition in a state of immaturity. That the Bolsheviks had succeeded in seizing power was little but 'a fluke' and a sign of the occasional 'freakishness of ... history'.[126] Lenin's internationalism testified in Schumpeter's mind to his insight that socialism would never succeed in the Soviet Union on its own: it desperately needed the support of socialist revolutions in other countries. Stalin, on the other hand, was just a nationalist and a 'modernized tsar'. Stalin had realized that there had to be 'millions of victims' if the Soviet form of 'alleged socialism' was to survive – and he was willing to pay that price.[127]

The rest of Schumpeter's argument about socialism is phrased as a sharp rebuttal to three common objections to socialism: that socialism is impossible because it violates the logic of economic analysis; that human nature is such that socialism will never work; and that socialists will not be able to handle a complex modern economy. That socialism would be incompatible with economic theory is firmly rejected by Schumpeter. There is no reason to believe that economists like Ludwig von Mises are right when they argue that socialism will not work since rational economic behaviour presupposes markets and these supposedly only exist in capitalist societies. Perfectly satisfactory economic theorems for socialist economies have been worked out by people like Enrico Barone, Schumpeter says, and it is clear that a rational socialist economic system with its own equivalents to prices, salaries and markets can be constructed.

Indeed, there are good reasons, according to Schumpeter, to believe in the *superiority* of the socialist economy as compared to the capitalist economy. Business cycles with their disturbing ups and downs will, for example, be eliminated, and business firms will be operating in an atmosphere of much less uncertainty. There will also be much less unemployment, since there will be no depressions and since the government will be in a position to deal more effectively with technological unemployment. All this amounts to 'a strong case for believing in the superior economic efficiency [of socialism]'.[128]

The second objection to socialism that Schumpeter takes up for discussion has to do with human nature. The way some socialists talk about socialist society, he says, one would think that human beings have to be 'demigods and archangels' for it to work.[129] But this is not the case; and socialism is perfectly feasible with human nature as it is. This, however, does not mean that 'human nature'

1 Schumpeter in 1898 at the age of 15 at Theresianum. (Courtesy of the Harvard University Archives.)

2 The House in Triesch where Schumpeter was born in 1883. It is now a run-down grocery store. (Courtesy of Professor Yuichi Shionoya.)

3 Schumpeter in 1909 at the age of twenty-six, just after having finished his first book in economics. (Courtesy of the Harvard University Archives.)

4 Schumpeter in 1919 as finance minister. (Courtesy of the National-bibliothek, Vienna.)

5 Annie Reisinger, Schumpeter's second wife and great love. (Courtesy of the Harvard University Archives.) This entry (in Gabelsberger shorthand) is from October 1931 and begins: 'O Mutter und Herrin—o seid über mir. Und lasst mich nicht blamieren in der Mathematik' ('Oh, Mother and Mistress—please protect me. And let me not make a fool of myself in mathematics').

6 Schumpeter in high spirits, probably in his home in Bonn around 1925. (Courtesy of the Harvard University Archives.)

7 Schumpeter at work, probably in his home in Bonn around 1930. (Courtesy of the Harvard University Archives.)

8 Schumpeter, probably around 1[...]
Archives.)

9 Schumpeter in 1935 at Harvard University. (Courtesy of the Harvard University Archives.)

10 Schumpeter during the difficult years of World War II. Photograph taken in 1943. (Courtesy of the Harvard University Archives.)

11 Elizabeth Boody Schumpeter, Schumpeter's third wife. (Courtesy of the Harvard University Archives.)

Elizabeth B. Schumpeter

12 The house at 7 Acacia Street in Cambridge, Massachusetts, where Schumpeter lived with Elizabeth during 1938–1950. (Courtesy of the Harvard University Archives.)

13 Schumpeter in the Harvard Yard, with Memorial Church in the background, late 1940s. (Courtesy of the Harvard University Archives.) The quote comes from Schumpeter's private diary in June 1948: 'We all of us like a sparkling error better than a trivial truth.'

(cautiously defined by Schumpeter as fundamental patterns of human behaviour) can be ignored. 'We had better realize from the start that exclusive reliance on a purely altruistic sense of duty is as unrealistic as would be a wholesale denial of its importance and its possibilities.'[130] People always need some form of social recognition and prestige; and this is not something that is unique to capitalism. What is unique to capitalism is merely the form that 'the prestige motive' takes, namely that people in capitalist society want to be rewarded with huge sums of money.[131] In a socialist society the prestige motive would therefore have to be reconditioned: 'successful performers may conceivably be satisfied nearly as well with the privilege – if granted with judicious economy – of being allowed to stick a penny stamp on their trousers as they are by receiving a million a year.' And it probably would work: 'Why not? Trotsky himself accepted the Order of the Red Flag.'[132]

The last major objection to socialism that Schumpeter discusses is that socialism would not be able to cope with the complexity of a modern economy. But there exists a perfect remedy for this complexity, Schumpeter says, and there is no reason why the socialists would not use it: *bureaucracy*. The idea that bureaucracies are efficient and competent, Schumpeter says, goes against the grain of what most people think. Does not the very term 'bureaucracy' evoke inefficiency, 'red tape' and the like? But this is just superficial, Schumpeter says, and bureaucracy has a worse reputation than it deserves, a little bit like monopoly. In reality, a bureaucratic machine is very efficient, and it is just impossible to imagine a socialist or a capitalist economy being run without the help of huge organizations. When capitalism is exhausted, socialism will also inherit the very competent bureaucracies of the huge corporations; and with their help the socialist economy will be run in a most efficient manner. Indeed, there is good reason to believe that socialism, by eliminating some inefficiencies, will eventually produce even more competent economic bureaucracies than the huge capitalist corporations. In Schumpeter's formulation:

> the whole of our argument may be put in a nutshell by saying that socialization means a stride beyond big business on the way that has been chalked out by it or, what amounts to the same thing, the socialist management may conceivably prove as superior to big-business capitalism as big-business capitalism has proved to be to the kind of competitive capitalism of which the English industry of a hundred years ago was the prototype.[133]

It is important to stress that for Schumpeter it was perfectly conceivable that socialism could be democratic. He defined socialism as 'an institutional pattern in which the control over the means of production and over production itself is vested with a central authority', and there is nothing in this definition that says anything about the political character of socialism.[134] Indeed, 'a society may be fully and truly socialist and yet be led by an absolute ruler or be organized in the most democratic of all possible ways; it may be aristocratic or proletarian; it may be a theocracy and hierarchic or atheist and indifferent to religion' and so on.[135] Schumpeter referred to this fact as 'the cultural indeterminateness of socialism'.[136]

What makes Schumpeter's ideas on the possibility of a 'socialist democracy' even more interesting is that they are connected to his famous theory of democracy, which forms the magnificent centrepiece of the political analysis in *Capitalism, Socialism and Democracy*. Schumpeter, as we know, develops his own theory of democracy in contrast to what he called 'the classical doctrine of democracy'. This latter theory is more or less synonymous with the eighteenth-century philosophy of democracy; and it is defined in the following way by Schumpeter: 'the democratic method is that institutional arrangement for arriving at political decisions which realizes the common good by making the people itself decide issues through the election of individuals who are to assemble in order to carry out its will.'[137] The focus in this type of democratic theory is primarily on 'the common good' of the people. This common good will be realized via the individuals who have been elected; and their task is therefore to carry out the will of the people.

To Schumpeter the classical doctrine of democracy has many flaws. For one thing, it is unrealistic and bound to give birth to dangerous illusions. For example, what exactly is this 'common good' of the people? Schumpeter's own answer is that the common good does not exist, since it is bound to mean different things to different people. The very notion of a common good is also impossibly confused in his opinion. It presupposes that we can know what an individual 'really' wants; that we then can add up all these 'true' opinions; and that they merge into a single 'common good' (and not just into a majority of opinions, which is something different). All of this is preposterous according to Schumpeter. He also points out that in the classical doctrine of democracy, the politician hardly exists; there are only representatives of the people who do what they are told and who see to it that the common good is properly realized. Anyone who knows anything about politics knows that this is nonsense; politicians have interests of their own.

Schumpeter's own, alternative theory of democracy is defined in the following way: 'the democratic method is that institutional arrangement for arriving at political decisions in which individuals acquire the power to decide by means of a competitive struggle for the people's vote.'[138] We notice immediately the difference between this definition and the earlier definition of the classical doctrine of democracy. While the latter emphasizes democracy as a value and underplays democracy as a method, Schumpeter's own definition does exactly the opposite. He makes no bones about the fact that democracy in his mind is primarily a way of electing candidates and of handing over the power to them. The voters can indeed choose to elect a certain candidate at one point in time and then withdraw their support at another time. But as long as the candidate is in parliament, it is the candidate and not the voters who has the power. 'The voters ... must understand that once they have elected an individual, political action is his business and not theirs.'[139] 'Political back-seat driving' is not possible.

Schumpeter sometimes refers to his theory of democracy as a 'theory of competitive leadership'. This captures an important part of it, namely that for Schumpeter the politician always has his own interests, which are distinct from those of the voters. As Schumpeter sees it, the politician produces democracy in about the same way as a merchant satisfies the needs of his customers – indirectly and as a byproduct. Paraphrasing Adam Smith, one can say that, according to Schumpeter, we do not owe our daily democratic system to the personal convictions of the Liberal, the Conservative and the Socialist, but to their egoistic interests as politicians. What drives a politician is in Schumpeter's mind not the same as that which drives a business man; it is power and not money. But the result is the same. The politician collects votes like the businessman pursues dollars. At one point in *Capitalism, Socialism and Democracy* Schumpeter cites a politician as saying, 'What businessmen do not understand is that exactly as they are dealing in oil so I am dealing in votes.'[140] There is clearly only a short step from this type of reasoning to the analysis of the Public Choice School – a step Schumpeter incidentally did not want to take.[141] The notion that one can use economic theory to solve problems in political science was totally against Schumpeter's principles; there was also the fact that political science has its own, very useful tradition for problem-solving.

The most neglected part of all in *Capitalism, Socialism and Democracy* is probably the one that deals with the possibility of having a socialist democracy. Schumpeter, as we already know, felt that socialism could be despotic as well as democratic. The way he outlined the general structure of a socialist democracy shows, however, that he took it quite seriously. A general condition for a socialist democracy to be introduced is that society has reached a certain level of economic and social development; a successful transition to a socialist democracy can only take place in 'a state of maturity'. The argument that democracy has its origin in capitalist society, Schumpeter said, does not mean that it will vanish together with capitalism:

The present-day forms and organs of democratic procedure are as much the outgrowth of the structure and the issues of the bourgeois world as is the fundamental principle of democracy itself. But this is no reason why they should have to disappear along with capitalism. General elections, parties, parliaments, cabinets and prime ministers may still prove to be the most convenient instruments for dealing with the agenda that the socialist order may reserve for political decisions.[142]

Schumpeter's ideas on socialist democracy are first of all to be found in a section of *Capitalism, Socialism and Democracy* entitled 'Democracy in the Socialist Order'.[143] From this and a few other places in the book it is possible to reconstruct the broad institutional structure of Schumpeter's socialist democracy (see figure 7.1). There would first of all have to be general and recurrent elections in which different political parties compete. The government would include a Ministry of Production (or a Central Board), responsible for the economy. The government would decide on such issues as the amount of investment and then hand them over for execution to the Ministry of Production. The latter would be in charge of developing a concrete plan within this framework. That the Ministry of Production must not have unlimited power over the economy is clear from two features of Schumpeter's plan. First, there may exist a special supervisory and checking authority ('a kind of *cour des comptes*'), which may have the right to veto decisions by the Ministry of Production.[144] The Ministry is also primarily a political organ and should therefore not interfere with the actual workings of the economic institutions. It 'controls and coordinates' the Industrial Managing Boards (or industrial managers), but it will allot substantial freedom to them. 'Almost any amount of freedom might be left to the "men on the spot"', Schumpeter says.[145] Inside the individual factories, however, there is only one will that counts: that of the manager. Schumpeter always felt that industrial democracy was sheer folly, and he often said that one of the great advantages with socialism was that it allowed you to impose much more discipline on the workers than you could ever hope to do in capitalism.[146]

Schumpeter was convinced that the economy could be managed in a perfectly efficient manner in a socialist democracy. He stressed that there would probably be clashes between different economic interests in socialist society, but that these would be less difficult to deal with than in capitalist society. 'Political life would be purified [in socialism].'[147] But he also foresaw special dangers in a socialist democracy. 'The task of keeping the democratic course', he said, 'may prove to be extremely delicate.'[148] This was especially due to one structural fact: the concentration of power is very high in socialist society. As soon as there is a political crisis, Schumpeter felt,

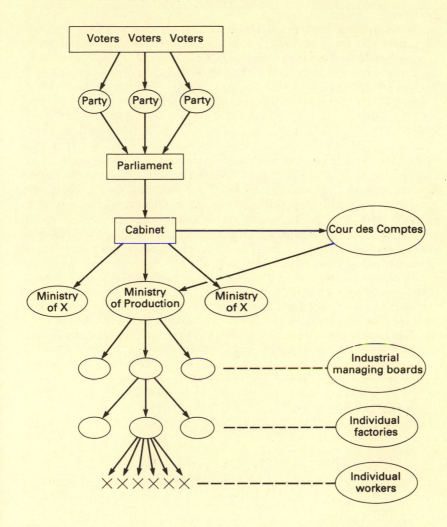

Figure 7.1 Schumpeter's blueprint for a socialist democracy.
(*Source*: Joseph A. Schumpeter, *Capitalism, Socialism and Democracy* (1942–50),
especially the section 'Democracy in the Socialist Order'.)

there would be a temptation for the politicians to extend their power illegitimately and thereby end the political democracy. From an economic viewpoint, as we know, it was good that there was strict discipline in the factories. But the politicians might also exploit this discipline in various undemocratic ways. 'Socialist democracy', Schumpeter summed up, has as much chance – or even more of a chance – than 'capitalist democracy' to end up 'as a sham'.[149]

Schumpeter made such a vigorous case for socialism in *Capitalism, Socialism and Democracy* that one reviewer declared outright that 'Schumpeter is a socialist.'[150] This, of course, is not true. It does, however, testify to the fact that Schumpeter had played the devil's advocate in a rather convincing manner. Some of his arguments for monopoly were in all likelihood also a bit tongue in cheek. Confronted with the accusation that he never told the reader what should be done about things, Schumpeter responded in the preface to the second edition of *Capitalism, Socialism and Democracy* that the book had been written in order to make the reader *think*:

> We resent a call to thinking and hate unfamiliar argument that does not tally with what we already believe or would like to believe. We walk into our future as we walked into the war, blindfolded. Now this is precisely where I wanted to serve the reader. *I did want to make him think*. And in order to do so it was essential not to divert his attention by discussions about what from any given standpoint 'should be done about it' which would have monopolized his interest. Analysis has a distinct task and to this task I wished to keep though I was fully aware of the fact that this resolve would cost me a great deal of the response a few pages of practical conclusions would have evoked.[151]

In the final analysis, it is also this particular quality of *Capitalism, Socialism and Democracy* – the capacity to make the reader look at familiar problems and facts with fresh eyes – that makes the book into the classic it has become. This is what Joan Robinson argued in her review from 1943 in *The Economic Journal*, which mixed critique with profound appraisal:

> The reader is swept along by the freshness, the dash, the impetuosity of Professor Schumpeter's stream of argument. But pause on the brink a moment and look around the contemporary scene. On reflection some rather large elements seem to be missing from the analysis. First, what about U.S.S.R. ... And then, what about Fascism? Does present-day experience really lead us to expect that capitalism is destined to a quiet and pious death? But, no matter whether it convinces or not, *this book is worth the whole parrot-house of contemporary orthodoxies, right, left, or centre.*[152]

8

Last Years, Last Work

When queried about his future plans, Schumpeter leaned back in his swivel chair and said softly, 'My research program grows longer and my life shorter. My *History of Economic Analysis* drags, and I am always hunting other hares. Time presses upon one and I am not getting any younger, you know. The program drags.'
(Interview with Schumpeter in *The Harvard Crimson*, 1944)

During the years after the Second World War until his death on 8 January 1950, Schumpeter worked feverishly to complete his third great work while in the United States, the monumental *History of Economic Analysis*. He felt that he had little time left to live and he desperately wanted to finish the book before he died. What makes this book so special, however, is not only that Schumpeter takes on the enormous task of telling the full story of economics from the Greeks onwards, but that he also tried to sum up his own vision of what he felt that economics should be like. It is consequently in *History of Economic Analysis* that we find his most complete statement about *Sozialökonomik* and how it relates to the other social sciences, despite the fact that Schumpeter never quite succeeded in finishing the book. Another important development during these last years was that Schumpeter reformulated his theory of the entrepreneur. In a couple of essays, written towards the end of the 1940s, Schumpeter presented a new version of his theory of the entrepreneur. On several points this differs so much from the original theory from 1911 (which had been brought up to date in 1926 in the second edition of *Theorie der wirtschaftlichen Entwicklung*) that we are justified in referring to it as *Schumpeter's last theory of the entrepreneur*.

I

After the war, Schumpeter more or less taught the same courses he had during the war: advanced economic theory, business cycles, economics of socialism, and history of economic thought. The new graduate students at Harvard, however, did not appreciate his teaching very much. They wanted to learn the new type of formalized economic theory and Schumpeter had very little to teach them on that score. Schumpeter appeared to them as something out of the past; as 'someone who could say "marginal utility" in seventeen languages', to cite one uncharitable comment.[1] The students felt that Schumpeter was past his prime and they were annoyed by his long-winded excursions about this or that fourteenth-century Italian economist.[2]

If one looks at Schumpeter's writings from these years, it is however clear that he was not past his prime at all. He was actually in a very creative stage of his life, tackling new problems and solving old ones. Still, it is clear that the broad and historical approach to economics that fascinated Schumpeter so much was increasingly out of tune with the times. This fact also accounts for some of the difficulties that Schumpeter encountered with his fellow economists at Harvard. It is true that he continued to annoy some of his colleagues, especially someone like Burbank, just by virtue of his personality. There was his customary 'lack of tact', his 'tendency towards exhibitionism', his 'desire to be the center of attention', and so on.[3] But there was also the fact that he was increasingly seeing things differently from his colleagues; and just as they felt put off by his wide and historical approach to economics, he felt estranged by their narrow-mindedness. In 1949, Schumpeter wrote to a colleague in Japan, 'I ... cannot say that I experience very much stimulus from my surroundings [at Harvard]. Scientifically, Leontief is the only man who is really alive and even he is now so much buried in administrative work, running the big research organization which he has built up, that not so very much remains of him either.'[4] Or, to cite Schumpeter's diary from about the same time: 'I give up Harvard. In this soil no more do any of my roses blossom.'[5]

As a result of this disenchantment with his colleagues in the economics department, Schumpeter turned elsewhere for inspiration. He, for example, got increasingly involved with Arthur H. Cole and his Research Center for Entrepreneurial Studies, which attracted an interesting mixture of people. He gave plenty of public lectures, and by the time of his death he was scheduled to give a lecture series at the Charles Walgreen Foundation, which was Chicago's equivalent to the Lowell Institute in Boston. After the war Schumpeter also started to travel abroad a little. As early as November 1945 he gave some lectures in Montreal, and in the winter of 1948 he visited Mexico, where he taught at the National University in Mexico City. By the time of his death, he was also scheduled to visit Europe. To go to Europe was a big decision for Schumpeter, and something he felt quite apprehensive about. As late as January 1949 he had written to von Beckerath, his old colleague at the University of Bonn, that 'I have simply not the moral courage to go to Europe because everything, beginning from bureaucratic vexations to the wanton ill-treatment of Germany, would keep me in a transport of indignation that would be very harmful to my blood pressure.'[6] In July 1949, however, Schumpeter was elected to be the first president of the newly founded International Economic Association. This was a great honour and Schumpeter was scheduled to visit the association's headquarters in Paris in 1950.

The fact that Schumpeter was elected president of the International Economic Association shows that even if he was not appreciated at Harvard, he was still very popular abroad. That many of his American colleagues also felt that he was a great economist became, however, clear in 1948 when he was elected president of the American Economic Association. Schumpeter appreciated this honour very much and put in a tremendous amount of work to organize the traditional annual meeting. As president of the American Economic Association Schumpeter was particularly interested in establishing better contacts between economics and the other social sciences, such as sociology and economic history. The result was a series of joint sessions at the annual meeting, which took place in December 1948 in Cleveland, Ohio. There was, for example, a roundtable in commemoration of the centenary of the Communist Manifesto ('The Sociology and Economics of Class Struggle').[7] One of the people who presented a paper here was Talcott Parsons, an old friend and admirer of Schumpeter.[8] For the economic historians Schumpeter had arranged a session entitled 'Possibilities for a Realistic Theory of Entrepreneurship'. The meeting in Cleveland was a success, and Schumpeter himself gave a celebrated presidential address on the role of ideology in economics, entitled 'Science and Ideology'.

Once the Second World War was over, Schumpeter's political attitudes softened considerably. By the end of 1945 a change in his thinking was already visible. At this time, as we have mentioned, he went to Montreal to give some lectures. The person who had arranged his trip was Emile Bouvier, a Jesuit priest who had been Schumpeter's student in the early 1940s. After his studies Bouvier had returned to Canada, where he became involved in a Catholic association for employers which advocated a corporatist ideology in the tradition of *Quadragesimo Anno* (1931) by Pope Pius XI. When

Schumpeter gave the key address at a meeting of this association on 19 November 1945, he surprised his audience of Canadian businessmen by coming out very strongly for just the kind of Catholic corporatism that Pope Pius XI had proclaimed in *Quadragesimo Anno*.[9] Society, Schumpeter said, was threatened by 'social decomposition' and lack of leadership, and the only solution was 'vocational associations'. 'The corporatist principle', he explained, allows for private property and competition as well as for cooperation and solidarity. Very importantly, it also avoids the danger of centralization that is inherent in socialism. What corporatism can give to society, and what society needs so desperately, is not social reform or economic reform, but '*moral reform*'. Schumpeter also made explicit and positive references to Catholic corporatism in *History of Economic Analysis* and in a speech he gave at the American Economic Association in December 1949.[10] During his last years Schumpeter, in other words, defined himself as a conservative thinker in the corporatist tradition.

Even though there is a more conciliatory tone to Schumpeter's political statements after the war, he was still a staunch conservative with a bit of a weakness for Germany. He strongly opposed the war crime trials, and he thought that the number of Jews who had been killed during the war was much inflated.[11] The big danger for the world, he wrote in 1946, was 'Russian imperialism' and he bemoaned the fact that the Allied troops had not turned on Russia once Hitler was defeated. 'Surely this is a case', he said, 'where a job half done is worse than nothing.'[12] Schumpeter was also very upset that while public opinion had been so quick to condemn Hitler, there was no equivalent fury over Stalin's gradual takeover of Europe. The European countries were exhausted and impoverished by the war, and this might explain their defeatist attitude towards Russia. The United States, on the other hand, did not have this excuse. But whatever the reason, no country was ready to stand up and counter Stalin's plans to take over Europe and Asia.

Schumpeter was also as disgusted as ever with social legislation and the liberals. He railed against the taxes: they amounted to a 'confiscation ... comparable with that effected by Lenin'; and he said that 'the present distribution of disposable incomes [in the United States] compares well with the one actually prevailing in Russia.'[13] In a speech entitled 'The March into Socialism', which Schumpeter gave at the American Economic Association in December 1949, he warned that the country was slowly becoming socialist. Schumpeter described this 'march into socialism' as 'the migration of people's economic affairs from the private into the public sphere', and he was particularly afraid that inflation would speed it up.[14]

About two weeks after Schumpeter gave the speech on 'The March into Socialism' he died. According to some people, he was writing up his notes for the speech on the evening before his death; according to others, he was working on the Walgreen Lectures, which he was scheduled to start delivering on 9 January 1950, the day after his death. Whichever is true, it is clear that Schumpeter died in the midst of a hectic and active working period and that he had plenty left to say. Schumpeter often used to tell his friends that he planned to write several books in his old age. First of all, there was the eternal book on money. In November 1949 Schumpeter promised S. E. Harris, who was editing a series of handbooks in economics, that by the summer of 1951 it would definitely be ready.[15] The title was to be *Theory of Money and Banking*. According to Elizabeth, Schumpeter was very serious about this ('he had taken out of the brown trunk, in which it was kept, the manuscript of the book on money, which he abandoned on his return from Europe at the end of the summer in either 1934 or 1935').[16] Wolfgang Stolper recalls that Schumpeter also had plans to write a novel on the theme of 'how a student who had flunked his exams shot his professor'.[17] It seems that the title would have been either *The Smile of the Idiot* or *Fun*. To John Kenneth Galbraith, Schumpeter wrote in 1948 that he was planning a book called *The Meaning of Conservatism* ('I am pretty sure that no conservative I have ever met would recognize himself in the picture I am going to draw').[18] And to Paul Samuelson, Schumpeter said that he planned to write 'a grand work on economic theory', 'a book on mathematical logic' and 'a sociological novel'. The last of these three works, Samuelson describes in the following way:

> As relaxation for really old age, he [that is, Schumpeter] spoke of writing a sociological novel in his eighties. He even once did field work on the latter: after a long and rather tiring walk, Mrs. Schumpeter with some difficulty persuaded him to ride on the subway back to Harvard Square. This, he reported, had been a very interesting experience; and what was more, when he came to write his sociological novel, he was going to do it again.[19]

II

Besides writing *History of Economic Analysis*, Schumpeter wrote about fifteen articles during the years 1945–50. Some of these are still very much worth reading, such as his superb portraits of Keynes and Pareto. What is most important about these articles, however, is that they contain what we earlier referred to as Schumpeter's last theory of the entrepreneur. By this we mean that during his last years Schumpeter reformulated his theory of the entrepreneur in such a way that we are justified in talking about a new version, if not a totally new theory, of entrepreneurship in his work. Schumpeter's reformulation is mainly to be found in three articles: 'The Creative

Response in Economic History' (1947), 'Theoretical Problems of Economic Growth' (1947) and 'Economic Theory and Entrepreneurial History' (1949).[20] A mention should also be made of a speech that Schumpeter gave before the National Bureau of Economic Research Conference on Business Cycles in 1949 and in which some of these ideas were presented in a very provocative form.[21]

There are already signs in Schumpeter's work from the late 1930s that he was dissatisfied with his theory of the entrepreneur, as formulated in *Theorie der wirtschaftlichen Entwicklung* (1911, 2nd edn 1926). This comes out very clearly in *Business Cycles*, where the emphasis is more on innovations than on the entrepreneur. The economic chapters in *Capitalism, Socialism and Democracy* also show that Schumpeter was in the process of questioning his old theory. In all likelihood, however, the immediate impetus for Schumpeter to reformulate his theory of the entrepreneur did not come so much from within as from his involvement during the late 1940s with the Research Center in Entrepreneurial Studies at Harvard. The moving force behind this whole enterprise was Arthur H. Cole, an economic historian at Harvard. By the mid-1940s Cole had decided that economic history needed to be reinvigorated and that studies of entrepreneurship would be a good way to go about this.[22] Cole succeeded in getting together a very competent group with this as its goal, 'The East Coast Group in Entrepreneurial History', and soon the idea emerged of forming an interdisciplinary centre for the study of entrepreneurship. Cole needed funding and support from various authorities, and turned among others to Schumpeter for help. Schumpeter did what he could and also became one of the four 'senior members' at the Center (the others were Cole, Thomas C. Cochran and Leland H. Jenks). He gave the first talk to the Center and its guests, and he attended nearly all of its meetings. 'Without his zeal and support', Cole was later to write, 'the Center might readily have "died aborning".'[23]

The Center was interdisciplinary in nature and no single approach dominated.[24] Cole himself drew no hard boundary lines between the social sciences and encouraged different perspectives. His own ideas about the entrepreneur came more from business history than from economic history; and he had also developed a functional approach to entrepreneurship, which was very different from Schumpeter's ideas. Leland Jenks and Thomas Cochran were first of all fascinated by the possibility of using sociology in the study of entrepreneurship and suggested that one could see the entrepreneur as a 'social role'. R. Richard Wohl, one of the junior members, was interested in anthropology and introduced a cultural approach. According to Hugh Aitken, another junior member, Schumpeter's idea that entrepreneurship and innovations were closely related influenced the people at the Center, but his ideas were far from being generally accepted. Especially the junior members showed resistance to Schumpeter's ideas; they wanted to work out new approaches to entrepreneurship themselves and not take over somebody else's ideas.[25]

Schumpeter's new theory of the entrepreneur, it should first of all be noted, has several traits in common with the version one can find in *Theorie der wirtschaftlichen Entwicklung*. The entrepreneur is still defined as an innovator as opposed to an inventor. The entrepreneur is not a risk-taker; it is the capitalist who takes the risk by putting up the capital. And the entrepreneur is always creative; when his work has become routine, he is not an entrepreneur any longer but a manager. There, however, also exist substantial differences between Schumpeter's early theory and his new ideas. The version of the entrepreneur that we can find in the three key articles from the 1940s is first of all much less individualistic. The new theory is also less firmly tied to the other parts in Schumpeter's system. And, finally, Schumpeter's new approach is considerably more relativistic in nature and open to empirical testing than his earlier one.

Schumpeter's new theory is less individualistic in that he now emphasized that the entrepreneur did not have to be a single person. 'The entrepreneurial function need not be embodied in a physical person and in particular in a single physical person. Every social environment has its own way of filling the entrepreneurial function.'[26] This meant, among other things, that a collection of individuals or a whole team could be 'the entrepreneur'. 'The entrepreneurial function', Schumpeter stressed, 'may be and often is filled co-operatively.'[27] Even the state could play the role of the entrepreneur, he said, and referred to how the US Department of Agriculture many times had 'revolutionized' the practice of farmers by introducing new methods of cultivation. A second important change in Schumpeter's theory of the entrepreneur was that he now, as opposed to earlier, did not try to base his other theorems about the economy directly on his theory of the entrepreneur. In *Theorie der wirtschaftlichen Entwicklung* he had constructed a series of other theorems – about profit, interest, banking and so on – with his theory of the entrepreneur as a basis. In his articles from the 1940s, however, there is much less of this. In particular we find a reformulation of the relationship between entrepreneurship and banking. In Schumpeter's original formulation, the banks had supplied the new capital via credit creation. Now, however, Schumpeter emphasized that the relationship between banks and entrepreneurs differed from country to country. In order to carry out their business, as Schumpeter also pointed out, banks had to keep a rather close check on their customers, and this was often resented by the entrepreneurs. This check could easily turn into control, and this was resented even more. 'Entrepreneurs and industrialists generally have fought against the restrictions imposed upon their freedom of action by bankers' interference, and important features of modern industrial policy are precisely explainable by the wish of industrialists to free themselves from it.'[28] A poll of entrepreneurs, Schumpeter added, would probably show that the average business leader prefers self-financing to bank credit.

The third important change in Schumpeter's theory of the entrepreneur has to do with a fundamental change in his attitude towards empirical data. In most of Schumpeter's works we are simply told that the entrepreneur behaves in a specific way and that this has certain consequences. This is the usual way to proceed in theoretical economics and the purpose is not so much to describe reality as to make sense of reality with the help of a theoretical construction. But however much one may admire Schumpeter's boldness and imagination as an economic theorist, one also often wishes that he would present some data in support of his hypotheses, say, that since the old type of entrepreneur is about to be replaced by bureaucratic managers, the whole capitalist system is in decline. And it is precisely a step in this direction that Schumpeter takes with his essays from the late 1940s. 'Does the importance of the entrepreneurial function decline as time goes on?', he asks.[29] And the answer is: 'There are serious reasons for believing that it does ... But this is at present only an impression. It is for the historian to establish or to refute it.' This emphasis on the need to confront his theories with empirical data can be found in many of his statements about the entrepreneur in the late 1940s. There only exist a few studies of entrepreneurship today, he says, but

> we do not know enough in order to form valid generalizations or even enough to be sure whether there are any generalizations to form. As it is, most of us as economists have some opinions on these matters. But these opinions have more to do with our preconceived ideas or ideals than with solid fact, and our habit of illustrating them by stray instances that have come to our notice is obviously a poor substitute for serious research.[30]

The kind of data that Schumpeter felt was needed could not, however, be supplied by the economist. Mathematics might be useful to get at the logic of the economic system, Schumpeter stressed, but its importance was clearly limited when it came to empirical studies. One reason for this was simply that much of what went on in the economy could not be quantified. 'It need hardly be added', he said, 'that, giving in to human weakness, economists are prone to treat as nonexistent what is not quantifiable and sometimes even what is not measurable.'[31] The kind of data that was missing could in Schumpeter's opinion best be supplied by economic historians. Over and over again in the 1940s Schumpeter kept repeating that economic theorists should try to establish better contact with economic historians. Only through an intimate collaboration between facts and theory, he stressed, would it be possible to make substantial advances in the study of entrepreneurship. Economic historians, he specified, could for one thing help the economist better to understand the institutional forms of entrepreneurship. With the help of economic history one could also get a better view of entrepreneurship in the different fields of the economy, such as finance, commerce and industry. Historical data could be useful in mapping out the different functions of entrepreneurship and in understanding the different types of entrepreneurs. Finally, Schumpeter was very enthusiastic about the potential use of industrial monographs and biographies of industrial leaders in research on entrepreneurship. This type of study was invaluable to the economic theorist, he said, especially if it had been carried out according to some general plan.

Even though Schumpeter constantly referred to economic history as an important ally for economic theory, he was not interested in replacing economic theory with economic history. Instead, he brought forward one of his key ideas from the Schmoller essay, namely that a new type of 'concretized' economic theory would result from an intensive interaction between economic theory and economic history. He noted that economic historians tended to be atheoretical and deterministic, while economic theorists often made room for choice and alternative strategies in their analyses. Though it was true enough that economic theory should be a 'servant' and not a 'master of historical research', economic theoreticians could be of particular assistance to economic historians by providing 'orderly schemata of possibilities and problems'.[32] In one of his three key articles from the 1940s Schumpeter says that what he wanted to accomplish by mixing economic theory with economic history was a kind of *general economic history*. This term gives associations to Weber's masterful exposition of economic history in *Wirtschaftsgeschichte*, which Frank Knight had translated into English in 1927 under the title *General Economic History*. Perhaps Schumpeter was thinking of Weber's work with its mixture of ideal types and historical erudition when he was referring to 'general economic history' in the 1940s. There is no way of knowing this, of course, even if we do know that Schumpeter had a copy of Knight's translation in his personal library and that he now and then referred to Weber's economic history in his own works.[33]

Schumpeter's attempt to redefine his theory of the entrepreneur was hardly noticed by his economic colleagues, most of whom had made up their minds long ago that Schumpeter's ideas could not be formulated in mathematical terms and were therefore of limited value.[34] That they would not have liked Schumpeter's new ideas, however, if they had read his articles (most of which were published in economic history journals) is clear from the reaction of some of Schumpeter's former students. Both Richard Goodwin and Paul Samuelson were thoroughly shocked when they heard about a speech that Schumpeter gave at a conference on business cycles in 1949 and in which he presented some of his new ideas. What made Goodwin and Samuelson so upset, however, was not that Schumpeter had become more empirical in his approach or that he had changed some of his original ideas about the entrepreneur, but that all of this implied that mathematical model-building was not the only road to the future in economics. 'It came as a great shock to me', Goodwin later said, 'that in the very last paper he ever wrote ... he said that the future of research lay in the study of the records of great business enterprises – no mention of econometric model building and testing!'[35] Samuelson was equally shocked. But while Goodwin was eventually to realize that Schumpeter's opinion was 'the logical culmination of his own unique contribution', Samuelson just thought that the whole thing was a fluke and that Schumpeter had played the devil's advocate in his usual manner. He even hints that Schumpeter might have been a bit senile (if only immediately to retract it): 'I do not think we have to invoke old age as an explanation for this uncharacteristic performance. He [just] loved to oppose the popular side.'[36]

The economic historians at Harvard reacted in a different way to Schumpeter's new ideas. But also they were fixated by Schumpeter's old theory of the entrepreneur and did not really give him credit for the changes he was trying to make. This was natural enough with the younger members at the Center for Entrepreneurial Studies: they wanted to develop their own ideas and not take over a ready-made system. Aitken adds a few other reasons why Schumpeter did not get a very good hearing from the younger members:

> There was ... much in the Schumpeterian system that we found hard to digest. Our positivistic stomachs rebelled at the taint of mysticism in Schumpeter's concept of creativity; and our ideological palates, conditioned during the late 1930s, found the heroic and aristocratic elements in his thinking distasteful. None of this was reasonable, of course; but it is perhaps understandable.[37]

It is, however, a little harder to understand why the senior members at the Center were also so insensitive to the new signals that Schumpeter was giving out. Alexander Gerschenkron, Harvard's most formidable economic historian, was, for example, very pleased with Erik Dahmén's pioneering attempt in 1950 to test some of Schumpeter's ideas.[38] Still, Gerschenkron would continue to point out that banks have *not* played the role in history that Schumpeter would have us think, disregarding the fact that Schumpeter had changed his mind on precisely this score.[39] To Gerschenkron, Schumpeter's theory of the entrepreneur was always the one that he had presented in *Theorie der wirtschaftlichen Entwicklung*. As late as the mid-1960s Gerschenkron would say that 'essentially Schumpeter's entrepreneur is equipped with some romantic traits. He has some resemblance to the medieval knight errant, who rides out in search of exciting adventures, ready to slay the dragons of routine and stagnation.'[40] This misperception of Schumpeter's ideas on entrepreneurship is still very much around in the Schumpeterian literature, and it is clear that Schumpeter's last theory of the entrepreneur is still waiting for a fair hearing.[41]

III

One reason why Schumpeter did not elaborate further on his new ideas about the entrepreneur was that he was totally immersed in working on his *History of Economic Analysis*. Exactly when Schumpeter made the decision to embark on this latter project is unclear, but it was probably some time in the 1930s. In 1939 he wrote, for example, to a grants authority that 'I propose to rewrite my *Epochs of the History of Economic Thought*, first published, in German, in 1914'.[42] The same year he also started to give a half-course in the history of economic thought at Harvard, something he would continue to do until 1949. By 1941 or 1942, Elizabeth tells us, Schumpeter had started to work furiously on his history. One reason why he worked so hard, she says, was that he wanted to blot out the war: 'I remember his telling one or two friends that he found work on the *History* a rather soothing occupation for wartime. It removed him temporarily from a grim reality which grieved him beyond measure.'[43] By the time the war was over the book had grown into a tremendously ambitious undertaking – it would end up being ten times longer than the version from 1914 – and it demanded all his energy. He often cursed the 'blasted History' and in 1949 he wrote to a friend that, 'this History of Economic Analysis is like an illness and I cannot get myself to make short work of it, which of course would not be impossible.'[44]

When Schumpeter died, the book was not finished. Elizabeth knew very little about the actual state of the manuscript since Schumpeter had not wanted her to read anything before the whole thing was ready. Her first task, after his death, was therefore to try to establish how far he had reached. This turned out to be much more laborious than one would think. The manuscript was scattered in many places – in Schumpeter's rooms in Windy Hill, in the house on Acacia Street and in his office at Harvard. After some time Elizabeth had found all the pieces, but there was no table of contents and it was by no means always clear in which order the different sections should be placed. After a few months, however, Elizabeth could conclude that even though Schumpeter had not finished the work, he had come very close; and she also decided that what existed could be published. Although Elizabeth had quite a bit of experience as an editor of economic works, she found the task of putting together the manuscript extremely taxing. Some parts of the manuscript were in longhand, which meant that they had to be deciphered and typed. Some of the typed material had been revised by Schumpeter, while others had not. In a few cases there existed alternative versions. There was also the fact that Schumpeter had not had time to complete the introductory and the concluding parts.

Elizabeth was helped in her work on the manuscript by several of Schumpeter's friends, such as Richard Goodwin, Paul Sweezy and Wassily Leontief. Still, she did the lion's share of the job herself, and she also spent a considerable sum of money in the process of turning the manuscript into a book. Eventually, she had to sell the house where she and Schumpeter had lived on Acacia Street, and she used half of the proceeds to put Schumpeter's work in order. By mid-1952 she could finally sign the preface to *History of Economic Analysis* and she had also started to read galley proofs and get the indexes in order. But before the book could be published, she died. According to the publisher, 'up to the last weeks of her prolonged illness, Mrs. Schumpeter devoted most of her time to preparing this book for publication.'[45] Even when she was hospitalized, Elizabeth worked on the book; and when she was too weak to type herself, she dictated her letters to the publisher.[46]

It 'had originally been planned that *History of Economic Analysis* was to be published in two volumes. When it finally appeared in the bookshops, however, its 1250 pages had been squeezed into one huge volume. The content naturally defies any quick summary. Schumpeter himself, however, once described his book in the following concise manner in a letter to his publisher:

The book will describe the development and the fortunes of scientific analysis in the field of economics, from Graeco-Roman times to the present, in the appropriate setting of social and political history and with some attention to the developments in other social sciences and also in philosophy. The ideas on economic policy that float in the public mind or may be attributed to legislators and administrators, whether or not embodied in elaborate systems, such as liberalism or solidarism and the like, which are commonly referred to as economic thought, come in only as part of that setting. The subject of the book is the history of the efforts to describe and explain economic facts and to provide the tools for doing so.[47]

Schumpeter then goes on to describe how his book consists of five major parts. In Part I or the introduction Schumpeter says that he will raise some methodological questions, such as whether economics is a science; what we mean by 'economics'; how we can study economics; and the like. Then come three huge historical parts, which constitute the main bulk of the book:

> Part II ... tells the story of the growth of historical, statistical, and theoretical knowledge of economic phenomena from its beginnings in ancient Greece to the emergence of economics as a recognized special field and to the consequent appearance in the second half of the eighteenth century of systematic treatises, of which A. Smith's *Wealth of Nations* proved to be the most successful one. Part II covers the period between 1776 [later changed to 1790] and 1870, and Part IV the period between 1870 and 1914.[48]

'Part V', Schumpeter told his publisher, 'is to help the reader to relate the present state of economics to the work of the past.'

The similarity between *History of Economic Analysis* and Schumpeter's book from 1914, *Epochen der Dogmen- und Methodengeschichte*, is quite obvious. Schumpeter's first book on the history of economics had started with an account of 'the development of economics (*Sozialökonomik*) as a science' and this answers exactly to Part II in *History of Economic Analysis*, called 'From the Beginnings to the First Classical Situation (1790)'. Also the other parts in the two books are similar, even if *History of Economic Analysis* – for natural reasons – ends a few decades later. Still, there also exist interesting differences between the two works, apart from the sheer size and detail of *History of Economic Analysis*. Schumpeter's general approach to economics is much more self-conscious and sophisticated in the latter work, where he, for example, makes an effort to look at economics with the help of the sociology of science. The difference between economics as a history of analytical thought, as opposed to a history of economic ideas or a history of economic schools, is, for example, spelled out with great clarity. If one sets the 1914 book next to *History of Economic Analysis*, one can also find a significant shift in Schumpeter's judgement of what constitutes the major accomplishments in economics. In 1914 Schumpeter had seen the Physiocrats as making the great breakthrough in economics with their idea of the economy as a circular flow. In *History of Economic Analysis*, however, the whole account is centred around Walras and the idea of general equilibrium. And, finally, the contributions by certain economists – such as Ricardo and the Scholastics – are presented in a new way in Schumpeter's last work.

Part I or the introduction to *History of Economic Analysis* is usually passed over very quickly, as if it did not contain very much of

interest. This, however, is a misperception; and Part I does not only
hold the key to an understanding of Schumpeter's *History* but to his
whole work in economics. Schumpeter wrote the introduction after
he had completed the main parts of the history, and it is clear that he
wanted to sum up his view of economics in the introduction – a little
like Max Weber had done in the two famous opening chapters in
Wirtschaft und Gesellschaft, which were also written last. The first
question that Schumpeter addresses in his introduction is why do we
need to study the history of economics? 'Cannot the old stuff be
safely left to the care of a few specialists who love it for its own
sake?'[49] But Schumpeter does not agree, and he gives several reasons
for this. First of all, it is not possible to just take a book on economics
and understand it without any knowledge whatsoever of its place in
the history of economics. 'The significance and validity of both problems and methods cannot be fully grasped without a knowledge of
the previous problems and methods to which they are the (tentative)
response.'[50] And Schumpeter emphasizes: 'Scientific analysis is not
simply a logically consistent process that starts with some primitive
notions and then adds to the stock in a straight-line fashion.'[51] There
is also the fact that an economist has much to learn from the history
of economics for the simple reason that economics is not a self-
sufficient and independent doctrine but part of society. It is, for
example, very important for an economist to contemplate the fact
that economics is socially grounded, since this fact explains much
of what goes on in the economist's world. By studying the history of
economic thought:

> we learn about both the futility and the fertility of controversies;
> about detours, wasted efforts, and blind alleys; about spells of
> arrested growth, about our dependence on chance, about how not
> to do things, about leeways to make up for. We learn to understand
> why we are as far as we actually are and also why we are not
> further. And we learn *what succeeds and how and why* – a question
> to which attention will be paid throughout this book.[52]

It is exactly at this point that Schumpeter's ideas about the sociology of science come in. Already in *Capitalism, Socialism and Democracy* Schumpeter had said that *Wissenssoziologie* was very useful for
the economist in order to understand the relationship between ideas
and social structures.[53] He, however, did not elaborate but just referred the reader to the works of Max Scheler and Karl Mannheim.
History of Economic Analysis, on the other hand, contains a long and
thoughtful discussion of how the sociology of science can be used to
separate out what is valid in a work from what is flawed by advocacy
and other biases. Schumpeter was particularly concerned with the
influence of 'ideology' on economics; and in so far as the sociology

of economics is concerned, 'the problem of ideology is the most important.'[54] In his presidential address to the American Economic Association in 1948, 'Science and Ideology', the message was the same.

The way in which Schumpeter defines ideology comes close to Marx, even if he also subjects the Marxist notion of ideology to sharp criticism: Marx did not apply the concept of ideology to what he wrote himself, only to the work of others; Marx thought that something was invalid just because it was ideological; and he oversimplified things by portraying ideology as part of a superstructure, which reflected objective reality. Still, Marx was right in his general intuition that people have a tendency to rationalize events or otherwise engage in ideological behaviour, 'comforting ourselves and impressing others by drawing a picture of ourselves, our motives, our friends, our enemies, our vocation, our church, our country, which may have more to do with what we like them to be than with what they are'.[55] In the final analysis, however, Schumpeter does not seem to have been very interested in supplying an exact definition of 'ideology'. What was much more important to him was to make the economist aware that he must be on his guard against ideological influences. One of the most urgent tasks for contemporary economics was therefore to devise 'a set of rules by which to locate, diagnose, and eliminate ideological delusion'.[56]

One concept, Schumpeter says, that might be useful in this context is that of *'Vision'*. Every great economist has an original vision of what the world is like. Keynes's vision, for example, was that of English capitalism in decline. And Schumpeter's own vision, we might add, was that of the pre-First World War bourgeoisie with its feeling that time was up and that socialism was just around the corner. A vision helps the economist to pick out topics, Schumpeter says, which are then analysed according to the rules of science. The vision itself, however, is not scientific; it is rather a 'preanalytic cognitive act that supplies the raw material for the analytic effort'.[57] As opposed to ideology, Schumpeter did not want to root out vision from economics. It is true that vision is 'ideological almost by definition'.[58] But without visions there would be no economics; and visions are both an integral and a useful part of economics. The point is rather that the vision should be laid bare in order that the limits to an economist's work should become clear and visible to everyone.

Another important question that Schumpeter raises in the introduction is how to define economics as a science. It is here that Schumpeter introduces his famous definition of economics as 'a box of tools'. He had borrowed the idea of 'tools' from Joan Robinson, and by this expression he basically meant that economics consists of a series of specialized techniques and concepts which can be used to analyse economic phenomena. Schumpeter was not interested in

specifying very much more than this when discussing what characterized economics as a science. One reason for this was that economics,
in his opinion, was the result of an accidental historical evolution
rather than of conscious efforts on the part of the economists. One
of the absolute key passages in *History of Economic Analysis*
reads as follows:

> Science as a whole has never attained a logically consistent
> architecture; it is a tropical forest, not a building erected according
> to blueprint . . . One of the consequences of this is that the frontiers
> of the individual sciences or of most of them are incessantly shift-
> ing and that there is no point in trying to define them *either by
> subject or by method*. This applies particularly to economics, which
> is not a science in the sense in which acoustics is one, but is rather
> an agglomeration of ill-coordinated and overlapping fields of
> research in the same sense as is 'medicine'. Accordingly, we shall
> indeed discuss other people's definitions – primarily for the pur-
> pose of wondering at their inadequacies – but we shall not adopt
> one for ourselves. Our closest approach to doing so will consist in
> the enumeration presented below of the main 'fields' . . . But even
> this epideiktic definition must be understood to carry no claim to
> completeness. In addition we must always leave open the possibil-
> ity that, in the future, topics may be added to or dropped from any
> complete list that might be drawn up as of today.[59]

With this 'list of fields' we have come to the very heart of *History of
Economic Analysis*, namely to Schumpeter's attempt to spell out his
own vision of a broad-based economics. Of all of Schumpeter's
works, it should be emphasized, *History of Economic Analysis* contains the most complete discussion of what he meant by *Sozialökonomik*. At the risk of repeating some of the things which have already
been said in the earlier chapters, we shall nevertheless present
Schumpeter's argument in the introduction to *History of Economic
Analysis* as fully as possible.

Economics, Schumpeter says, can be conceptualized in many different ways. There is, for example, the idea of 'political economy'.
But political economy, in Schumpeter's mind, represents an illegitimate mixture of economic analysis and political ideology. Economics
has to be kept as free as possible from politics, which always
threatens to destroy its scientific character. 'The first thing a man
will do for his ideals', Schumpeter says, 'is to lie.'[60] There is also the
fact that by focusing on what is politically or socially important,
rather than on what is scientifically important, science is led astray.
Therefore, economics has to be sharply separated from politics, and
exclusively deal with scientific questions. Following Marshall,
Schumpeter calls the kind of economics he has in mind '(scientific)
economics'. This term, he notes, was introduced in the 1890s in

England and the United States. 'Later on', Schumpeter points out, 'a parallel usage was introduced, though less firmly established, in Germany. The word was Social Economics, *Sozialökonomie*, and the man who did more than any other to assure some currency to it was Max Weber.'[61]

Scientific economics or *Sozialökonomik* consists, first of all, of 'tooled knowledge' or of special techniques that the economist must learn. Schumpeter firmly rejects the charge that this view implies what Hayek has called 'scientism' or an uncritical copying of the methods of physics in the belief that economics is a natural science. It is indeed true that economics, just like physics, has to be rigorously scientific. But that is also where the parallels between physics and economics end, Schumpeter says. You can, for example, not use laboratory experiments in economics. This may be a drawback, but on the other hand economics 'enjoys ... a source of information that is denied to physics, namely, man's extensive knowledge of the *meanings* of economic action'.[62] The introduction of 'meaning' into the economic analysis does not mean that economics should become a branch of psychology. What it does mean, however, is that economic theorems can be constructed either on the basis of logic (or assigned meanings) or on the basis of observation (or observed meanings). Schumpeter rejects the idea that all of economics can be reduced to observations of people involved in economic activities and to the meanings they assign to their activities. He also says that it would be wrong to view 'economic theorems that are logical' as basically identical to 'economic theorems that are based on observations'. These two types of theorems both involve 'meaning', but should be kept separate:

> It would no doubt be possible to assimilate both types of theory by interpreting the logical norms also as 'purifying' generalizations from observational data, if need be, from observations that are subconsciously stored up by common experience. On the whole, however, it seems better not to do so but to recognize frankly that we have, or think we have, the ability to understand meanings and to represent the implications of these meanings by appropriately constructed schemata.[63]

Even though Schumpeter addresses the question of a *verstehende Nationalökonomie* (to use a term by Werner Sombart), it is clear that he feels uncomfortable with the notion of *verstehen* and of straying too far from a positivistic notion of science.[64] Schumpeter raises the problem of the role of meaning in economic life in his *History of Economic Life*, but he does not do very much more with it than has just been reported. Weber's idea that economics should consist of several fields is, however, fully developed in Schumpeter's last work.

As noted earlier, Schumpeter says that there is no reason why economics should consist of a fixed number of fields. Instead we can expect to add some fields and drop others as history progresses. In *History of Economic Analysis* Schumpeter discusses primarily four fields: economic theory, economic history, economic sociology and statistics.[65] Anthropology, he says, can be seen as part of history, and business economics is part of economics in general.[66]

An important theme that runs through Schumpeter's discussion of the different fields is that none of them should be allowed to monopolize economics at the expense of the others. If Schumpeter shows favouritism towards any one of the fundamental fields in his last work, however, it is towards economic history. It is in the methodological introduction to *History of Economic Analysis* that he makes the famous statement that, 'I wish to state right now that if, starting my work in economics afresh, I were told that I could study only one [of the fundamental fields] but could have my choice, it would be economic history that I should choose.'[67] There are three reasons, Schumpeter says, why he thinks so highly of economic history. First, any economic event always takes place in historical time, and this means that the economist has to be well versed in history in order to do good economics. Again, this is a point where Schumpeter and Weber agree; also Weber had argued that it was analytical insight in combination with profound historical knowledge that was needed to do good social science. Schumpeter writes in his history: 'Nobody can hope to understand the economic phenomena of any, including the present, epoch who has not an adequate command of historical *facts* and an adequate amount of historical *sense* or of what may be described as *historical experience*.'[68] The second reason why economic history is crucial to the economist is that history crosses disciplinary boundaries in a very natural way: 'it affords the best method for understanding how economic and non-economic facts *are* related and how the various social sciences *should* be related to one another.'[69] Schumpeter's third reason for having such a high opinion of economic history was that most errors in economics were due precisely to a lack of knowledge in history.

But it was not enough for the economist to be knowledgeable in history, he must also be able to carry out historical research himself in order to be a good economist. It was the same with statistics, the second fundamental field in economics. Only by knowing how to compile statistics could one use them correctly:

> It is impossible to understand statistical figures without understanding how they have been compiled. It is equally impossible to extract information from them or to understand the information that specialists extract for the rest of us without understanding the methods by which this is done – and the epistemological back-

grounds of these methods. Thus, an adequate command of modern statistical methods is a necessary (but not a sufficient) condition for preventing the modern economist from producing nonsense.[70]

Schumpeter realized that one could not demand that the average economist should be competent in economic theory, economic history, statistics and economic sociology, but he emphasized that it was very important to have this as a goal and to see to it that they were all represented in the training of economists.

According to *History of Economic Analysis*, economic theory constitutes not the first, but the 'third fundamental field' in economics.[71] Schumpeter notes that theoretical economics, as opposed to theoretical physics, always involves *'meanings'* – be it assigned meaning (as in formal economic theory) or observed meaning (as in empirical economics).[72] The point that Schumpeter was most eager to make in the section on economic theory was, however, a different one. And this is that there exist two kinds of economic theory. According to the first, which is the more trivial one, theory is synonymous with 'explanatory hypotheses'. By this type of hypothesis Schumpeter means the kind of theory that an economist may propose with a particular problem in mind, say that the price of a certain commodity tends to stabilize in a certain range under certain conditions. To Schumpeter, however, this kind of economic theory is only the tip of the iceberg, and the less interesting part of the iceberg at that. The second kind of economic theory is very different and focuses on the concepts or ideas themselves, in this case that there is something called a 'price' and that it indeed 'stabilizes'. These kinds of concepts or ideas are what Schumpeter calls 'tools'; and they are used to work on reality and shape it in our minds. He writes that concepts of this type 'differ from the hypotheses of the first kind in that they do not *embody* final results of research that are supposed to be interesting for their own sake, but are mere instruments or tools framed for the purpose of *establishing* interesting results.'[73] But the theorist does more than just 'frame' the hypotheses: 'Just as important is the devising of the other gadgets by which results may be extracted from the hypotheses – all the concepts (such as "marginal rate of substitution", "marginal productivity", "multiplier", "accelerator"), relations between concepts, and methods of handling these relations, all of which have nothing hypothetical about them.'[74]

Economic sociology constitutes the last major field in Schumpeter's scheme. It is true that a combination of theory, history and statistics covers the economic phenomenon rather well, but there are also some aspects that elude them. And this is where economic sociology comes in. 'Borrowing from German practice', Schumpeter says, 'we shall find it useful, therefore, to introduce a fourth fundamental field to complement the three others, although positive work in this field also leads us beyond mere economic analysis: the field that we shall call Economic Sociology (*Wirtschaftssoziologie*).'[75] Economic sociology primarily deals with 'social institutions' of relevance to economic action, such as property, inheritance, contract and government. These are topics which the economic historian is also interested in studying; and in one sense one can say that economic sociology is 'a sort of generalized or typified or stylized economic history'.[76] Schumpeter adds that economic sociology can only prosper if there is plenty of cooperation between economists and sociologists. But this type of cooperation has rarely come about: 'it is the fact that ever since the eighteenth century both groups have grown steadily apart until by now the modal economist and the modal sociologist know little and care less about what the other does, each preferring to use, respectively, a primitive sociology and a primitive economics of his own to accepting one another's professional results.'[77] As usual, Schumpeter's plea for more cooperation is not to be seen as an encouragement to merge the two fields. 'Cross-fertilization', as he says, 'might easily result in cross-sterilization.'[78]

The introduction to *History of Economic Analysis* is only about 50 pages long, and the rest of the book is devoted to a very detailed and learned account of the development of economics from the Greeks till the early twentieth century. What makes Schumpeter's work even more impressive is that he tried not only to write the history of economics, as conventionally conceived, but the history of *Sozialökonomik*. This was clearly a tremendously difficult task, and after having finished the main bulk of the manuscript, Schumpeter felt that he had only succeeded with this task 'in a fragmentary manner'.[79] The reason why his account was not more systematic, he said, had to do with the fact that he lacked the necessary knowledge and that the book would have become much longer. Still, there is a conscious effort throughout Schumpeter's work not only to tell the history of theoretical economics, but also of economic history, of economic sociology and of statistics.

The difficulties that this project entailed for the structuring of Schumpeter's history were solved in different ways in the three main parts of the book. In the first of these (Part II), which dealt with economics from the Greeks to 1790, Schumpeter essentially tried to present each author's contribution to the different 'fields', a little like he had done with Marx in *Capitalism, Socialism and Democracy*. If we take Aristotle as an example, there is first a section on Aristotle's economic sociology with a discussion of his theories about the origin of the state, private property and slavery. This is followed by an account of Aristotle's contribution to 'pure economics', where Schumpeter discusses his ideas on value, money, interest and so on. Economic history is part of the whole account only in the sense that Schumpeter has inserted a few descriptions here and there about the economic conditions in Ancient Greece. Statistics did not exist in Aristotle's day, but Part II has a chapter about the 'econometricians' of the seventeenth and eighteenth centuries, such as Sir William Petty and the Physiocrats. Their main contribution, Schumpeter says, was to have shown that numerical analysis should be part of economics.

Part II also contains some accounts which are very memorable, especially of the Scholastics and of Adam Smith. Schumpeter had a very high opinion of the Scholastics and argued that if any group could be said to have founded economics, it was they. The Scholastics had worked out a sophisticated theory of utility, a theory of interest and a theory of money. They had even produced an 'embryonic demand–supply apparatus'.[80] Adam Smith, on the other hand, got more of a whipping from Schumpeter than a hearing. '*The Wealth of Nations*', we are told, 'does not contain a single *analytic* idea, principle, or method that was entirely new in 1776.'[81] Smith's main feat was to have synthesized an enormous amount of material; and this is something he did very, very well. Indeed, Schumpeter savagely continues:

> his very limitations made for success. Had he been more brilliant, he would not have been taken so seriously. Had he dug more deeply, had he unearthed more recondite truth, had he used difficult and ingenious methods, he would not have been understood. But he had no such ambitions; in fact, he disliked whatever went beyond plain common sense. He never moved above the head of even the dullest reader.[82]

Part III of *History of Economic Analysis* is devoted to the classical period (1790–1870). Economic history is again present mainly in the form of background material on the economic development. There is a section on statistics, where Schumpeter argues that even though great progress was made during these years, 'the statisticians' pure theory and the economists' pure theory were almost completely divorced.'[83] Economic sociology is discussed in a section called 'The Institutional Frame of the Economic Process', where Schumpeter says that the classical authors basically took the social institutions for granted. As a consequence, they did not realize that their economic analyses were only valid under certain conditions: that the state did not intervene in the economy; that there was free competition; and so on. Schumpeter also notes that the classical authors failed to develop a theory of social class. In so far as their economics is concerned, Schumpeter was rather negative. The most creative theoretician of the period was clearly Ricardo, but Schumpeter did not have a very high opinion of his work. For one thing, Ricardo confused values and facts; and he had an annoying tendency to pile arguments on top of each other in order to hide this ('the Ricardian Vice').[84] Ricardo also failed to make any real progress on the main problem in economics, namely how to develop a general equilibrium model. In brief, Ricardo's work was a 'detour'.[85]

The next period that Schumpeter dealt with began in 1870 and ended in 1914 (Part IV). During these years the economists just took over the institutional assumptions of the classical authors and failed to make any use of the works produced by their sociological colleagues. And even though there was 'a boom in statistical theory', most economists totally ignored it.[86] In economic theory, however, a great revolution took place around the turn of the century when Jevons, Menger and Walras developed the theory of marginal utility. Schumpeter paid homage to them for this, but he reserved his highest praise for Walras's theory of general equilibrium. After the discovery of economics as a science, he said, the great difficulty had been to discover *the fundamental problem* of economics.[87] Over the centuries many efforts had been made in this direction, but with little success:

> The scholastics had an inkling of it. The seventeenth-century businessmen-economists came nearer to it. Isnard, A. Smith, J. B. Say, Ricardo, and others all struggled or rather fumbled for it, every one of them in his own way. But the discovery was not fully made until Walras, whose system of equations, defining (static) equilibrium in a system of interdependent quantities, is the Magna Carta of economic theory.[88]

The last hundred pages of *History of Economic Analysis* are devoted to developments after the First World War. This section is fragmentary in nature, and it is clear that it would have looked very different if Schumpeter had had the time to complete it and revise it. Nevertheless, it is possible to get a general idea of what Schumpeter thought about the most recent developments in economics. With the emergence of econometrics, for example, an 'alliance between statistics and theoretical economics' had finally been achieved.[89] It is also clear, Schumpeter said, that in terms of technique, the economic theory of 1945 is 'greatly superior' to the economic theory of the turn of the century.[90] 'At the same time', he adds, 'it must be admitted that fundamentally new ideas have been almost wholly absent.'[91] Today's economists basically live off the heritage of the generation of Walras, Menger and Jevons. Schumpeter was particularly disappointed by the failure of his contemporaries to develop a general dynamic theory:

> the thing to do is not to supplement static theory ... but to replace it by a system of general economic dynamics into which statics

would enter as a special case. The realization of the fact that even a static theory cannot be fully developed without an explicit dynamical schema (Samuelson) ... is a first step in this direction, and if space permitted, a few others could be mentioned. However, no attack on the whole front of Walrasian theory has as yet developed and the analogy with a building plot is still painfully apposite: an increasing number of workers see the new goal; but for the time being this is practically all.[92]

When *History of Economic Analysis* was published, it was reviewed by all the major historians of economic thought, such as Jacob Viner, Lionel Robbins, Frank Knight and others.[93] The general verdict was that Schumpeter had produced an immensely learned work, which constituted a major contribution to the literature. Elizabeth was praised for all the work she had put in, even if some questions were also raised about the quality of her editing.[94] Much was said about Schumpeter's idiosyncrasies and his unfair treatment of certain economists, especially Adam Smith and Ricardo. It was also noted that Schumpeter had his own favourites, such as the Scholastics and Walras. Nothing, however, was said about Schumpeter's vision of a broad-based science of economics and of his attempt to write the history of *Sozialökonomik*. For this reason – and since *History of Economic Analysis* is Schumpeter's last work – it might be in place to make a brief appraisal of this aspect of Schumpeter's enterprise.

The general idea behind *Sozialökonomik* is that economics is both broader and richer than theoretical economics, especially formalized economic theory. That Schumpeter chose constantly to remind us of this fact, with his notion of *Sozialökonomik*, is clearly something to be grateful for. One could perhaps argue that the division of labour in the social sciences is such that the works of economists, historians, sociologists and statisticians will automatically complement each other. 'How nice it would be', Paul Samuelson has said, 'if in fact you could have a division of labor, and one man would hold the tumbler and the other man would do the somersaults. We are all looking for that other fellow, I think, as we look for the good broker – the man in the other discipline who matches with our interests.'[95] But 'the man in the other discipline' is, of course, never there when he is needed, and this is why Schumpeter's idea of a *Sozialökonomik* is very useful. One might perhaps argue that what is needed is rather a radically new perspective in economics, which would encompass all that is useful in the different social sciences. But as things stand today, this is little but wishful thinking. And, in the meantime, Schumpeter's main intuition makes quite a lot of sense, namely that economics should be in constant contact with economic history, economic sociology and statistics. There is also something to be said for Schumpeter's proposal that economists should be exposed to all of these topics as part of their training. If mainstream economics is ever to break out of its current isolation from the other social sciences – and we are talking about a much more worrisome situation than in Schumpeter's day – it will probably be done by economists who have some knowledge of what is happening in the other social sciences. *All in all*: Schumpeter's work reminds us of the necessity of discussing these questions and that economics is first of all a social science.

IV

This chapter will close with a few words about Schumpeter's personal life after the Second World War until his death in 1950. In general, Schumpeter's last years were peaceful and calm. Apart from the trips abroad that he and Elizabeth took, they had a well-established routine, alternating between the house in Cambridge and the one in Connecticut. When he was not teaching, Schumpeter worked on his history of economics; he played a little tennis; took walks with Elizabeth; and then worked again. Elizabeth took care of most details in Schumpeter's life; 'Elizabeth is managing my wordly affairs', as he used to say.[96] But there were also some sorrows during these years. In the autumn of 1948 Elizabeth discovered that she had breast cancer and was immediately operated upon. The operation was successful, but Schumpeter was still very much disturbed by the episode. 'The lightning from blue skies has struck me ... I could not go on without her', he wrote in his diary.[97] At about the same time, Schumpeter also received a letter which confirmed the rumours that Mia Stöckel, his housekeeper and companion during a few years in Bonn, had died during the war.[98] In January 1942 a huge number of people had been executed in Novi Sad, Yugoslavia, where Mia and her family lived, on the ground of potential disloyalty to the Nazis. All Jews, priests and – like Mia and her husband – members of the English Club were among those who were shot.

If we look at Schumpeter's mental state during these last years, it is clear that once the war was over, it improved considerably. In some ways, however, Schumpeter was never able fully to recover. He still felt isolated, alone and unhappy. 'Why am I so disgusted? Why am I so sad? Why do I feel that those people and I have nothing in common?', he wrote in his diary in 1947.[99] His sense that his own death was imminent was also growing. 'I am dying', reads one notation from 1946 to 1947.[100] He kept telling his friends that he soon would be dead, but he must have done it with a smile on his lips, for they did not take him seriously. 'In the home of Alvin H. Hansen one evening [in 1947]', Ragnar Frisch says, 'he spoke of himself as "staggering towards his grave", but nobody talking with him that evening could believe that that was anything more than one of his usual jokes.'[101] As during the war, Schumpeter was tormented by the fact that he had failed in life. 'It is a poor result of a life's work', he wrote to himself, 'to arrive in the realization that the whole damn thing is not worth the trouble of breathing.'[102] At times Schumpeter would explode in anger and disgust as during the war. One note, written with huge, scrawling letters, as if Schumpeter had held the pen the way you grip a knife, reads as follows: 'For this is all it all amounts to: the prototype from which to draw the picture of mankind is the prostitute.'[103]

In relation to *die Hasen*, Schumpeter continued to communicate on a daily basis with his beloved Annie and mother during these last years.[104] As before, he turned to them when he faced some difficulty, and he thanked them when things went well. After he had given his celebrated presidential address at the American Economic Association in December 1948, he wrote for example in his diary:

> Thank you, Hasen, for supporting me and for one of the richest presents. Everyone rose for my presidential address. The whole of the Cleveland ballroom audience rose and gave me applause. That was not poor and that was not small. And yet so undeserved. Thank you, Hasen. O give me strength. O Gott and Hasen.[105]

A few years before his death Schumpeter also began to address some of his prayers directly to God, rather than to Annie and his mother, and to observe the Christian holidays. By one of Schumpeter's commentators this has been interpreted as a further sign that he was in reality 'a profoundly religious person, albeit in an unorthodox fashion'.[106] According to this interpretation, the reason why Schumpeter's most intimate friends always thought that he was *not* religious was that Schumpeter very successfully kept his religion to himself. But at heart – so the argument goes – Schumpeter admired the Catholic Church, was a truly religious man, and so on.

This, however, is to make too much of a few scattered statements in Schumpeter's private diary. There were no doubt religious overtones to Schumpeter's relationship with *die Hasen*, especially during the late 1940s. But whether this is enough to label him 'a profoundly religious man' is an entirely different matter. If we, by this expression, mean someone whose worldview is profoundly influenced by his religion, Schumpeter was definitely not a religious man. Indeed, that Schumpeter was not particularly religious comes out with great clarity if one goes through another part of Schumpeter's diary from these years, namely the sections which contain his aphorisms. An aphorism is by definition an attempt to express a general truth about the world and human affairs (in a certain stylistic manner), and it therefore expresses the moral universe of the author. Schumpeter wrote something like a hundred aphorisms in the 1940s (most of which are reproduced in Appendix I of this book), and we shall now use these to get a glimpse of what Schumpeter's *Weltanschauung* was really like and what kind of mental world he actually lived in during his last years.

When one reads through Schumpeter's aphorisms one is immediately struck by how few values there were in his universe. Love, victory, revenge and hate – that was pretty much all. These were '*the four pivots of life*'.[107] He wrote: 'The first value in life is Victory, the second is Revenge.'[108] All human motivation, Schumpeter said, boiled down to this: 'To hunt for food and women and to kill enemies that is and always was what man wanted and was fitted for, and this is the greatest happiness for the greatest number.'[109] A certain elitism was also part of Schumpeter's worldview, where people were firmly divided into leader and mass. Equality was an illusion: 'Equality is the ideal of the subnormal but even the subnormals do not really desire equality but only that there be nobody better.'[110] Time and time again Schumpeter came back to the 'subnormals' and the danger they represented to society.

The role of knowledge in human affairs is fused with Schumpeter's elitism in a predictable manner. The mass is fond of its ignorance, while the true man of knowledge fights his way to knowledge: 'What matters to man are his illusions'; 'mankind is prepared to believe anything except the truth.'[111] At times there is an element of *fröhliche Wissenschaft* in Schumpeter's aphorisms. '*We all of us like a sparkling error better than a trivial truth*', reads one of the better aphorisms.[112] And who knows which colleagues at Harvard Schumpeter had in mind when he penned another memorable aphorism: 'Don't ask the donkey to sing.'[113]

The reference to Nietzsche's *fröhliche Wissenschaft* is not idle; and to some extent one can say that Schumpeter lived in a similar universe to that of the German philosopher. Also Nietzsche's world was inhabited by demonic forces, heroic individuals and a weak, despicable mass. Like Nietzsche, Schumpeter felt that true creation demanded huge sacrifices from the artist, even illness. 'Most creation is pathological'; 'only the sick oyster produces pearls.'[114] There was sometimes a strange sexual element in Schumpeter's aphorisms, which pointed to disturbances and distortions: 'If you ever doubt the sexual sense of "beauty", only imagine you find two growths exactly like "beautiful" breasts on a man or simply when they have no sexual connotation.'[115] And, finally, there was the dive into the depths of the pool of human emotions. Schumpeter wrote the following aphorism twice: '*I wonder if the vermins that live on the decomposing corpse also believe that they are reforming it*.'[116]

Another person who comes to mind when one enters Schumpeter's mental universe is Vilfredo Pareto.[117] There are actually quite a few

parallels between Schumpeter and Pareto. They were both prominent economists and they had a great interest in sociology as well as
in politics. Both felt that while economics should deal with individual, rational behaviour, sociology and politics were about irrational, collective behaviour. They were both cynical about human
affairs and neither believed in democracy. Pareto would have been
happy to stand as the author of the following aphorism, which
Schumpeter repeated over and over in his diary, 'Democracy is
government by lying.'[118] He would probably also have agreed with
Schumpeter that 'there is not only the one enemy of humanity – the
subnormal – there is another, the idealist.'[119] That Schumpeter himself had a certain affinity for Pareto is clear from a biographical essay
that Schumpeter wrote in 1949 on the Italian economist. As in most
of his portraits of other economists, Schumpeter projected something
of himself onto the person he wrote about. When Schumpeter calls
Pareto a 'bourgeois Karl Marx' and when he says that Pareto 'cannot
be pigeonholed; he paid court to no "ism"', it is hard not to feel
that these descriptions also fit Schumpeter.[120] Writing about Pareto's
personality, Schumpeter kept referring to 'the deep pool of personality' and how it can never be drained 'so as to show what is
at the bottom of it'.[121] Perhaps this was also how Schumpeter saw
himself.

If we now try to assemble all the different threads of what has just
been said about Schumpeter's private *Weltanschauung*, as it can be
reconstructed on the basis of his aphorisms, we arrive at something
like the following. The world that Schumpeter lived in during his last
years was a pre-Christian, nearly pagan kind of world. It was clearly
not a religious world in any meaningful sense of this word. It was a
universe of few and strong values, such as love and hate and victory
and revenge. But there was no morality, no mercy, no forgiveness in
Schumpeter's world. These were all signs of weakness; and weak
people were subnormals, just as idealists were fools. Might was right,
and the man of the pen was a relative to the man with the sword.
This was not an attractive world or one in which it was possible to
live in peace with oneself and with others. It was an inhuman universe and it lets us understand how Schumpeter must have suffered
from having to live in it. 'It is, of course, your mind much more than
your body which makes you feel ill and weak', as Elizabeth once
wrote to Schumpeter.[122]

Schumpeter died, at the age of 66, on the night between 7 and 8
January 1950 in his own bed in the house in Taconic. The medical
reason was cerebral haemorrhage, even if some suspected overwork
in combination with a lack of will to live. Elizabeth arranged for an
Episcopalian funeral service on 10 January at St John's Church in
Salisbury, Connecticut. A memorial service was also held a few
weeks later in Memorial Church at Harvard Yard in Cambridge.

Epilogue

For the next few years Elizabeth spent most of her time honouring Schumpeter's memory in various ways. We have already described how she laboured over his *History of Economic Analysis*. It was also a giant task to put Schumpeter's papers in order, including the thousands of little slips with notes that Schumpeter had accumulated since the early 1930s. Elizabeth did all of this and also saw to it that the bulk of Schumpeter's papers were given to Harvard, where they can still be consulted in the archives. Harvard was not willing to take care of Schumpeter's books in the way that Elizabeth wanted, so she gave a choice collection to the Kress Library and some 2,000 less valuable volumes to the Hitotsubashi Library in Tokyo.[123] She also arranged to have whatever was left of Schumpeter's belongings in Jülich shipped to the United States. Most had been destroyed during the Second World War when Jülich was bombed ('by the American Air Force', as Elizabeth used to add), but some 80 odd books were finally sent to Cambridge.[124] Most of these were economic books in English, but there was also a full set of *Grundriss der Sozialökonomik*.

At first Elizabeth tried to arrange for a Schumpeter Memorial Room in the Littauer Center at Harvard, but this turned out to be impossible for administrative and bureaucratic reasons. She was initially more successful in having a Schumpeter Prize Fund established. The general idea was to collect money for a Schumpeter Prize of $1,000, which was to be awarded to someone who had made an original contribution to economics, especially to 'the study of economic development, and its interrelations with historical, social, and political evolution, and the interrelations between economic theory, statistics, and history'.[125] Haberler, Smithies and Leontief helped Elizabeth with the Fund and by 1953 $11,600 had been collected. When Elizabeth died, all of her estate – estimated at $150,000 – also went to the Department of Economics at Harvard, where it has been used to support graduate students in her husband's name.[126]

That Elizabeth worked so hard to put Schumpeter's manuscripts and papers in order has usually been seen as a sign of her love for Schumpeter. And so it was. But it was also a sign of her own lifelong commitment to science, scholarship and truth. When she was given the opportunity to eliminate certain passages in Schumpeter's work, which could be seen as pro-Nazi, she politely refused. Among the papers that she handed over to Harvard were Schumpeter's private diaries, memorabilia from Schumpeter's second wife and letters from a former mistress. She also included letters from herself to Schumpeter, which she had every right in the world to consider private. Eventually Elizabeth had spent so much money on getting

Schumpeter's things in order that she could not afford to live in Cambridge any longer. She now withdrew to her beloved Windy Hill, where she ran a small nursery. After a long and painful struggle with cancer, she died in July 1953. Memorial services were held for her in St John's Episcopal Church in Salisbury, Connecticut, where she a few years earlier had said goodbye to her husband.

APPENDICES

Appendix I

Aphorisms from Schumpeter's Private Diary

Schumpeter's aphorisms can be found in his private diaries and on some of the famous little slips of paper that he always carried with him in case an idea occurred to him. The diaries cover the years when Schumpeter was in the United States and were deposited by Elizabeth Boody Schumpeter in the Harvard University Archives, where they can still be consulted.[1]

Schumpeter often wrote aphorisms, and the first one in this appendix comes from 1936. In 1943 he decided to write them on a more regular basis, and the majority of the aphorisms are from the years 1943–6.[2] Occasionally Schumpeter would insert an aphorism directly into an article or a book and at other times he would just express himself in such a poignant manner, that the end product would look very much like an aphorism. This was as true for his spoken language as for his written language. Take, for example, the following statement from Schumpeter's diary in 1931: 'Catch a parrot, teach him to say "Supply and Demand" and you have an economist.'[3] Or, to take another example, Schumpeter's answer to a student who asked him about the state of economics, just after the Second World War: 'Economics is getting better and better, but economists are getting worse and worse.'[4] Many people have commented on Schumpeter's brilliant style, and it is clear that he had a superb talent for language. But, according to Böhm-Bawerk, Schumpeter's capacity to express himself so easily could also get him into trouble – he had been graced with 'a dangerous gift by the gods'.[5]

1

The trouble with progressives is that they are always a hundred years behind their time.

2

A political scientist is a man who understands neither law nor economics nor sociology.

3

Democracy is government by lying.

4

Beauty obeys Law – Freedom is Ugliness.

5

Dishonesty is the most human of all characteristics.

6

Never judge a man by what he says or a party by its program or a religion by its articles of faith.

7

Just as travelling once was picturesque, so were revolutions; we have changed all of that; travelling is no longer picturesque and our revolution is drab and mechanized.

8

Mankind is prepared to believe anything except the truth.

9

Common sense is a method to arrive at workable conclusions from false premisses by nonsensical reasoning.

10

Success is not valuable and, as a matter of fact, not valued for what we get by it but for what it proves to us and others what we are.

11

The essential fact about life is death.

12

Don't ask the donkey to sing.

13

The doctor who is dying and puts down the symptoms – *that* is man at his best.

14

Humanity does not really care for freedom, the mass of the people quickly realize that they are not up to it: what they want is being fed, led, amused and, above everything, drilled. But they do care for the phrase.

15

If you ever doubt the sexual sense of 'beauty', only imagine you find two growths exactly like 'beautiful' breasts on a man or simply when they have no sexual connotation.

16
Why do people fight?
Because they enjoy it.

17
To fight – the most human of all characteristics.

18
To lie – what distinguishes man from animals.

19
You can't convince anyone who is not deep down convinced already.

20
Leave all the fighting to the soldiers and the barking to the dogs.

21
Art is but a technique to bring out our vision from a heap of rubbish.

22
To hunt for food and women and to kill enemies that is and always was what man wanted and was fitted for, and this is the greatest happiness for the greatest number.

23
People do not reason on facts but on creations of their fancies.

24
Why form a party when you can as well form a pressure group?

25
Jurisprudence is the attempt to make sense of foolish rules.

26
A woman or a workman longs for something.

27
Capitalism pays the people that strive to pull it down.

28
We are only dogs chasing cars.

29
A master-horseman never pulls his horse about.

30
Wisdom is the ability to be intelligent without a lag.

31
The first value in life is Victory, the second is Revenge.

32
Two kinds of people I distrust: architects who profess to build cheaply, economists who profess to give simple answers.

33

The Art of the theorist is introducing restrictions which do make problems manageable without making them trite (and valueless).

34

Let's never forget: Propositions that are known to be wrong have nevertheless been 'proved' in the past to the satisfaction of those best able to judge!

35

What is this interval between two sleeps? What is a day and what is life? A block of marble that God gives you to make a work of art.

36

It's the escapist who talks about escapism.

37

Have you ever seen a sign-post that walks the way in which it points?

38

The more I study modern humanity the more am I impressed by the comparative gentleness of Jinghis Khan.

39

To live is to love
but also to hate.
To live is to fight
but also to lie.

40

Nations are like vicious children – and idiotic ones at that.

41

Whoever is resolved to believe in miracles, needs them.

42

Politicians are like bad horsemen who are so preoccupied with keeping in the saddle that they can't bother about where they go.

43

Love that hates
bliss that hurts.

44

Victory–revenge ⎫
Love–hate   ⎬ the four pivots of life
                 ⎭

45

Humanity can never see a point without making nonsense of it.

46

In a sense politics is more serious than anything else.
In another it is less serious than anything else.

47

A statesman is the animal who works with phrases instead of with the burglar's jimmy.

48

Equality is the ideal of the subnormal but even the subnormals do not really desire equality but only that there be nobody better.

49

The Essence of Position is the Power to abuse it.

50

Strength wins not by being used but by being there.

51

Foreign policy is domestic politics.

52

Bureaucracy is an engine for the Production of Regulation.

53

It is the type of man and not his deed that justifies his being hanged.

54

I wonder if the vermins that live on the decomposing corpse also believe that they are reforming it.

55

No denying the fact that most politically operative values are national.

56

Criminal foolishness is foolish criminality?

57

The great task of the Cultivated mind: To find meaning in the meaningless.

58

How close relations, after all, are wisdom and stupidity.

59

Most tragic of all sights: a blind man who hits his seeing-eye dog.

60

How we hate those whom we have injured.

61

For this is all it all amounts to: the prototype from which to draw the picture of humanity is the prostitute.

62

The economist's difficulty in speaking of practical measures is that he talks to – if he is not himself – a vicious child that screams and kicks and never wants the means when it wants an end.

63

Principle is something we appeal to if we do not know a reason.

64

Most creation is pathological.

65

Only the sick oyster produces pearls.

66

What matters to man are his illusions.

67

There is not only the one enemy of humanity – the subnormal – there is another, the idealist.

68

He who understands mankind and still writes for them to read it is a fool, but he may be God's fool.

69

The best way to spoil a point of view is to make it a matter of principle.

70

Messages succeed more by the errors than by the truths they contain.

71

Truth cannot walk without the help of error any more than a lame man can walk without the help of crutches.

72

Mankind is a lame beggar and error its crutch.

73

The man who can read and write is *more* of a slave than the man who cannot.

74

Scientific medicine and scientific engineering would be impossible if their questions were decided by politicians and the popular vote.

75

A series of tactical successes often sums up to a strategic defeat.

76

In political and socio-political analysis, as you meet a statement of one of the parties observed – look for the opposite: it may be the truth.

77

Most common reason for being dissatisfied with an environment is not being able to meet its standards.

78

You can't substantiate what you love to assert? Never mind, economist, simply say: it is commonly known and you will be allright.

79

The most specifically human is $\left\{ \begin{array}{l} \text{sadism} \\ \text{beastliness} \end{array} \right.$

80

An economist who is not unpopular like hell is not worth his salt.

81

To lead men you must say certain lies.

82

Economics deals only with surface forms.

83

The meaning of each move is in the countermove.

84

He who talks about his vision tells you the limits of his range of vision.

85

Whatever other advantages Math may have, it is certainly the purest of human pleasures.

86

We all of us like a sparkling error better than a trivial truth.

87

Freedom – the ideal of the slave.

88

Advice to economists: boldly deny the obvious.

89

There is a kind of human tolerance that is nothing but lack of dignity.

90

Explanation is linking up more complex things with more simple things.

91

A friend is a man to whom you can be rude.

92

The victory of the soldier is the defeat of the general.

93

When people feel they cease to think.

94

Knowledge is restriction of possibilities.

95

Civilization is whipped out of the masses and declines with the incisiveness of the whip.

96

In order to be really stupid one does need a certain amount of cleverness.

97

Equality of men is the most stupid of all credos.

98

The enemy is the substandard.

99

The true problem is the problem of the subnormal, but instead of solving it, we take them into consideration.

100

It is our mind that looks for simplicity, not nature.

101

Planning means planlessness and waste.

102

Of all the reasons for the failure of able men the most important is the inability to wait.

103

Sanguinary revolution is the sadism of the well-behaved radical.

104

Politics is the art to change our mind gracefully.

105

Why do religions persecute?
Why, because men delight in persecuting.

106

The trouble is capitalism does not believe in itself.

Appendix II

Schumpeter's Novel Ships in Fog *(a Fragment)*

In the 1930s Schumpeter planned to write a novel, tentatively called **Ships in Fog.** *He only sketched the outline of the novel, which is reproduced here.[1] The outline is mainly of interest for its thinly veiled autobiographical content.*

Now let me be quite pedantic about it. Or else you'll never take in what I'm going to paint. Now backgrounds, racial and social, are essential in order to understand what a man is ...

Well he – let's call him Henry – was an Englishman by birth. But by race only on his mother's side. His father, before he acquired English citizenship would have called himself an Italian. But the matter is more complicated than that. The family belonged to the fringe end of the commercial and financial set of Trieste which racially was a mixture defying analysis. Greek, German, Serb and Italian elements. And presumably all of them contributed towards making our hero's paternal ancestry. His father had emigrated to England as an exponent of Triestian shipping interests and married an English girl with a great pedigree and absolutely no money.

Their only child was four years old when, well on the way to a considerable financial position, the father was killed on the hunting field. And the mother was henceforth the one great human factor in Henry's life. She was an excellent woman, strong and kind and amply provided with the delightful blinkers of English society. She did her duties in a way which can only be called manful though it was truly womanly when I come to think of it. To make him an English gentleman was her one aim in life.

She had not much money ... But she had connections which she resolutely exploited for her darling – that was among other [reasons] why to her dying day he belonged to one of the four or five best clubs though he hardly ever set foot in it and why he was seen on terms of equality in houses that rank much above what is referred to as the smart set, though, at the time of this story, he had ceased to frequent them and the corresponding country houses. But I want to make this quite clear – the social world was open to him from the beginning and shut only when he did not trouble to go and that meant much. No complexes. No faked contempt. No hidden wistfulness [...]

Oh mother, mother ... But let's go on. Disappointment was in store for her. Disappointment all the more bitter because realization was so near; all the more bitter, in a sense, precisely because in every other respect he gave her satisfaction and always not only felt [...] but also manifested in every word and act his unconditioned attachment to her, his unbounded confidence in her. Confidence – not the right word ...

Henry went through Eton and through two years of Oxford with flying colors. Then he broke away [...] That's it! ... Where was he at home? Not really in England! Often he had thought so but ancestral past had asserted itself each time. But neither in France or Italy though he found himself drifting to both whenever he had a week or a month to spare. Certainly not in Germany or what had been the Austro-Hungarian Empire.

But that was not the salient point. More than country means class – but he did not with subconscious allegiance belong either to society or the business class or the professions or the trade union world all of which provided such comfortable homes for everyone he knew. Yes – his mother's corner of society had been his as long as she lived.

And for modern man his work is everything – all that is left in many cases [...] Doing efficient work without aim, without hope.

No family [...]

No real friends though plenty of them.

No woman in whose womanhood to anchor.

According to Arthur Smithies, who has tried to reconstruct the outline to Schumpeter's novel on the basis of his notes, Henry's mother wanted him to enter politics.[2] Henry agreed, but for some reason he realized that he just could not do it. After a few years of reflection and confusion, he decided to go into business in the United States. He was more interested, it seems, in business as a kind of challenge than as a way to make money. Henry's Schumpeter-like character comes out in the following anecdote. Henry had asked his secretary to buy up a corporation on the stock exchange. When the secretary objected that Henry had a very low opinion of the management, Henry answered, 'How good must be a business that can stand such directors.' How the whole novel was supposed to end, Smithies says, we do not know.

Appendix III

Letters by Schumpeter

Schumpeter wrote a huge number of letters throughout his career and whatever remains of these are today scattered in private and public collections throughout the world. No attempt has been made to publish Schumpeter's full correspondence, an enterprise which would also be made difficult by the fact that Schumpeter often tore up the letters he received and used the pieces for his own notes. A few of his letters, however, have been published, notably some personal letters from Schumpeter's stay in Germany, 1925–31. These letters come from Gottfried Haberler's private collection and can be found in Eduard März' book on Schumpeter.[1] The letters which have been included in this Appendix, on the other hand, were mainly written during Schumpeter's stay in the United States, more precisely during the years 1933–49. All but three letters come from the Schumpeter Collection at Harvard University. Most of the letters at Harvard are neatly typed (the carbon copies were kept) and are less private in tone than the ones in the März volume. They have primarily been included here to give a picture of how Schumpeter viewed his own scientific production; a few also supply some information about his personal situation and his political preferences. The 1912 letter to John Bates Clark and the 1926 letter to Wesley Clair Mitchell come from the Butler Library at Columbia University, and the 1946 letter to Irving Fisher from Yale University Library. All letters are reprinted by permission of the respective library or archive.

Graz
Parkstrasse 17   March 10, 1912

My dear Professor Clark,[1]

When I had my book sent to you, I had the intention to write you a
few remarks about it, which I am now about to do.[2] Well, in the first
Chapter, I have developed the theory, that there would be no interest
in the static state and that there would be no other incomes but wages
and rents from natural agents. I know you don't agree with that,
though your conception of the industry being 'synchronized' in the
normal course of things plays an important part in it. In the second
chapter I then proceed to analyze what the essential forces of progress are *under the assumption* that population, technical knowledge,
tastes and so on *don't vary* – for, if they do, there is undoubtedly also
a sort of development but one which does not present new problems,
for the whole social economy adapts itself to the ever-altering data in
a well-known manner. I don't like to say anything about the results
reached in this and the next chapter.[3] But the fourth brings a theory
of entrepreneur's gain very like your own theory and the fifth, a
theory of interest, of which the fundamental thought is, that the
source of interest are the ever-varying profits, which crop up and
disappear constantly in a dynamic society and which cause an agio
on present *purchasing power* as such – as heretic a view as has ever
been committed to the flames. This 'dynamic' view of interest leads
to the result that interest is the child of progress and would disappear if society stood still and that neither workmen nor landlords
sacrifice a penny for interest paying. The sixth chapter gives a theory
of crises, based on the idea that progress is, as it were, a separate
phenomenon which essentially and necessarily causes a reaction in
those strata, which don't take part in it and the data of whose
existence are altered by it by sudden jerks. The seventh chapter
treats of some general questions especially of the influence of progress on all classes.[4]

This is what I understand by my 'dynamic theory', which I have
called – to humour German readers, who react[5] to the word 'dyna-

1   John Bates Clark (1847–1938). This letter is today to be found in the John
Bates Clark Papers, Rare Books and Manuscript Library, Columbia University.
2   Schumpeter here refers to *Theorie der wirtschaftlichen Entwicklung* (1911).
3   'Kredit und Kapital'.
4   'Das Gesamtbild der Volkswirtschaft'.
5   This word is difficult to make out.

mic' – 'Theorie der wirtschaftlichen Entwicklung'. It is mainly a theory of capital, interest, profits and crises. And I should love to know some day what you think of it. There would perhaps be some advantage in publishing a short paper on the main points, but I am so occupied that I could not think of doing it so far.

Last autumn we moved to Graz, when I have been called to this University. I like this pretty town surrounded by woody hills and my wife feels very well in its damp and English climate.

I hope you have been pleased by the little article I wrote in Schmollers Jahrbuch on American Economics.[6] I did not think it well to acknowledge the kind help you gave me in connection with it, for I thought it my duty to emphasize your personal share in the development of American thought and have been afraid that if I acknowledged your help, readers might infer that the prominence given to your work was somehow suggested by yourself.

Remember me, please, to Mrs. Clark and do me the favour to devote a leisure hour to my new book.

Very cordially yours,

Joseph A. Schumpeter

6   Joseph A. Schumpeter, 'Die neuerer Wirtschaftstheorie in den Vereinigten Staaten', *Jahrbuch für Gesetzgebung*, 1910.

Bonn (Germany)
Aug. 30th 1926
Coblenzerstrasse 39

My dear Mitchell,[1]

In sending you a paper, one of the aims of which was to say, what I have to say on the subject of your Presidential Address – and the subject of some private talks in times gone by – I cannot refrain from telling you, how often I thought of you ever since we parted in 1914 and how the lapse of time has been powerless to efface what was one of the instances, so rare in my life, of a genuine friendship. As such feeling is but rarely onesided I guess you often wondered

1   Wesley Clair Mitchell (1874–1948). This letter is today to be found in the Wesley Clair Mitchell Papers, Rare Books and Manuscript Library, Columbia University.

why I did not write. There were many reasons for this – it is not now interesting except for strict 'behaviorists'. It always was my intention to return to science as soon as it got possible again to live on a professorship – the measure of worldly success that beyond merit fell to my share never compensating me for what for me was work unpalatable well nigh beyond endurance, but it was not until the summer 1925 that an acceptable occasion to do so offered itself in the shape of the chair vacant at this University because of Dietzel's retirement on account of age.[2] I entered upon my duties in Nov. 1925, feeling extremely happy.[3] And I should, I believe, have kept on feeling happy, trying to make up for lost time and to exploit my 'practical experience' as well as new ideas.[4] Only I had married, about the same time, a wife twenty years my junior, whom I adored and who taught me the possibility of a paradise on earth. And four weeks ago, giving birth, before the time, to a boy she met a terrible death. This is one of the first letters I write. Of course, my days are falling slowly into their new order, but of course all light has gone out of them.

I have been delighted, all these years, to observe the steady growth of your fame in America as well as in Europe. I do think your work and teaching will make an epoch in the life of our science. Round your hearth, I trust, health and happiness are always present.

Kindly rem. me to Mrs. Mitchell and Snyder and believe me cordially yours

Joseph Schumpeter

P.S.: Excuse me for putting in a postscript what I really ought to have said in a most official way. The 'Archiv für Sozialwissenschaft', of which I am a coeditor, requests most insistently the honor of a contribution from you. My coeditors press me to ask you – and, as the Archiv is an acceptable platform, as far as German periodicals go, I think I may join my request to theirs: You will be widely read.

There is another similar thing: On October 2nd is to appear the first number of a new economics weekly, Der Deutsche Volkswirt, which aims at being – not too modestly – what the Nation and the Economist are in England. It will be well done, by the first economic Journalist of Germany, Dr. Stolper, will be absolutely independent, strictly

2   Schumpeter is referring to the chair after Heinrich Dietzel (1857–1935) at the University of Bonn.
3   Here follow a few illegible words.
4   Schumpeter here refers to his forays into politics and business, 1919–25.

respectable, of the best level attainable here and it is sure to be widely read. I shall contribute regularly and have been asked for advice as to foreign contributors. Now first: Could I have something from you? And secondly: Could you help to advice in getting other people to contribute? Besides economic questions, such as the trust problem (interstate commerce comm. and so on) it is questions of constitutional practice, cultural trends, political facts and tendencies, which would be of the highest importance. Of course, mere name counts for something, but good stuff will be taken also from unknown people. As to pay I expect them to be satisfactory, anyhow considerably over the German 'market rate'. The invitation to you is 'official', excuse me for being so informal about it. I should be happy to contribute a little towards some better understanding of American viewpoints.

2 Scott Street
Cambridge, Massachusetts

20 March 1933

Privat-Docent Dr. Gottfried V. Haberler
Piaristeng 60
Vienna, VIII, Austria

Dear Haberler:

Very many thanks for your letter which I hope you will forgive me for answering in English for if I have got to answer it in German, which means by my own hand, it would again lie about unanswered for months. There is no reason for you to have a bad conscience for it is really I who owe you a letter. But it is always the same tale with me. My inexorable program of work takes out of me what steam I have and then there is hardly anything left for other things. I hope you will explain this to Mrs. Haberler and ask her to forgive me for not having answered her gracious lines for all this time.

I wish to congratulate you heartily on having finished your book on International Trade which I greatly look forward to.[1] So it will come out before Ohlin after all, or at least pretty much at the same time.[2] I can figure your sense of relief. As to my book on Money to which you are good enough to refer, I really do not know whether I shall finish it in this academic year. It would probably be possible but in order to

1 Gottfried Haberler, *Der internationale Handel: Theorie der weltwirtschaftlichen Zusammenhänge sowie Darstellung und Analyse der Aussenhandelspolitik* (J. Springer, Berlin, 1933).
2 The reference is to Bertil Ohlin, *Interregional and International Trade* (Harvard University Press, Cambridge, 1933).

get rid of it I have to sacrifice so much that I take no pleasure whatsoever in what is left. It will be a thoroughly bad performance and greatly disappoint you. At least it will have the merit of being short for the continuous operations performed on it reduce the whole thing really to bare bones. I have made some progress in other respects, but this made me all the more impatient with this particular piece of work which I ought never to have undertaken. The depression exhaling from this manuscript has nearly spoiled my first year at Harvard which otherwise would have been very pleasant and all that I could have wished or expected.

I am greatly interested in what you tell me about your thoughts and plans. I only wish that I could do something to remove that evil spirit of critical doubt from your mind. It is melancholy to reflect that with your great powers you could do things for our science which you will never do if you look so icily on all the pioneers' work which in our days, through errors and failures, lays the foundation of a new economics, the contour lines of which I think I see fairly clearly. I sometimes feel like Moses must have felt when he beheld the Promised Land and knew that he himself would not be allowed to enter it but you do not see that Promised Land which you, being young, could certainly enter but always insist on denying its existence. Forgive my preaching. It was your remarks about measuring utility which prompted it.

I feel the same way about what you say with reference to the hypothesis of people maximising utility. We obviously can not do without a function which it would perhaps be best to call the 'economic potential' and which need not have any psychological significance but only certain formal properties. To attempt to do without it would be tantamount to denying that there is any connected whole of theoretical propositions about economic behavior at all. To interpret it as meaning utility or welfare may be useful for some problems, superfluous for others, and wrong for still others. But then, tautologies which may occur in this connection are perfectly harmless if they are tautologies at all. Now the endeavours to evaluate numerically that potential or in most cases difference between potentials and that kind is obviously the next step on the way of economics towards the status of a fully quantitative science and if we confine ourselves to telling each other that it is impossible, we shall never get beyond what is a rather uncomfortable transition stage. It is supreme courage which is wanted just now. Later generations may do the critical work and it is the presence of that courage which makes the greatness of Frisch, although I am sorry to say that he has quite a full measure of criticism for the products of other people. If the mathematicians and physicists a hundred years ago had been in possession of the critical apparatus of modern mathematics the greatest physical discoveries would never have been made, for the first thing that strikes one when one reads those old chaps is that what they were doing was, mathematically speaking, nonsense. It is the greatest of the many misfortunes which seem to beset the way of our science that its heroic stage falls in a time when all the other sciences around it have passed that stage and settled down to critique which may be quite the thing for them but which would spell sterility if transplanted into our field at this juncture.

On the other hand, I greatly approve of your plan to make all our empirical assumptions explicit. I think we shall have to add to them considerably as we go along. Nothing is more striking than the presence of unexplained invariants in economic life such as Pareto's 'Alpha' or what Keynes calls 'The Gibson Paradox' or Carl Snyder's 'Steady Rate of Increase in Total Production', and so forth. These things point to the presence of very constant relations between a few fundamental quantities and to the possibility of expressing them by very simple factual hypotheses.

I am greatly looking forward to reading your contribution to the Spiethoff volume. I am not astonished that you begin to find fault with the Mises–Hayek theory. What I was astonished about is that you ever had a taste for it even to the point of expounding it in your Chicago address which I was very sorry to read for really you ought to tell people of results of your own and if you allow me to say so, that address would have been a mistake even if that theory were more valuable than it is.

But about all these things it would be much better to talk than to write.

I was very glad to hear that the times do not affect the scientific activity of the Viennese circle which I shall ever look upon as a most signal instance of the truth that scientific and artistic achievement has but a very indirect connection with the economic and political environment. As to Germany, I find it very difficult to form an opinion. Recent events may mean a catastrophe but they also may mean salvation. I do not know that your personal chances are unfavorably affected for most of those who before would have been invincible competitors for professorships drop out now and it is by no means certain that equally invincible ones will be substituted for them.

Kindly remember me to Madam and believe me

Very cordially yours,

Joseph A. Schumpeter

P.S. I was very glad what you say about Sweezy. I shall look after him proportionately when he returns.

J. A. S.

2 Scott Street
Cambridge, Massachusetts

April 19, 1933

The Reverend Harry Emerson Fosdick
Riverside Church
Riverside Drive, New York City

Dear Sir:

   Your name has been suggested to me in connection with my plan
for forming a Committee to take care of some of those German scientists who are now being removed from their chairs by the present
government on account of their Hebrew race or faith. There is, of
course, nobody whose name and position would command as universal respect as yours in an action of this kind but not having the
privilege of your personal acquaintance I have no means of judging
whether and how far you are willing to interest yourself in this
matter. My friend Professor Wesley Clair Mitchell of Columbia University, is cooperating with me and would be glad to give you any
particulars you may desire. In any case, I beg to enclose a list of
names, the bearers of which are in that particular predicament. They
are all economists for, being an economist myself, I have naturally in
the first instance their fate at heart.
   In order to avoid what would be a very natural misunderstanding,
allow me to state that I am a German citizen but not a Jew or of
Jewish decent. Nor am I a thorough exponent of the present German
government, the actions of which look somewhat differently to one
who has had the experience of the regime which preceded it. My
conservative convictions make it impossible for me to share in the
well-nigh unanimous condemnation the Hitler Ministry meets with
in the world at large. It is merely from a sense of duty towards men
who have been my colleagues that I am trying to organise some help
for them which would enable them to carry on quiet scientific work
in this country should necessity arise.
   I beg to apologise for intruding upon you and beg to remain

               Very sincerely yours,

               Joseph A. Schumpeter

2 Scott Street
Cambridge, Massachusetts

May 18, 1934

Mr. Stewart S. Morgan
Department of English,
College City, Texas.

My dear Mr. Morgan:

It is with great pleasure that I give my consent, if such be required, to the reprinting of my essay on 'Depressions' in your collection.[1] To be frank I rather feel flattered at your wish to do so, for it is certainly the greatest compliment that has yet been paid to my handling of what is for me a foreign language. I do think that, if you will allow such a colloquialism, I muddle along all right both in writing and in talking, but I had no idea that my English was eligible for a collection to be used in courses in composition.

You want to have some facts about myself. Well, I am an Austrian by birth, born in 1883 in a village called Triesch in what was then a province of the Austro-Hungarian Empire, viz. Moravia, which now forms part of the Czechoslovakian Republic. I was educated in Vienna, and following up an impulse which very early asserted itself, I then travelled about for a few years studying economics from various standpoints and began to give lectures on Economic Theory at the University of Vienna in 1909, in which year I also was appointed to a chair of Economics in Czernowitz, then the most eastern town of Austria, now belonging to Roumania. I was called to the University of Graz in 1911, and in 1913–14 I acted as what was called an exchange professor to Columbia University, when I first made acquaintance with and fell in love with this country. Later on I entered politics and took office as Minister of Finance in Austria after the war. I did not return to scientific life until 1925, when I accepted a professorship at the University of Bonn, Germany. In 1927–28 and again in 1930 I visited Harvard University, which I joined as a member of her permanent staff in 1932. I think this is as much as you will want to know about my past history and type of life.

At present my interests are exclusively in Economic Theory and in the analysis of the phenomena of the business cycle, about which I hope to publish a rather portly volume within a year. Other things

1 Joseph A. Schumpeter, 'Depressions – Can We Learn from Past Experience?', in *The Economics of the Recovery Program*, ed. D. V. Brown et al. (Whittlesey House, McGraw-Hill, New York and London, 1934), pp. 3–21.

partly or entirely outside the economic sphere will engage my attention later on. As to publications, if everything be counted they probably run into something like two hundred items, but most of the results of my work have been published in two books, the one entitled The Nature and Essence of Theoretical Economics (1908), the other The Theory of Economic Evolution (1912). The latter has been translated into French, Italian and English (the Italian translation has appeared already; the French and English ones will do so shortly, while Russian and Japanese translations are in hand). Perhaps I may also mention a History of Economics (1914) and two sociological pieces of work: The Sociology of Imperialism and The Theory of Social Classes which, originally intended for books, actually appeared only in a German scientific periodical called the Archiv für Sozialwissenschaft und Sozialpolitik of which I was also co-editor and to which also I contributed half a dozen other papers. There is of course a lengthy series of papers which probably mean something to the specialist, but for our purpose I do not think I need mention any more titles.

Sincerely yours,

Joseph A. Schumpeter

2 Scott Street
Cambridge, Massachusetts

June 4, 1934

Mr. David T. Pottinger,
Publishing Department Harvard University Press,
38 Quincy Street,
Cambridge, Massachusetts.

Dear Mr. Pottinger,

Enclosed please find some material summarizing my forthcoming book in the Harvard Economic Studies.[1] I hope that it is the sort of thing you want, yet I am not at all sure. It is of course quite easy to characterize briefly any monograph on a limited subject. But in this case I confess that I felt considerably embarrassed and I had better explain my difficulties to you.

1   Joseph A. Schumpeter, *The Theory of Economic Development: An Inquiry into Profits, Capital, Credit, Interest, and the Business Cycle*, tr. Redvers Opie (Harvard University Press, Cambridge, 1934). Originally published as volume XLVI in the Harvard Economic Studies Series.

When this book first appeared in 1911, both the general view of the economic process embodied in it and about half a dozen of the results it tried to establish seemed to many people so strikingly uncongenial and so far removed from traditional teaching that it met almost universal hostility. But since then both the general view and some of the individual theorems have been gaining ground and have exerted considerable influence on contemporaneous work in Germany. It is this that prompted friends or pupils in many countries to undertake translations. An abbreviated Italian one has already appeared; the French is about to appear; a Japanese is in preparation; and at the instigation and friendly encouragement of Professor Taussig I have even been induced to sanction the English one which you are about to publish, although I feel misgivings in submitting such a purely theoretical structure to the Anglo-American public in a form with which I have partly grown out of sympathy myself. For although the translation is made on the second German edition which has been revised (the third German edition is merely a reprint of the second), it is in substance still the book of 1911, which it has to remain if its original message was worth conveying at all. Now I am frankly ill at ease in trying to explain what the thing really means. What I am going to say will unavoidably repeat in the main what is said in the prefaces, but I trust to your superior experience to make something out of it that will serve the purpose.

Thanking you for all the trouble you take on behalf of this child of mine which has almost grown a stranger to me.

Sincerely yours,

Joseph A. Schumpeter

HARVARD UNIVERSITY
DEPARTMENT OF ECONOMICS

Cambridge, Massachusetts
March 19, 1936

Professor Irving Fisher
460 Prospect Street
New Haven, Conn.

My dear Fisher:

Ever so many thanks for your kind letter. I feel immensely relieved by gathering from it that although perhaps somewhat annoyed, as you may well be, you are not really cross with me. Let us then leave it with Hotelling and Bowley and I am still ready to obey the call of duty in case Hotelling should fail after all.[1]

I am deeply grateful for the generous interest you take in the hygienic background of my case. You are right on all essential points. My work is my only interest in life and I do try, as you put it, to get the maximum performance out of my machine. I admit that it is reasonable to try to deal as rationally with one's organism as one does with one's motor car and that attention to a set of rational rules is a very essential thing which may make all the difference between success and failure.

I have often felt annoyed that doctors fail to realize that. When I try in the summer to get into working form again and for the purpose consult some doctor, the result has been so far invariably that there is nothing organically the matter with me and that hence nothing ought to be done. This is precisely the reverse of the truth. It is before a definite breakdown has occurred that investigation ought to show the weak points in order to take them in hand while there is time. I am therefore looking forward with the greatest possible interest to the new edition of your book from which I hope to learn a lot.

Very Sincerely Yours,

Joseph A. Schumpeter

1   The reference is probably to some business concerning the Econometric Society. Harold Hotelling was its president in 1936–7.

HARVARD UNIVERSITY
DEPARTMENT OF ECONOMICS

Cambridge, Massachusetts
December 23, 1936

In re: Mr. Talcott Parsons' manuscript: *Sociology and the Elements of Human Action*.[1]

To the Committee on Research in the Social Sciences:

Having completed a study of the above manuscript as the Committee wished me to do, I beg to report as follows:

1   Schumpeter had been asked by Harvard's Committee on Research in the Social Sciences to comment on a project by Parsons that the Committee had

There is no doubt whatsoever in my mind but that this book will fill a definite function in the American literature. In particular, the critical exposition of the ideas of Max Weber will do much to put before the American scientific public a body of doctrine which is very difficult of access and has therefore been unduly neglected as compared with the structure of Pareto or Durkheim. The scholarly care with which the main elements of Max Weber's thought are analyzed and followed to their sources and displayed in their significance cannot be too highly commended. The author has in fact so deeply penetrated into the German thicket as to lose in some places the faculty of writing clearly in English about it, and some turns of phrase become fully understandable only if translated into German.

Precisely because Pareto and Durkheim, still more of course Marshall, are better known, the exposition of their thought will not fulfill precisely the same function. But in the case of Marshall, where the author sums up an earlier published work of his,[2] it must be admitted that much of which he has to say is illuminating and novel. The laborious disquisitions about Durkheim have, to me, opened many nooks and crannies in a system which I did not notice or understand before. It should be added that understanding Durkheim involves understanding the Comtest tradition from which much of his work arose and that Mr. Parsons seems to me to meet that test successfully. Both his introduction and his concluding chapters are eminently sensible and scholarly, although I do not put them as high as those which are devoted to critical exposition. I am not enough of a philosopher, however, to appreciate the necessity of expressing oneself quite at that length. Personally, I think the work would considerably gain by being shortened. Much space seems to me to be needlessly lost in getting to the point.

On the whole, therefore, my opinion is definitely favorable to publication of this work which not everyone will appreciate, but which everyone must recognize as a very serious piece of research. Commercial publication seems to me pretty much out of the question, but I may be wrong in this. American thought has of late so much turned in those directions that sales may be after all more favorable than I expect.

J. A. Schumpeter

funded. Parsons manuscript was later published as *The Structure of Social Action: A Study in Social Theory with Special Reference to a Group of Recent European Writers* (McGraw-Hill Book Company, Inc, New York, 1937).
2 Talcott Parsons, 'Wants and Activities in Marshall', *Quarterly Journal of Economics*, 46 (1931), pp. 101–40.

May 12, 1937

Mr. Albert Pratt
Goodwin, Proctor & Hoar
84 State Street
Boston, Mass.

My dear Pratt:

There are two points which I want to add to what otherwise would
be mere thanks for your too kind letter.

First: No, no satisfactory exposition of the rationale of the conservative creed exists. The old little book by Lord Hugh Cecil is quite
out of date and never was very much.[1] It appeared in some collection
(like Everyman's Library, but I don't think it was that) almost thirty
years ago. There is a certain amount of literature from the specifically Roman Catholic standpoint, but this would probably not serve
the purpose.

Views closely related to ours are sometimes expounded in this
country in the American Review, which seems to me to merit more
attention than it gets, but is not quite the thing either. Much can be
found in general histories of politics, biographies of politicians and
so on, but this is not more than material. It is one of the humors of
the situation that conservatism has never satisfactorily formulated
itself. This is indeed an important task, for no party can attract that
is not sure of its own intellectual ground.

It must be done on many levels: a scientific and truly philosophic
exposition of doctrine is as important in a time where the intellectual
counts for so much, as are popular formulations, accessible and
attractive to everybody. All this work is antecedent to formulating
any particular programs. That this is so you can easily see from the
history of the socialist movement. Surely, there was no lack of practical spirit and tactical skill about it. But nevertheless socialists
always realized that it is necessary to have a broad background of
ideas to draw on. And they went into the discussions of detailed and
refined points of doctrine with a zest from which conservatives have
much to learn.

The second point I want to mention because I was unable to do so
at our dinner, or rather I did not wish to do so since, with time as
limited as it was, it would have hardly been possible to avoid misunderstandings, is the cause of Spain. It is instructive for a number
of reasons, but I want to mention only one, the tremendous efficiency
of radical propaganda.

1   Lord Hugh Cecil, *Conservatism* (Williams and Norgate, London, 1912).

Nothing proves more how far conservative spirit and conservative organization have already decayed than the fact that radical lies and distortions not only have access to, but command the international press, with the result that many good conservatives in this country perfectly innocently and honorably take sides with the anarchist and communist rabble. They seriously believe that the movement headed by Franco, which is really the most national and democratic imaginable and means nothing else but the revolt of the very soul of Spain against barbarism and crime, is nothing but the plot of a group of mercenaries paid by foreign fascism.

When such distortion becomes possible, conservative thinking, as well as conservative action, must be at the mercy of its enemies. No marshalling of conservative forces and no clear purpose in action is possible under such circumstances.

Cordially yours,

Joseph A. Schumpeter

7 Acacia Street
March 12, 1940

Mr. W. W. Rostow
Department of Economics
Barnard College
Columbia University
New York, N.Y.

Dear Mr. Rostow:

I have your letter of February 26 and will touch upon the points you raise in your order.[1]

Ad. 1. Yes, on principle the opening date of a long wave should be the inflection point in the ascending interval of the curve (not necessarily a sine curve: see Chapter 5 of 'Business Cycles') which would theoretically indicate its sweep. For the first Kondratieff which I have stated in some detail, that inflection point should come somewhere in the 80's of the eighteenth century. But at that time, still more than in the two subsequent cases, disturbing factors have to be taken account of which make the exact location of that inflection point extremely doubtful, even apart from the scantiness of

---

1   Rostow must have written to Schumpeter just after having read *Business Cycles* (1939).

information. I date from 1786. As to the maxima (upper turning
points) you are almost exactly right. According to my account the
first Kondratieff reaches its maximum or upper turning point in
1801, the second in 1857, the third in 1911. I quite agree with you
that the process of testing such a schema involves approximate dating. That is why I dated every single juglar, and for a few intervals of
time at least, also the kitchins.

Ad. 2. Yes, it is my opinion that the price level should normally rise
in the prosperity phases of Kondratieffs and fall during recession and
depression. I am less positive about recovery; though this has not
been actually the case in the first and second Kondratieffs, it is
conceivable that the downward excess of depressions might produce
a corrective rise in recession. You are right in assuming that the
upward movement of prices, in the absence of counter-acting forces,
more than cancelling the other three phases, should last about four-
teen years. Yes, I do hold that the increases in price level in the
1790's, and especially in the 1850's, and in the sixteen years pre-
ceeding the World War were essentially caused by the Kondratieff
prosperity process.

Ad. 3. The long wave describes what I like to call the great recurrent industrial revolutions. Perhaps I should be more explicit about
that but I confine myself now to answering your special question. I
do think that the downgrades (recessions and depressions) of the
Kondratieffs are among other things characterized by abnormal unemployment, which each generation that lives through it, as a matter
of fact, believes practically to be chronic. This is statistically quite
clear, beyond any doubt, concerning the current Kondratieff. It is
also clear for the second Kondratieff, especially in the 70's and 80's.
And we may infer from such stray data as we have, that unemployment was unusually severe in the 20's of the nineteenth century. Or,
in fact since the close of the Napoleonic Wars, which would of course,
by virtue of the well known mechanism of war economy, obscure
that effect for the time between 1800 and 1815. But I do not believe it
correct to say that 'secularly falling prices', as such, are to be blamed
for that. I should be interested to know what evidence induces you to
deny the prevalence of unemployment from 1815 to 1850 (Why 1850?
The 30's were already in the recovery phase, though there was also
plenty of unemployment then, and the Kondratieff ends with 1842.
Of course, there was no abnormal unemployment in the time of the
English railroad mania of the 40's). And in the 70's and 80's. The
article in the Economic History Review, which I look upon for very
nice verifications, speaks of investment of real wage rates, also of real
wage bill; but all of this is perfectly compatible with abnormal
unemployment as evidenced by the English trade-union percentage. I
agree with you that the Thorpe–Mitchell measurement is impaired
by the periods they choose.

Ad. 4. Of course I would not object. It is of the essence of my theory that innovation includes the opening of new areas, sources of supply, outlets, new organizations, and so on. I thought I had made that quite clear.

Ad. 5. I do think that on the whole the long wave conception works well. In particular, my partiality for it has been increased by the fact that it clears up phenomena which otherwise would constitute unexplained problems, such as the Gibson paradox or the 'breaks in trend' which many students find in their series, for instance in the 90's of the nineteenth century.

Like all great disturbances such as the Civil War or the World War, 1914–1918, the Napoleonic Wars distort all cycles, repeatedly turning into booms what otherwise would have been depressions, and displaying both peaks and troughs. The behavior, relative to each other, of producers goods' and consumers goods' output is theoretically an extremely delicate question, which on some occasions is made hopeless by the defects of our material. On the whole, however, I think it possible to show that the increase in producers goods' output in the downward phase of the long wave tends, relative to the increase in consumers goods' output, to be less rather than more rapid. This would require a lot of discussion, however.

Post-war innovations were primarily 'induced and completing'. This is most obviously seen in the utility and motor car developments, together with all their subsidiaries. This does not mean that there were not a few fundamentally new things. But they don't amount to much, at least not for the time being. Many quite new things turn out to be 'induced and completing' if, for instance, the electrification of the household is put into its proper setting as a side-show of the general electrical development.

Yes, I have come to the conclusion that innovation was on a sufficient scale from 1786 to 1801 to account for what I mean it to account. But you must never forget, first, that I only claim 'igniting' importance for innovations and that I do not deny that the bulk of the prosperity phenomena comes about through processes not themselves of an innovatory character (see the post-war building boom in this country). And, second, that the innovation of that period did not simply consist in cotton textile and in iron and steel developments, but also in the further canal building and in the spread of the factory system as such. If this is properly taken into account, the thing is not so inadequate as those historians seem to think who always point out that the Watts engines were of small quantitative importance before 1820.

Sincerely yours,

Joseph A. Schumpeter

7 Acacia Street
March 16, 1940

Professor Simon Kuznets
Wharton School of Finance and Commerce
University of Pennsylvania
Philadelphia, Pennsylvania

Dear Kuznets:

Needless to say I am delighted to hear that you are going to review my 'Business Cycles'.[1] I hope you will not hesitate to put me right on many points on which you know very much more than I do, and particularly if, in the last two chapters, I have made improper use of your work on 'National Income'.[2]

It has been very kind of you to take that trouble about my dating. I believe indeed, that at least an attempt at dating is essential for the testing of any realistic business cycle theory. That is why I have tried to date not only the Kondratieffs but also *all* the Juglars and, if I have not done the same with the Kitchins (but have dated these only in a number of cases and over limited periods), that was because it was simply beyond my time and means.

You will understand, however, that my dating is frankly experimental, and in many cases only approximate. For instance, I feel fairly confident that a new wave of development started in the three countries studied by me in the 80's of the eighteenth century. The evidence is strong for England, although weaker for this country, and weakest for Germany, for which country the information I could gather was not adequate. But I feel not much confidence in the particular year (1786) I have chosen.

I feel particularly obliged because my own count differs somewhat from the one you have derived from my volumes. You state correctly that as far as I can see, the differences between the countries are only small. But difficulties are somewhat increased if dating is by the whole year. You will, therefore, find that in what follows I have inserted fractional years in two cases.

The phases of the Kondratieff of the Industrial Revolution I date as follows:

Prosperity	1787–1800
Recession	1801–1813

1 Kuznets's review turned out to be devastatingly critical. See Simon Kuznets, 'Schumpeter's *Business Cycles*', *American Economic Review*, 30 (1940), pp. 257–71.
2 Simon Kuznets, *National Income and Capital Formation, 1919–1935: A Preliminary Report* (National Bureau of Economic Research, New York, 1937).

| Depression | 1814–1827 |
| Revival | 1828–1842 |

The phases of the bourgeois Kondratieff are:

Prosperity	1843–1857
Recession	1858–1869
Depression	1870–1884/5
Revival	1886–1897

The phases of the Neo-Mercantilist Kondratieff

Prosperity	1898–1911
Recession	1912–1924/5
Depression	1926–1938

I know that I have been sticking my neck out in being so positive about a doubtful matter, but I think I can say this for myself: wherever the schema does not fit I am prepared to prove in detail the presence of disturbances which seem to me to be adequate to account for the deviations.

Cordially yours,

Joseph A. Schumpeter

7 Acacia Street
May 21, 1941

Mr. Charles C. Burlingham
Burlingham, Veeder, Clark & Hupper
27 William Street
New York City

Dear Burlingham,

Enclosed please find a reprint of the memoir of our departed friend.[1] My co-authors did not interfere with my text at all but I still wish you to understand that the fact that I was writing in the name of a committee prevented me from adding a personal touch which would have been there if I had written over my single signature. I will certainly send a copy to Mrs. Alfred Brandeis who by the way I visited once in Louisville – delightful old lady, charming milieu.

I read with sorrow that you are in a pretty low state of mind. So

1   Joseph A. Schumpeter (with Arthur H. Cole and Edward S. Mason) 'Frank William Taussig', *Quarterly Journal of Economics*, 55 (1941), pp. 337–63.

am I, of course. In a sense every one of us must necessarily be an Anglophile, but it is the state of the future of this country which primarily weighs upon my mind. After all, readjustment in Europe was over-due and I never believed in the possibility of upholding indefinitely arrangements and spheres of influence which fundamentally date from the 18th century. In part, Hitler seems to me to be nothing but the creature of that maladjustment. Now this fact is, of course, irrelevant for England but it is not irrelevant for this country which is going to stake her everything on an attempt to keep up an obsolete state of things. This, however, is only part of my troubles. When I see how the government goes about defense and when I consider what kind of fiscal policy and what kind of government control over industry is likely to emerge once the President becomes absolute on our entry into the war, I cannot help feeling that this will be the end of the American way of life. A ten-years' war and a ten-years' Roosevelt dictatorship will completely upset the social structure. That the likes of us will disappear is, of course, in itself of small moment. But that tremendous possibilities for human happiness should be destroyed (and destroyed without necessity) seems to me one of the great tragedies of history. Well, the dies are cast and all we can now do is, I suppose, to hope for national success.

Cordially yours,

Joseph A. Schumpeter

May 26, 1941

Mr. Lloyd S. Huntsman
570 South Sixth Street
San Jose, California

My dear Mr. Huntsman,

First I have to apologize for the fact that pressure of work has prevented me from answering your letter of April 29 until today. I hope that my letter does not arrive too late to help you in framing your term report.

You have chosen a difficult task. My notions on the subject of value and distribution can be gleaned from that old book of mine which appeared first in 1911 and was translated into English in 1930 or so.[1] There I tried to show that distribution in capitalist society is dominated by the fact that capitalism is an evolutionary process and therefore displays phenomena which we cannot hope to discover in a study of a stationary economy.

---

1 *Theorie der wirtschaftlichen Entwicklung* (1911, tr. into English in 1934).

My theory of profits is really very simple and the theory of interest, which encountered so many objections, should be easier to swallow now since Mr. Keynes has adopted one which in important respects is much on the same lines. Both these theories you will find also expounded in my book on 'Business Cycles'.

If I had time I should be glad to go more fully into the matter and to tell you how the whole thing looks to me now. But since you ask for data about myself I will confine myself to telling you briefly that I am an Austrian and that I was born in 1883 in a place that since has fallen within Czechoslovakia. I was educated in Vienna where I took my doctor's degree in Law and Political Science and after practicing law in Cairo, Egypt, I became lecturer at the University of Vienna and then Professor of Economics at a few other Austrian universities, after which I entered politics and became Minister of Finance in 1919. I returned to teaching and research in 1925 when I accepted the Chair at the University of Bonn in the Rhineland. In 1930 I accepted a call to Harvard where I have been since the fall of 1932. I think that's all but it would be difficult to give you a survey of my scientific development. Dropping early sociological and historical interests, I became an economic theorist and the work of my youth is summed up in a book I published in 1907.[2] Then I worked at that theory of economic evolution into which personal observation, historical studies, and theoretical work enter in proportions which it is difficult to define. I have written dozens of other things but fortunately you are not concerned with this.

Sincerely yours in a hurry,

Joseph A. Schumpeter

2   *Das Wesen und der Hauptinhalt der theoretischen Nationalökonomie* (1908).

February 16, 1942

Miss Edna Lonegan
3714 Avenue I
Brooklyn, N.Y.

Dear Colleague:

Many thanks for your too kind letter. It is in fact a constant source of wonder to me how it is possible for other sensible people to try to build far-reaching fundamental theories on material drawn from the last decade or at best from the last two decades. If they looked a little farther back they could not fail to discover that the depression, 1929–32, was anything but unprecedented and that the only thing that was really new about it was the spirit in which it was met.

Now so far as there are any scientific reasons (as distinguished from political preferences) the only remedy for it is a greater place for economic history in the training and the intellectual furniture of our economists. I have been primarily a theorist all my life and feel quite uncomfortable in having to preach the historian's faith. Yet I have arrived at the conclusion that theoretical equipment, if uncomplemented by a thorough grounding in the history of the economic process, is worse than no theory at all.

With kind regards and in the hope of meeting you somewhere and somewhen.

Very sincerely yours,

Joseph A. Schumpeter

December 6, 1943

Professor David McCord Wright
James Wilson School of Economics
University of Virginia
Charlottesville, Virginia

Dear Wright:

Thanks for your letter, which I do not wish to leave unanswered.

I am in hopes that the Quarterly Journal of Economics will accept your paper. Concerning the 'tremendous' stock of actual knowledge with which you are good enough to credit me, I can give a very simple piece of advice: never miss an opportunity to add to it, and furthermore choose your leisure-hour reading so as to add to the historical part of it, and the stock will automatically grow beyond your own expectations.

I experienced a moment of real pleasure when I read your brief reference to your own family history. This is, indeed, the one thing in my theoretical (so far as it is not purely technical) writing on which I pride myself; it is all seen, and in this sense there is nothing in my structures that has not a living piece of reality behind it. This is not an advantage in every respect. It makes, for instance, my theories so refractory to mathematical formulations. They can never be so cut and dried as Keynes' schema is; but there are compensating advantages, and one of them is that so many people have told me, as you have done: 'Yes, that is so. I know that from my own experience and observation'. Your family seems to be a particularly typical case.

This answers, in part, your remark about Keynes' use of the marginal propensity to consume. There are two reasons why I do not think much of it. The first is that so far as such a propensity, having become set, plays any causal role, it is just one of those many hitches which must indeed be taken account of in the analysis of a particular situation, but which have no place among the great factors that produce the contour lines. The second reason is that whenever such a propensity does play such a role and means more than the temporary persistence of a habit, then it is only a word for the really operative causes which must be found in the individual situations of the bourgeois families that display the phenomena. In other words, the concept only marks the door to the real problem.

I ought really to go more into this and, in particular, into the equivocation by which Keynes arrives at the result that 'saving' necessarily reduces the total amount of consumption and produces the result that consumers goods remain unsold (which as a general proposition seems to me to be completely wrong) and by which his followers arrive at the result that after any single injection of money, natural income must after a time fall back to its previous level. Instead of going into this, I wish, however, to point out that the difference between myself and Hansen concerning the problem of the stagnating economy is, so far as the theoretical aspect of this problem is concerned, not so great as it seems. Perhaps you will remember that in my Business Cycles I envisaged the possibility of what I called 'prosperityless' cycles. That would be cycles which would really consist only of slumps interrupted by temporary recoveries. This model proves that, however I may differ from Hansen in the diagnosis in the facts of the thirties, there is no unbridgeable gulf between us theoretically.

Cordially yours,

Joseph A. Schumpeter

August 7, 1944

Professor C. A. Gulick
119 South Hall
University of California
Berkeley, California

Dear Professor Gulick,

I do not envy you your arduous task.[1] It must be awfully difficult to reconstruct from inevitably inadequate and partly unreliable

1 C. A. Gulick had asked Schumpeter about his role in the scandal surrounding Alpine Montan during Schumpeter's time as finance minister in 1919. Schumpeter disagreed with the conclusions that Gulick drew from this letter and wrote another one to Gulick, dated 18 October, 1944. Excerpts from both of Schumpeter's letters can be found in volume 1 of C. A. Gulick, *Austria from Habsburg to Hitler* (Berkeley, University of California Press, 1948), pp. 140–1.

material the true course of events during the troubled time [in Austria after the First World War]. All I can remember concerning the incident to which you refer is this.

The Alpine-Montan Corporation, the largest iron producer of Austria and the owner of by far the most important source of iron ore in that country, naturally loomed large in all the plans of socialization that were discussed in 1918 and 1919. I have never been able to make up my mind how serious those discussions were, considering that in the position of what was left of the Austrian state it was clearly impossible to carry any measure that would unfavorably affect any interest able to secure foreign support. Of this the leading men of the socialist party were fully aware, but they found it difficult to make the point clear to the rank and file, which might easily have suspected prevarication behind any such argument. Under these circumstances, I find it perfectly understandable that Dr. Bauer, in the book from which you quote,[2] repeated what then was a current rumor, although from my knowledge of him I absolve him from any charge of conscious dishonesty. But the fact is that I had neither a motive nor the power to initiate or to prevent any buying campaign on the stock exchange which was perfectly free. The banker you mentioned needed no authorization from me, nor would such authorization have helped him.[3] All the Minister of Finance was concerned with was that foreign exchange acquired by means of sales of stock to foreigners should be duly delivered at the legal rate to the public treasury, a rule which was enforced as far as possible. To this criticism by the Volkswirt (I know of it only from your letter) must be reduced. I never published anything either officially or unofficially on the matter, but, if my memory serves me, the government commissioner of the stock exchange did. That is to say, he published, I think, a notice warning the public against speculative excesses that have no other basis than rumors about foreigners who were supposed to interest themselves in Austrian industries. If such a notice was published, it must have been sometime in the spring of 1919.

Allow me to add a word on a more interesting matter. In conditions of advanced inflation, which has, however, not yet taken full effect on prices, there is an argument for a capital levy which does not apply in other circumstances. For a few weeks I thought it possible to break the spiral of inflation by such a measure, but the idea had to be given up for two reasons. First, owing to the political alliance between socialists and Christian socialists, the agrarian sector would have been practically exempted from its proper share in the burden. Second, socialist opinion was in favor of using the levy as

2   Otto Bauer, *Die Österreichische Revolution* (Wiener Volksbuchhandlung, Vienna, 1923).
3   Richard Kola.

a means of socialization. For both reasons, the measure would have been futile as a means of combatting inflation, as, in fact, it proved to be when enacted under my successor. This explains the fate of the bill during my tenure in office, which is difficult to understand without those two factors. In another sense and for another purpose, a capital levy played a role as a part of my program of reconstruction which was embodied in the budget that never got beyond the cabinet and over which I resigned.

I have no objection to your using the information contained in this letter or any part of it in any way you please.

Sincerely yours,

Joseph A. Schumpeter

**Joseph A. Schumpeter
7 Acacia Street
Cambridge, Massachusetts**

February 18, 1946[1]

Dear Fisher,[2]

No, I have not been abroad nor sick in any technical sense of the word, and have really no excuse to offer for my unpardonable silence except that I found it so difficult to formulate an answer.

I consider you one of the dozen or so first economists of all times and countries, and, if I did not know that, my work on the history of economic analysis which I hope to complete in the current year would have brought the fact home to me. Moreover I entertain feelings of admiration and affection toward you personally which I reserve for a still smaller number of people. Therefore, anything that might redound to the honor of your name is bound to appeal to me most strongly. Also, feeling thus toward you, I am grateful for your invitation to join the Advisory Board which I consider an honor.

Nevertheless I do not feel I can accept and, in order to avoid misunderstandings which I should greatly regret, I must allude to personal convictions with which I hate to bother you: I am not, like you, hale, strong, and in fundamental – and hopeful – sympathy with

1 The date has been added to the letter, presumably by the librarian in charge of ordering the Irving Fisher Papers at the Department for Manuscripts and Archives at Yale University Library, from where this letter comes.
2 Irving Fisher (1867–1947).

modern mankind. On the contrary I feel ill in mind and body (and not only because of what happened in the war), always tired and downcast and am dragging myself through work which nevertheless is *all I do not hate*. This of course is for you alone. But it is not, you will realize, the condition in which one can accept a call of hope like yours. I should be utterly useless – in fact an impediment because I now always function in the way of which you have just had an example.

But this does not mean that I am not grateful.

Let me thank you, then, and allow me to remain

affectionately yours

Joseph Schumpeter

P.S.: Many thanks for your book – wish I could profit by it!

December 4, 1948

Mr. George Maiswinkle, Assistant Treasurer
Chilton Company
Chestnut and 56th Street
Philadelphia 39, Pennsylvania

Dear Mr. Maiswinkle:

In reply to your letter of November 26, I beg to inform you that I am not planning any revisions in my two volumes on BUSINESS CYCLES. The reason is that it covers all the relevant material nearly up to the year in which war demand began to assert itself. Ever since, the economic process has been under the influence of this war demand and the attendant inflation, so that the phenomena characteristic of the normal business cycle have been entirely overshadowed. As regards the scientific groundwork and the methods of approach, I have nothing to alter. Allow me to add that the prognosis which would follow from my three cycle schema seems to be fully borne out by postwar events so far, and that I am as convinced as ever that, barring wars, revolutions and so on, the business process will run on a rising trend of prosperity for about the next fifteen years, though we may expect this general prosperity to be interrupted two or three times by short and sharp recessions.

Very truly yours,

Joseph A. Schumpeter

April 22, 1949

Professor Lewis H. Haney
Graduate School of Business Administration
New York University
90 Trinity Place
New York 6, New York

Dear Professor Haney:

I have always refused to answer questions such as the one you have addressed to me in your letter of April 18th, and also to participate in a German publication that was issued about fifteen years ago by a publishing firm (I forget the name) and consisted in a series of autobiographical papers by a number of economists.[1] My reason was that nobody is an unbiased judge of what he has done himself. I feel, however, that I should not adhere to this principle when such a question is addressed to me by a colleague whom I respect so sincerely as I do you and when refusal to answer would look like an attempt to thwart an evidently generous intention. Therefore, I will try to characterize how my own work in technical economics looks to me. I am going to leave out my excursions into sociology, particularly my papers on imperialism and on social classes and also the argument of my CAPITALISM, SOCIALISM AND DEMOCRACY, although the latter contains also some purely economic chapters.

All economists, including the English classics (especially Ricardo and John Stuart Mill) of course paid some attention, more or less, to phenomena of economic development. But the scientific core of their systems was invariably economic statics, the only outstanding exception being Marx. Myself, I began at an early age to look upon economic life essentially as a process of change, and I tried to make the main features of this change the center of my own type of theory. In doing so, I discovered that a number of phenomena such as entrepreneurial profits, interest, and credit found ready explanation within such an evolutionary schema. The theory of business cycles had, of course, always been 'evolutionary' by nature, but even in this case a new explanation occurred to me that differed from others in showing that the mechanism of evolution so works as to produce a wave-like movement of its own even when there are no external disturbances to produce them. Results were first published systematically (there were a few articles before that) in a book entitled THE THEORY OF ECONOMIC DEVELOPMENT that I published in 1911

1   Haney must have written to Schumpeter as part of preparing for the new edition of his standard work *History of Economic Thought: A Critical Account of the Origin and Development of Economic Theories of the Leading Thinkers in the Leading Nations* (Macmillan, New York, 1949).

(although the year actually printed on the first edition was 1912). Systematic expansion and the bulk of the necessary historical and statistical complements were published in the two volumes that appeared in 1939.

My line of thought created no school, although elements that hail from it are to be found in the writings of a great many economists, many of whom do not share my general views. Thus, for instance, my theory of credit became a generally accepted commonplace and the view that interest is a monetary phenomenon has been carried to success by Keynes and his school with whom, in other respects, I have little in common (although from a passage in the TREATISE ON MONEY I infer that Keynes personally accepted my theory of the cycle).[2] And it would take a great amount of labor in order to form an opinion how much or how little my work has helped in producing modern economics – a question that does not interest me enough to waste trouble upon answering it. But of late, to my surprise, there has been a sort of revival of interest in it, especially in France.

Please understand that I have dictated the above in order to fulfill your wish and out of respect for you, but not in order to advertise for myself. Any recognition of my cooperation would, therefore, only embarrass me and also draw upon me understandable remonstration from correspondents whose analogous wishes have not been fulfilled.

Wishing you all possible success for the new edition of your excellent history,

Sincerely yours,

Joseph A. Schumpeter

P.S. A small point that always has interested me just happens to occur to me: about a year after the publication of my THEORY OF ECONOMIC DEVELOPMENT and about three years after the publication of my first article on business cycles there appeared in the Journal of the Royal Statistical Association an article by D. H. Robertson that hinted at, although it did not fully develop, the same idea. Robertson then produced a fuller version in his book entitled A STUDY OF INDUSTRIAL FLUCTUATIONS and some of the ideas in his BANKING POLICY AND THE PRICE LEVEL also show affinity to my way of thinking. Nothing could be farther from my mind than accusing that excellent economist of having borrowed from me. All my publications up to that time had been in German, which he doesn't read and the differences in argument are much too great to

2   For the relevant passage, see volume 2 of John Maynard Keynes, *A Treatise on Money* (St Martin's Press, London, 1971), pp. 85–6. Keynes' work was originally published in 1930.

warrant assumption of anything else but a chance affinity. But precisely because I am convinced of his independence, this little fact is of some interest.

August 10, 1949

Prof. Shigeto Tsuru
Tokyo University of Commerce
Kunitachi
Tokyo, Japan

Dear Friend Tsuru:

Many thanks for your letter of July 30. It is with particular pleasure that I welcome you back to academic activities which as in the 5th century in Rome are perhaps the least distasteful ones to indulge in, in the world as it is. Studies in mathematics and statistics will complement most usefully your theoretical achievements and I greatly look forward to the results. Of course, distance always beautifies but I who am near enough to Harvard cannot say that I experience very much stimulus from my surroundings. Scientifically, Leontief is the only man who is really alive and even he is now so much buried in administrative work, running the big research organization which he has built up, that not so very much remains of him either. The fundamental ideas, methods and approaches you know, and original achievement can be built upon this in Tokyo as well as in Boston. What is added to them year by year is not so very much.

It was very good of you to give me news of our friends. Please convey my best regards to Professors Nakayama, Tobata, Araki and Shibata.

With kind regards and best wishes from both of us to both of you.

Cordially yours,

Joseph A. Schumpeter

November 8, 1949

M. le Professeur René Roux
52 Boulevard Magenta
Paris 10, France

My dear colleague:

Of course I shall be delighted if you will undertake the task of writing a sketch on my views on the theory on money. It will be a difficult task however, for apart from my German article in *Archiv für Sozialwissenschaft*,[1] of which I do not think much myself, I have never treated the problems of money per se: my views on money have been presented only incidentally in works of mine which were primarily devoted to other subjects. Thus I have published both of my theories of money and credit in my *Theory of Economic Development* which first appeared in 1911 and also contains an exposition of my monetary theory of interest. Since 1934 I do not think that I have written anything about the subject except in Chapters 8, 11, 12 and 13 of my book on *Business Cycles*. The fifth section of Chapter 14 is also pertinent to the matter, but within a year or two I hope to write a book on money that will give my latest views.

With kind regards.

Sincerely yours,

Joseph A. Schumpeter

1   Joseph A. Schumpeter, 'Das Sozialprodukt und die Rechenpfennige: Glossen und Beiträge zur Geldtheorie von heute', *Archiv für Sozialwissenschaft und Sozialpolitik*, 44 (1917), pp. 627–715.

Bibliography of
Schumpeter's Works

This bibliography focuses primarily on Schumpeter's scientific works and less on his political writings. Everything that Schumpeter wrote in the original, be it in English or German (or in some other language) has been included. Whenever an item has been translated into English, a notation indicates where to find the translation. To compile the bibliography I have mainly drawn on three already existing bibliographies: Elizabeth Boody Schumpeter's 'Bibliography of the Writings of Joseph Alois Schumpeter', *Quarterly Journal of Economics*, 64 (1950), pp. 373–84; Michael I. Stevenson's *Joseph Alois Schumpeter: A Bibliography, 1905–1984* (Westport, Conn.: Greenwood Press, 1985); and Massimo M. Augello's extremely detailed bibliography in *Joseph Alois Schumpeter: A Reference Guide* (Berlin: Springer-Verlag, 1990), which is also reprinted in Joseph A. Schumpeter, *The Economics and Sociology of Capitalism*, edited with an introduction by R. Swedberg (Princeton: Princeton University Press, 1991).

There exist several collections of Schumpeter's scientific articles; and whenever an article can be found in one of these, it will be added after the original bibliographic notation. Three in English are: *Essays*, edited with an introduction by R. V. Clemence (Cambridge: Addison-Wesley, 1951); *Ten Great Economists: From Marx to Keynes*, edited with an introduction by Elizabeth Boody Schumpeter (New York: Oxford University Press, 1951); and *The Economics and Sociology of Capitalism* (Princeton: Princeton University Press, 1991). There is also *Imperialism and Social Classes*, edited with an introduction by Paul Sweezy (New York: A. M. Kelley; Oxford: Blackwell, 1951). Some of Schumpeter's articles, which originally appeared in German, have been collected in anthologies as well: in *Aufsätze zur ökonomischen Theorie*, edited by Erich Schneider and Arthur Spiethoff (Tübingen: J. C. B. Mohr, 1952); in *Aufsätze zur Soziologie*, edited by Erich Schneider and Arthur Spiethoff (Tübingen: J. C. B. Mohr, 1953) and in *Dogmenhistorische und biographische Aufsätze*, edited by Erich Schneider and Arthur Spiethoff (Tübingen: J. C. B. Mohr, 1954). A few original items can also be found in *Beiträge zur Sozialökonomik*, edited with an introduction by Stephan Böhm (Vienna: Böhlau Verlag, 1987).

Since this bibliography only contains the most important of Schumpeter's political writings and of his writings in the popular press, the reader's attention should be drawn to the many items in *Aufsätze zur Wirtschaftspolitik*, edited with an introduction by Wolfgang F. Stolper and Christian Seidl (Tübingen: J. C. B. Mohr, 1985). There is also the fact that Schumpeter wrote a huge number of book reviews, of which only the most important have been included. A full list of the reviews can be found in Massimo M. Augello's excellent bibliography. Most of the collections of Schumpeter's essays as well as his books, it should finally be added, are still in print.

Books

Das Wesen und der Hauptinhalt der theoretischen Nationalökonomie (Munich and Leipzig: Duncker & Humblot, 1908).
Theorie der wirtschaftlichen Entwicklung (Leipzig: Duncker & Humblot, 1912). (The book actually appeared in 1911.) The second revised edition was published in 1926 as *Theorie der wirtschaftlichen Entwicklung: Eine Untersuchung über Unternehmergewinn, Kapital, Kredit, Zins und den Konjunkturzyklus* (same publisher). An English translation of the second edition has appeared under the title *The Theory of Economic Development: An Inquiry into Profits, Capital, Credit, Interest, and the Business Cycle*, tr. Redvers Opie (Cambridge: Harvard University Press, 1934).
Epochen der Dogmen- und Methodengeschichte (Tübingen: J. C. B. Mohr, 1914). This work originally appeared as part of Volume I of *Grundriss der Sozialökonomik*, ed. Max Weber. An English translation has appeared under the title *Economic Doctrine and Method: An Historical Sketch*, tr. R. Aris (London: George Allen & Unwin; New York: Oxford University Press, 1954).
Vergangenheit und Zukunft der Sozialwissenschaften (Munich and Leipzig: Duncker and Humblot, 1915).
Business Cycles: A Theoretical, Historical and Statistical Analysis of the Capitalist Process. 2 vols. (New York and London: McGraw-Hill, 1939).
Capitalism, Socialism and Democracy (New York: Harper & Brothers, 1942). Second rev. ed. 1947. Third enlarged ed. 1950. Schumpeter also wrote a new preface to the third English edition 1949.
(with William Leonard Crum) *Rudimentary Mathematics for Economists and Statisticians* (New York: McGraw-Hill Book Company, 1946).
History of Economic Analysis. Edited with an introduction by Elizabeth Boody Schumpeter (London: Allen & Unwin; New York: Oxford University Press, 1954).
Das Wesen des Geldes. Edited with an introduction by Fritz Karl Mann. (Göttingen: Vandenhoeck und Ruprecht, 1970).

Articles

As noted in the introduction to this bibliography, there exist several collections of Schumpeter's articles and whenever an article can be found in one of these, it will be added after the original bibliographic notation. For the full reference, the reader is referred to the introduction.

1905

'Die Methode der Standard Population', *Statistische Monatschrift*, 31 (1905): 188–91.
'Die Methode der Index-Zahlen', *Statistische Monatschrift*, 31 (1905) : 191–7.
'Die internationale Preisbildung', *Statistische Monatschrift*, 31 (1905): 923–8.

1906

'Über die mathematische Methode der theoretischen Ökonomie', *Zeitschrift für Volkswirtschaft, Sozialpolitik und Verwaltung*, 15 (1906): 30–49. Reprinted in *Aufsätze zur ökonomischen Theorie*.
'Professor Clarks Verteilungstheorie', *Zeitschrift für Volkswirtschaft, Sozialpolitik und Verwaltung*, 15 (1906): 325–33.
'Rudolf Auspitz', *Economic Journal*, 16 (1906): 309–11.

1907

'Das Rentenprinzip in der Verteilungslehre', *Jahrbuch für Gesetzgebung, Verwaltung und Volkswirtschaft im Deutschen Reich*, 31 (1907): 31–65, 591–634. Reprinted in *Aufsätze zur ökonomischen Theorie*.

1908

'Einige neuere Erscheinungen auf dem Gebiete der theoretischen Nationalökonomie', *Zeitschrift für Volkswirtschaft, Sozialpolitik und Verwaltung*, 17 (1908): 402–20. (Reviews of books by Seligman, Jevons, Carver and others.)
'J. B. Clark, *Essentials of Economic Theory*', *Zeitschrift für Volkswirtschaft, Sozialpolitik und Verwaltung*, 17 (1908): 653–9.

1909

'Bemerkungen über das Zurechnungsproblem', *Zeitschrift für Volkswirtschaft, Sozialpolitik und Verwaltung*, 18 (1909): 79–132. Reprinted in *Aufsätze zur ökonomischen Theorie*.
'On the Concept of Social Value', *Quarterly Journal of Economics*, 23 (1909): 213–32. Reprinted in *Essays*.
'Irving Fisher, *The Nature of Capital and Income*', *Zeitschrift für Volkswirtschaft, Sozialpolitik und Verwaltung*, 18 (1909): 679–80.

1910

'Über das Wesen der Wirtschaftskrisen', *Zeitschrift für Volkswirtschaft, Sozialpolitik und Verwaltung*, 19 (1910): 271–325.
'Marie Esprit Léon Walras', *Zeitschrift für Volkswirtschaft, Sozialpolitik und*

Verwaltung, 19 (1910): 397–402. Reprinted in *Dogmenhistorische und biographische Aufsätze* and translated in *Ten Great Economists*.
'Die neuere Wirtschaftstheorie in den Vereinigten Staaten', *Jahrbuch für Gesetzgebung, Verwaltung und Volkswirtschaft im Deutschen Reich*, 34 (1910): 913–63.
Wie studiert man Sozialwissenschaft? Czernowitz: H. Pardini, 1910. Reprinted in *Aufsätze zur ökonomischen Theorie*.
'V. Pareto, *Manuel d'économie politique*', *Archiv für Sozialwissenschaft und Sozialpolitik*, 31 (1910): 257.
'G. Schmoller, *Grundriss der allgemeinen Volkswirtschaftslehre. 1. Teil*', *Archiv für Sozialwissenschaft und Sozialpolitik*, 31 (1910): 257–8.
'E. von Böhm-Bawerk, *Kapital und Kapitalzins*', *Archiv für Sozialwissenschaft und Sozialpolitik*, 31 (1910): 271.

1913

'Zinsfuss und Geldverfassung', *Jahrbuch der Gesellschaft Österreichischer Volkswirte* (1913): 38–63. Reprinted in *Aufsätze zur ökonomischen Theorie*.
'Eine "dynamische" Theorie der Kapitalzinses: Eine Entgegnung', *Zeitschrift für Volkswirtschaft, Sozialpolitik und Verwaltung*, 22 (1913): 599–639. Reprinted in *Aufsätze zur ökonomischen Theorie*.
'Meinungsaüsserung zur Frage des Werturteils', pp. 49–50 in *Äusserungen zur Werturteilsdiskussion im Ausschuss des Vereins für Sozialpolitik*. Düsseldorf: Privately printed, 1913.

1914

'Die "positive" Methode in der Nationalökonomie', *Deutsche Literaturzeitung*, 35 (1914): 2101–8. Reprinted in *Aufsätze zur ökonomischen Theorie*.
'Das wissenschaftliche Lebenswerk Eugen von Böhm-Bawerks', *Zeitschrift für Volkswirtschaft, Sozialpolitik und Verwaltung*, 23 (1914): 454–528. Reprinted in *Dogmenhistorische und biographische Aufsätze* and translated (partly) in *Ten Great Economists*.
'Die Wellenbewegung des Wirtschaftslebens', *Archiv für Sozialwissenschaft und Sozialpolitik*, 39 (1914–15): 1–32. Reprinted in *Beiträge zur Sozialökonomik*.

1916

'Das Grundprinzip der Verteilungstheorie', *Archiv für Sozialwissenschaft und Sozialpolitik*, 42 (1916–17): 1–88. Reprinted in *Aufsätze zur ökonomischen Theorie*.

1917

'Das Bodenmonopol – Eine Entgegnung auf Dr. Oppenheimers Artikel', *Archiv für Sozialwissenschaft und Sozialpolitik*, 44 (1917–18): 495–502.
'Das Sozialprodukt und die Rechenpfennige: Glossen und Beiträge zur Geldtheorie von heute', *Archiv für Sozialwissenschaft und Sozialpolitik*, 44

(1917–18): 627–715. Reprinted in *Aufsätze zur ökonomischen Theorie* and translated in *International Economic Papers*, 6 (1956): 148–211.

1918

Die Krise des Steuerstaates (Graz and Leipzig: Leuschner and Lubensky, 1918). Reprinted in *Aufsätze zur Soziologie* and translated into English in *International Economic Papers*, vol. 6 (1954): 5–38 (reprinted in *The Economics and Sociology of Capitalism*).
'Karl Marx, der Denker', *Arbeiterwille*, 29 (5 May, 1918). Reprinted in *Beiträge zur Sozialökonomik*.

1919

'Zur Soziologie der Imperialismen', *Archiv für Sozialwissenschaft und Sozialpolitik*, 46 (1918–19): 1–39, 275–310. Reprinted in *Aufsätze zur Soziologie* and translated into English in *Imperialism and Social Classes* (reprinted in *The Economics and Sociology of Capitalism*).

1920

'Sozialistische Möglichkeiten von heute', *Archiv für Sozialwissenschaft und Sozialpolitik*, 48 (1920–1): 305–60. Reprinted in *Aufsätze zur ökonomischen Theorie*.
'Max Webers Werk', *Der Österreichische Volkswirt*, 12 (August 1920): 831–4. Reprinted in *Dogmenhistorische und biographische Aufsätze* and translated in *The Economics and Sociology of Capitalism*.

1921

'Carl Menger', *Zeitschrift für Volkswirtschaft und Sozialpolitik*, 1 (1921): 197–206. Reprinted in *Dogmenhistorische und biographische Aufsätze* and translated in *Ten Great Economists*.

1923

'Angebot', pp. 299–303 in Volume 1 *Handwörterbuch der Staatswissenschaften*, 4th edn (Jena: Verlag von G. Fischer, 1923).
'Kapital', pp. 582–4 in Volume 5 *Handwörterbuch der Staatswissenschaften*, 4th edn (Jena: Verlag von G. Fischer, 1923).

1924

'Der Sozialismus in England und bei uns', *Der Österreichische Volkswirt*, 16 (December 1924): 295–7, 327–30. Reprinted in *Aufsätze zur ökonomischen Theorie*.

'Eugen von Böhm-Bawerk', pp. 63–80 in vol II of *Neue Österreichische Biographie 1815–1918* (Vienna: Amalthea Verlag, 1925). Reprinted in *Dogmenhistorische und biographische Aufsätze* and translated in *The Development of Economic Thought*, ed. H. W. Spiegel (New York: John Wiley and Sons, 1952), pp. 569–80.

'Edgeworth und die neuere Wirtschaftstheorie', *Weltwirtschaftliches Archiv*, 22 (1925): 183–202. Reprinted in *Dogmenhistorische und biographische Aufsätze*.

'Kreditkontrolle', *Archiv für Sozialwissenschaft und Sozialpolitik*, 54 (1925): 289–328. Reprinted in *Aufsätze zur ökonomischen Theorie*.

'The Currency Situation in Austria', pp. 225–31 in United States Senate. Commission of Gold and Silver Inquiry. Foreign Currency and Exchange Investigation. Serial 9 (Volume 1) by J. P. Young, *European Currency and Finance*. Washington: Government Printing Office, 1925.

1926

'Gustav v. Schmoller und die Probleme von heute', *Schmollers Jahrbuch für Gesetzgebung, Verwaltung und Volkswirtschaft*, 50 (1926): 337–88. Reprinted in *Dogmenhistorische und biographische Aufsätze*.

'G. F. Knapp', *Economic Journal*, 36 (1926): 512–14. Reprinted in *Ten Great Economists*.

1927

'Die sozialen Klassen im ethnisch homogenen Milieu', *Archiv für Sozialwissenschaft und Sozialpolitik*, 57 (1927): 1–67. Reprinted in *Aufsätze zur Soziologie* and translated into English in *Imperialism and Social Classes* (reprinted in *The Economics and Sociology of Capitalism*).

'Cassels Theoretische Sozialökonomik', *Schmollers Jahrbuch für Gesetzgebung, Verwaltung und Volkswirtschaft*, 51 (1927): 241–60. Reprinted in *Dogmenhistorische und biographische Aufsätze*.

'Die Arbeitslosigkeit', *Der Deutsche Volkswirt* (March 1927): 729–32. Reprinted in *Aufsätze zur Wirtschaftspolitik*.

'Sombarts dritter Band', *Schmollers Jahrbuch für Gesetzgebung, Verwaltung und Volkswirtschaft*, 51 (1927): 349–69. Reprinted in *Dogmenhistorische und biographische Aufsätze*.

'Zur Frage der Grenzproduktivität: Eine Entgegnung auf den vorstehenden Aufsatz von Willen Valk', *Schmollers Jahrbuch für Gesetzgebung, Verwaltung und Volkswirtschaft*, 51 (1927): 671–80.

'Unternehmerfunktion und Arbeiterinteresse', *Der Arbeitsgeber*, 17, 8 (1927): 166–70. Reprinted in *Aufsätze zur Wirtschaftspolitik*.

'Zur Einführung der folgenden Arbeit Knut Wicksells: Mathematische Nationalökonomie', *Archiv für Sozialwissenschaft und Sozialpolitik*, 58 (1927–8): 238–51. Reprinted in *Dogmenhistorische und biographische Aufsätze*.

'Friedrich von Wieser', *Economic Journal*, 37 (1927): 328–30. Reprinted in *Ten Great Economists*.

'Die goldene Bremse an der Kreditmaschine', pp. 80–106 in vol. I of *Kölner Vorträge* (No publisher: Cologne, 1927). Reprinted in *Aufsätze zur ökonomischen Theorie.*

'The Explanation of the Business Cycles', *Economica*, 7 (1927): 286–311. Reprinted in *Essays.*

'Deutschland', pp. 1–30 in vol. I of F. A. Fetter and R. Reisch (eds) *Die Wirtschaftstheorie der Gegenwart* (Vienna: J. Springer, 1927). Reprinted in *Dogmenhistorische und biographische Aufsätze.*

1928

'Staatsreferendar und Staatsassessor', *Schmollers Jahrbuch für Gesetzgebung, Verwaltung und Volkswirtschaft*, 52 (1928): 703–20. Reprinted in *Aufsätze zur ökonomischen Theorie.*

'The Instability of Capitalism', *Economic Journal*, 38 (1928): 361–86. Reprinted in *Essays.*

'International Cartels and Their Relation to World Trade', in P. T. Moon (ed.) *America as a Creditor Nation* (New York: Columbia University, 1928).

'Der Unternehmer in der Volkswirtschaft von heute', pp. 295–312 in B. Harms (ed.) *Strukturwandlungen der deutschen Volkswirtschaft* (Berlin: Reimer Hobbing, 1928). Reprinted in *Aufsätze zur Wirtschaftspolitik.*

'Unternehmer', pp. 476–87 in vol. VIII of *Handwörterbuch der Staatswissenschaften*, 4th edn (Jena: G. Fischer, 1928). Reprinted in *Beiträge zur Sozialökonomik.*

1929

'Das soziale Anlitz des Deutschen Reiches', *Bonner Mitteilungen*, 1 (1929): 3–14. Reprinted in *Aufsätze zur Soziologie.*

'Die Wirtschaftslehre und die reformierte Referendarprüfung', *Schmollers Jahrbuch für Gesetzgebung, Verwaltung und Volkswirtschaft*, 53 (1929): 637–50. Reprinted in *Aufsätze zur ökonomischen Theorie.*

'Ökonomie und Soziologie der Einkommensteuer', *Der Deutsche Volkswirt*, 4 (December 1929): 380–5. Reprinted in *Aufsätze zur Wirtschaftspolitik.*

1930

'Mitchell's Business Cycles', *Quarterly Journal of Economics*, 45 (1930): 150–72. Reprinted in *Essays.*

'Auspitz, Rudolf (1837–1906)', p. 317 in Vol. 2 of *Encyclopaedia of the Social Sciences* (New York: The Macmillan Company, 1930).

'Böhm-Bawerk, Eugen von (1851–1914)', pp. 618–19 in Vol. 2 of *Encyclopaedia of the Social Sciences* (New York: The Macmillan Company, 1930).

1931

'The Present World Depression: A Tentative Diagnosis', *American Economic Review*, Supplement (March 1931): 179–82. Reprinted in *Essays.*

246   BIBLIOGRAPHY OF SCHUMPETER'S WORKS

'Les possibilités actuelles du socialisme', *L'Année Politique Française et Etrangère*, 24 (1931): 385–418.
'The Theory of the Business Cycle', *Keizaigaku Ronshu – The Journal of Economics*, 4, 1 (1931): 1–18.
'The Present State of International Commercial Policy', *The Kokumin Keizai Zasshi – Journal of Economics and Business Administration*, 50 (1931): 481–506.
'The Present State of Economics. Or on Systems, Schools and Methods', *The Kokumin Keizai Zasshi – Journal of Economics and Business Administration*, 50 (1931): 679–705.
'Das Kapital im wirtschaftlichen Kreislauf und in der wirtschaftlichen Entwicklung', pp. 187–208 in vol. I of B. Harms (ed.) *Kapital und Kapitalismus* (Berlin: Veröffentlichungen der deutschen Vereinigung für Staatswissenschaftliche Fortbildung, 1931).

1932

'A German View: World Depression and Franco-German Economic Relations', *Lloyds Bank Limited Monthly Review*, Supplement (March 1932): 14–35.
'Ladislaus von Bortkiewicz', *Economic Journal*, 42 (1932): 338–40. Reprinted in *Ten Great Economists*.
'G-H Bousquet, *Institutes de science économique*', *Economic Journal*, 42 (1932): 449–51.

1933

'The Common Sense of Econometrics', *Econometrica*, 1 (1933): 5–12. Reprinted in *Essays*.
'Der Stand und die nächste Zukunft der Konjunkturforschung', pp. 263–7 in *Festschrift für Arthur Spiethoff* (Munich: Duncker & Humblot, 1933).
'J. M. Keynes, *Essays in Biography*', *Economic Journal*, 43 (1933): 652–7.

1934

'Imperfect Competition', *American Economic Review*, Supplement 24 (March 1934): 21–32.
'Depressions – Can We Learn from Past Experience?', pp. 3–21 in D. V. Brown et al. (eds) *The Economics of the Recovery Program* (New York and London: Whittlesey House, McGraw-Hill, 1934). Reprinted in *Essays*.
'Joan Robinson, *The Economics of Imperfect Competition*', *Journal of Political Economy*, 42 (1934): 249–57.

1935

'The Analysis of Economic Change', *Review of Economic Statistics*, 17 (1935): 2–10. Reprinted in *Essays*.
'Young, Allyn Abbott (1876–1929)', pp. 514–15 in Vol. 15 of *Encyclopaedia of the Social Sciences* (New York: The Macmillan Company, 1935).

1936

'Professor Taussig on Wages and Capital', pp. 213–22 in *Explorations in Economics: Notes and Essays Contributed in Honor of F. W. Taussig* (New York and London: McGraw-Hill, 1936). Reprinted in *Essays*.

'J. M. Keynes, *General Theory*', *Journal of the American Statistical Association*, 31 (1936): 791–5. Reprinted in *Essays*.

Can Capitalism Survive? (Washington, DC: United States Department of Agriculture Graduate School, 1936).

1937

'Preface' to the Japanese translation of *Theorie der wirtschaftlichen Entwicklung* (1926 edn). Reprinted in *Essays*.

1940

'The Influence of Protective Tariffs on the Industrial Development of the United States', *Academy of Political Science – Proceedings*, 19 (May 1940): 2–7. Reprinted in *Essays*.

1941

(with Arthur H. Cole and Edward S. Mason) 'Frank William Taussig', *Quarterly Journal of Economics*, 55 (1941): 337–63. Reprinted in *Ten Great Economists*.

'Alfred Marshall's Principles: A Semi-Centennial Appraisal', *American Economic Review*, 31 (1941): 236–48. Reprinted in *Ten Great Economists*.

1942

'G. J. Stiegler, *The Theory of Competitive Price*', *American Economic Review*, 32 (1942): 844–7.

1943

'Capitalism in the Postwar World', pp. 113–26 in S. E. Harris (ed.) *Postwar Economic Problems* (New York and London: McGraw-Hill, 1943). Reprinted in *Essays*.

1946

'The Decade of the Twenties', *Papers and Proceedings of the American Economic Review*, 36 (1946): 1–10. Reprinted in *Essays*.

'John Maynard Keynes, 1883–1946', *American Economic Review*, 36 (1946): 495–518. Reprinted in *Ten Great Economists*.

'Keynes and Statistics', *Review of Economic Statistics*, 28 (1946): 194–6.

'L'Avenir de l'entreprise privée devant les tendances socialistes modernes', pp. 103–8 in *Comment sauvegarder l'entreprise privée* (Montreal: L'Association Professionelle des Industriels, 1946). An English translation from the 1975 volume of *History of Political Economy* is reprinted in *The Economics and Sociology of Capitalism.*

'Capitalism', pp. 801–7 in Vol. 4 of *Encyclopaedia Brittanica* (Chicago, London and Toronto: Encyclopaedia Brittanica Ltd, 1946). Reprinted in *Essays.*

'F. A. Hayek, *The Road to Serfdom*', *Journal of Political Economy*, 54 (1946): 269–70.

1947

'The Creative Response in Economic History', *Journal of Economic History*, 7 (1947): 149–59. Reprinted in *Essays* and (in the original, longer version) in *The Economics and Sociology of Capitalism.*

'Theoretical Problems of Economic Growth', *Journal of Economic History*, Supplement 7 (1947): 1–9. Reprinted in *Essays.*

'Keynes, the Economist', pp. 73–101 in S. E. Harris (ed.) *The New Economics: Keynes' Influence on Theory and Public Policy* (New York: A. A. Knopf, 1947).

1948

'There is Still Time to Stop Inflation', *Nation's Business*, 36 (June 1948): 33–5, 88–91. Reprinted in *Essays.*

'Irving Fisher's Econometrics', *Econometrica*, 16 (1948): 219–31. Reprinted in *Ten Great Economists.*

1949

'Science and Ideology', *American Economic Review*, 39 (1949): 345–59. Reprinted in *Essays.*

'Vilfredo Pareto, 1848–1920', *Quarterly Journal of Economics*, 63 (1949): 147–73. Reprinted in *Ten Great Economists.*

'The Communist Manifesto in Economics and Sociology', *Journal of Political Economy*, 57 (1949): 199–212. Reprinted in *Essays.*

'English Economists and the State-Managed Economy', *Journal of Political Economy*, 57 (1949): 371–82. Reprinted in *Essays.*

'Economic Theory and Entrepreneurial History', pp. 63–84 in *Change and the Entrepreneur: Postulates and Patterns for Entrepreneurial History*, ed. by the Research Center for Entrepreneurial History (Cambridge: Harvard University Press, 1949). Reprinted in *Essays.*

'The Historical Approach to the Analysis of Business Cycles', pp. 149–62 in *Conference on Business Cycles* (New York: National Bureau of Economic Research, 1949). Reprinted in *Essays.*

1950

'Wesley Clair Mitchell, 1874–1948', *Quarterly Journal of Economics*, 64 (1950): 139–55. Reprinted in *Ten Great Economists*.
'The March into Socialism', *American Economic Review*, 40 (1950): 446–56.

Published posthumously

1951

'Review of the Troops', *Quarterly Journal of Economics*, 65 (1951): 149–80.

1952

'Das Woher und Wohin unserer Wissenschaft', pp. 598–608 in *Aufsätze zur ökonomischen Theorie*. Schumpeter gave this speech in 1932.

1982

'The "Crisis" in Economics – Fifty Years Ago', *Journal of Economic Literature*, 20 (1982): 1049–59. Based on a lecture delivered in Japan in 1931.
'Recent Developments of Political Economy', *Kobe University Economic Review*, 28 (1982): 1–15. Based on a lecture delivered in Japan in 1931. Reprinted in *The Economics and Sociology of Capitalism*.

1983

'American Institutions and Economic Progress', *Zeitschrift für die gesamte Staatswissenschaft*, 139 (1983): 191–6. This outline was written in 1949. Reprinted in *The Economics and Sociology of Capitalism*.

1984

'The Basic Lines of Financial Policy for Now and the Next Three Years', pp. 566–85 in Eduard März, *Austrian Banking and Financial Policy: Creditanstalt at a Turning Point, 1913–1923* (London: Weidenfeld and Nicolson, 1984). The original version of this article from 1919 can be found in Schumpeter, *Aufsätze zur Wirtschaftspolitik*.
'The Meaning of Rationality in the Social Sciences', *Zeitschrift für die gesamte Staatswissenschaft*, 140 (1983): 577–93. A fuller version of this article from 1940 can be found in *The Economics and Sociology of Capitalism*.

1985

'Memorandum I'. First published in *Aufsätze zur Wirtschaftspolitik*, pp. 251–72.
'Memorandum II'. First published in *Aufsätze zur Wirtschaftspolitik*, pp. 273–89.
'Memorandum III'. First published in *Aufsätze zur Wirtschaftspolitik*, pp. 289–310.

1987

'Some Questions of Principle', *Research in the History of Economic Thought and Methodology*, 5 (1987): 93–116. This constitutes a different version of chapter 1 in *History of Economic Analysis* than the one Elizabeth Boody Schumpeter chose to publish.
An Economic Interpretation of Our Time: The Lowell Lectures, pp. 339–400 in *The Economics and Sociology of Capitalism*, ed. R. Swedberg (Princeton, N.J.: Princeton University Press, 1991). Schumpeter gave the Lowell Lectures in 1941.
'Wage and Tax Policy in Transitional States of Society', pp. 429–37 in *The Economics and Sociology of Capitalism*, ed. R. Swedberg (Princeton, N.J.: Princeton University Press, 1991). This is the outline for a course Schumpeter gave in 1948 at the National University in Mexico City.
'Can Capitalism Survive?', pp. 298–315 in *The Economics and Sociology of Capitalism*, ed. R. Swedberg (Princeton, N.J.: Princeton University Press, 1991). A verbatim transcription of a speech Schumpeter gave in 1936 (and the discussion afterwards).

Notes

Introduction

1 Max Weber, '"Objectivity" in Social Science and Social Policy', in *The Methodology of the Social Sciences*, tr. E. A. Shils and H. A. Finch (The Free Press, New York, 1949), p. 63.
2 Joseph A. Schumpeter, *The Theory of Economic Development: An Inquiry into Profits, Capital, Credit, Interest, and the Business Cycle*, tr. R. Opie (Cambridge, Harvard University Press, 1934), p. 3.
3 Joseph A. Schumpeter, 'Vilfredo Pareto, 1848–1923', in *Ten Great Economists: From Marx to Keynes* (New York, Oxford University Press, 1951), pp. 112–13.

Chapter 1   Childhood and Youth

1 Joseph Schumpeter to Stewart S. Morgan, 18 May 1934. This letter, like all other letters from the Joseph Schumpeter Collection, is cited by permission of the Harvard University Archives (HUA), Cambridge, Massachusetts. The quote at the opening of the chapter comes from 'Professor Schumpeter, Austrian Minister, Now Teaching Economic Theory Here', *The Harvard Crimson*, 11 April 1944, pp. 1, 4.
2 Elizabeth Schumpeter to Therese Dautzenberg, 15 January 1951. This letter, like other letters from the Elizabeth Boody Schumpeter Collection, is cited by permission of the Schlesinger Library, Cambridge, Massachusetts. All of Schumpeter's material left behind in Jülich was destroyed during the Second World War (with the exception of a few books that were sent to his wife).
3 Schumpeter's birth certificate can be found in the Schumpeter Collection at the Harvard University Archives. The collection consists of some 130 boxes of articles, manuscripts, letters and the like, which Elizabeth Boody Schumpeter put together and donated to Harvard University after her husband's death.

4 Here, as elsewhere, I have drawn on Christian Seidl's careful scholarship when it comes to dates in Schumpeter's life. See Christian Seidl, 'Joseph Alois Schumpeter: Character, Life and Particulars of his Graz Period', in *Lectures on Schumpeterian Economics*, ed. Christian Seidl (Springer-Verlag, Berlin, 1984), p. 189.

5 Edda Gigers to Elizabeth Boody Schumpeter, 6 March 1951 (HUA). Edda Gigers was born Edith Schumpeter (1900–?) and was a distant relative of Schumpeter, being the daughter of the son of one of Schumpeter's grandfather's children. (Some obvious language errors and some overly awkward sentence constructions in the letter have been corrected.)

6 Here as elsewhere, when discussing the history of the Schumpeters in Triesch, I have mainly drawn on Yuichi Shionoya, 'The Schumpeter Family in Trest', *Hitotsubashi Journal of Economics*, 30 (2) (1989), pp. 157–71; Frank Meissner, 'The Schumpeters and Industrialization of Trest', *Zeitschrift für die gesamte Staatswissenschaft*, 135 (1979), pp. 256–62; and Robert Loring Allen, *Opening Doors: The Life and Work of Joseph Schumpeter* (Transaction Publishers, New Brunswick, 1991), vol. 1, pp. 7–30.

7 Gigers to Elizabeth Boody Schumpeter.

8 Gottfried Haberler, 'Joseph Alois Schumpeter, 1883–1950', *Quarterly Journal of Economics*, 64 (1950), p. 334.

9 See e.g. Richard Goodwin, 'Schumpeter: The Man I Knew', *Ricerche Economiche*, 4 (1983), p. 610.

10 Arthur Smithies, 'Memorial: Joseph Alois Schumpeter, 1883–1950', in *Schumpeter, Social Scientist*, ed. Seymour Edwin Harris (Cambridge, Harvard University Press, 1951), p. 11.

11 Seidl, 'Schumpeter', p. 190; Allen, *Opening Doors*, vol. 1, p. 17.

12 Smithies, 'Memorial', p. 11. Others have said the same; see e.g. Haberler, 'Schumpeter', p. 354.

13 Schumpeter, *Ships in Fog* (HUA). Emphasis added. The whole outline is reproduced in Appendix II.

14 Ibid.

15 Wolfgang F. Stolper, 'Joseph Alois Schumpeter', *Challenge*, 21 (1979), p. 65. See also William M. Johnston, *The Austrian Mind: An Intellectual and Social History 1849–1938* (Berkeley, University of California Press, 1972).

16 Stolper, 'Schumpeter', *Challenge*, p. 65.

17 Schumpeter's contribution to *Stammbuch (II) des Philosophischen Fakultät der Universität Bonn* of the Archives of the University of Bonn.

18 Joseph A. Schumpeter, *Imperialism and Social Classes* (Meridian Books, New York, 1955), p. 102.

19 Haberler, 'Schumpeter', p. 335.

20 Felix Somary, *Erinnerungen aus meinem Leben*, 2nd edn (Manesse Verlag, Zürich, 1959), pp. 170–1.

21 Schumpeter, *Stammbuch*.

22 Ibid.

23 Joseph A. Schumpeter, 'Die Wirtschaftslehre und die reformierte Referendarprüfung', *Schmollers Jahrbuch* (1926), as cited in Haberler, 'Schumpeter', p. 336.

24 Joseph Schumpeter, 'Eugen von Böhm-Bawerk', in *Ten Great Economists* (Oxford University Press, New York, 1951), pp. 143–4.

25 Haberler, 'Schumpeter', p. 338.
26 Schumpeter, *Stammbuch*.
27 Schumpeter as cited in Haberler, 'Schumpeter', p. 342.
28 Smithies, 'Schumpeter', p. 11.
29 As cited in Schumpeter, *Ten Great Economists*, p. xi.
30 The reason that we know this is that Schumpeter often bragged about his sexual adventures to his friends. Richard Goodwin says that 'he [that is, Schumpeter] once told me an awe-inspiring, specific number for the women he had known sexually.' Schumpeter was clearly impressed by himself on this score. 'OK', he once wrote in his diary, 'I have a gift for women.' See Goodwin, 'Schumpeter: The Man I Knew', p. 611. For the diary quote as well as Schumpeter's and Gladys's extramarital affairs, see Allen, *Opening Doors*, vol. 1, pp. 89, 98, 294.
31 I first thought that Christian Seidl had settled the whole matter when he found proof that Gladys was two years younger than Schumpeter (see Christian Seidl, *Joseph Alois Schumpeter in Graz*, Department of Economics, University of Graz, Research Memorandum Nr. 8201, 1982, p. 4). Prof. Yuichi Shionoya, however, then kindly sent me an article in which a copy of the marriage certificate between Schumpeter and Gladys is reproduced. Here it says that on 5 November 1907 Schumpeter ('24 years') married Gladys Ricarde Seaver ('36 years'). Till Gladys's birth certificate is found, we may therefore assume that she was indeed 12 years older than Schumpeter.
32 Stolper, 'Schumpeter', *Challenge*, p. 65.
33 Ibid.
34 Schumpeter's vita in Akt Nr. 9501 vom 8 März 1909 des k.k. Ministeriums für Kultus und Unterricht, Dep. Nr. VII, Allgemeines Verwaltungsarchiv, Vienna.
35 Haberler, 'Schumpeter', p. 338.
36 See Allen, *Opening Doors*, vol. 1, p. 97.
37 Smithies, 'Schumpeter', p. 12.
38 Maximilian Koessler to Elizabeth Boody Schumpeter, 9 January 1950 (HUA). Koessler was a lawyer who at one point was contemplating writing a biography of Eugen Ehrlich.
39 Seidl, 'Schumpeter', p. 194.
40 Schumpeter to Paul Siebeck, 16 June 1916 (HUA).

Chapter 2 Early Economic Works

1 Arthur Spiethoff, 'Josef Schumpeter in Memoriam', *Kyklos*, 3 (1950), p. 291. The quote at the opening of this chapter comes from Schumpeter's *Theorie der wirtschaftlichen Entwicklung* (1911), as translated in Joseph A. Schumpeter, *The Theory of Economic Development: An Inquiry into Profits, Capital, Credit, Interest, and the Business Cycle*, tr. R. Opie (Harvard University Press, Cambridge, 1934), p. 3.
2 See e.g. Joseph A. Schumpeter, *Ten Great Economists* (Oxford University Press, New York, 1951), p. 87.
3 Léon Walras, *Correspondence of Léon Walras and Related Papers*, edited by William Jaffé (North-Holland Publishing Company, Amsterdam, 1965), vol. III, p. 385.

4   Erich Schneider, 'Schumpeter's Early German Works, 1906–1917', in
    Schumpeter, Social Scientist, ed. Seymour Edwin Harris (Harvard Uni-
    versity Press, Cambridge, 1951), pp. 54–8.
5   Ibid., p. 54.
6   See e.g. Richard Swedberg, 'Joseph A. Schumpeter and the Tradition of
    Economic Sociology', *Journal of Institutional and Theoretical Economics*,
    145 (1989), pp. 510–11.
7   Schumpeter's vita in Akt Nr. 9501 vom 8 März 1909 des k.k. Minister-
    iums für Kultus und Unterricht, Dep. Nr. VII, Allgemeines Verwaltungsar-
    chiv, Vienna. Schumpeter also refers to this experience in a footnote in
    Business Cycles. See Joseph A. Schumpeter, *Business Cycles: A Theoreti-
    cal, Historical, and Statistical Analysis of the Capitalist Process* (McGraw-
    Hill, New York, 1939), vol. I, p. 223.
8   Joseph A. Schumpeter, 'Über die internationale Preisbildung (Auszug)',
    Statistische Monatschrift, 10 (1905), pp. 923–8.
9   Ibid., p. 923.
10 Ibid., p. 925.
11 Schumpeter's contribution to *Stammbuch (II) des Philosophischen Fakul-
    tät der Universität Bonn* of the Archives of the University of Bonn.
12 Schumpeter to Lloyd S. Huntsman, 26 May 1941 (HUA).
13 Joseph A. Schumpeter, *Das Wesen und der Hauptinhalt der theoretischen
    Nationalökonomie* (Duncker & Humblot, Leipzig, 1908, p. 20.
14 Ibid., p. xxi.
15 Ibid., p. xiv.
16 Ibid., p. vii.
17 Ibid., pp. 91, 575. Later in life, as we shall see in chapter 8, Schumpeter
    would re-evaluate his position and have a more positive opinion of the
    role of ideology in economics. Ideology would still be seen as detrimental
    to economics – but without a *vision* (which inevitably includes ideo-
    logy), there would be no progress in economic theory, Schumpeter now
    adds.
18 Ibid., p. 90. Emphasis in the text has been removed.
19 See Max Weber, '"Objectivity" in Social Science and Social Policy'
    (1904), in *The Methodology of the Social Sciences*, tr. E. A. Shils and H. A.
    Finch (The Free Press, New York, 1949), pp. 49–112.
20 Schumpeter, *Das Wesen*, p. 45.
21 Ibid., p. 536.
22 Ibid., p. 540.
23 Ibid., p. 553.
24 Ibid., p. 536.
25 Ibid., p. 28.
26 Schumpeter uses the term '*Beschreibung*' for theoretical economics. For
    the kind of description that historians engage in, he reserves the term
    '*Deskription*'. See e.g. ibid., pp. 29, 37, 42.
27 Ibid., p. 43.
28 Ibid., p. 44.
29 Ibid., p. 94.
30 Ibid., p. 573. I thank Murray Milgate for telling me about the intellectual
    history of the 'sea level' and 'equilibrium' analogy. According to Milgate,
    Walras got it from Turgot; and it actually goes back to at least some of
    the English mercantilists.

31 I owe this important point to Prof. Yuichi Shionoya.
32 *Das Wesen*, pp. 184, 567.
33 Ibid., pp. 182–3.
34 Ibid., p. 626.
35 Schumpeter in a letter to Edwin R. Seligman in 1913 as cited in Robert Loring Allen, *Opening Doors: The Life and Work of Joseph Schumpeter* (Transaction Publishers, New Brunswick, 1991), vol. 1, p. 132.
36 Friedrich von Wieser, 'Review of Schumpeter, *Das Wesen und der Hauptinhalt der theoretischen Nationalökonomie*', *Jahrbuch für Gesetzgebung, Verwaltung und Volkswirtschaft*, 35 (1911), pp. 395–417; Léon Walras to Georges Renard, 24 December 1908, *Correspondence of Léon Walras*, Vol. III, p. 384.
37 Othmar Spann, 'Die mechanisch-mathematische Analogie in der Volkswirtschaftslehre', *Archiv für Sozialwissenschaft und Sozialpolitik*, 30 (1910), pp. 786–824.
38 'Professor Schumpeter, Austrian Minister, Now Teaching Economic Theory Here', *The Harvard Crimson*, 11 April 1944, pp. 1, 4. See also Schumpeter to Taksyasu Kimura and Takumam Yasui, 12 August 1936 (HUA).
39 Von Wieser, 'Review of Schumpeter', p. 417.
40 See e.g. Schumpeter, *Das Wesen*, pp. 94, 198.
41 Schumpeter to Léon Walras, 9 October 1908, *Correspondence of Léon Walras*, vol. III, p. 378.
42 Joseph A. Schumpeter, *Essays* (Transaction Press, New Brunswick, 1989), p. 166. Schumpeter describes how he changed his opinion about Walras in his preface to the Japanese translation of *Theorie der wirtschaftlichen Entwicklung*, which is signed June 1937.
43 Ibid.
44 Ibid.
45 Joseph A. Schumpeter, *Theorie der wirtschaftlichen Entwicklung* (Duncker & Humblot, Leipzig, 1912), p. x.
46 Ibid., p. xi.
47 Ibid., p. 487.
48 Joseph A. Schumpeter, *The Theory of Economic Development: An Inquiry into Profits, Capital, Credit, Interest, and the Business Cycle*, tr. R. Opie (Harvard University Press, Cambridge, 1934), pp. 21–2. I shall often cite this English edition when discussing Schumpeter's 1911 book, since it represents the best-known version. The English translation is based on the second edition of *Theorie*, which appeared in 1926. According to Schumpeter's preface to the second edition, 'the argument itself has nowhere been altered' (even if there exist some other changes between the two editions), see Schumpeter, *Theory*, p. xii. The two books, however, are often different; and it is, for example, often pointed out that the concept of innovation is missing from the 1911 version. But even if this is true, the *idea* of innovation is clearly present in the 1911 version. Already in the first edition, Schumpeter thus defines entrepreneurship in terms of putting together new 'combinations', and he distinguishes very clearly between entrepreneurs and inventors. See Schumpeter, *Theorie* (1912), pp. 158–9, 178–9.
49 Ibid., p. 64.
50 Ibid., p. 74.

51   Ibid., p. 88.
52   Ibid., p. 66.
53   Schumpeter, *Theorie*, p. 529.
54   Ibid.
55   Schumpeter, *Theory*, p. 65.
56   This quote, as well as the one in the preceding line, comes from ibid., p. 82.
57   For a comparison between Schumpeter and Weber on this point, see especially Edward Carlin, 'Schumpeter's Constructed Type', *Kyklos*, 9 (1956), pp. 27–42.
58   Schumpeter, *Theory*, p. 93.
59   Here, as elsewhere in the text, I have decided not to present an overly detailed (and thereby technically correct) picture of Schumpeter's economic theory. Credit and capital are, for example, not identical in Schumpeter's scheme. For exact definitions, see ibid., pp. 107, 116–17.
60   Ibid., p. 212.
61   Ibid., p. 224.
62   Schumpeter, *Theorie* (2nd edn, 1926), p. xiii. For an analysis of Chapter 7 in *Theorie* from 1911, see also the important article by Yuichi Shionoya in the 1990 volume of *JITE*.
63   Schumpeter, *Theorie* (1912), p. 464.
64   Ibid., p. 518.
65   Ibid., p. 515.
66   Ibid., p. 525.
67   Ibid., p. 526.
68   Ibid., p. 535.
69   Ibid., p. 538.
70   Ibid., p. 546–7.
71   Ibid., p. 548.
72   Schumpeter to David T. Pottinger, 4 June 1934 (HUA).
73   Eugen von Böhm-Bawerk, 'Eine "dynamische" Theorie des Kapitalzinses', in *Eugen von Böhm-Bawerks kleinere Abhandlungen über Kapital und Zins*, ed. Franz X. Weiss (Hölder-Pichler-Tempsky A. G., Vienna, 1926), vol. II, p. 585.
74   Joseph A. Schumpeter, 'Eine "dynamische" Theorie des Kapitalzinses: Eine Entgegnung', in *Aufsätze zur ökonomischen Theorie* (J. C. B. Mohr, Tübingen, 1952), pp. 411–12.
75   Schumpeter to Pottinger.
76   See the bibliography by Massimo M. Augello in Joseph A. Schumpeter, *The Economics and Sociology of Capitalism*, ed. R. Swedberg (Princeton University Press, Princeton, N.J., 1991), pp. 445–81.
77   Joseph A. Schumpeter, *Economic Doctrine and Method: An Historical Sketch* (George Allen & Unwin Ltd, London, 1954), p. 25.
78   The 'irreparable error' was repaired in Schumpeter's later book on the history of economic thought; see Joseph A. Schumpeter, *History of Economic Analysis* (George Allen & Unwin, London, 1954), p. 344.
79   Schumpeter, *Economic Doctrine*, p. 24.
80   Ibid., p. 62.
81   Ibid., p. 63.
82   Ibid., p. 65.

83 Ibid., p. 97.
84 Ibid., pp. 119–22.
85 Ibid., p. 119.
86 Ibid., p. 120.
87 See also Schumpeter's article on Marx from 1918: Joseph A. Schumpeter, 'Karl Marx, der Denker', in *Beiträge zur Sozialökonomik*, ed. S. Böhm (Böhlau Verlag, Vienna, 1987), pp. 89–93.
88 See e.g. Schumpeter, *Das Wesen*, p. 9.
89 Schumpeter, *Economic Doctrine*, p. 167.
90 Ibid., p. 159.
91 Ibid., pp. 91, 169.
92 Ibid., p. 173. Emphasis added.
93 Ibid. Emphasis added.

Chapter 3　In Politics

1 Joseph A. Schumpeter, *Aufsätze zur Wirtschaftspolitik* (J.C.B. Mohr, Tübingen, 1985), p. 271. Emphasis added. The quote at the opening of this chapter comes from a letter written by Theodore Morgan which was published in *The Economist*, 24 December 1983, p. 4.
2 Schumpeter to Carl Landauer, 21 December 1940 (HUA).
3 Stephan Verosta, 'Joseph Schumpeter gegen das Zollbündnis der Donaumonarchie mit Deutschland und gegen die Anschlusspolitik Otto Bauers (1916–1919)', in *Festschrift für Christian Boda* (Europaverlag, Vienna, 1976), pp. 373–404.
4 Ibid., p. 381. The full text of the note and the secret appendix can be found in Verosta.
5 Ibid., p. 385.
6 Schumpeter, *Wirtschaftspolitik*, p. 253.
7 Ibid., p. 255.
8 Ibid., p. 257.
9 Ibid., p. 259.
10 Ibid., p. 269.
11 Ibid., p. 271. Emphasis added at the end of the quote.
12 Ibid., p. 272.
13 Ibid., p. 281.
14 Ibid., p. 309.
15 Ibid., p. 302. Emphasis added.
16 Josef Redlich, *Schicksalsjahre Österreichs, 1908–1919*, vol. II, p. 237, as cited in Christian Seidl, 'Joseph Alois Schumpeter: Character, Life and Particulars of his Graz Period', in *Lectures on Schumpeterian Economics*, ed. Christian Seidl (Springer-Verlag, Berlin, 1984), p. 203.
17 Ibid., pp. 203–4. Seidl's translation has been slightly altered.
18 Gottfried Haberler, 'Joseph Alois Schumpeter, 1883–1950', *Quarterly Journal of Economics*, 64 (1950), p. 345.
19 Theodor W. Vogelstein, *Joseph A. Schumpeter and the Sozialisierungskommission: An Annotation to Gottfried Haberler's Memoir of Schumpeter* (unpublished manuscript, Harvard University Archives, 1950), pp. 4–5.

20 Felix Somary, *Erinnerungen aus meinem Leben*, 2nd edn (Manesse Verlag, Zürich, 1959), p. 171.
21 Gottfried Haberler to Theodor M. Vogelstein, 20 December 1950 (HUA).
22 Somary, *Erinnerungen*, p. 171.
23 *Bericht der Sozialisierungskommission über die Frage der Sozialisierung des Kohlenbergbaues vom 31. Juli 1920. Anhang: Vorläufiger Bericht vom 15. Februar 1919* (Verlag Hans Robert Engelmann, Berlin, 1920), p. 35.
24 Ibid., p. 38.
25 Ibid., p. 36.
26 Joseph A. Schumpeter, 'The Crisis of the Tax State', in Joseph A. Schumpeter, *The Economics and Sociology of Capitalism* (Princeton University Press, Princeton, NJ, 1991), p. 131.
27 Ibid., p. 123.
28 Schumpeter, *Wirtschaftspolitik*, p. 5.
29 Ibid., pp. 5–6.
30 Karl Kraus, *Die Fackel*, 508–13 (April 1919), p. 158.
31 'Professor Schumpeter, Austrian Minister, Now Teaching Economic Theory Here', *The Harvard Crimson*, 11 April 1944, pp. 1, 4.
32 See e.g. Schumpeter's speech on 25 April 1919 in the Constituent National Assembly, as cited in Schumpeter, *Wirtschaftspolitik*, p. 320. See also Robert Loring Allen, *Opening Doors: The Life and Work of Joseph Schumpeter* (Transaction Publishers, New Brunswick, 1991), vol. 1, pp. 176–7.
33 Joseph A. Schumpeter, 'The Basic Lines of Financial Policy for Now and the Next Three Years', in Eduard März, *Austrian Banking and Financial Policy: Creditanstalt at a Turning Point* (Weidenfeld and Nicolson, London, 1984), p. 567. Emphasis in the original text removed.
34 Ibid., p. 585. The translation has been slightly altered.
35 See e.g. Eduard März, 'Joseph A. Schumpeter as Minister of Finance of the First Republic of Austria, March 1919–October 1919', in *Schumpeterian Economics*, ed. Helmut Frisch (Praeger Publishers, New York, 1981), p. 171. The material on Schumpeter and Oppenheimer comes from Robert Hoffman, 'Die wirtschaftlichen Grundlagen der britischen Österreichpolitik', in *Mitteilungen des Österreichischen Staatsarchiv* (Vienna, 1977). See also Francis Oppenheimer, *Stranger Within: Autobiographical Pages* (Faber and Faber, London, 1960), pp. 369–71. According to Oppenheimer, 'He [that is, Schumpeter] wanted, if possible, a strong Allied Finance Commission to take charge of Austria along the lines of the British financial administration in Egypt' (p. 369).
36 März, 'Schumpeter', pp. 172–3.
37 For the Kola Affair, see especially März, 'Schumpeter', pp. 174–5; März, *Austrian Banking*, pp. 333–9; and Charles A. Gulick, *Austria from Habsburg to Hitler* (University of California Press, Berkeley, 1948), pp. 134–41.
38 Joseph A. Schumpeter to Karl Renner, undated letter (probably written towards the end of August or early September 1919), as cited in März, *Austrian Banking*, p. 335. It should be added that Schumpeter had been in contact with Kola from the very beginning of his term as finance minister. Kola claims that he became Schumpeter's unofficial adviser on practical aspects of finance policy; and that the two had early engaged together in an illegal and secret (though probably government-

sponsored) scheme of strengthening the Austrian Crown. See Richard
Kola, *Rückblick ins Gestrige. Erlebtes und Empfundenes* (Rikola Verlag,
Vienna, 1922), pp. 229–55.

39 See especially Allen, *Opening Doors*, vol. 1, pp. 168, 186.

40 Schumpeter, *Wirtschaftspolitik*, p. 6.

Chapter 4   The Difficult Decade

1 Arthur Smithies, 'Memorial: Joseph Alois Schumpeter, 1883–1950', in
   Schumpeter, Social Scientist, ed. Seymour Edwin Harris (Cambridge,
   Harvard University Press, 1951), p. 14. The quote at the opening of this
   chapter comes from Joseph A. Schumpeter, *Aufsätze zur ökonomischen
   Theorie* (J.C.B. Mohr, Tübingen, 1952), p. 600.

2 The following account draws mainly on Bernd Kulla, 'Spiethoff,
   Schumpeter und '*Das Wesen des Geldes*', *Kyklos*, 42 (1989), pp. 431–4.

3 Schumpeter to Arthur Spiethoff, 17 April 1924 as cited in ibid., p. 432.

4 The section on the Biedermann Bank draws primarily on Robert Loring
   Allen, *Opening Doors: The Life and Work of Joseph Schumpeter* (Transaction Publishers, New Brunswick, 1991), vol. 1, pp. 184–9. More information about Schumpeter and the Biedermann Bank is to be expected from
   Wolfgang Stolper's forthcoming book on Schumpeter's economic policy.

5 Allen, *Opening Doors*, vol. 1, p. 190. Allen also says: 'This encounter with
   ladies of the evening was only one of many.'

6 This happened in 1883 according to Johannes Winkelmann, *Max Webers
   hinterlassenes Hauptwerk* (J.C.B. Mohr, Tübingen, 1986), p. 12. The term
   '*Sozialökonomik*' is generally thought to have originated with Jean-
   Baptiste Say's *Cours complet d'Economie politique* (1828–9); in German
   economics it can be found before this in a work by Dühring from 1865,
   Kapital und Arbeit. Kursus der National- und Sozialökonomie. See Schumpeter, *Epochen der Dogmen- und Methodengeschichte* in *Grundriss
   der Sozialökonomik. I. Abteilung*, ed. Max Weber (J.C.B. Mohr, Tübingen,
   1914), p. 56.

7 Christian Seidl, 'Joseph Alois Schumpeter: Character, Life and Particulars of his Graz Period', in *Lectures on Schumpeterian Economics*, ed.
   Christian Seidl (Springer-Verlag, Berlin, 1984), p. 192. See also the
   folder with documents on Schumpeter's Bonn appointment at the Zentrales Staatsarchiv in Merseburg.

8 Gustav Stolper to Arthur Spiethoff, 22 August 1925 in Joseph A.
   Schumpeter, *Aufsätze zur Wirtschaftspolitik* (J.C.B. Mohr, Tübingen,
   1985), pp. 33–4.

9 Ibid., p. 33.

10 Schneider, *Joseph A. Schumpeter* (Bureau of Business Research Mono-
    graph No. 1, University of Nebraska-Lincoln, Nebraska-Lincoln, 1975),
    p. 29. The translation has been slightly altered.

11 Schumpeter to 'St . . .', 11 November 1925 as cited in Eduard März,
    Joseph Alois Schumpeter – Forscher, Lehrer und Politiker (R. Oldenbourg
    Verlag, Munich, 1983), p. 169. The full names of the people that
    Schumpeter wrote to have often been deleted in März's book and
    replaced with the first letters of their names.

12   Schumpeter to Shigeto Tsuru, 10 August 1949 (HUA).
13   M. Ernst Kamp and Friedrich H. Stamm, *Bonner Gelehrte – Beiträge zur Geschichte der Wissenschaften in Bonn: Staatswissenschaften* (H. Bouvier u. Co. Verlag/Ludwig Röhrscheid Verlag, Bonn, 1969), p. 55.
14   Ibid.
15   The following section draws heavily on Allen, *Opening Doors*, vol. 1, pp. 139–41. I am also grateful for material, such as the copy of Annie's and Schumpeter's marriage certificate, which was supplied to me by Prof. Yuichi Shionoya.
16   'For a time in the early post-war period, Schumpeter kept steady company ... with a lady of the street named Nelly. She not only shared his bed, but dined and was seen in public with him. She took it upon herself to assume, without his permission or authority, the name of Nelly Schumpeter and told everyone that she was Joseph Schumpeter's wife. On more than one occasion, while drunk, she made scenes in coffee houses, demanding that Schumpeter's friends seek him out and bring him to her' – Allen, *Opening Doors*, vol. 1, p. 190.
17   Richard M. Goodwin, 'Schumpeter: The Man I Knew', *Ricerche Economiche*, 4 (1983), p. 611.
18   This diary covers the years 1919–26 and supposedly only exists in the form of a series of copies that Schumpeter made. Schumpeter's re-copies were first read and commented upon by Erica Gerschenkron (married to Alexander Gerschenkron) and later also by Robert Loring Allen. Much of the information on Annie Reisinger comes consequently from Erica Gerschenkron, 'The Diaries of Anna Reisinger-Schumpeter: A Report' (unpublished manuscript, Harvard University Archives, no date) and from Allen, *Opening Doors*, vol. 1, pp. 192–8, 217–18.
19   Annie Reisinger to Schumpeter, 30 September 1920 (HUA).
20   Schumpeter to 'G...', 22 August 1926 in März, *Schumpeter*, p. 171. Emphasis added.
21   The death certificate can be found in the Harvard University Archives. Annie's condition when giving birth may have been complicated by an abortion she had had in 1924 after an unhappy affair with a married man, only identified as 'Gerhard L.' in her diary. See Allen, *Opening Doors*, vol. 1, p. 194.
22   Schumpeter to 'G ...', 3 August 1926 in ibid., p. 170.
23   Arthur Spiethoff, 'Josef Schumpeter', *Kyklos*, 3 (1950), pp. 289–90.
24   Schumpeter to 'G ...', August 1926 in März, *Schumpeter*, p. 170.
25   These letters are reprinted in März, *Schumpeter*, pp. 169–84. They originally come from Gottfried Haberler's personal collection.
26   Schumpeter to 'G ...', Friday 1926 and 22 August 1926 in ibid., p. 171.
27   The information in this section comes from Allen, *Opening Doors*, vol. 1, pp. 224–7 and from Gerschenkron, 'The Diaries of Anna Reisinger-Schumpeter'.
28   Robert Loring Allen, to some extent following in the footsteps of Erica Gerschenkron, was the first to study the role of 'die Hasen' in Schumpeter's life. Erica Gerschenkron wrote a confidential report on the diaries of Annie Schumpeter for the Department of Economics in the early 1960s, which Robert Loring Allen found and deposited in the Harvard University Archives. See, e.g., Allen, *Opening Doors*, vol. 1, pp. 199, 226–8, 238.
29   Schumpeter to 'L.G.' in ibid., pp. 171–2.

30 Schumpeter to 'G . . .', probably September 1929 in ibid., p. 181.
31 Gottfried Haberler, 'Joseph Alois Schumpeter, 1883–1950', *Quarterly Journal of Economics*, 59 (1950), p. 354.
32 It is not known how large Schumpeter's debt was. One estimate is that it amounted to some two or three times his annual income. See Allen, *Opening Doors*, vol. 1, p. 219.
33 Schumpeter to 'G . . .', 25 March 1927 in März, *Schumpeter*, p. 174.
34 Schumpeter to 'G . . .', in ibid., p. 179. Through writing and lecturing, Schumpeter hoped to add some 5–6,000 marks per year to his salary of 11,550 marks as a professor. All in all, he would then have been making about $4–5,000, which was a respectable income in the 1920s. See Allen, *Opening Doors*, vol. 1, p. 215.
35 Schumpeter to Arthur Spiethoff, 19 September 1929 as cited in Kulla, 'Spiethoff', p. 433.
36 Schumpeter to Arthur Spiethoff, 2 April 1930 as cited in ibid.
37 Schneider, *Schumpeter*, p. 33.
38 Kulla, 'Spiethoff', p. 431.
39 Schumpeter to René Roux, 8 November 1949 (HUA).
40 Schneider, *Schumpeter*, p. 30.
41 Wolgang F. Stolper, 'Joseph Alois Schumpeter – a Personal Memoir', *Challenge*, 21 (January-February 1979), p. 68.
42 Ibid. The house referred to is the one on Coblenzerstrasse.
43 'Professor Schumpeter, Austrian Minister, Now Teaching Economic Theory Here', *The Harvard Crimson*, 11 April 1944, pp. 1, 4.
44 Schumpeter to Moore, 13 February 1931 (HUA). The full name is probably Clifford H. Moore.
45 Schumpeter to 'G . . .', 13 March 1931 in März, *Schumpeter*, p. 183.
46 This section draws primarily on Allen, *Opening Doors*, vol. 1, pp. 230, 289–91.
47 Ibid., p. 289.
48 See the excellent bibliograpy of Schumpeter's writings by Massimo M. Augello, as reproduced in Joseph A. Schumpeter, *The Economics and Sociology of Capitalism*, ed. R. Swedberg (Princeton University Press, Princeton, NJ, 1991), pp. 445–81. Political speeches and book reviews are not included in the numbers mentioned.
49 Schumpeter to René Roux, 8 November 1949 (HUA). The full letter is reproduced in Appendix III.
50 Joseph A. Schumpeter, 'Das Sozialprodukt und die Rechenpfennige: Glossen und Beiträge zur Geldtheorie von heute', *Archiv für Sozialwissenschaft und Sozialpolitik*, 44 (1917–18), pp. 627–715.
51 Schumpeter to Réne Roux, 8 November 1949 (HUA).
52 Joseph A. Schumpeter, *Das Wesen des Geldes* (Vandenhoeck and Ruprecht, Göttingen, 1970), p. 1.
53 Ibid., p. 2.
54 I here follow Erich Schneider's clear account in his review of Schumpeter's book. See Erich Schneider, 'Review of Joseph A. Schumpeter, *Das Wesen des Geldes*', *German Economic Review*, 8 (1970), pp. 348–52.
55 Schumpeter, *Das Wesen des Geldes*, p. 224. Emphasis in the original text removed; the translation is mainly that of Erich Schneider. It can be added that Schumpeter's money book was not well received when it was published in 1970. Attempts to revive Schumpeter's theory of money

have also been severely criticized. See, e.g., Barbel Näderer, *Die Entwick-lung der Geldtheorie Joseph A. Schumpeters* (Duncker & Humblot, 1990), p. 175.

56   See e.g. Joseph A. Schumpeter, 'The Present World Depression: A Tentative Diagnosis', *American Economic Review Supplement*, 21 (1931), p. 179; and *Das Wesen des Geldes*, p. 121.

57   Joseph A. Schumpeter, 'The Instability of Capitalism', *Economic Journal*, 38 (1928), p. 361.

58   Ibid., p. 386.

59   Paul A. Samuelson, 'Schumpeter's *Capitalism, Socialism and Democracy*', in *Schumpeter's Vision: Capitalism, Socialism and Democracy after 40 Years*, ed. Arnold Heertje (Praeger, New York, 1981), pp. 1–22.

60   Max Weber, *The Methodology of the Social Sciences*, tr. E. A. Shils and H. A. Finch (The Free Press, New York, 1949), pp. 63, 90.

61   Ibid., pp. 63–6. See also p. 45 in Weber's 'The Meaning of "Ethical Neutrality" in Sociology and Economics'.

62   Joseph A. Schumpeter, 'Gustav von Schmoller und die Probleme von heute', *Schmollers Jahrbuch für Gesetzgebung, Verwaltung und Volkswirt-schaft*, 50 (1926), p. 381.

63   Ibid., p. 355.

64   Ibid., p. 357.

65   Ibid., p. 375.

66   Ibid., p. 362.

67   Ibid.

68   Ibid., pp. 351–2.

69   Ibid., p. 360. Emphasis added.

70   Ibid., pp. 353–4.

71   Ibid., p. 354.

72   Ibid., p. 358.

73   Ibid., p. 375.

74   Ibid., p. 353.

75   Ibid., p. 367.

76   Ibid., p. 370. Emphasis added. In his 1914 book Schumpeter uses the term 'ökonomische Soziologie' rather than 'Wirtschaftssoziologie'.

77   See, e.g., the following two works in which Sombart comes out very strongly for a sociological theory of economics: Werner Sombart, *Nationalökonomie und Soziologie* (Gustav Fischer, Jena, 1930) and *Die drei Nationalökonomien* (Duncker & Humblot, Munich, 1930).

Chapter 5   Excursions in Economic Sociology

1   Paul M. Sweezy, 'Schumpeter on *Imperialism and Social Classes*', in *Schumpeter, Social Scientist*, ed. Seymour Edwin Harris (Cambridge, Harvard University Press, 1951), p. 119. The books Schumpeter mentioned were *Das Wesen* (1908), *Theorie* (1911), *Business Cycles* (1939) and *Capitalism, Socialism and Democracy* (1942). A list written after Schumpeter's death would naturally have to include *History of Economic Analysis* (posthumously published in 1954). The quote at the opening of this

chapter comes from H. Stuart Hughes, *Consciousness and Society*: *The Reorientation of Social Thought 1890–1930* (Alfred A. Knopf, New York, 1958), p. 314.

2   See Schumpeter to Stewart S. Morgan, 18 May 1934 (HUA) where he refers to them as his 'two sociological pieces of work' (HUA); and Schumpeter to Lewis H. Haney, 22 April 1949 (HUA) where he refers exclusively to these two articles as his 'excursions into sociology'.

3   'My interest for sociology and philosophy was awakened already while at high school ("Gymnasiezeit")', Schumpeter's contribution to *Stammbuch (II) des Philosophischen Fakultät der Universität Bonn* of the Archives of the University of Bonn.

4   Joseph A. Schumpeter, *Imperialism and Social Classes*, tr. H. Norden (Meridian Books, New York, 1955), p. 102.

5   Schumpeter's vita in Akt Nr. 9501 vom 8 März 1909 des k.k. Ministeriums für Kultus und Unterricht, Dep. Nr. VII, Allgemeines Verwaltungsarchiv, Vienna.

6   See e.g. Joseph A. Schumpeter, 'Die 'positive' Methode in der Nationalökonomie', in *Aufsätze zur ökonomischen Theorie* (J.C.B. Mohr, Tübingen, 1952), pp. 549–52.

7   Schumpeter's vita in Akt Nr. 9501.

8   Joseph A. Schumpeter, *Das Wesen und der Hauptinhalt der theoretischen Nationalökonomie* (Duncker & Humblot, Leipzig, 1908), p. 539.

9   Ibid.

10 Joseph A. Schumpeter, *Economic Doctrine and Method*, tr. R. Aris (George Allen & Unwin Ltd, London, 1954), p. 103.

11 Joseph A. Schumpeter, 'Wie studiert man Sozialwissenschaft?' (1915), in *Aufsätze zur ökonomischen Theorie*, p. 556.

12 See e.g. Joseph A. Schumpeter, 'Recent Developments of Political Economy', in *The Economics and Sociology of Capitalism*, ed. R. Swedberg (Princeton University Press, Princeton, NJ, 1991), pp. 284–97.

13 For an excellent attempt at this, see Jürgen Osterhammel, 'Spielarten der Sozialökonomik: Joseph A. Schumpeter und Max Weber', in *Max Weber und seine Zeitgenossen*, ed. Wolfgang J. Mommsen and Wolfgang Schwentker (Vandenhoeck & Ruprecht, Göttingen, 1988), pp. 147–95. A slightly shorter version of Osterhammel's article has been published as 'Varieties of Social Economics: Joseph A. Schumpeter and Max Weber', in *Max Weber and His Contemporaries*, ed. Wolfgang J. Mommsen and Jürgen Osterhammel (The German Historical Institute, London, 1987), pp. 106–20.

14 Schumpeter was probably already present at the 1909 meeting. That he at least was a member of the *Verein* in 1910 is clear from the member list for this year as reproduced in *Verhandlungen des Vereins für Sozialpolitik in Wien, 1909* (Schriften des Vereins für Sozialpolitik – Band 132, Duncker & Humblot, 1910), p. 635. Schumpeter was also one of the people asked to prepare a written text for the 1914 meeting. See in this context Randall Collins, *Weberian Sociological Theory* (Cambridge University Press, Cambridge, 1986), p. 120; and Joseph A. Schumpeter, 'Meinungsäusserung zur Frage des Werturteils', in *Äusserungen zur Werturteildiskussion im Ausschuss des Vereins für Sozialpolitik* (no place, privately printed, 1913), pp. 49–50.

15 Osterhammel, 'Varieties of Social Economics', pp. 106, 118.

16 Weber wrote to the Vienna Faculty that, 'It is my absolute duty to state that the Faculty would injure itself badly if it does not appoint the most prominent theoretical talent – and as I have understood it from all the accounts of the students, also the most eminent teaching talent – Joseph Schumpeter.' See Max Weber, 'Gutachen' (Rep. 92, Nr. 30, Bd. 13) in the Weber Collection at the Zentrales Staatsarchiv in Merseburg. I thank Dr Dieter Krüger for telling me about this document. Schumpeter apparently had quite a few enemies at the University of Vienna and the person who was finally appointed was Othmar Spann.

17 Schumpeter became a member of the editorial board in 1916 according to a letter from Schumpeter to Paul Siebeck, 16 June 1916 (HUA). His contract with the journal was apparently redrawn in the early 1920s. Schumpeter was on the editorial board of *Archiv* till the last issue of this journal appeared in 1933. (I am grateful to Günther Roth for having explained the intricacies of the editorial policies of *Archiv* to me.)

18 Ibid. It can be added that only a few and inconsequential letters exist between Weber and Schumpeter, according to information supplied to the author by Wolfgang Mommsen on June 1, 1989.

19 See Walther Tritsch, 'A Conversation between Joseph Schumpeter and Max Weber', *History of Sociology*, 6 (1985), pp. 167–72. As the translator points out on p. 172, there is some doubt as to the accuracy of Tritsch's assertion that the meeting took place in 1919 in Vienna.

20 Karl Jaspers, *Three Essays: Leonardo, Descartes, Weber*, tr. R. Manheim (Harcourt, Brace & World, Inc., New York, 1964), p. 222. Jaspers had found the anecdote in Felix Somary, *Erinnerungen aus meinem Leben*, 2nd edn (Manesse Verlag, Zürich, 1959), pp. 171–2.

21 Fritz Karl Mann, 'Einführung des Herausgebers', in Joseph A. Schumpeter, *Das Wesen des Geldes* (Vandenhoeck and Ruprecht, Göttingen, 1970), p. xii.

22 See Joseph A. Schumpeter, 'Max Weber's Work', in *The Economics and Sociology of Capitalism* (1991), pp. 220–9. The translation (which has been slightly altered here) is by Guy Oakes.

23 Schumpeter does not talk about this aspect of Weber's work in his 1920 article. In his posthumously published *History of Economic Analysis*, however, he explicitly says apropos 'Sozialökonomie' that Weber 'did more than any other to assure some currency to [this concept]'; and that '[Weber's] work and teaching had much to do with the emergence of Economic Sociology'. See Joseph A. Schumpeter, *History of Economic Analysis* (George Allen & Unwin, London, 1954), pp. 21, 819.

24 Schumpeter, 'Max Weber's Work'. 'The Social Psychology of the World Religions' is the title given to Weber's '*Die Wirtschaftsethik der Weltreligionen. Vergleichende religionssoziologische Versuche*' (1920–1) in *From Max Weber*, translated and edited by H. H. Gerth and C. Wright Mills (The Free Press, Glencoe, Ill., 1951).

25 Schumpeter, 'Max Weber's Work'. Schumpeter would later reiterate that Weber 'was not an economist at all' and underline Weber's 'almost complete ignorance [of economic theory]'. See Schumpeter, *History of Economic Analysis*, p. 819.

26 For Weber's definitions of "economic organization" and "economically

active organization", see Max Weber, *Economy and Society: An Outline of Interpretive Sociology*, ed. Günther Roth and Claus Wittich (University of California Press, 1978), p. 74–5.

27 Joseph A. Schumpeter, 'The Crisis of the Tax State', *International Economic Papers*, 4 (1954), p. 7.
28 Ibid., p. 6.
29 Ibid.
30 Ibid., p. 15.
31 Ibid., p. 16.
32 Rudolf Braun, 'Taxation, Sociopolitical Structure, and State-Building: Great Britain and Brandenburg-Prussia', in *The Formation of National States in Western Europe*, ed. Charles Tilly (Princeton University Press, Princeton, NJ, 1975), p. 245.
33 Ibid., pp. 245–6. The quote comes from a 1934 article by Fritz Karl Mann, 'Finanzsoziologie: Grundsätzliche Bemerkungen', in *Kölner Vierteljahreshefte für Soziologie*.
34 Schumpeter, 'The Crisis of the Tax State', p. 38.
35 Ibid., p. 24. The translation has been slightly altered.
36 Ibid. The translation has been slightly altered.
37 James O'Connor, *The Fiscal Crisis of the State* (St Martin's Press, New York, 1973), p. 10.
38 Schumpeter, *Imperialism*, p. 6. Emphasis added.
39 See in this context Schumpeter's contribution to the debate around the turn of the century on whether prices were set through power or through economic laws. Schumpeter argued that power could, at the most, have a minor impact on the key problem in economics, which was to formulate economic laws. To illustrate his thought on this point he used the example of a card game. In a card game, he said, every player is dealt different cards at the beginning of the game, just as power is bound to influence how an individual starts out in society. But once the players have their cards, they all have to play by the rules; and these rules are the equivalent of the laws of the economist. See Joseph A. Schumpeter, 'Das Grundprinzip der Verteilungstheorie', *Archiv für Sozialwissenschaft und Sozialpolitik*, 42 (1916–17), p. 26.
40 Schumpeter, *Imperialism*, p. 61.
41 Ibid.
42 Ibid., pp. 11–12.
43 Ibid., p. 69.
44 Ibid., p. 68.
45 Ibid., p. 73. Emphasis added.
46 The works that Schumpeter probably had in mind were *Finanzkapital* (1910) by Hilferding and *Die Nationalitätenfrage und die Sozialdemokratie* (1907) by Bauer. Paul Sweezy argues that Schumpeter 'almost certainly' had not read Lenin's *Imperialism, the Highest Stage of Capitalism* when he wrote his article. Lenin wrote *Imperialism* in 1916 and it was published in Russia before the end of the war. It did not, however, appear in German and French translation until 1920. One may, of course, question Sweezy's assertion on the ground that some of Schumpeter's acquaintances read Russian (for example Weber) and might have told Schumpeter about Lenin's argument. Schumpeter, it may finally be added, was

never particularly impressed by Lenin (see Sweezy, 'Schumpeter', p. 120). Finally, whether Schumpeter was familiar with Rosa Luxemburg's analysis of imperialism is not known.

47   Schumpeter, *Imperialism*, p. 46.

48   Ibid., p. 65.

49   See e.g. E. M. Winslow, 'Marxian, Liberal, and Sociological Theories of Imperialism', *Journal of Political Economy*, 39 (1931), pp. 713–58; and Murray Greene, 'Schumpeter's Imperialism – a Critical Note', *Social Research*, 19 (1952), pp. 453–63. Greene makes the important point that since Schumpeter by definition says that imperialism has to involve 'forcible expansion', he rules out many forms of economic imperialism.

50   Raymond Aron, *War and Industrial Society* (Oxford University Press, London, 1958), p. 19.

51   Karl W. Deutsch, 'Joseph Schumpeter as an Analyst of Sociology and Economic History', *Journal of Economic History*, 16 (1956), p. 50. It may finally be added that Schumpeter touched on imperialism also in *Business Cycles* (the famous note on p. 696!) and in *Capitalism, Socialism and Democracy*. At the time of his death he had plans to write an article on imperialism for *Foreign Affairs*. In my opinion, however, Schumpeter always believed that capitalism was inherently anti-imperialistic; and Schumpeter added little in his later works to his original formulation from 1918–19.

52   Schumpeter, *Imperialism*, p. 101.

53   Ibid.

54   See e.g. Joseph A. Schumpeter, *Capitalism, Socialism and Democracy* (Harper and Row, New York, 1975), p. 204.

55   Schumpeter, *Imperialism*, p. 103.

56   Ibid., p. 105.

57   Ibid., p. 106.

58   Ibid., p. 105.

59   Ibid., p. 107.

60   Ibid.

61   Ibid., p. 113.

62   Ibid., p. 107. The translation has been slightly altered.

63   Ibid., p. 126.

64   Ibid., p. 120.

65   Ibid., p. 134. The emphasis in the text has been deleted and the translation has been slightly altered.

66   Ibid., p. 146.

67   Ibid., p. 150.

68   Ibid., p. 149.

69   Ibid., p. 166.

70   Ibid., p. 167. Emphasis in the original text removed.

71   An excerpt from Schumpeter's essay is available in *Class, Status, and Power*, a standard work in the stratification literature. See *Class, Status, and Power: Social Stratification in Comparative Perspective*, ed. Reinhard Bendix and Seymour Martin Lipset (The Free Press, New York, 1966).

72   Robert K. Merton as cited on the back of Schumpeter, *Imperialism*. Merton is referring to Schumpeter's essays on imperialism and social classes (the essay on the tax state is not included in this collection).

Chapter 6   In the United States

1   Schumpeter to anonymous, 18 October 1930 in Eduard März, *Joseph Alois Schumpeter: Forscher, Lehrer und Politiker* (R. Oldenbourg Verlag, Munich, 1983), p. 182. The expression Schumpeter used about the United States was 'ein unglaublich ungemütliches Land'. The quote at the opening of this chapter comes from 'Professor Schumpeter, Austrian Minister, Now Teaching Economic Theory Here', *The Harvard Crimson*, 11 April 1944, pp. 1, 4.

2   Schumpeter to Adolph Löwe, 19 November 1932 (HUA).

3   Schumpeter to Dennis H. Robertson, 24 December 1932 (HUA).

4   The list is today in the Schumpeter Collection at Harvard.

5   'I have almost none of the early works of my husband published in German. He left them behind in Jülich', Elizabeth Boody Schumpeter to Arthur Spiethoff, 16 April 1952 (The Schlesinger Library, Radcliffe College). It could perhaps be argued that leaving behind one's possessions, in the manner that Schumpeter did, is not so peculiar for someone who is engaged in an international career. The fact that Schumpeter never contemplated leaving the United States in combination with the fact that he had ample opportunity to take his things in Jülich to the United States, indicate, however, that Schumpeter indeed wanted to leave behind his life in Europe.

6   See e.g. Schumpeter to Waldemar Gurian, 5 February 1943 (HUA), in which Schumpeter says that his main reason for leaving Germany were 'motives of scientific work'.

7   Arthur Smithies, 'Memorial: Joseph Alois Schumpeter, 1883–1950', in *Schumpeter, Social Scientist*, ed. Seymour Edwin Harris (Cambridge, Harvard University Press, 1951), p. 14.

8   Schumpeter to Irving Fisher, 19 March 1936 (HUA).

9   Ibid.

10 Joseph A. Schumpeter, 'John Maynard Keynes', in *Ten Great Economists: From Marx to Keynes* (Oxford University Press, New York, 1951), p. 272.

11 Schumpeter to Gottfried Haberler, 20 March 1933 (HUA). According to Haberler, Schumpeter stopped working on the book on money in 1934–5. See Gottfried Haberler, 'Joseph Alois Schumpeter, 1883–1950', *Quarterly Journal of Economics*, 64 (1950), p. 355.

12 The letter is dated 27 November 1912 and can be found in the Harvard University Archives. It is also discussed by Elizabeth Boody Schumpeter in her foreword to *Ten Great Economists*. See Schumpeter, *Ten Great Economists*, pp. xi–xii.

13 Schumpeter, 'Frank William Taussig, 1859–1940', in *Ten Great Economists*, pp. 217–18.

14 Schumpeter to 'G...', 5 January 1931 in März, *Schumpeter*, p. 183.

15 Allyn A. Young to Dean Clifford H. Moore, 23 March 1927 (HUA). I thank Larry Nichols for having drawn my attention to this letter.

16 Edward S. Mason, 'The Harvard Department of Economics from the Beginning to World War II', *The Quarterly Journal of Economics*, 97 (1982), pp. 419ff.

17 Allyn A. Young to Dean Clifford H. Moore, 23 March 1927 (HUA).
18 See e.g. Schumpeter, 'Taussig', pp. 202–3, 214–15; and Paul Samuelson, 'Schumpeter as a Teacher and Economic Theorist', in *Schumpeter, Social Scientist*, ed. Seymour Edwin Harris (Cambridge, Harvard University Press, 1951), p. 51.
19 Samuelson, 'Schumpeter', pp. 50–1.
20 Ibid., p. 51.
21 Ibid., p. 52. For another, quite similar, impression of Schumpeter as a teacher in 1935, see Robert Triffin, 'Schumpeter, Souvenirs d'un Etudiant', *Economie Appliquée*, 3 (1950), pp. 413–16.
22 This anecdote comes from an interview with Carl Kaysen, who took courses with Schumpeter in the 1940s. The interview took place at MIT in Cambridge, Mass., on 23 February 1988.
23 The jokes in this section come from interviews with Carl Kaysen and John Kenneth Galbraith. The interview with Galbraith took place in his home in Cambridge, Mass., on 8 January 1988.
24 Schumpeter to Lawrence J. Henderson, 1 February 1937 (HUA). Schumpeter sometimes gave imaginary grades, and Paul Samuelson received the highest of these: A++. See Robert Loring Allen, *Opening Doors: The Life and Work of Joseph Schumpeter* (Transaction Publishers, New Brunswick, 1991), vol. 2, p. 41.
25 Author's interview with Galbraith.
26 Edward S. Mason, 'The Harvard Department of Economics', p. 422.
27 Schumpeter to Henry Schultz, March 9, 1933 (HUA).
28 *Harvard University Catalogue 1933–34* (Cambridge, Harvard University, 1933), p. 306.
29 Schumpeter to E. B. Wilson, 24 May 1934 (HUA).
30 Schumpeter cited in Wolfgang F. Stolper, 'Joseph Alois Schumpeter – A Personal Memoir', *Challenge*, 21 (January-February 1979), p. 67.
31 See e.g. Schumpeter to Henry Schultz, 9 March 1933 (HUA); and to Abraham Flexner, 8 May 1934 (HUA).
32 Samuelson, 'Schumpeter', p. 49.
33 Schumpeter cited in Richard Goodwin, 'Schumpeter: The Man I Knew', *Ricerche Economiche*, 4 (1983), p. 609.
34 Interview with Abram Bergson in Cambridge, Mass., January 22, 1988.
35 Schumpeter to Gottfried Haberler, 20 March 1933 (HUA).
36 Schumpeter to David McCord Wright, 6 December 1943 (HUA).
37 Joseph A. Schumpeter, 'The Common Sense of Econometrics', in *Essays* (Addison-Wesley, Cambridge, 1951), p. 100.
38 John Kenneth Galbraith, *A Life in Our Time* (Houghton Mifflin, Boston, 1981), p. 90.
39 Schumpeter to Arthur W. Marget, 24 February 1937 (HUA).
40 See John Kenneth Galbraith, *A History of Economics: The Past as the Present* (Hamish Hamilton, London, 1987), p. 238; and Albert O. Hirschman, 'How the Keynesian Revolution was Exported from the United States, and Other Comments', in *The Political Power of Economic Ideas: Keynesianism Across Nations*, ed. Peter Hall (Princeton University Press, Princeton, NJ, 1989), pp. 347–59. Samuelson's textbook originally appeared in 1948.
41 Schumpeter to Irving Fisher, 17 July 1944 (HUA).

42 Joseph A. Schumpeter, 'Review of Keynes's *General Theory*', in *Essays*, p. 154.
43 Schumpeter to Oscar Lange, 24 February 1937 (HUA); and to Arthur W. Marget, 24 February 1937.
44 Schumpeter to Oscar Lange, 24 February 1937 (HUA).
45 Joseph A. Schumpeter, 'John Maynard Keynes, 1883–1946', in *Ten Great Economists*, pp. 260–91.
46 Simon Kuznets, 'Schumpeter's Business Cycles', *American Economic Review*, 30 (1940), pp. 257–71.
47 Stolper, 'Schumpeter', p. 69.
48 Schumpeter to Kenneth Boulding, 15 March 1939 (HUA).
49 Allen, *Opening Doors*, vol. 2, p. 4.
50 See, e.g., ibid., vol. 2, pp. 18, 47.
51 Schumpeter to Fisher, 19 March 1936 (HUA).
52 Schumpeter's private diary, 20 June 1936 (HUA).
53 The following is based primarily on two sources: an application for federal employment that Elizabeth Boody Schumpeter filled in, probably in 1950, and which has been preserved among her papers at the Schlesinger Library at Radcliffe College; and Elizabeth Waterman Gilboy, 'Elizabeth Boody Schumpeter, 1898–1953', in Elizabeth Boody Schumpeter, *English Overseas Trade Statistics, 1697–1808* (Oxford, The Clarendon Press, 1960), pp. v–vii. It should be noted that on many points, Waterman Gilboy contradicts Elizabeth Boody Schumpeter. The errors are presumably on Waterman Gilboy's side.
54 Based on the author's conversations in 1987–8 with various people who were at Harvard in the 1930s.
55 Waterman Gilboy, 'Elizabeth Boody Schumpeter', p. v.
56 Ibid., p. vi.
57 Application for federal employment, p. 11 (Schlesinger Library, Radcliffe College).
58 Elizabeth Boody Firuski to Joseph A. Schumpeter, undated letter from the summer of 1937 (HUA).
59 Elizabeth Boody Firuski to Joseph A. Schumpeter, 8 July 1937 (HUA).
60 Elizabeth Boody Schumpeter to J. C. Roraback, 2 June 1939 (HUA).
61 Ibid.
62 Schumpeter to Albert G. Hart, 8 November 1949 (HUA).
63 Elizabeth Boody Schumpeter to Joseph A. Schumpeter, 31 October 1949 (HUA).
64 See Allen, *Opening Doors*, vol. 2, pp. 57–61.
65 Smithies, 'Schumpeter', p. 15.
66 The original English version of the preface to the Japanese translation can be found in Schumpeter's *Essays*.
67 According to a grant application, Schumpeter 'began [the work on this project] in 1927 and ... worked intermittently ever since [on it], finishing the greater part of a first draft in 1930'. See Joseph A. Schumpeter, Application for Grant addressed to the Harvard University Committee on Research in the Social Sciences, Department of Economics, 3 February 1936 (HUA).
68 Schumpeter to H. L. Swart, 13 June 1935 (HUA).

69 Schumpeter to Mr Kittredge, Rockefeller Foundation, 16 March 1936 (HUA).

70 Schumpeter, Application, 3 February 1936 (HUA). Harvard's Committee on Research in the Social Sciences, it may be added, was funded by the Rockefeller Foundation as well.

71 Schumpeter, Application for Grant addressed to the Harvard University Committee on Research in the Social Sciences, Department of Economics, 11 February 1938 (HUA).

72 Schumpeter to the Chairman of the Harvard University Committee on Research in the Social Sciences, 22 June 1945 (HUA). Schumpeter wrote: 'The main ideas are worked out; the general scaffolding stands; and in a number of particular points, especially on saving and investment, most of the research and calculations have been done, which I shall do at all within the project.'

73 Schumpeter to Chester Barnard, 6 January 1939 (HUA).

74 For more details, see the introduction to Joseph A. Schumpeter, *The Economics and Sociology of Capitalism*, ed. R. Swedberg (Princeton University Press, Princeton, NJ, 1991), pp. 69–70, 96.

75 Reprinted in Schumpeter, *The Economics and Sociology of Capitalism*, pp. 316–38. A shorter version can be found in the 1984 issue of the *Journal of Institutional and Theoretical Economics*.

76 Joseph A. Schumpeter, *Business Cycles: A Theoretical, Historical, and Statistical Analysis of the Capitalist Process* (McGraw-Hill, New York, 1909), p. v.

77 Schumpeter to Wesley Clair Mitchell, 6 May 1937 (HUA).

78 John Kenneth Galbraith, 'Near or Far Right (Review of *Capitalism, Socialism and Democracy*)', *New Society*, 758 (April 14, 1977), p. 74.

79 Joseph A. Schumpeter, 'Die Wirtschaftstheorie der Gegenwart in Deutschland', in *Dogmenhistorische und biographische Aufsätze* (J. C. B. Mohr, Tübingen, 1954), p. 269.

80 Schumpeter, *Business Cycles*, p. 279.

81 Ibid., p. 96.

82 Ibid., pp. 144–5. See also ibid., pp. 96–7.

83 Ibid., p. 30.

84 Ibid., p. 32.

85 Ibid., p. 31. Robert K. Merton approvingly cites this passage in his *Social Theory and Social Structure* (The Free Press, New York, 1968), p. 144. (I thank Robert K. Merton for having drawn my attention to this passage.)

86 Schumpeter, *Business Cycles*, p. 13.

87 Ibid.

88 Ibid., pp. 906–7.

89 Ibid., p. 106.

90 Ibid., pp. 138, 222.

91 Schumpeter to Simon Kuznets, 16 March 1940 (HUA). Kuznets later used this information for his review.

92 Schumpeter, *Business Cycles*, p. 1050.

93 See e.g. the review by Hans Neisser in *Annals of the American Academy*, 205 (1940), pp. 205–6; by Oskar Morgenstern in *The New Republic*, 102 (May 1940), p. 615; and by Simon Kuznets in *The American Economic Review*, 30 (1940), pp. 257–71.

94 At the risk of straying too far from the topic, it may be added that when one assesses the reception of *Business Cycles*, there is one personal letter from Ragnar Frisch to Schumpeter that sticks in one's mind. Schumpeter had sent a copy of his book to Frisch in Oslo, Norway; and it reached Frisch in the midst of much anxiety over a possible attack by the Nazis. Frisch wrote: 'My dear friend Schumpeter ... This is a sad morning. Outside it is raining and inside the air is filled with thoughts of the negotiations between Finland and Russia which have just begun. We follow them with extreme attention, and also with apprehension because we do not know whether Norway will be next and because of our deep sympathy with the Finnish people. – But on my table I have your book. And so nevertheless this is a cheerful morning. Your book has brought me a greeting from a world of intellect and kindness and beauty where the course of affairs is not determined by motorized armies. Will this tell you what feelings your book has released with me?', Ragnar Frisch to Joseph A. Schumpeter, 13 October 1939 (HUA). Norway was occupied by Hitler five months later, on 9 April 1940.

95 For some recent additions to the debate about *Business Cycles*, see e.g. Alfred Kleinknecht, *Innovation Patterns in Crisis and Prosperity: Schumpeter's Long Cycle Reconsidered* (St Martin's Press, New York, 1987); and W. W. Rostow's review of Kleinknecht's book in the March 1988 issue of *The Journal of Economic Literature*.

96 Kuznets, 'Schumpeter's Business Cycles', pp. 262–3.

97 Ibid., p. 265.

98 Ibid., pp. 266–7.

99 Ibid., p. 269.

100 Ibid., p. 270.

101 Paul Samuelson, 'Joseph Alois Schumpeter', in *Dictionary of American Biography; Supplement Four, 1946–1950*, ed. John A. Garraty and Edward T. James (Charles Scribner's Sons, New York, 1974), p. 723.

102 Author's interview with Erik Dahmén at Skandinaviska Enskilda Banken in Stockholm on 10 July 1987. See also Erik Dahmén, 'Schumpeterian Dynamics: Some Methodological Notes', *Journal of Economic Behavior and Organization*, 5 (1984), pp. 25–34.

103 See e.g. Schumpeter, *Business Cycles*, pp. 327, 355.

104 Ibid., p. 220. Emphasis added.

Chapter 7 Capitalism, Socialism and Democracy

1 Joseph A. Schumpeter, *Business Cycles: A Theoretical, Historical, and Statistical Analysis of the Capitalist Process* (McGraw-Hill, New York, 1939), p. 279. The quote at the opening of this chapter comes from an unpublished manuscript in the Schumpeter Collection at Harvard, entitled 'The Future of Gold', which represents a speech that Schumpeter gave on 14 April 1941 before The Economic Club of Detroit.

2 Author's interview with John Kenneth Galbraith in his home in Cambridge, Mass., on 8 January 1988.

3 Fritz Karl Mann, 'Einführung des Herausgebers', in Joseph A. Schumpeter, *Das Wesen des Geldes* (Vandenhoeck & Ruprecht, Göttingen, 1970), p. xxvi. There also exist many references in *Business Cycles* to

'the writer's treatise on money'. See e.g. Schumpeter, *Business Cycles*, pp. 109, 176, 226.

4 Joseph A. Schumpeter, *An Economic Interpretation of Our Time*, Lecture 8 (28 March 1941), p. 14. Emphasis added.

5 Author's interview with James Duesenberry in his office in Littauer Center in Cambridge on 10 March 1988.

6 Schumpeter's private diary 1941–2 (HUA). (Unless an exact date has been given in this and other footnotes which refer to Schumpeter's diary, it has not been possible to establish it.)

7 John Kenneth Galbraith, 'Near or Far Right (Review of Schumpeter, *Capitalism, Socialism and Democracy*)', *New Society*, 758 (14 April 1977), p. 74.

8 See e.g. Edward S. Mason, 'The Harvard Department of Economics from the Beginning to World War II', *The Quarterly Journal of Economics*, 97 (1982), p. 413; Leonard Silk, *The Economists* (Avon Books, New York, 1978), p. 12; Richard Goodwin, 'Schumpeter: The Man I Knew', *Ricerche Economiche*, 4 (1983), p. 610.

9 Goodwin, 'Schumpeter', p. 610.

10 Ibid.; Silk, *The Economists*, p. 13 – Samuelson had apparently been offered an instructorship at Harvard. See Robert Loring Allen, *Opening Doors: The Life and Work of Joseph Schumpeter* (Transaction Publishers, New Brunswick, 1991), vol. 2, p. 95.

11 Author's interview in 1987–8; see also Allen, *Opening Doors*, vol. 2, p. 95.

12 E. S. Furniss to Joseph A. Schumpeter, 18 May 1940 (HUA). With his $ 12,000 a year, Schumpeter was one of the dozen or so best paid professors at Harvard at this time. When he was appointed George F. Baker Professor of Economics in September 1935, he received a salary of $ 10,000. In 1948 (when Schumpeter's retirement – at $ 4,000 a year – should have begun), his salary was increased to $ 14,000, again the highest salary that Harvard was paying. It has finally been estimated that between 1939 and 1950 Schumpeter received some $ 12,400 in royalties. See Allen, *Opening Doors*, vol. 2, pp. 27, 110, 114, 188–9, 234.

13 Edward Chamberlin et al. to Joseph A. Schumpeter, 3 June 1940 (HUA).

14 Paul A. Samuelson et al. to Joseph A. Schumpeter, 3 June 1940 (HUA).

15 Wassily Leontief to Joseph A. Schumpeter, 7 September 1940 (HUA).

16 Elizabeth Boody Schumpeter to Imrie de Vegh, 3 January 1952 (Schlesinger Library).

17 Schumpeter, private diary, 9 October 1942 (HUA).

18 Schumpeter to Dean Paul H. Buck, 18 May 1945 (HUA).

19 Ibid. Schumpeter refers to Dunlop's book as *Wages and Trade Unions*.

20 'Interview with Paul M. Sweezy', *Monthly Review*, 38 (April 1987), pp. 3–4. Sweezy sums it up like this: 'The department was sharply divided. Not between radicals and conservatives, but between those who were adamantly opposed to having any radicals in the department and those, like Schumpeter for example, who were very friendly.'

21 Schumpeter, private diary, 25 April 1943 (HUA).

22 Schumpeter, private diary, 5 January 1942 (HUA).

23 Goodwin, 'Schumpeter', p. 610.

24 Gottfried Haberler, 'Schumpeter's *Capitalism, Socialism and Democracy*

after Forty Years', in *Schumpeter's Vision: Schumpeter's Capitalism, Socialism and Democracy after Forty Years*, ed. Arnold Heertje (Praeger, New York, 1981), p. 74.

25 The first statement was probably written in 1941, while the second comes from 1945–6 (see Schumpeter's private diary in the Harvard University Archives). When writing in his diary Schumpeter sometimes wrote in English, sometimes in German, and sometimes in Gabelsberger shorthand. Erica Gerschenkron knew how to read Schumpeter's shorthand, and Robert Loring Allen makes use of much material in shorthand. For a discussion of Schumpeter's diary, see Erica Gerschenkron, 'The Diaries of Anna Reisinger-Schumpeter: A Report' (unpublished manuscript, Harvard University Archives, no date) and Allen, *Opening Doors*, vol. 2, pp. 53–61.

26 Schumpeter's private diary, 1942–3 (HUA).

27 This section builds on information in Gerschenkron, 'The Diaries of Anna Reisinger-Schumpeter', and Allen, *Opening Doors*, vol. 2, pp. 108–10.

28 Allen, *Opening Doors*, vol. 2, p. 108.

29 Author's interview with Paul Samuelson on 11 January 1988. See also, e.g., Toni Stolper, *Ein Leben in Brennpunkten unserer Zeit: Wien, Berlin, New York – Gustav Stolper, 1888–1947* (Rainer Wunderlich Verlag, Tübingen, 1962), p. 420.

30 Elizabeth Boody Schumpeter to Frederick L. Allen, *Harper's Magazine*, 7 March 1939 (Schlesinger Library).

31 Elizabeth Boody Schumpeter to R. F. Williams, 5 September 1939 (Schlesinger Library).

32 She contributed the following chapters: 'Government Policy and Recovery in Japan', 'The Population of the Japanese Empire', 'Japan, Korea and Manchukuo, 1936–1940', and 'Industrial Development and Government Policy, 1936–1940'.

33 See Elizabeth Boody Schumpeter to George S. Pettee, 15 December 1941 (Schlesinger Library).

34 Though J. Edgar Hoover personally put pressure on his agents to bring the Schumpeters to trial, no evidence was ever found to warrant their prosecution. The Bureau was mainly interested in Elizabeth. Schumpeter, as opposed to his wife, was never interviewed by the FBI. As of 1991, the FBI has released 325 pages of its files on Joseph and Elizabeth Schumpeter (see FBI-FOIPA nos. 335,669 and 335,670).

35 See page 12 in Elizabeth Boody Schumpeter's application for public employment, which is probably from 1950 (Schlesinger Library).

36 Schumpeter's private diary, c. 1934 (HUA).

37 Schumpeter's private diary, 19 November 1936 (HUA).

38 Schumpeter's private diary, 23 October 1935 (HUA). The next to last line also consists of three dots in the original.

39 Schumpeter's private diary, 6 September 1941 (HUA).

40 Schumpeter's private diary, 14 December 1941 (HUA).

41 Schumpeter's private diary, 17 December 1941; 3 December 1941; and 25 April 1943 (HUA).

42 Schumpeter's private diary, 12 July 1941, as cited in Allen, *Opening Doors*, vol. 2, p. 108.

43 Schumpeter's private diary, probably 10 June 1942. A few words

between brackets after some of the individual interests have been eliminated since they were hard to decipher.

44 Schumpeter's private diary, 1941–2 (HUA).
45 Schumpeter's private diary, 23 November 1942 (HUA). See also the entry for 30 October 1942.
46 Schumpeter's private diary, 30 October 1942 (HUA).
47 Schumpeter's private diary, 25 September 1942 (HUA).
48 Joseph A. Schumpeter, *Can Capitalism Survive?* (unpublished lecture, 1936, HUA), p. 17. The lecture can also be found in Joseph A. Schumpeter, *The Economics and Sociology of Capitalism*, ed. R. Swedberg (Princeton University Press, Princeton, NJ, 1991), pp. 298–315.
49 Joseph A. Schumpeter, *An Economic Interpretation of Our Time*, Lecture 7 (25 March 1941), p. 13 (HUA). This version of the lectures (as opposed to the one cited in some later notes) can also be found in Joseph A. Schumpeter, *The Economics and Sociology of Capitalism*, ed. R. Swedberg (Princeton University Press, Princeton, NJ, 1991), pp. 339–400.
50 Joseph A. Schumpeter, *An Economic Interpretation of Our Time*, Lecture 2, p. 31 (HUA). This version of the Lowell Lectures is much longer than the one referred to in note 49 and only exists in the Schumpeter Collection. It will henceforth be referred to as *An Economic Interpretation of Our Time* (expanded version).
51 Schumpeter to Redvers Opie, probably 1933. Emphasis added. I thank Wolfgang Stolper for having drawn this letter to my attention. It may be added that there was also a sharply realistic side to Schumpeter's conservatism (he basically saw democracy as a way for the voters to agree on a leader) as well as a romantic-charismatic side (as evidenced, for example, by his belief during the First World War that the Austro-Hungarian Empire could only be saved by a nobleman).
52 See especially Joseph A. Schumpeter, 'Sozialistische Möglichkeiten von heute', in *Aufsätze zur ökonomischen Theorie* (J.C.B. Mohr, Tübingen, 1952), pp. 455–510. That Schumpeter was also pro-British when it came to socialism is clear from 'Der Sozialismus in England und bei uns', *Aufsätze*, pp. 511–26. The first essay is from 1920–1 and the second from 1924.
53 Schumpeter to Redvers Opie, probably in 1933. I thank Wolfgang Stolper for having drawn this letter to my attention.
54 Joseph A. Schumpeter, 'The Problem of Europe' (Yale University, 20 February 1928, synopsis of speech). This document is today to be found in the Beinecke Rare Book and Manuscript Library at Yale University.
55 Schumpeter, *An Economic Interpretation of Our Time*, Lecture 6 (21 March 1941), p. 3. On 5 September 1941 Schumpeter wrote in his diary: 'Why am I so pro-German? . . . and this hate against Russia, where is it coming from?', cited in Allen, *Opening Doors*, vol. 2, p. 103.
56 Schumpeter, *An Economic Interpretation of Our Time* (expanded version), Lecture 2, p. 3.
57 Ibid., p. 10.
58 Schumpeter as cited in 'Clashing Views on Austrian Situation Presented by Langer and Schumpeter', *Harvard Crimson*, February 15, 1934. I thank William Buxton for having drawn this article to my attention.

59 Schumpeter, *An Economic Interpretation of Our Time* (expanded version), Lecture 2, p. 3.

60 Schumpeter, *An Economic Interpretation of Our Time*, Lecture 7 (25 March 1941), p. 3.

61 Schumpeter, *An Economic Interpretation of Our Time* (expanded version), Lecture 2, p. 11.

62 Erich Schneider, *Joseph A. Schumpeter* (Bureau of Business Research, University of Nebraska-Lincoln, 1975), p. 59. 'He [that is, Schumpeter] still believed up to the time of his departure that the federal German government and the Prussian Braun government would prevail.'

63 Joseph A. Schumpeter, 'Das soziale Anlitz des Deutschen Reiches', in *Aufsätze zur Soziologie* (J.C.B. Mohr, Tübingen, 1953), pp. 214–25.

64 Schumpeter to Waldemar Gurian, 5 February 1943 (HUA).

65 Schumpeter, 'The Problem of Europe' (1928).

66 See e.g. Galbraith, 'Near or Far Right', p. 74.

67 Joseph A. Schumpeter, 'Depressions – Can We Learn from Past Experience', in *Essays* (Addison-Wesley, Cambridge, 1951), p. 117. Schumpeter's article was published in a book called *The Economics of the Recovery Program* (1934), which was a product of the group called (by themselves) the Seven Wise Men at Harvard. The members of this group (some of whom saw themselves as positive to the New Deal) were Schumpeter, Douglass V. Brown, Edward Chamberlin, Seymour E. Harris, Wassily Leontief, Edward S. Mason and Overton H. Taylor.

68 Schumpeter to Charles C. Burlingham, 21 May 1941 (HUA).

69 Joseph A. Schumpeter, 'Das Woher und Wohin unserer Wissenschaft' in *Aufsätze zur ökonomischen Theorie*, p. 606. The exact wording is 'Katastrophe oder Glorie'. In the original transcript of the speech (which Schumpeter owned, but never corrected), it says 'Katastrophe *und* Glorie'. The 'und' was exchanged for 'oder' on the suggestion of Gottfried Haberler when Schumpeter's speech was published in the early 1950s in *Aufsätze*. In 'Das Woher und Wohin unserer Wissenschaft' Schumpeter also says that the rise to power of the Nazis will give young economists plenty of opportunity for good jobs. Schumpeter also suggested to some of his students that they should join the Nazi party and thereby promote their careers. See Allen, *Opening Doors*, vol. 1, p. 248.

70 Schumpeter to Gottfried Haberler, 20 March 1933 (HUA). It can be added that the Reichstag fire took place on 27 February 1933; national elections were held on 5 March (the Nazis polled 43.9 per cent); and on 23 March an enabling bill was passed in the Reichstag which gave full power to Hitler.

71 Both Robert Triffin and John Kenneth Galbraith say that Schumpeter had 'contempt' for Hitler. Author's interview with Galbraith on 8 January 1988; Robert Triffin, 'Schumpeter, Souvenirs d'un Etudiant', *Economie Appliquée*, 3 (1950), p. 414. According to an entry in Schumpeter's diary from 17 March 1940 (HUA) he felt that 'only religion can fight hitlerism on its own ground, for people accept the Hitlerian religion a) because it is *this* religion they want b) because it is *a* religion they want.' Other entries support the claim that Schumpeter saw Hitlerism as a religion.

72 Schumpeter to Edmund E. Day, 2 May 1933 (HUA). In order to round

off the picture of Schumpeter and Nazism, it should be noted that Schumpeter, according to Haberler, was 'violently attacked by National Socialist economic writers on the ground that his economic theories were not German in spirit'. According to the same source, Schumpeter also 'knew and said repeatedly that if he had remained in Germany he would have been one of the first candidates for the concentration camp.' See Gottfried Haberler, 'Joseph Alois Schumpeter, 1883–1950', 64 (1950), *Quarterly Journal of Economics*, pp. 356–7.

73   Schumpeter to Reverend Harry Emerson Fosdick, 19 April 1933 (HUA). According to Wolfgang Stolper, Schumpeter urged people in Germany to stay and fight Hitler from within: 'Schumpeter told people: collaborate, collaborate and bore from within' (telephone interview with Wolfgang Stolper on 5 February 1988).

74   Author's interview with Paul Samuelson on 11 January 1988. 'Up to a very late date Schumpeter thought Hitler was going to win the war.'

75   Schumpeter, *An Economic Interpretation of Our Time*, Lecture 7 (March 25, 1941), pp. 14–15. In 1939 Schumpeter also said in an interview that 'the best way to solve European problems would be to halt the present war and leave the Greater German boundaries as they are today' (*Boston Herald*, 20 October, 1939, p. 17).

76   Author's interview with Paul Samuelson on 11 January 1988. As late as 1944, however, Schumpeter would tell friends that Germany might still win. See Allen, *Opening Doors*, vol. 2, p. 154.

77   Schumpeter's private diary, 1945 (HUA).

78   Schumpeter's private diary, 1945 (HUA). Schumpeter was extremely upset by the United States decision to drop two atom bombs on Japan: 'It is a stupid bestiality or a bestial stupidity', Allen, *Opening Doors*, vol. 2, p. 155.

79   When I conducted interviews for this book in 1987–8, I heard quite a few stories about remarks Schumpeter had made about the Jews. The question is also touched upon in Silk, *The Economists*, pp. 13–14; Goodwin, 'Schumpeter', p. 610–11.

80   Schumpeter to Ragnar Frisch, 3 December 1932 (HUA).

81   Author's interview with Galbraith on 8 January 1988.

82   Author's interview with Samuelson on 11 January 1988.

83   John Kenneth Galbraith, *A View from the Stands of People, Politics, Military Power and the Arts* (Houghton Mifflin Company, Boston, 1986), p. 288.

84   Paul A. Samuelson, 'Joseph Schumpeter', *Newsweek*, 13 April 1970, p. 75.

85   Schumpeter to the Committee on Research in the Social Sciences, 8 June 1940 (HUA).

86   Elizabeth Boody Schumpeter, 'Editor's Introduction' in Joseph A. Schumpeter, *History of Economic Analysis* (George Allen & Unwin, London, 1954), pp. v–vi.

87   Daniel Bell, 'The Prospects of American Capitalism: On Keynes, Schumpeter, and Galbraith', in *The End of Ideology: On The Exhaustion of Political Ideas in the Fifties* (The Free Press, Illinois, 1960), p. 73.

88   Galbraith, 'Near or Far Right', p. 74.

89   Schumpeter to the Committee on Research in the Social Sciences, 8

June 1940 (HUA); Schumpeter to Harper & Brothers, Publishers, 7 June 1939 (HUA); and Joseph A. Schumpeter, *Capitalism, Socialism and Democracy*, 3rd edn (Harper & Row, New York, 1950), p. xiii. (I shall in most cases use the 1975 edition with a preface by Tom Bottomore. This edition, however, lacks Schumpeter's prefaces to the first two editions in the United States).

90 Schumpeter, *Capitalism, Socialism and Democracy* (1950), p. xiii.
91 Ibid.
92 Schumpeter, *Business Cycles*, p. 666.
93 Joseph A. Schumpeter, *Economic Doctrine and Method: An Historical Sketch*, tr. R. Aris (George Allen & Unwin, London, 1954), p. 119.
94 See also Joseph A. Schumpeter, 'Karl Marx, der Denker' in *Beiträge zur Sozialökonomik*, ed. Stephan Böhm (Böhlau Verlag, Vienna, 1987), pp. 89–93.
95 See especially Schumpeter, 'Die sozialistische Möglichkeiten von heute' and 'Der Sozialismus in England und bei uns' in *Aufsätze*.
96 Joseph A. Schumpeter, *Essays* (Addison-Wesley, Cambridge, 1951), p. 160.
97 Ibid.
98 Weber does this, for example, in his 1904 essay on objectivity where he says that Marx is one of the forerunners of 'die sozialökonomische Wissenschaft': Max Weber, 'Die "Objektivität" sozialwissenschaftlicher und sozialpolitischer Erkenntnis', in *Gesammelte Aufsätze zur Wissenschaftslehre* (J.C.B. Mohr, Tübingen, 1988), p. 163.
99 Schumpeter, *Capitalism, Socialism and Democracy* (1975), p. 44.
100 Ibid., p. 10.
101 Ibid., p. 12.
102 Ibid., pp. 25, 27, 40.
103 Ibid., p. 43.
104 Ibid., p. 46.
105 Ibid., p. 6.
106 Ibid., p. 81.
107 Ibid., p. 77.
108 Ibid.
109 Ibid., p. 83.
110 Ibid., p. 84.
111 Ibid., p. 102.
112 Two standard works on the Schumpeterian hypothesis are Morton I. Kamien and Nancy L. Schwartz, *Market Structure and Innovation* (Cambridge University Press, 1982) and F. M. Scherer, *Innovation and Growth: Schumpeterian Perspectives* (The MIT Press, Cambridge, 1984).
113 Kamien and Schwartz, *Market Structure*, pp. 53, 217.
114 Schumpeter, *Capitalism, Socialism and Democracy* (1975), p. 133.
115 Ibid., p. 157.
116 Ibid., p. 138.
117 Ibid., p. 161.
118 See e.g. *Schumpeter's Vision* which contains a series of articles in honour of Schumpeter's book.
119 Gary Becker, 'Pressure Groups and Political Behavior', in *Capitalism and Democracy: Schumpeter Revisited*, ed. R. D. Coe and C. K. Wilbur (University of Notre Dame Press, Notre Dame, 1985), p. 120.

278 NOTES TO PP. 159—66

120 Gottfried Haberler, 'Schumpeter's *Capitalism, Socialism and Democracy*' in *Schumpeter's Vision*, p 87.
121 Schumpeter, *Capitalism, Socialism and Democracy* (1975), pp. 221–8.
122 Ibid., e.g., p. 364.
123 Ibid., p. 233.
124 Ibid., p. 221.
125 Ibid., p. 226.
126 Ibid., p. 359.
127 Ibid., p. 362.
128 Ibid., p. 188.
129 Ibid., p. 202.
130 Ibid., p. 207.
131 Ibid., p. 208.
132 Ibid.
133 Ibid., pp. 195–6.
134 Ibid., p. 167.
135 Ibid., p. 170.
136 Ibid.
137 Ibid., p. 250.
138 Ibid., p. 269.
139 Ibid., p. 290.
140 Ibid., p. 285.
141 See e.g. William C. Mitchell, 'Schumpeter and Public Choice, Part I', *Public Choice*, 42 (1984), p. 76. Schumpeter may be seen as one of the fathers of the Public Choice School, as e.g. Anthony Downs acknowledges ('Schumpeter's profound analysis of democracy forms the inspiration for our whole thesis') in *An Economic Theory of Democracy* (Harper and Row, New York, 1957), p. 29. It would also be interesting (as Murray Milgate has pointed out to me) to find out whether there exists a direct or indirect relationship between Schumpeter and the rent-seeking literature. It is, finally, often noted that Schumpeter took the idea of 'the political entrepreneur' from Weber. One, however, does not have to go as far as Turner and Factor who argue that Schumpeter's analysis of democracy could only become so celebrated because Weber's ideas on this topic were unknown in the United States! See Stephen P. Turner and Regis A. Factor, *Max Weber and the Dispute Over Reason and Value: A Study in Philosophy, Ethics, and Politics* (Routledge & Kegan Paul, London, 1984), p. 184.
142 Schumpeter, *Capitalism, Socialism and Democracy* (1975), pp. 300–1.
143 Ibid., pp. 296–302; see also pp. 167–86.
144 Ibid., p. 168.
145 Ibid.
146 Ibid., pp. 210–18, 300.
147 Ibid., p. 302.
148 Ibid.
149 Ibid.
150 Edgar Salin, 'Einleitung', in Joseph A. Schumpeter, *Kapitalismus, Sozialismus und Demokratie* (Verlag A. Francke A. G., Bern, 1946), p. 8.
151 Schumpeter, *Capitalism, Socialism and Democracy* (1950), p. xi.
152 Joan Robinson, 'Review of Joseph A. Schumpeter, *Capitalism, Socialism*

and Democracy', The Economic Journal, 53 (1943), p. 383. Emphasis added towards the end of the quote.

Chapter 8   Last Years, Last Work

1   From an interview I conducted in 1987–8. The quote at the opening of this chapter comes from 'Professor Schumpeter, Austrian Minister, Now Teaching Economic Theory Here', *The Harvard Crimson*, 11 April 1944, pp. 1, 4.

2   From interviews I conducted in 1987–8. It has been argued that Schumpeter was considerably less arbitrary in his teaching of the history class than it was rumoured on the Harvard campus. See Charles E. Staley, 'Schumpeter's 1947 Course in the History of Economic Thought', *History of Political Economy*, 15 (1983), pp. 25–37.

3   Seymour E. Harris, 'Introductory Remarks', in *Schumpeter, Social Scientist*, ed. Seymour E. Harris (Harvard University Press, Cambridge, 1951) p. 6.

4   Schumpeter to Shigeto Tsuru, 10 August 1949 (HUA).

5   Schumpeter in July 1949 as cited in Robert Loring Allen, *Opening Doors: The Life and Work of Joseph Schumpeter* (Transaction Publishers, New Brunswick, 1991), vol. 2, p. 237.

6   Schumpeter to Herbert von Beckerath, 24 January 1949 (HUA).

7   See the May 1949 issue of *The American Economic Review*, which contains the papers and proceedings from the meeting in Ohio, December 27–30, 1948.

8   Parsons had been an instructor at the economics department when Schumpeter first arrived. 'In the first year I was at Harvard [that is, in 1927] Joseph Schumpeter was there as a visiting professor. I sat in on his course on "General Economics", and it was here that I first began to get a clear conception of what a theoretical system was' (Talcott Parsons, 'A Short Account of My Intellectual Development', *Alpha Kappa Deltan*, 29 (1959), p. 6). 'For some years', Parsons has confirmed in a letter, 'I stood rather close to the conception of pure economics which I first learned from Schumpeter', Parsons to Adolf Löwe, 27 January 1941 (HUA). Schumpeter was also one of the original reviewers of Parsons's famous work, *The Structure of Social Action*. In his report to the Committee on Research in the Social Sciences (which had funded part of Parsons's research), Schumpeter commended Parsons on the section on Max Weber: 'The scholarly care with which the main elements of Max Weber's thought are analyzed and followed to their sources and displayed in their significance cannot be too highly commended.' Schumpeter then adds, tongue in cheek: 'The author has in fact so deeply penetrated into the German thicket as to lose in some places the faculty of writing clearly in English about it, and some turns of phrase become fully understandable only if translated into German' (Schumpeter to the Committee on Research in the Social Sciences about Talcott Parsons's manuscript *Sociology and the Elements of Human Action*, 23 December 1936 (HUA); the full report is reprinted in Appendix III).

9   Joseph A. Schumpeter, 'L'Avenir de l'entreprise privée devant les

tendances socialistes modernes', in Association professionelles des industriels, *Premier congrès patronal: Comment sauvegarder l'entreprise privée* (L'Association, Montreal, 1946), pp. 103–8.

10 Joseph A. Schumpeter, *History of Economic Analysis* (George Allen and Unwin, London, 1954), p. 765; *Capitalism, Socialism and Democracy* (Harper and Row, New York, 1975), p. 416.

11 See Allen, *Opening Doors*, vol. 2, p. 166. In Schumpeter's opinion two million Jews – not six million – had been killed.

12 Schumpeter, *Capitalism, Socialism and Democracy* (1975), p. 401. This section is based on chapter 28, 'The Consequences of the Second World War', which was written in July 1946.

13 Ibid., p. 381.

14 Ibid., p. 415.

15 Schumpeter to Seymour E. Harris, 16 November 1949 (HUA).

16 Schumpeter, *History of Economic Analysis*, p. 1194.

17 Wolfgang F. Stolper, 'Joseph Alois Schumpeter – A Personal Memoir', *Challenge*, 21 (January-February 1979), p. 69.

18 Schumpeter to John Kenneth Galbraith, 28 October 1948 (HUA).

19 Paul Samuelson, 'Schumpeter as a Teacher and Economic Theorist', in *Schumpeter, Social Scientist*, p. 48.

20 All essays are reprinted in Schumpeter's *Essays*. See Joseph A. Schumpeter, *Essays* (Addison-Wesley, Cambridge, 1951), pp. 216–27, 227–35, 248–66.

21 Schumpeter, 'The Historical Approach to the Analysis of Business Cycles', in *Essays*, pp. 308–15.

22 The following account builds on the standard sources on the Center, including Hugh G. J. Aitken, 'Entrepreneurial History: The History of an Intellectual Innovation', in *Explorations in Enterprise*, ed. Hugh G. J. Aitken (Harvard University Press, Cambridge, 1965), pp. 3–19; Ruth Crandall, *The Research Center in Entrepreneurial History at Harvard University, 1948–1958. A Historical Sketch* (unpublished manuscript, Harvard University Archives, 1960); and Adrien Taymans, 'Le "Research Center in Entrepreneurial History"', *Economie Appliquée*, 3 (1959), pp. 615–35. The author is also grateful for relevant information from Hugh G. J. Aitken, Thomas C. Cochran and David Landes in 1988.

23 Arthur H. Cole, 'Joseph A. Schumpeter and the Research Center in Entrepreneurial History', *Explorations in Entrepreneurial History*, 2, 2 (1950), p. 56.

24 See especially Aitken, 'Entrepreneurial History'.

25 Ibid., pp. 8–10.

26 Schumpeter, 'Economic Theory and Entrepreneurial History', in *Essays*, p. 255.

27 Ibid., p. 256.

28 Ibid., p. 262.

29 Schumpeter, 'The Creative Response in Economic History', in *Essays*, p. 224.

30 Ibid., p. 226.

31 Schumpeter, 'Theoretical Problems of Economic Growth', in *Essays*, p. 231.

32 Ibid., p. 235.

33 *The Catalogue of Prof. Schumpeter's Library* (Hitotsubashi University
    Library, Tokyo, 1962), column 72. For references to Weber's economic
    history, see e.g. Joseph A. Schumpeter, *Das Wesen des Geldes* (Van-
    denhoeck and Ruprecht, Göttingen, 1970), pp. 22, 36; and Schumpeter,
    History of Economic Analysis, p. 817. It can be added that Schumpeter
    would in all likelihood have been quite critical of the current tendency
    to centre research in economic history around questions that can be
    solved through sophisticated, quantitative methods. He had, after all,
    been trained in the German tradition of historiography which empha-
    sized a series of other problems.
34 During my interviews in 1987–8 with Schumpeter's students and
    colleagues I was repeatedly told that it was more or less impossible
    to express Schumpeter's theory of the entrepreneur in mathematical
    terms.
35 Richard M. Goodwin, 'Schumpeter – The Man I Knew', *Richerche
    Economiche*, 4 (1983), p. 609.
36 Samuelson, 'Schumpeter', p. 30.
37 Aitken, 'Entrepreneurial Research', p. 10.
38 Dahmén does this in his doctoral dissertation, 'Entrepreneurial Activity
    and the Development of Swedish Industry, 1919–1939' (1950, tr. 1970).
    Briefly, Dahmén found in his study of Swedish industry that new
    enterprises had indeed been the ones that introduced new commodities
    but not necessarily the ones that had introduced new methods of pro-
    duction. Gerschenkron comments favourably on Dahmén's research
    e.g. in 'Discussion' in *Papers and Proceedings of The American Economic
    Review*, 58 (1968), pp. 96–7.
39 See e.g. Alexander Gerschenkron, 'Comments', in *The Transfer of Tech-
    nology to Developing Countries*, ed. Daniel L. Spencer and Alexander
    Woroniak (Frederick A. Praeger, New York, 1967), pp. 85–6.
40 Ibid., p. 84.
41 As one reviewer of the manuscript for this book pointed out, it may
    be argued that even though Schumpeter towards the end of his life
    changed his mind about the social role of the entrepreneur, the under-
    lying analytical-economic model for his theorizing still remained the
    same. And, if this is the case, Gerschenkron's earlier cited comment
    would, for example, appear in a different light.
42 Schumpeter, application to the Committee on Research in the Social
    Sciences at Harvard, 15 February 1939 (HUA). Schumpeter's plans,
    however, go further back than 1939. There exists, for example, a letter
    from 1935 in which it is confirmed that Schumpeter will hand in the
    manuscript to a book called *History of Economic Thought* by 30 June
    1936. See Justin H. Moore to Schumpeter, 18 January 1935 (HUA).
43 Elizabeth Boody Schumpeter, 'Editor's Introduction', in Schumpeter,
    History of Economic Analysis, p. vi.
44 Schumpeter to Edward S. Mason, 10 August 1949 (HUA); Allen, *Open-
    ing Doors*, vol. 2, p. 189.
45 Elizabeth Boody Schumpeter, 'Editor's Introduction', in Schumpeter,
    History of Economic Analysis, p. xiii.
46 See e.g. Elizabeth Boody Schumpeter to R. B. Landauer, George Allen
    and Unwin Ltd, 2 June 1953. I thank Michael Bott of the Library of the

University of Reading (where the Schumpeters' correspondence with George Allen and Unwin is to be found) for having located this letter for me.

47 Schumpeter to Allen & Unwin in 1949 as cited in Schumpeter, *History of Economic Analysis*, p. vii.
48 Ibid.
49 Ibid., p. 4.
50 Ibid.
51 Ibid.
52 Ibid., p. 5.
53 Schumpeter, *Capitalism, Socialism and Democracy* (Harper & Row, New York, 1975), p. 11.
54 Schumpeter, *History of Economic Analysis*, p. 33.
55 Ibid., pp. 34–5.
56 Ibid., p. 44.
57 Ibid., p. 41.
58 Ibid., p. 42.
59 Ibid., p. 10. An 'epideiktic' definition, Schumpeter explains in a footnote, is the kind of definition where one defines something by pointing to a specimen of the general class. To define an 'elephant', in other words, one points at an elephant.
60 Ibid., p. 43.
61 Ibid., p. 21.
62 Ibid., p. 16.
63 Ibid., p. 17.
64 Werner Sombart, *Die drei Nationalökonomien* (Duncker & Humblot, Munich, 1930), pp. 140–276.
65 According to Elizabeth Boody Schumpeter, Schumpeter only saw economic sociology as 'a *possible* fourth [field]'. The background to this qualification is the following. When Schumpeter started to write *History of Economic Analysis* he did not include economic sociology among his fundamental fields. The reason for this was probably that work in economic sociology led beyond economics. As the writing progressed, Schumpeter, however, changed his mind and he now started to refer to economic sociology as a 'fourth fundamental field'. See Schumpeter, *History of Economic Analysis*, pp. 21, 1190.
66 See e.g. ibid., pp. 13, 22.
67 Ibid., p. 12.
68 Ibid., pp. 12–13. Emphasis in text.
69 Ibid., p. 13. Emphasis in text.
70 Ibid., p. 14.
71 Ibid.
72 Ibid., pp. 14ff.
73 Ibid., p. 15. Emphasis in text.
74 Ibid.
75 Ibid., p. 21.
76 Ibid., p. 20.
77 Ibid., pp. 26–7.
78 Ibid., p. 27.
79 Ibid., p. 25.

80 Ibid., p. 101.
81 Ibid., p. 184.
82 Ibid., p. 185.
83 Ibid., p. 525.
84 Ibid., p. 473.
85 Ibid.
86 Ibid., pp. 961–2.
87 Ibid., p. 242. Emphasis added.
88 Ibid.
89 Ibid., p. 1141.
90 Ibid., p. 1145.
91 Ibid.
92 Ibid., p. 1160.
93 See e.g. Frank Knight, 'Schumpeter's *History of Economics*', *Southern Economic Journal*, 21 (1954–5), pp. 261–72; Lionel Robbins, 'Schumpeter's *History of Economic Analysis*', *Quarterly Journal of Economics*, 69 (1955), pp. 1–22; Jacob Viner, 'Schumpeter's *History of Economic Analysis*', *American Economic Review*, 44 (1954), pp. 894–910. Several other well-known economists reviewed Schumpeter's work, including Joseph Dorfman, G. B. Richardson, George J. Stigler and I. M. D. Little.
94 See e.g. Knight, 'Schumpeter's *History*', p. 263. According to my interview with John Kenneth Galbraith on 8 January 1988, Elizabeth had done 'a rather mediocre editing job'. Paul Samuelson has said that *History of Economic Analysis* consitutes a 'magnificent torso' which, however, needs to be 'pruned and completed', see Paul Samuelson, 'Schumpeter, Joseph Alois', in *Dictionary of American Biography. Supplement Four, 1946–1950*, ed. John A. Garraty and Edward T. James (Charles Scribner, New York, 1974), pp. 722–3.
95 Samuelson as cited in Leonard Silk, *The Economists* (Avon Books, New York, 1978), p. 29.
96 Schumpeter to Albert G. Hart, 8 November 1949 (HUA).
97 Schumpeter's diary, autumn 1948, as cited in Allen, *Opening Doors*, vol. 2, p. 220.
98 Otto Stöckel to Joseph A. Schumpeter, 1 May 1947 (HUA). According to rumours in Cambridge, Mia and her husband were shot because they had been members of the resistance. See Allen, *Opening Doors*, vol. 2, p. 176.
99 Schumpeter, private diary, 25 June 1947 (HUA).
100 Schumpeter, private diary, 1946–7 (HUA).
101 Ragnar Frisch, 'Some Personal Reminiscences of a Great Man', in *Schumpeter, Social Scientist*, p. 8.
102 Schumpeter, private diary, 1946–7 (HUA).
103 Schumpeter, private diary, 1946 (HUA). Emphasis added.
104 See Erica Gerschenkron, 'The Diaries of Anna Reisinger-Schumpeter: A Report' (unpublished manuscript, Harvard University Archives, no date) and Allen, *Opening Doors*, vol. 2, pp. 199–200.
105 Cited in Allen, *Opening Doors*, vol. 2, p. 221.
106 Allen, *Opening Doors*, vol. 2, p. 60; see also pp. 42, 48, 58–61, 199–200.
107 This, like all the other aphorisms cited in this chapter, comes from

Schumpeter's private diary. We shall, however, refer to their number in Appendix I. This aphorism (where emphasis has been added) is thus Aphorism 44.

108   Aphorism 31.
109   Aphorism 22.
110   Aphorism 48.
111   Aphorisms 66 and 8.
112   Aphorism 86. Emphasis added.
113   Aphorism 12.
114   Aphorisms 64 and 65.
115   Aphorism 15.
116   Aphorism 54. Emphasis added.
117   I am thankful to Albert O. Hirschman as well as Paul Samuelson for having pointed this out to me.
118   Aphorism 3. Emphasis added.
119   Aphorism 67.
120   Joseph A. Schumpeter, 'Vilfredo Pareto, 1848–1923', in *Ten Great Economists* (Oxford University Press, New York, 1951), p. 111.
121   Ibid., p. 115.
122   Elizabeth Boody Firuski to Schumpeter, summer 1937 (HUA).
123   For more details, see *The Catalogue of Prof. Schumpeter's Library*.
124   Elizabeth Boody Schumpeter, 'Editor's Introduction', in *History of Economic Analysis*, p. xi.
125   'Schumpeter Prize Fund', p. 2, as appended to a letter from Imrie de Vegh to Gottfried Haberler et al., 2 June 1953 (The Schlesinger Library, Radcliffe College).
126   The Schumpeter Prize is each year awarded to a promising graduate student in economics at Harvard. Since 1988 the International Joseph A. Schumpeter Society also bestows an annual Schumpeter Prize. When Schumpeter died, it may finally be added, his personal estate was valued at $ 18,000 (of which $ 8,000 represented future copyrights income). See Allen, *Opening Doors*, vol. 2, pp. 234, 247.

Appendix I   *Aphorisms from Schumpeter's Private Diary*

1   Most aphorisms can be found in HUG (FP) 4.1, boxes 4, 5 and 7, which cover the years 1940–4, 1945–8 and 1932–43. Aphorisms 80–82, 97–100 come from Robert Loring Allen, *Opening Doors: The Life and Work of Joseph Schumpeter* (Transaction Publishers, New Brunswick, 1991), vol. 2, pp. 146, 182, 190–1; and 101–103 come from Arthur Smithies, 'Memorial: Joseph Alois Schumpeter, 1883–1950' in *Schumpeter, Social Scientist*, edited by Seymour Edwin Harris (Harvard University Press, Cambridge, 1951), p. 23.
2   An attempt has been made to place the aphorisms in chronological order: 1–3 (1936–7); 4 (1939); 5 (1941); 6 (1941–2); 7–9 (1942); 10 (1942–3); 11–33 (1943); 34–42 (1944); 43–52 (1945); 53–69 (1946); 70–72 (1946–7); 73–82 (1947); 83–89 (1948); 90–106 (no date; probably the late 1940s). Whenever Schumpeter wrote the same aphorism several times in the diary, the first date has been used.
3   The notation continues: 'Not quite. It is better today: The parrot cries

"Planning". But it is the old parrot all the same', cited in Allen, *Opening Doors*, vol. 1, p. 288.
4 The student's name was Dallas Steinthorsen. See Allen, *Opening Doors*, vol. 2, p. 173.
5 Eugen von Böhm-Bawerk, 'Eine "dynamische" Theorie des Kapitalzinses' (1913), in *Kleinere Abhandlungen über Kapital und Zins* (Halder-Pichler-Tempsky, Vienna, 1926), 585.

Appendix II   *Schumpeter's Novel* Ships in Fog *(a Fragment)*

1 This excerpt is reconstructed from HUG (FP) 4.3 in the Harvard University Archives and should replace the version reproduced in Arthur Smithies, 'Memorial: Joseph Alois Schumpeter, 1883–1950' in *Schumpeter, Social Scientist*, edited by Seymour Edwin Harris (Harvard University Press, Cambridge, 1951), pp. 16–17. Schumpeter also considered the title *Ships Passing in the Fog*.
2 Smithies, 'Schumpeter', p. 17. The author has inspected Schumpeter's original notes but has nothing to add to Smithies' summary, which forms the basis for what is said in this section.

Appendix III   *Letters by Schumpeter*

1 Edward März, *Joseph Alois Schumpeter – Forscher, Lehrer und Politiker* (R. Oldenbourg, Munich, 1983), pp. 169–84. Thirty-eight letters by Schumpeter have been included in this book.

Index

Adler, Max, 23
Adler, Siegmund, 23
Aitken, Hugh, 172, 280 n.22
Allen, Robert Loring, 120, 260
    n.18, 260 n.28, 273 n.25
Alpine Montan Gesellschaft,
    62–3, 231–3,
American Economic Association,
    169–70, 181, 191, 279 n.7
*Archiv für Sozialwissenschaft und
    Sozialpolitik*, 20, 79, 92, 98,
    100, 102, 212, 218, 264 n.17
Aristotle, 186
Aron, Raymond, 101–2
Augello, Massimo M., 239–40
Austria, 46–64, 145–7
Austrian School in Economics,
    14–15,
Austrian Social Democratic
    Party, 58–63, 146–7
Austro-Hungarian Empire *see*
    Austria

banking *see* credit
Barnard, Chester, 126
Barone, Enrico, 160
Bauer, Otto, 14, 58–63, 99, 232
Becker, Gary, 159
Beckerath, Herbert von, 71, 169
Bergson, Abram, 117
Berlin, University of *see*
    University of Berlin

Biedermann Bank, 67–8, 76, 259
    n.4
Böhm, Stephan, 239
Böhm-Bawerk, Eugen von,
    14–15, 17–19, 23, 39, 46, 70,
    153, 200
Bonn, University of *see*
    Schumpeter, Joseph A., at
    the University of Bonn
    (1925–1932)
Bouvier, Emile, 169
Braun, Rudolf, 96
Brown, Douglass V., 275 n.67
Bryce, Robert, 118
Bücher, Karl, 41
Bullock, Charles J., 112
Burbank, H. H., 139, 168
Bureau of International Research
    at Harvard University and
    Radcliffe College, 122, 142
bureaucracy, 161
Burlingham, Charles C., 227–8
business cycles, 35–6, 82–3, 140,
    148, 151, 155–6, 160, 223–5,
    235
    see also Schumpeter, Joseph A.,
    Works: *Business Cycles*

Cannan, Edwin, 112
capitalism, 32, 36, 82–3, 98–9,
    128 ff., 159
    see also Schumpeter, Joseph A.,

Works: *Business Cycles* and
*Capitalism, Socialism and
Democracy*
*Capitalism, Socialism and
Democracy see* Schumpeter,
Joseph A., Works: *Capitalism,
Socialism and Democracy*
(1942–50)
Carver, T. N., 112
Cassel, Gustav, 112
Cecil, Hugh, 222
Chamberlin, Edward, 275 n.67
Christian Social Party (Austria),
58–9
Churchill, Winston, 141
Clark, John Bates, 29, 113,
209–11
class, social, 154
see also Schumpeter, Joseph A.,
Works: Social Classes in an
Ethnically Homogenous
Environment' (1927)
Clemence, R. V., 239
Cochran, Thomas C., 172, 280
n.22
Cole, Arthur H., 168, 172
Columbia University *see*
Schumpeter, Joseph A., at
Columbia University
(1913–14)
competition, 26, 156–7, 187
conservatism *see* Schumpeter,
Joseph A., political opinions
consumers, 33–4
contract, 158, 186
corporatism, 169–70
see also Schumpeter, Joseph A.,
political opinions
Cournot, Antoine Augustin, 70,
116
creative destruction, 157
credit, 33, 35–6, 81, 173–4, 235–6
Crum, William Leonard, 116–17
Czernowitz, University of *see*
Schumpeter, Joseph A., at
the University of Czernowitz
(1909–11)

Dahmén, Erik, 135, 176, 281 n.38
democracy, theory of, 162–6, 200

Deutsch, Karl, 102
Dietzel, Heinrich, 69, 212
Downs, Anthony, 278 n.141
Dunlop, John, 140
Durkheim, Emile, 91, 104, 221
dynamic theory, 29–39, 188–9,
235–6

Econometric Society, 77, 117–18
econometrics *see* mathematical
economics; Schumpeter,
Joseph A., Works: 'The
Common Sense of
Econometrics' (1933)
economic development *see*
Schumpeter, Joseph A.,
Works: *Theorie der
wirtschaftlichen Entwicklung*
(1911, 1926, tr. 1934) and
Business Cycles (1939)
economic history, 12–13, 15,
23–4, 33, 37, 44–5, 81, 85–7,
111, 115, 129–30, 135, 154,
169, 171–7, 184–6, 229–30,
281 n.33
see also Methodenstreit
economic policy *see* Schumpeter,
Joseph A., as finance minister
(1919)
economic sociology, 41, 43, 81,
88, 90–107, 129, 152, 185–7,
262 n.76, 282 n.65
economic theory *see* dynamic
theory; Econometric Society;
mathematical economics;
Sozialökonomik; static
theory; theoretical economics
Edgeworth, Francis Y., 15–16, 70,
116
Ehrlich, Eugen, 18
England *see* Schumpeter, Joseph
A., in England (1906–7) *and*
political opinions
entrepreneur, 34–6, 38, 83,
104–6, 111–12, 158, 167,
171–7, 255 n.48, 281 n.44
see also innovations
equilibrium, concept of, 28 ff.,
131, 134, 179, 188
see also Walras, Léon

fascism *see* Hitler; Schumpeter,
    Joseph A., political opinions
FBI (Federal Bureau of
    Investigation), 143, 273 n.34
Firuski, Elizabeth Boody *see*
    Schumpeter, Elizabeth
    Boody
Firuski, Maurice, 122
fiscal sociology *see* Goldscheid,
    Rudolf; Schumpeter, Joseph
    A., Works: 'The Crisis of the
    Tax State' (1918)
Fisher, Irving, 22, 115–16, 121,
    209, 219–20, 233–4
Fosdick, Harry Emerson, 216
Franco, Francisco, 223
Frisch, Ragnar, 77, 113, 134, 150,
    190–1, 214, 270 n.94

Galbraith, John Kenneth, 115,
    118–19, 139, 150–1, 157, 171
Germany *see* Hitler; Schumpeter,
    Joseph A., political opinions
Gerschenkron, Alexander, 176–7,
    281 nn.38, 41
Gerschenkron, Erica, 260 nn.18,
    28, 273 n.25
Gigers, Edda, 252 n.5
Goldscheid, Rudolf, 90, 95
Goodwin, Richard, 72, 175, 178
Graz, University of *see*
    Schumpeter, Joseph A.,
    childhood *and* at the
    University of Graz (1911–21)
Gulick, C. A., 231–3
Gumplowicz, Ludwig, 11, 91
Gutman, Franz, 69

Haberler, Gottfried, 11, 18, 56–7,
    75, 110, 126, 141, 148, 159,
    194, 209, 213–15
Haney, Lewis H., 235–7
Hansen, Alvin, 118–19, 190, 231
Harris, Seymour E., 171, 275 n.67
Harvard University *see*
    Schumpeter, Joseph A., at
    Harvard University (1927–8,
    1930, 1932–50)
Harvard University Archives,
    194, 199, 209, 251 n.3

Hayek, Friedrich A. von, 183, 215
Heimann, Eduard, 55
Hildebrand, Bruno, 19
Hildebrand, Richard, 19–20
Hilferding, Rudolf, 14–15, 55–6,
    99
Hirschman, Albert O., 284 n.117
Historical School of Economics
    see Methodenstreit;
    Schmoller, Gustav von
history *see* economic history
History of Economic Analysis see
    Schumpeter, Joseph A.,
    Works: *History of Economic
    Analysis* (1954)
history of economics *see*
    Schumpeter, Joseph A.,
    Works: *Epochen der
    Dogmen- und
    Methodengeschichte* (1914)
    and *History of Economic
    Analysis* (1954)
Hitler, Adolf, 147–50, 170, 216,
    228, 275 nn.69, 71, 72, 276 n.76
Hoover, J. Edgar, 273 n.34
Hotelling, Harold, 220
human nature, 160–1
Huntsman, Lloyd S., 228–9

ideology, 86, 92, 136, 169, 180–2,
    254 n.17, 263 n.14
imperialism *see* Schumpeter,
    Joseph A., Works: 'The
    Sociology of Imperialisms'
    (1918–19)
Inama-Sternegg, Karl Theodor
    von, 13, 23–4
industrial society, 101–2
innovations, 34, 106, 131, 135,
    157, 172–3, 225, 255 n.48,
    271 n.95, 277 n.112, 281 n.38
    see also entrepreneur
Institute of Pacific Relations, 142
institutions *see* economic
    sociology
interest, 35, 39, 131, 133, 210,
    235–6
International Economic
    Association, 169
International Joseph A.

Schumpeter Society, 2, 284
    n.126
Isnard, A. N., 188

Japan, 77–8, 142–3, 147, 194, 276
    n.78
Jenks, Leland H., 172
Jevons, Stanley, 13–14, 188
Joslyn, C. S., 112
Juglar Cycle, 36, 82, 131–2
    see also Schumpeter, Joseph A.,
        Works: Business Cycles (1939)
Juraschek, Franz von, 13

Kamien, Morton I., 157
Kautsky, Karl, 55
Keler, Sigismund von, 8–10
Keynes, John Maynard, 16, 76,
    110, 118–19, 171, 215,
    229–31, 236
Keynesianism, 1, 118–19, 138–9
Kitchin Cycle, 82, 131–2
    see also Schumpeter, Joseph A.,
        Works: Business Cycles (1939)
Knight, Frank H., 175, 189
Kola, Richard, 62–4, 232, 258
    n.38
Kondratieff Cycle, 82, 131–4,
    223–7
    see also Schumpeter, Joseph A.,
        Works: Business Cycles (1939)
Kraus, Karl, 60
Kuznets, Simon, 119, 133–5,
    226–7

Lammasch, Heinrich, 13, 50,
    54–5
Landes, David, 280 n.22
Langer, William, 138
Laski, Harold, 122
Lederer, Emil, 14, 55–7, 79
Lenin, Vladimir, 99, 160, 170, 265
    n.46
Leontief, Wassily, 116–17, 126,
    168, 178, 194, 237, 275 n.67
Lonegan, Edna, 229–30
Lotz, Walter, 69
Löwe, Adolph, 108

McGrannahan, David, 126
Machiavelli, Niccolo, 64

Maiswinkle, George, 234
Mann, Fritz Karl, 69, 80, 93, 96
Mannheim, Karl, 180
marginal utility see utility
market, 156, 160
    see also competition
Marshall, Alfred, 16, 27, 116, 182,
    221
Marx, Karl, 15, 38, 43, 152–6,
    235, 257 n.87
    see also Marxism
Marxism, 14–15, 38, 43, 99, 101,
    140, 152–6, 235, 265 n.46
März, Eduard, 47, 209
Mason, Edward S., 275 n.67
mathematical economics, 13, 15,
    18, 22, 70, 115–18, 168,
    174–6, 187–8, 214, 230, 281
    n.34
Maurois, André, 138
Menger, Carl, 13–15, 22–3, 25–6,
    46, 188
Merton, Robert K., 107
Methodenstreit, 2, 13, 22–3, 44,
    83–4, 88
methodological individualism,
    26, 104
Milgate, Murray, 254 n.30, 278
    n.141
Mill, John Stuart, 29, 235
Milles, Thomas, 41, 256 n.78
Mises, Ludwig von, 14, 69, 160,
    215
Mitchell, Wesley Clair, 20, 82, 84,
    127, 209, 211–13, 216
money see Schumpeter, Joseph
    A., Works: book on money
    (Das Wesen des Geldes, 1970)
monopoly, 34, 101, 156–8, 161,
    166
Montesquieu, Baron de la Brède
    et de, 101
Moore, H. L., 115
Moore, Wilbert E., 126
Moore Jr, Barrington, 101, 106
Morgan, Stewart S., 5, 217–18
Musgrave, Richard, 115

Naumann, Friedrich, 49
Nietzsche, Friedrich, 192

objectivity *see* ideology
O'Connnor, James, 97–8
Ohlin, Bertil, 213
Opie, Redvers, 125
Oppenheimer, Francis, 62, 258
    n.35

Pareto, Vilfredo, 3, 15, 107, 116,
    171, 192–3, 221
Parsons, Talcott, 126, 169, 220–1,
    279 n.8
Pearson, Karl, 16
Petty, William, 187
Philippovich, Eugen von, 14, 46
Physiocrats, 42, 179, 187
Pigou, A. C., 82, 113, 116
Pius XI, 169–70
political science, 162–6
Pottinger, David T., 218–19
power, 265 n.39
Pratt, Albert, 222–3
profit, 36, 105, 235
property, 152, 158, 186
psychology, 27, 183
public choice, 127, 163, 278 n.141

Quesnay, François, 42

rationality, 98–9, 135, 155, 163,
    278 n.141
    see also Schumpeter, Joseph A.,
    Works: 'The Meaning of
    Rationality in the Social
    Sciences' (1941)
Redlich, Joseph, 54–5
Reisinger, Anna *see* Schumpeter,
    Anna ('Annie')
religion *see* Schumpeter, Joseph
    A., attitude towards religion
Renner, Karl, 58, 258 n.38
Research Center for
    Entrepreneurial Studies, 168,
    172–3, 176, 280 n.22
Ricardo, David, 42–3, 85, 179,
    187–8, 235
Richard Kola and Co. *see* Kola,
    Richard
Ripley, William Z., 112
Robbins, Lionel, 189
Robertson, Dennis H., 108

Robinson, Joan, 166, 181
Roosevelt, F. D., 141–2, 147–8,
    228
Rostow, Walt W., 223–5
Roux, René, 237–8
Russian Revolution, 59–60, 93,
    146, 160, 274 n.55
    see also Schumpeter, Joseph A.,
    political opinions

Saint-Simon, Henri de, 101
Salin, Edgar, 76, 278 n.150
Samuelson, Paul A., 83, 113–15,
    118, 135, 139, 149–50, 171,
    177, 189, 268 n.24, 272 n.10,
    284 n.117
Say, Jean-Baptiste, 188
Scheler, Max, 180
Scherer, F. M., 277 n.112
Schmoller, Gustav von, 13, 22–3,
    25, 30, 66, 70, 98, 104, 107
    see also Methodenstreit
Schneider, Erich, 22, 77, 239
Scholastics, 41, 179, 187, 189
Schultz, Henry, 115–16
Schumpeter, Alois, 6–9
Schumpeter, Anna ('Annie'; born
    Reisinger), 72–5, 109, 124,
    141–2, 190, 193–5, 260 nn.18,
    21, 28
Schumpeter, Elizabeth Boody
    (born Boody), 6, 8, 110,
    121–4, 140, 142, 177–8, 190,
    239
Schumpeter, Gladys (born
    Seaver), 16–17, 20, 72, 253
    n.31
Schumpeter, Hugo, 78
Schumpeter, Johanna (born
    Grüner), 6–10, 17, 72–5, 124,
    141–2, 190
Schumpeter, Josef (1777–1848;
    Schumpeter's great-
    grandfather), 7
Schumpeter, Josef (1855–1887;
    Schumpeter's father), 6, 8–9
Schumpeter, Joseph A.
    (1883–1950)
    attitude towards religion, 6, 73,
    124, 141, 155–6, 169–70,
    191–3, 275 n.71

political opinions, 46–64, 137, 162 ff., 169–71, 222–3, 231–3, 273 n.34, 274 n.51, 276 nn.71, 73

Biographical:
childhood, 1–11
at Theresianum (1893–1901), 8, 10–11, 68, 91, 263 n.3
at the University of Vienna (1901–6), 12–15, 17–18, 22–4
in England (1906–7), 15–16
in Egypt (1907–8), 17, 67
at the University of Czernowitz (1909–11), 18–19, 91, 102
at the University of Graz (1911–21), 19–20, 46–8, 67, 69, 211
at Columbia University (1913–14), 20, 91
as finance minister in Austria (1919), 58–64, 258 nn.35, 38
in the Socialization Commission in Berlin (1919), 55–8
in banking and other business ventures (1921–4), 67–9
at the University of Bonn (1925–32), 69–71, 73, 78–9, 115–16, 261 n.34
at Harvard University (1927–8, 1930, 1932–50), 65, 77–9, 108–22, 125, 137–41, 148, 168–9, 176–7, 192, 194, 272 nn.12, 20, 275 n.67, 284 n.126

Works:
Das Wesen und der Hauptinhalt der theoretischen Nationalökonomie (1908), 17, 19, 21, 24–32, 91, 109, 125, 218, 229, 237–8
Theorie der wirtschaftlichen Entwicklung (1911, 1926, tr. 1934 as *The Theory of Economic Development*), 18–19, 21–2, 32–40, 66, 92, 102, 119, 125, 127, 131, 152–3, 167, 172–3, 210–11, 218–19, 228–9, 235–6
Epochen der Dogmen- und Methodengeschichte (1914; tr.

1954 as *Economic Doctrine and Method*), 14, 20–1, 40–5, 92, 177, 179
Vergangenheit und Zukunft der Sozialwissenschaften (1915), 19, 91
'Memorandum I, II and II' (1916–17), 48–54
'The Crisis of the Tax State' (1918), 59, 90, 94–8, 107
'Money and the Social Product' (1918–19), 80–1, 238
'The Sociology of Imperialisms' (1918–19), 90, 98–102, 107, 126, 218, 265 n.46, 266 nn.49, 51
'Gustav von Schmoller und die Probleme von heute' (1926), 73, 80, 83–9
'Social Classes in an Ethnically Homogenous Environment' (1927), 90–1, 102–7, 154, 218
'The Economic Instability of Capitalism' (1928), 82–3
'The Common Sense of Econometrics' (1933), 118, 125
'The Analysis of Economic Change' (1935), 125
Business Cycles (1939), 22, 87, 110–11, 119–21, 124, 126–36, 151–2, 156, 234, 271 n.95
An Economic Interpretation of Our Time (The Lowell Lectures) (1941), 110–11, 136, 138, 143, 145, 149, 155, 274 n.50
'The Meaning of Rationality in the Social Sciences' (1941), 111, 126–7
Capitalism, Socialism and Democracy (1942–50), 43, 64, 96–7, 105, 111, 121, 128–9, 135–8, 143, 145, 150–66, 180
'The Creative Response in Economic History' (1947), 171 ff.
'Theoretical Problems of Economic Growth' (1947), 171 ff.
'Economic Theory and

Schumpeter, Joseph A.
   (1883–1950) (cont.):
   Entrepreneurial History'
      (1949), 171 ff.
   'The Historical Approach to the
      Analysis of Business Cycles'
      (1949), 172, 280 n.21
   'Science and Ideology' (1949),
      169, 181
   'The March into Socialism'
      (1950), 170
   History of Economic Analysis
      (1954), 16, 22, 111, 121, 167,
      177–90, 281 n.42, 283 nn.93,
      94
   book on money (Das Wesen des
      Geldes, 1970), 71, 75–6,
      79–82, 110, 138, 171, 213–14,
      261 n.55, 271 n.3
   The Theoretical Apparatus of
      Economics (incomplete), 110,
      125–6, 269 n.67, 270 n.72
Schumpeter, Maria, 8
Schumpeter, Nelly (fictitious
   name), 72, 260 n.16
Schwartz, Nancy L., 157
Seaver, Gladys Ricarde see
   Schumpeter, Gladys
Seidl, Christian, 47–8, 240, 252
   n.4
Seipel, Ignaz, 58
Seven Wise Men, 120–1
Shionoya, Yuichi, 252 n.6, 253
   n.31, 255 n.31, 256 n.62, 260
   n.15
Siebeck, Paul, 20
Simiand, François, 91
Simmel, Georg, 81, 91, 104
Skocpol, Theda, 106
Smith, Adam, 42, 163, 179, 187–8
Smithies, Arthur, 109, 124, 194,
   208
Snyder, Carl, 215
socialism, 59, 138, 146, 159–66
   see also Marxism; Russian
      Revolution; Schumpeter,
      Joseph A., Works: Capitalism,
      Socialism and Democracy
      (1942–50)
Socialization Commission see

Schumpeter, Joseph A., in
   the Socialization
   Commission in Berlin (1919)
sociology, 11, 17, 24, 27, 37–8, 43,
   81, 90–108, 115, 118–19, 129,
   133, 136–7, 171, 180, 218,
   229, 235, 263 n.3
   see also economic sociology
Somary, Felix, 11, 14, 56–7, 93
Sombart, Werner, 79, 88, 183, 262
   n.77
Sorokin, Pitirim, 115, 138
Sozialökonomik, 2, 29, 66, 79–80,
   84, 86–9, 93–4, 103, 107, 118,
   128, 138, 179, 182–6, 189,
   194, 259 n.6, 263 n.13, 264
   n.23, 277 n.98
Spann, Othmar, 30–1, 70, 104,
   264 n.16
Spencer, Herbert, 101
Spiethoff, Arthur, 21, 50, 67,
   69–71, 76, 82, 85, 112, 128,
   239
Stalin, Joseph, 160, 170
state, the, 94–102, 186
static theory, 28–30, 32–5, 37–9,
   235
statistics, 16, 23, 66, 82, 129–35,
   184–5, 188
Stevenson, Michael I., 239
Stöckel, Mia, 109, 190, 283 n.98
Stolper, Gustav, 69–70, 212
Stolper, Wolfgang F., 47, 77, 115,
   119, 171, 240
Swedberg, Richard, 239
Sweezy, Paul, 115–16, 126, 140,
   178, 215, 239, 272 n.20

tariffs, 101
Taussig, F. W., 20, 111–13, 123
taxation, 23
   see also Schumpeter, Joseph A.,
      Works: 'The Crisis of the Tax
      State' (1918)
Taylor, Overton H., 275 n.67
theoretical economics, 22–32,
   44–5, 81, 86–7, 98, 103–4,
   107, 113–14, 174, 183–5, 230
Theory of Economic Development
   see Schumpeter, Joseph A.,

Works: *Theorie der wirtschaftlichen Entwicklung* (1911, 1926, tr. 1934 as *The Theory of Economic Development*)

Theresianum *see* Schumpeter, Joseph A., at Theresianum (1893–1901)

Tilly, Charles, 106

Tobin, James, 115

Triesch (Trest, Czechoslovakia), 5–7

Tritsch, Walter, 92

Trotsky, Leon, 161

Tsuru, Shigeto, 237

Turgot, A. R. J., 42, 254 n.30

University of Berlin, 78–9, 82, 108

utility, 27, 43–4, 187–8

values in economics *see* ideology

Verein für Sozialpolitik, 25, 92, 263 n.14

Verosta, Stephan, 47

Viner, Jacob, 189

vision in economics, 181, 254 n.17

Vogelstein, Theodor, 56, 58

Walras, Léon, 13–15, 22, 29–32, 70, 81, 116, 153, 179, 188–9

Weber, Marianne, 92

Weber, Max, 2–3, 26, 35, 43, 64, 83–4, 88–93, 154, 175, 180, 183, 221, 256 n.57, 259 n.6, 263 nn.13, 14, 264 nn.16, 18, 23, 25, 278 n.141, 281 n.33

Westermarck, Edward, 16, 91

Wicksell, Knut, 70

Wieser, Friedrich von, 13–14, 17–18, 23, 30, 41, 46, 55, 70

Wilson, E. B., 116

Wohl, R. Richard, 172

Wright, David McCord, 230–1

Yale University, 139–40